This work is dedicated to my beloved and beautiful wife Kathryn.
For always standing by me. And for sitting through *Lucky Louie* with me.

Kathryn, I never have—*and never will*—get tired of dedicating books to you...

THE
PRIME-TIME
2005–2006
SEASON

TV YEAR

VOLUME 1

JOHN KENNETH MUIR

APPLAUSE THEATRE & CINEMA BOOKS
An Imprint of Hal Leonard Corporation
New York

Published in 2007 by

Applause Theatre & Cinema Books (an imprint of Hal Leonard Corporation)

19 West 21st Street, New York, NY 10010

Printed in the United States of America

Cover and interior design by Pearl Chang

ISBN 13: 978-1-55783-684-7

ISBN 10: 1-55783-684-1

ISSN: 1935-7486

www.applausepub.com

ACKNOWLEDGMENTS

Special thanks to my always-spectacular agent, June Clark.

And also to producer, author and friend Joe Maddrey.

My appreciation also to Brian Black, Pearl Chang, and Michael Messina at Applause

for their tender-loving care of this manuscript.

CONTENTS

TV YEAR VOLUME ONE: FOREWORD

BY LARRY BRODY

I was talking to my friend Bob Sabaroff the other day, and he said something that took me by surprise.

Bob's a veteran of what might be called the TV Writing Wars, having worked as a writer in the 1950s all the way up to the '90s. His top credits, "The ones that get people paying attention to me at cocktail parties," he says, "are *Star Trek* and *Star Trek: The Next Generation.*"

Frankly, those get me listening more closely too. It was Bob's experience, as well as his general intelligence, that led me to expect him to say just about anything but the words that came out of his mouth:

"This is a Golden Age for television," Bob said. "And especially for television writing."

Let me be honest here. My first reaction was, *This guy's gone bonkers. What's he talking about?*

I mean, if you want to call the 1950s the Golden Age of Television (as many people do), I certainly can understand that. Look at what was on the air during that remarkable TV decade:

Playhouse 90!

I Love Lucy!

Dragnet!

Gunsmoke!

Bonanza!

The Milton Berle Show!

Your Show of Shows!

Alfred Hitchcock Presents!

77 Sunset Strip!

Captain Kangaroo!

The Twilight Zone!

And a host of other shows I still remember as well as if I'd seen them all not yesterday but this morning.

I don't think anyone can deny that the '50s gave us some truly outstanding moments in entertainment. I'd even argue that watched today, the episodes of the shows I've mentioned still stand up as vastly entertaining.

Want to get your blood boiling abut the human condition? *Playhouse 90* will do the job. Feel like laughing for a solid half-hour? *Lucy's* got that covered. And *Twilight Zone* will keep you wondering, while *Bonanza* gives your body a dose of adrenalin that's probably more than you need. These were shows that made me love TV so much that I thought I would die if I didn't get to work in the medium.

A case can be made for the 1970s as another kind of Golden Age, and in fact was one night not all that long ago when I was reminiscing with another good friend of mine, Paul Wendkos.

Paul's a director, not a writer, but like Bob Sabaroff his credits stretch from the '50s through the '90s. If you ask him, he'll say his two biggies are *"The Mephisto Waltz* and the *Gidget* movie. They were feature films that influenced people and still are influencing them." I, on the other hand, love his work on such television series as *Police Story, Harry O,* and *The Invaders.*

"Those were high-class shows," Paul said as we sat

there in our metaphorical "Wayback Machine." '70s TV was totally professional. Medical shows, cop shows, lawyer shows, science fiction shows—each form was polished to a high sheen."

And there in the archives to testify for him are:

Police Story!

M*A*S*H!

The Bold Ones!

All in the Family!

The Magician!

Hawaii Five-0!

The Streets of San Francisco!

Harry O!

Ironside!

Sanford and Son!

Welcome Back, Kotter!

And dozens of other shows, many of which (like *Police Story, The Bold Ones, The Magician, Hawaii Five-0, The Streets of San Francisco, Ironside,* and many others) I had the joy of working on as a writer or producer or both.

The strength of '70s television was that it was suspenseful and moving, balancing characterization and humor and action so perfectly that no one ever would believe it was done instinctively and not as the result of deep, dark, secret research. And, above all, it was slick. Slickly written, slickly acted and directed, and oh-so slickly shot.

Police Story personified the now-familiar, "The cop works on the case and the case works on the cop" theme. *All in the Family* and *M*A*S*H* combined comedy with hard, often unpleasant reality. *The Bold Ones* gave us idealistic and socially conscious doctors, lawyers, cops, and politicians. And *The Magician* offered total escape from reality while masquerading as the ultimate crime solving series. (No "procedural" elements there. Not a one!)

Which brings us back to the idea of a third Golden Age of Television. One existing not in the past but in the present. *Today.*

When Bob Sabaroff brought it up I wanted to dismiss the idea outright. But he's not the kind of guy to talk through his hat, so I thought about it. And turned on my plasma screen (the one with the big burned-in CBS logo on it because CBS has so many of my wife's favorite shows) and watched what was out there. And bought a pile of DVD collections and watched them.

And what I saw, on the air as I write this (at least, most of them), and during the 2005–2006 season this book so brilliantly and completely covers as well (Quick Aside to John Muir: How'd you ever do this? Where'd you find the time? You had to be writing all the time you were *watching TV!),* was this:

Lost!

Curb Your Enthusiasm!

Desperate Housewives!

Arrested Development!

The Sopranos!

Nip/Tuck!

Entourage!

Deadwood!

South Park!

Rome!

The Office!

Battlestar Galactica!

Veronica Mars!

Medium!

House!

Six Feet Under!

And more and more and—

You get the point. The more I thought, the more I watched, the longer the list of series I found genuinely exciting grew. And what is it that's so exciting to me about the shows covered in this tome? What is it that grabs me and makes me say, "Whoa! This is really something?"

It's the fact that unlike the shows of the '50s and '70s (and '60s, '80s, and '90s too), these babies always surprise me. They may not be slick, but they sure are personal. Not corporate shills thrown at the audience to get it to watch the commercials, but strange, quirky manifestations of the sensibilities a.k.a. worldviews a.k.a. the talent and taste of their creators.

Lost, Curb Your Enthusiasm, Desperate Housewives, Arrested Development, The Sopranos, and all the others consistently turn the old rules of TV dramaturgy on their heads. They allow the audience to take absolutely nothing for granted, moving into unknown territory in a way unheard of until now.

The creators of these shows know that they're up against the most powerful foes any television series has ever had. The web. Video games. And, most insidious of all, that traitor to the medium, the remote control, which makes it so easy for any viewer who's not totally enthralled with what's on to effortlessly and painlessly click away.

Because of this, the showrunners throw out all the stops. Anything tried or true or, for that matter, too "polished" is a hindrance, not an asset. It's *old.* So to keep things new these shows give us the unexpected whenever possible, in moments big and small. No, it doesn't always work perfectly, but to me all is forgiven the minute I find myself staring at the screen, shocked by my awareness that I'm encountering the unknown.

Time now to cut to the chase—an old television

standby that so many of the new shows no longer need to do—and say it right out:

This *is* another Golden Age.

The Golden Age of Television Experimentation.

Oh, man, why couldn't it have been like this when I was around?

AN INTRODUCTION TO TV YEAR, VOLUME 1

THE *LOST* EFFECT
AND OTHER TRENDS

Welcome to the inaugural edition of *TV Year*, a survey of one full season's worth of television entertainment programming. Science fiction, drama, situation comedies, historical period pieces…they're all chronicled, remembered, and summarized in these pages. The successes, the failures, even the behind-the-scenes controversies.

"One full season," I wrote above. However, it's easier to type that description than it is to adequately explain it. To wit, in the contemporary television universe, new TV series are *constantly* premiering. The days of a network progam such as *Star Trek* (1966–1969) or *The Fugitive* (1964–1968) running for thirty weeks, from September through June—only to be repeated in the dog days of summer—are long gone.

Instead, in this hyper, fast-paced 21st century, one season begins in August (to get the jump on the series commencing in September), a *second* season—the so-called "midseason" picks up in January, and then a *third* season, the summertime season, begins just as school is letting out. It runs right up to the cusp of the next season, and the whole cycle repeats.

Honestly, things aren't even that cut and dry. Today, TV series remain on the air sometimes for as short a span as two weeks, or, as in the example of a notorious 2005-2006 failure, *Emily's Reasons Why Not*, a mere week—only one airing! So, essentially, new shows are now unspooling *all the time*; virtually every week, fifty-two weeks a year. Thus, *TV Year* is tasked to catalog an entire *calendar year's* worth of entertainment programming, from August 1, 2005 to July 31, 2006. Future editions shall pick up the gauntlet starting with August 1, 2006, and proceed from there.

With that organization business behind us, it's appropriate to focus on the most important matter that this book seeks to illuminate. What kind of a year was it for TV, anyway? In exploring that question, it is critically important to observe that the 2005–2006 season represents the first full season to follow on the heels of the 2004–2005 resurgence of scripted drama, after years and years of reality programming supremacy. This celebrated rebirth was blazed by such ABC initiatives as *Lost, Desperate Housewives*, and *Grey's Anatomy*.

Of those three, *Lost* in particular merits special consideration. It's the story of plane crash survivors trapped on an island that's part mystical; part magical. The important thing to understand about *Lost* is that the series is *high concept*; meaning simply that it's easy to explain to a newcomer. Plane crash. Mysterious island. Kind of sci-fi. Kind of not.

Witnessing the smash success of *Lost*, which earned an Emmy Award for best dramatic series, virtually every broadcast network scrambled—SCRAMBLED, *I say*—to create an equally high-concept program for the 2005–2006 docket. Some of those high concepts succeeded dramatically, while some crashed and burned. But "the Lost

Effect," as I've termed it, was the guiding and primary principle leading into this season's worth of television.

For instance, everything one needs to know about Paul Scheuring's FOX drama *Prison Break* is right there, contained in the title. *Prison. Break*. The concept is so simple, so crisp, that it's practically glorious. Intellectual yet taciturn Michael Scofield (Wentworth Miller) gets himself sent to prison intentionally after intricately planning to escape from it with his already-incarcerated brother, Lincoln (Dominic Purcell). The series charts his progress from the time he sets foot in Fox River Penitentiary to the moment he and his brother (and a few troublesome hangers on) scale the institution's walls.

The same network also gave the high concept another avenue to prove itself in a dramatic soap opera entitled *Reunion*. Just like the popular Kiefer Sutherland series *24* marshals the concept of "real time" to propel itself from one harrowing installment to another, *Reunion's* "high concept" was that each hour-long segment would represent one year in the life of several characters, spanning the epoch from 1986 to 2006. In this series, one of the *dramatis personae* was murdered in the present, and all the proceeding episodes, from 1986 to present (or until cancellation) developed the lives and relationships of the characters…who were all suspects in the crime. Unfortunately, the serialized and highly complex (but fascinating in terms of its structure) *Reunion* was pre-empted early in its run by a prime-time Presidential address. It never recovered, but the central premise—like *Prison Break*—was high concept all the way.

Other programs that aired in the 2005–2006 season remembered the example of *Lost* and dutifully registered another angle of the high concept. The series from J.J. Abrams was a serialized drama featuring a large ensemble cast and boasting science fiction overtones. Thus, ABC, NBC and CBS all devised new serialized dramas that featured—*surprise!*—large ensemble casts and science fiction overtones. These shows were called *Invasion, Surface,* and *Threshold. Invasion* concerned a large blended family facing a possible alien invasion conducted by cover of hurricane; *Surface* dramatized the story of a new breed of sea monsters teeming in the Earth's ocean; and the short-lived *Threshold* concerned *another* alien invasion and a government team assigned to stop it.

Another program, *Commander in Chief*—a new Geena Davis effort—was also a high concept enterprise, at least after a fashion. Specifically, it was *The West Wing* (1999–2006) *redux,* only with a woman as President of the United States. Again, the premise makes the series instantly recognizable to impatient channel surfers looking for a destination. Or how about *Book of Daniel,* a series concerning a pastor (Aidan Quinn) who carries on regular conversations with Jesus Christ? Distinctive enough for you? No? Then try *Ghost Whisperer,* another enterprise where the title says it all. *Ghost. Whisperer.*

Many of the aforementioned high concept series were canceled by the end of the season, but an intrepid viewer can detect in each venture how *Lost* (and to a lesser degree, *Desperate Housewives*) generated a ripple effect—an aftershock—that rumbled throughout the network schedules in 2005–2006.

BIG NAMES: BIG FAILURES

Another critical lesson of this year in television was that "big" Hollywood names don't necessarily generate impressive ratings. Geena Davis and Heather Graham are both established movie stars…and both of their TV series died inglorious, quick deaths. Former spouses and movie stars

Don Johnson and Melanie Griffith starred in TV series this year too (both on the defunct WB), and both *Just Legal* and *Twins* were canceled. Chris O'Donnell—formerly the Boy Wonder in the *Batman* movie franchise—also failed on television with his legal series, *Head Cases.* Dennis Hopper's network series, *E-Ring,* got the boot before the end of the season too. Ditto teen heartthrob Freddie Prinze, Jr. and his situation comedy, *Freddie.*

Furthermore, established and well-liked small-screen stars such as Jenna Elfman, Lisa Kudrow, Matt LeBlanc, Rebecca Romijn, John Stamos, Henry Winkler, and Seth Green also saw their newest efforts fail conspicuously. The misfires weren't just limited to actors either. Other highly recognizable faces and names in pop culture met with audience ennui too. *The Apprentice: Martha Stewart* starred America's favorite ex-con and happy homemaker, but the show drew tepid ratings and got the ax. So did inspirational singer Amy Grant's feel-good series, *Three Wishes.*

What's the lesson in such high-profile nonstarters? Perhaps only this: producers and creators need to make certain not merely that their series are well cast. For programs to succeed, they must actually be good; both solidly written, dominated by appealing and interesting concepts, and populated with interesting people. The fracturing of the TV world due to cable programming means more choices for viewers. And more choices means that even a star vehicle is not a sure thing.

After all, remind me again, who's the big name star of *Lost?* Or *Prison Break?*

CRIME TIME:
OR CRIME SOMETIMES PAYS

If you flip on the television at any point in prime time during an average week, you've probably got a better than 50-50 chance of spotting a crime drama right off the bat. In the 2005–2006 season, no less than twenty series involving some aspect of crime investigation aired regularly. Every aspect of crime, from the deed itself (*Law & Order: Criminal Intent*) to the assembling of the forensic evidence (*CSI*), to the arrest (*The Shield*), to the suspect interrogation (*The Closer*), to the trial (*Law & Order*) are featured on individual series. Missing persons cases (*Without a Trace*), deviant serial murders (*Killer Instinct; Criminal Minds*), sex crimes (*Law & Order: SVU*), cases related to the military (*NCIS*), old cases left unsolved and forgotten (*Cold Case*), cases in suburbia (*Close to Home*), and cases wrongly decided and in need of overturning (*In Justice*) are all depicted.

On television episodes, crimes are solved utilizing forensic science (*CSI: Miami; CSI: NY*), by studying bones (*Bones*), through post-mortem medical exam (*Crossing Jordan*), via the auspices of psychics (*Medium*); and prosecuted by attorneys of all stripes, including senile ones (*Boston Legal*), insane ones (*Head Cases*), drunks (*Just Legal*), and young hotties (*Conviction*). Considering all these examples, it's clear that as far as television is concerned, crime really does pay.

One hastens to add, virtually all of these shows seem to be created by Jerry Bruckheimer, the antichrist of crime television. Yet he's clearly onto something in his ruthless propagation of the form. These series often boast a long shelflife and viewers never seem to tire of crime investigation dramas.

In fact, when TV in 2005 and 2006 is bland or undistinguished, it is in part due to what could be dubbed the *Law & Order* effect. Instead of writers expending the energy to craft authentic and interesting human characters, they populate their shows with ciphers; these investigative "teams" or "units." You've seen the type: good-looking, athletic men in sharp business suits and ties, and lovely women in high heels who—while impeccably dressed—snap questions at suspects, babble techno-jargon about forensic science, and endlessly explain plot exposition to one another. Conveniently, there is no need for characters to talk to each other meaningfully or in original language; and no time to deal with their own humanity. Instead it's all about solving a misdeed and catching the "perp."

With so many crime shows dominating the airwaves, the same stories also get trotted out repeatedly. How often is a lead detective a broken man inside or a widower? How often are there episodes in which a cast member is framed for murder and his stalwart companions must clear his name? Or a segment wherein a crime investigator is shot in the line of duty? Or one featuring a new female boss who has a crush on the chief male investigator?! Or that other staple of the genre: a death row inmate is wrongly convicted and only has hours left before execution to clear his name. Yes, it's all been repeated endlessly.

Thankfully, 2005–2006 was also the year that—registering the imbalance perhaps, criminals struck back. Certainly, we've had the glorious HBO Mafia series *The Sopranos* for six years now, but 2005–2006 brought three freshman attempts to gaze at the flip side of the criminal investigation. These efforts concerned clever criminals successfully evading the suits. Crooks and thieves were the stars of AMC's *Hustle*, NBC's *Heist* and FX's *Thief*. At least two of those series, *Thief* and *Hustle*, are quite good. However, all but *Hustle* have been canceled. The cops win again.

In years to come, when *Law & Order: Breaking and Entering* airs every night, followed by *CSI: Des Moines*, don't say I didn't warn you…

KILLING WITH LAUGHTER:
THE DEATH OF THE AMERICAN SITCOM

The long-lived half-hour situation comedy, usually based around the central idea of the average "family" is in deep trouble in 2005–2006. It's no wonder, given the very unfortunate representatives of this format. Even on a close examination, it's painfully obvious that *According to Jim, King of Queens, Lucky Louie, Rodney*, and *Still Standing* are exactly the same show.

All these sitcoms feature a central male figure, always blue collar or "working class." He's not traditionally attractive; meaning he's overweight, fat, and balding. Yet he's married to the most gorgeous, fit, tolerant woman imaginable…basically a supermodel. Which is unrealistic, because he isn't even rich. Anyway, this beautiful woman finds her hapless mate's serial buffoonery, misbehavior, and willful ignorance amusing rather than irritating and—for some reason—wants to bear more children by him. At least she could spare the world that fate.

Other situation comedies aired this year are also off-the-shelf, cookie-cutter affairs that don't generate much in terms of interest. They're either uninspired efforts about siblings living together (*Twins, Related, What I Like About You*, etc.); *Friends*-wannabes concerning packs of friends sharing impossibly beautiful and spacious urban apartments (*Four Kings, Hot Properties*); or the newest trend: slacker love stories. *Free Ride, Love Monkey, The Loop, Teachers, Jake in Progress*, and *What About Brian* are just a few examples of comedies in which a man (either in his twenties or thirties) lusts after an inaccesible "dream" woman who doesn't appear to want anything to do with him.

Just take a gander at the comedy casualties from the 2005–2006 season. The tally is unreal. From ABC: *Crumbs, Emily's Reasons Why Not, Freddie, Hope & Faith, Hot Properties, Jake in Progress, Less Than Perfect, Love Monkey, Rodney, Sons & Daughters*. From CBS: *Courting Alex, Out of Practice, Still Standing, Yes Dear*. From NBC: *Four Kings, Joey, Teachers, Will & Grace*. From FOX: *The Bernie Mac Show, Free Ride, Malcolm in the Middle, That '70s Show, Stacked*. From the WB: *Blue Collar TV, Living with Fran, Pepper Dennis, Related, What I Like About You, Twins*. From UPN: *Cuts, Eve, Love Inc*. And from HBO: *The Comeback*.

For those who are counting, that's over *thirty* comedies canceled in one calendar year, a virtual massacre of the form. Yet all is not lost. There's hope for the half-hour comedy. NBC's *My Name is Earl*, Chris Rock's *Everybody Hates Chris* (UPN), HBO's *Extras* and established series such as *Curb Your Enthusiasm, The Office, Entourage*, and *Scrubs* continue to prove that comedies outside the cookie cutter mold can still make us laugh, and thereby thrive on television.

THE NEW GOLDEN AGE?

The 2005–2006 television season is a fascinating and appropriate time to begin *TV Year*, in part because so much about this sturdy old medium is changing…and for the better. This is a time of transition, however, and change is never easy. For instance, this is the last year for both UPN and the WB. Next year, these networks— both created in the 1990s—will officially be history;

merged into something called "The CW." The networks that birthed *Buffy the Vampire Slayer, Dawson's Creek, 7th Heaven,* and *Veronica Mars* are no more.

How else is TV changing? First and foremost, a wide variety of programming is today becoming available via downloads. Episodes of your favorite series are coming to hand-held devices, cell phones, and computers near you. That means, essentially, that TV has outgrown the confines of the box. The format as a vehicle for entertainment is now…ubiquitous. Some may see such a development as scary, but the easy availability of television programming means that old classics can come back; and that new shows can find alternative routes to popularity and fame.

Is America perched on the cusp of a "new golden age of television" as Jon Cassar remarked upon accepting his 2006 Emmy Award for best director for the drama series *24*? Well, yes. In some senses. There's a case to be made that television today is what the medium of film once was.

Consider the fact that once upon a time, television programming had to be homogenized to an alarming degree. There were only three broadcast networks, and that meant only three options for consumers. Yet in the 21st century, cable television has splintered television watching to a degree unimaginable two decades ago. Specifically, there now exist scads of niche channels and niche shows. And delightfully, these new series don't need to be viewed by more than a few million viewers to be deemed hits. *Eureka* and *Doctor Who* on The Sci-Fi Channel; *Monk* and *Psych* on USA; *The Closer* on TNT. These series might have been quickly canceled in decades past, but now they thrive.

By contrast, because of their unwieldy costs, cinematic outings now must appeal to the widest audiences possible to make a decent return on egregious investments. For example, *Superman Returns (*2006) reportedly cost over $250 million…considerably more than a season of the young Superman series, *Smallville.* Thus movies and TV have switched positions, and television is truly positioned to become a confident art form all its own; not the dirty red-headed cousin to cinema.

It's difficult to deny a looming golden age when one considers some of the programing airing today. Yes, the sitcom is still mostly dross and certainly the crime investigation milieu is played out. The high concept TV program is still hit or miss. But never forget, television today is the land of *Veronica Mars, 24, Scrubs, Rome, Brotherhood, Lost, My Name is Earl, The Office, Prison Break, Weeds, Deadwood, The Sopranos, Gilmore Girls*, and *Doctor Who*, to name just a few triumphs. Each of the aforementioned series is tops in its genre. Why go out and see a movie when a DVD box set of *Veronica Mars* is available? Why rent a movie from Blockbuster when *Weeds* is right there, "on demand"? Why bother Netflix when you can download an episode of *The Office* on your PC?

So 2005–2006 is not just the season of *TV Year*, it's the year of television. The golden age has arrived.

AMERICAN DAD!

(FOX) (RENEWED) (30 minutes) (Sundays at 9:30 pm EST; September 18, 2005–May 14, 2006) Atlantic Creative/Fuzzy Door Productions. Created by: Seth MacFarlane, Mike Barker, Matt Weitzman. Executive Producers: Mike Barker, Seth Mac-Farlane, Matt Weitzman. Co-Executive Producers: Jim Bernstein, Ethan Cohen, David Hemingson, Kenny Schwartz, Rick Wiener, David Zuckerman. Film Editor: Bobby Gibis. Written by: Jim Bernstein, Neal Boushell, Brian Boyle, Robert Cohen, Erik Durbin, Steve Hely, Nahnatchka Khan, Alison McDonald, Matt & Chris McKenna, Sam O'Neal, Kenny Schwartz, Craig Thomas, David Zuckerman. Directed by: John Aoshima, Albert Calleros, Rodney Clouden, Pam Cooke, Mike Kim, Anthony Loi, Seth MacFarlane, Caleb Meurer, Scott Wood, Brent Woods.

VOICE CAST

Seth MacFarlane (Stan Smith, Roger the Alien, George Corbin); Wendy Schaal (Francine Smith); Scott Grimes (Steve Smith); Rachael MacFarlane (Hayley Smith/ Melanie/Barb); Dee Bradley Baker (Klaus/Tony).

American Dad!, the new animated series from *Family Guy* creator Seth MacFarlane, actually aired its first episodes in Winter and Spring of 2005 as a kind of shakedown cruise, but the bulk of the first season unfolded during the 2005–2006 season, the reason it's covered here.

In essence *American Dad!* is a "family" comedy in the vein of *The Simpsons* or—again—*Family Guy.* As expected of such material, there's the doltish father figure in the lead, here named Stan (Seth MacFarlane); his long-suffering and sensible wife, Francine (Wendy Schaal); the brood of children, in this case a geek named Steve (Scott Grimes) and a "green" teen named Hayley (Rachael Mac-Farlane) and also the…*uh*…resident alien. In the manner that *Family Guy* features Stewie, the snobby, talking baby with the football-shaped head, *American Dad!* highlights

a snobby extraterrestrial with a pear-shaped head. His name is Roger. Subbing for *Family Guy*'s dog is Klaus, the family's loquacious goldfish!

American Dad! differs from *Family Guy* in some drastic ways. First, the enterprise is staged as a lampoon of all the "dumb dad" series populating television today (meaning *According to Jim, The Simpsons* [already a lampoon], *Rodney, Still Standing, King of Queens*…shall I go on?). Secondly, it provides Stan a specific agenda as the outlet for his stupidity. He's not just dumb by nature. No, he's a CIA agent and über-patriot who is constitutionally unable to view a situation from any angle but the extreme right wing. Stan is thus Oliver North on steroids, and he even looks like a parody of American icon Superman, with gigantic broad shoulders and jutting chin. But Stan is a parody of stereotypical American masculinity because he's infinitely foolish, utterly unable to communicate with his family, and an egregious failure in understanding the nature of any emotional situation he stumbles into.

So, *American Dad!* adopts all the tropes of the sitcom form and breathes new life into very old stories by gazing at them anew through the lens of 21st Century America, patriotism, and the War on Terror. In one episode ("Francine's Flashbacks"), Stan doesn't want Francine to realize he's forgotten their wedding anniversary again (a plot as old as *The Honeymooners*, 1955 or *I Love Lucy*, 1951), but how he attempts to get out of the predicament is a new (and funny) twist: he co-opts the CIA to fix the problem with a little memory wipe. Only problem, twenty years get erased from Francine's brain cells, not twenty minutes.

Another *American Dad!* episode finds Stan strongly suspecting that his new neighbors are terrorists. On *All in the Family,* Archie Bunker's fear would have likely been of

Stand up and salute **AMERICAN DAD!**, Seth MacFarlane's follow up to *Family Guy*.

an African-American family moving in next door, but the old "*there goes the neighborhood*" routine has been recast again, within MacFarlane's unique context.

In "All About Steve," Stan is ashamed that his son is a *Star Trek* fan and geek boy...until he realizes he could exploit his son's interest to help him capture a cyberterrorist, and so on. In another context and in another, less evolved era, this could have been the story of a prejudiced father fearing that his son is gay, right?

For the critics who claim that *American Dad!* is too much like *Family Guy*, the truth is that such reviewers simply aren't looking closely enough. *Family Guy* is wacky and funny, but scattershot. It takes aim at *everything*. The jokes there don't adhere to any single overriding philosophy or consistent leitmotif beyond pop culture allusions. By contrast, *American Dad!* offers a very distinct context and conceit, and all the humor emanates from that wellspring. We can't see it now, because we live in the age of "Terror," but someday, this series may be seen as the TV comedy that best expresses this time period in America.

The first season has been released on DVD.

AMERICAN INVENTOR

(ABC) (RENEWED) (60 minutes) (Thursdays at 9:00 pm, EST; March 16, 2006-May 11, 2006) Fremantle Media North America/Peter Jones Productions Inc./Syco Television. Executive Producers: Elizabeth Bronstein, Simon Cowell, Cecile Frot-Coutaz, Sibhan Greene, Nigel Hall, Daniel Soiseth. Produced by: Bob Gillan, James McNab, Darren R. Paletz, John Putro, Kate Richter, Jill Roozenboom. Camera: Mike Ansbush, Dane Lawing. Film Editors: Roger Bartlett, Devon Collins, Paul Coyne, James Fletcher, Paul Frazier, John Hoelle, John M. Larson, Matt McCartie, Hudson Smith. Directed by: Sharon Trojan Hollinger.

CAST
Matt Gallant (Host)
Doug Hall (Judge)
Ed Evangelista (Judge)
Mary Lou Quinlan (Judge)
Peter Jones (Judge)

CONTESTANTS
Robert Amore, Sharon Clemens, Darla Davenport-Powell, Ed Hall, Janusz Liberkowski, Mark Martinez, Sheryl McDonald, Francisco Patino, Jodi Pliszka, Jennifer Safuto, Joseph Safuto, Erik Thompson, Jerry Wesley.

Simon Cowell, the acerbic appraiser in residence on another TV series that includes the initials "A. I.," was the mastermind behind this unscripted ABC reality series that first aired in the Spring of 2006 and boldly went in search of America's next great invention. This sojourn was otherwise known as a quest for "the embodiment of the American dream!"

Wonder if the American dream includes getting a dressing down from unimpressed judges?

Host Matt Gallant takes the Ryan Seacrest role on *American Inventor,* and the series features a panel of four judges, rather than the customary three. In this case, the judges are Peter Jones, a British entrepreneur and the heir to Cowell's sarcasm legacy; Doug Hall, a best-selling author and radio personality; Ed Evangelista, a creative executive, and Mary Lou Quinlan, the CEO of a marketing company.

The format for *American Inventor* also apes *American Idol* in other ways…to an uncomfortably close degree. For instance, the judges fan out across the country, to Los Angeles, San Francisco, New York, Denver, Washington D.C., Chicago, and Atlanta in search of the "American Inventor," an opportunity for people to audition before the panels. As on *American Idol,* many of those who audition come across as strange, off-putting, demented or attention-seeking, which is sure to get a laugh at home. Too bad William Hung never built anything.

After the audition stage, fifty hopefuls return to Hollywood, and then that number is whittled down to two dozen. From there, twelve finalists are selected to become the next "American Inventor" and each given a stipend of $50,000. The grand prize winner receives $1 million, as well as the grateful recognition of the nation in this hour-long series which ran for ten episodes.

Among the contestants in the 2005–2006 sortie of *American Inventor:* Robert Amore, Sharon Clemens, Darla Davenport-Powell, Ed Hall, Janusz Liberkowski, Mark Martinez, Sheryl McDonald, Francisco Patino, Jodi Pliszka, Joe and Jennifer Safuto, Erik Thompson and Jerry Wesley. Among the top inventions: a "tone belt," a "word ace," "the un-brella," the "double-traction bike," an "EZ-X portable gym" and the "spherical safety seat."

At the end of the ten-episode run, Janusz Liberkowski, an engineer from San Jose, California was crowned the *American Inventor* for his creation of the spherical safety seat, a revolutionary new infant child car seat.

Not currently available on DVD.

AMERICA'S GOT TALENT

(NBC) (RENEWED) (60 minutes) (Wednesdays at 8:00 pm, EST; June 21, 2006–September 6, 2006) Fremantle Entertainment Ltd./Syco Television. Executive Producers: Simon Cowell, Cecile Frot-Coutaz, Ken Warwick. Co-Executive Producer: Jason Raff. Produced by: Michael H. Miller. Film Editors: Eric B. Shanks, Steve Zukerman. Directed by: Russell Norman.

CAST
Regis Philbin (Host)
David Hasselhoff (Judge)
Piers Morgan (Judge)
Brandy Norwood (Judge)

CONTESTANTS
All That, Celtic Spring, Cole Miller, L.D. Miller, Realis, Bianca Ryan, Vivian Smallwood, Taylor Ward.

The 2005–2006 season saw *American Idol* judge Simon Cowell successfully attempt to duplicate the reality/talent show/game show format of his famous FOX series. Not coincidentally, both of his network efforts included the word "America" in the title, and both simulated the style and format of *Idol. American Inventor* came in the spring (see above), and *America's Got Talent* became the unexpected hit of the summer of '06.

Affable former *Who Wants to Be a Millionaire* (1999) host Regis Philbin emceed this televised talent show that critics compared to *Star Search* and *The Gong Show.* It's not as innocent as the former, nor as crass as the latter. Which makes it merely pabulum.

After a series of auditions around the country (Los Angeles, New York, Chicago, Atlanta, etc.) contestants descend on Hollywood and step on stage to strut their bizarre stuff. Unlike *American Idol,* there is no age limit on the acts here, and singing isn't the only game in town. As the series web site notes: "From ventriloquists to contortionists, acrobats to animal acts, magicians to mimes,

America will prove (or not) just how talented they really are."[1]

Running for ten weeks, *America's Got Talent* pitted the weirdest and wildest acts imaginable against the now *de rigueur* panel of three magistrates. Sound familiar? In this case, there was the kindly pushover and Paula Abdul surrogate, pop star Brandy; acerbic Brit and Cowell clone, Piers Morgan, and finally washed-up TV star David Hasselhoff. Unlike *American Idol,* these judges could wield real power against the acts on stage and activate "buzzers" during any act deemed particularly lacking. If all three "X"-shaped buzzers went off during an act, that contestant was eliminated.

America's Got Talent's first season featured an array of oddities, from jugglers to an all-male troupe of clogdancers called "All That." Let's see: there were rapping grannies, a nose flutist(!), and a man called Bobby Badfingers who could utilize his digits like an organic musical instrument.

In the end, the victor (as selected by American voters at home…again, just like *Idol*), was eleven-year-old Bianca Ryan. She sang Janis Joplin's "Piece of My Heart" and walked away not just with America's heart, but the $1 million prize money. Kind of a shame to hold a massive talent contest separate from *American Idol* and then give the prize to a singer—just like that show—don't you think?

I was rooting for the nose flutist.

Not currently available on DVD.

THE APPRENTICE:
MARTHA STEWART

(NBC) (CANCELED) (60 minutes) (Wednesdays at 8:00 pm, EST; September 21, 2005-December 21, 2005) Mark Burnett Productions/Martha Stewart Living Omnimedia/Trump Productions, LLC. Executive Producers: Mark Burnett, Jay Bienstock, Martha Stewart, Donald Trump. Co-Executive Producers: Kevin Harris, Conrad Riggs. Produced by: Luciana Brafman-Bienstock, Jeff Cole, Rob La Plante, Bill Pruitt, Thomas B. Ruff. Camera: Alan Pierce. Film Editor: Michael Berkowitz.

CAST
Martha Stewart
Alexis Stewart

CONTESTANTS
Sarah Brennan, Jim Bozzini, Ryan Danz, Bethany Frankel, Howie Greenspan, Carrie Gugger, Amanda Hill, David Kavandish, Shawn Killinger, Jennifer Le, Juff Rudell, Dawn Silvia, Chuck Soldano, Marcella Valladolid.

To the bigwigs at NBC, it must have seemed like a sure thing to spin off the popular Donald Trump reality/game series *The Apprentice*; especially with another famous businessperson "celebrity" ensconced at the helm, in this case ex-con Martha Stewart...the unhappy homemaker who had just finished jail time for perjury. What happened instead makes for terrific TV history: a failed show, and some very public recriminations about it.

The Apprentice: Martha Stewart apes the format (down to the musical cues, it seems) of its elder brethren, *The Apprentice*. In this case, however, Martha Stewart is firmly "the boss," the CEO in search of a new apprentice. Sixteen candidates (or contestants) apply for that job, which comes with nice financial remuneration too: a $250,000 stipend! In the thirteen episodes that aired from September 21 to December 21, 2005, Martha would set out tasks for the contestants and then decide whom to eliminate after the completion of the assignment. Her tag line to the recently downsized was: "*You just don't fit in.*"

That euphemism for "You're fired!" (Trump's more enthusiastically delivered zinger) explains a serious problem with this series. Although the idea was to "focus on Martha the businesswoman"[2], the parolee was anything but the tough-as-nails corporate personality many perceived. Out of the slammer and apparently eager to prove she wasn't such a witch after all, Martha presented a soft-pedaled version of her already-established persona for TV consumption, and that didn't necessarily make for compelling television. Critics commented that the "kinder, gentler" Stewart "seemed a bit contrived."[3]

Also, many of the jobs that the applicants undertook during the course of the episodes weren't especially exciting. In one episode, the prospective interviewees dueled over development of a children's book. In another contest, they had to manage competing flower shops in the West Village ("Business is Blooming"). One episode involving baking a cake for a wedding expo ("Bake It Till You Make It"), and the nadir sequence was probably "Final Approach," which concerned making a promotional video for an airline. It isn't exactly scintillating material. A better show would have been *The Convict: Martha,* a reality show following Martha through her prison stint.

The Apprentice: Martha Stewart aired opposite *Lost* on Wednesday nights for a time in 2005...and was clobbered in the ratings, even when pitted against catch-up *Lost* "clip" shows (i.e. reruns). Also, whereas *The Apprentice* regularly drew over eleven million viewers to the TV, this distaff edition attracted just seven million (and the numbers plummeted from there).

In the end, Dawna Stone was the winner of the contest, but Martha Stewart herself was the big loser. NBC

Before the feud: Donald Trump and Martha Stewart on the set of **THE APPRENTICE:** MARTHA STEWART.

opted not to renew the show after the first run of thirteen episodes. The cancellation was a surprise that sent shockwaves through the industry (and the business world), and the real drama (the one audiences had wanted to see on TV) finally commenced when Martha Stewart informed *Newsweek* that she implicitly blamed Donald Trump for the failure. She suggested that her show was supposed to be the only version of *The Apprentice* and that in her first episode, she was supposed to fire Donald Trump. "Having two *Apprentices* was as unfair to him as unfair to me," she noted in one interview, "but Donald really wanted to stay…"[4]

Trump responded to these assertions with anger. "It's about time you started taking responsibility" he suggested in a letter to Martha he shared with *Newsweek*. "Your per-formance was terrible in that the show lacked mood, temperament, and just about everything else a show needs for success. I knew it would fail as soon as I first saw it."[5]

The war of words continued unabated—to the delight of the press—and Stewart called Trump's missive mean-spirited and reckless. Ultimately, the battle of the two business personalities proved far more interesting than the contest played out on *The Apprentice: Martha Stewart.*

Martha's version of *The Apprentice*—destined to go down in history beside other unsuccessful spinoffs such as *Joanie Loves Chachi*, is not yet available on DVD.

Not yet available on DVD.

BIG LOVE

(HBO) (RENEWED) (60 minutes) (Sundays at 10:00 pm, EST; March 12, 2006-June 4, 2006) Anima Sola Productions/ Playtone Productions. Created by: Mark V. Olsen, Will Scheffer. Executive Producers: Gary Goetzman, Tom Hanks, Alexa Junge, Shane Keller, Mark V. Olsen, Will Scheffer. Producers: Bernaette Caulfield, Jill Sprecher, Karen Sprecher. Directors of Photography: Ross Alsobrook, James Glennon. Film Editors: Amy Duddleston, Carole Kravetz, Tanya M. Swerling, Leo Trombetta. Music: Mark Mothersbaugh. Written by: Dustin Lance Black, Jeanette Collins, Mimi Friedman, Alexa Junge, Eileen Myers, Mark V. Olsen, Will Scheffer, Karen and Jill Sprecher, Doug Stockstill. Directed by: Julian Farino, Rodrigo Garcia, Mary Harron, Michael Lehmann, Charles McDougall, Alan Poul, Steve Shill, Alan Taylor.

CAST

Bill Paxton (Bill Henrickson)
Jeanne Tripplehorn (Barb Henrickson)
Chloë Sevigny (Nicolette/Nicki)
Ginnifer Goodwin (Margene)
Harry Dean Stanton (Roman)
Amanda Seyfried (Sarah)
Douglas Smith (Ben)
Melora Walters (Wanda)
Shawn Doyle (Joe)
Bruce Dern (Franklin)
Grace Zabriskie (Lois)
Mary Kay Place (Adaleen)
Matt Ross (Alby Grant)
Tina Marjorino (Heather)

If HBO continues to produce and air dramatic series of this caliber, the broadcast networks might as well fold up shop and pack it in. *Big Love* is the extraordinary, breathtaking and often harrowing drama about a polygamist entrepreneur and his family dealing with 21st century life in suburban Utah, the reddest of red states.

While ostensibly a family drama, *Big Love* remains even more daring than its subject matter suggests: it's a program that revolves around the very notion of freedom, and what can occur when a government dictates to people how they should live, and which arrangements are acceptable. Suddenly, the law creates a whole underclass of people living under the radar, and from there matters just spinwheel. People live their lives in secret, unable to feel proud of the values they hold dear. Worse, they must constantly lie to neighbors, family and friends about their "orientation," and—after awhile—dishonesty takes a toll on a person…and a family.

In specific terms, *Big Love* is the account of a Mormon fundamentalist named Bill Henrickson (Bill Paxton), a man who was kicked out of the polygamist compound called Juniper Creek when he was fourteen years old. Now, Bill is a self-made man, a proud and respected businessman who owns a franchise called Henrickson's Home Plus; a local variety of Lowe's or Home Depot. But Bill hides a desperate secret. In the tradition of his ancestors, he's chosen to live as a polygamist, to marry more than one woman. He didn't come to this decision easily, but when his wife of seventeen years, the lovely Barb (Jeanne Tripplehorn), developed cancer some years earlier, he came to believe he was called to the lifestyle. Bill has three children with Barb: a teenager who is desperately afraid of premarital sex and going to Hell because of it, a son named Ben (Douglas Smith); a level-headed teenage girl who disdains polygamy but keeps an open mind, Sarah (Amanda Seyfried); and a little tyke named Teenie.

Bill is also married to a second wife, the avaricious Nicki (Chloë Sevigny), who harbors such a dramatic and materialistic appetite for "things" that she's secretly gotten herself into $60,000 of credit card debt. Nicki also happens to be one of the many daughters of corrupt Roman Grant (Harry Dean Stanton), the current spiritual leader of Juniper Creek. She has two boys by Bill.

Margene (Ginnifer Goodwin) is Bill's third wife, a young, inexperienced and naïve woman who fell in love with Bill yet didn't quite understand what it would mean to be a "sister" bride in the polygamist tradition. During the course of *Big Love,* Margene copes with the isolation of hiding the lifestyle and learns, to her dismay, that her inclusion in the family was not a unanimous vote. Nonetheless, Margene embraces that her place is with Bill, Barb and Nicki, and in an episode called "The Baptism" is officially "born" into the life.

Big Love also examines the practical realities of Mormon fundamentalist polygamy. Basically, Bill is expected to have sexual intercourse every night because each wife only sees him twice a week or thereabouts due to the sleeping arrangements (three bedrooms in three houses). This is a difficult task for Bill and in "Viagra Blues," he acquires the medication to ensure he can satisfy all his brides. Squabbles also arise over whose night it is, where Bill spends his time, and how much authority Barb—as first wife—should wield over the sister brides. When Barb wants to accept a job as a teacher, for instance, Nicki objects because of the ways it will affect her.

Big Love also gazes at the seamy, unsavory side of Mormon fundamentalist polygamy, and many episodes reveal the depth of poverty infecting the Juniper Creek compound. Old men like Roman Grant scandalously marry women who are 13 to 14 years old, and who have no means of independence, of escaping the life, or choosing it for themselves. This aspect of the polygamist life is unattractive and exploitive. Yet in revealing that the Henrickson family is loving and tolerant, the series proves evenhanded in its assessment of this life. It sensitively explores *all* sides of the issue.

During the course of *Big Love*'s first season, Bill and Roman grapple for dominance over Bill's home improvement stores, which Roman owns a piece of as head of Bill's church. In the season finale, Bill had wheedled his way onto Roman's inner sanctum by getting a seat on "the council" at Juniper Creek and Roman responded in harsh fashion by "outing" Barb as a polygamist at a public forum where she was presented with the "Mother of the Year" award.

Big Love is often funny, especially in the manner in which it deals with Bill's estranged parents, Franklin (Bruce Dern) and Lois (Grace Zabriskie). In one episode, when Franklin is poisoned, the prime suspect is Lois. In another instance, after being evicted from Juniper Creek, Franklin comes to stay at Bill's compound and refuses to use a toilet when urinating. Instead—in full view of the children—he relieves himself in the kitchen sink.

Big Love asks pertinent questions about what constitutes a family in this day and age. Is America a nation that can only permit one kind of marriage, meaning one man with one woman? There's been much talk about gay marriage lately, but if that's a viable option, then surely polygamy is as well, right? *Big Love* forces one to honestly face such social issues. The Henrickson marriage works—though at times it looks like a chore (and quite exhausting). On the other hand, in a series of episodes (including "The Affair"), Bill and Barb run off to motel rooms together and carry on a secret affair separate from the other two wives. This development indicates that Bill favors one spouse above the others. Perhaps, *Big Love*, also speculates with intelligence, the human heart can only love one other person at a time.

The first season has been released on DVD.

BLACK. WHITE.

(FX) (CANCELED) (60 minutes) (Wednesdays at 10:00 pm; March 6, 2006–April 12, 2006) Actual Reality Pictures. Executive Producers: Matt Alvarez, Ice Cube, R.J. Cutler. Co-Executive Producers: Fernando Mills, Jude Weng. Produced by: Todd Lubin, Keith Vanderlan, Nisa Ahmad. Directors of Photography: Derth Adams, Andrei Cranach, Todd Dos Reis, John Tarver. Film Editors: Poppy Das, Greg Finton, Yaffa Lerea, Andy Robertson. Directed by: R.J. Cutler.

CAST
Rose Bloomfield
Bruno Marcotulli
Brian Sparks
Nicholas Sparks
Renee Sparks
Carmen Wurgel

Although many critics and viewers described the race-based scenario of this unusual reality series as incendiary or exploitative, others found the results of the self-described "social experiment" fascinating TV.

The premise of *Black. White.* is simple: two "average" American families (one Caucasian, one African-American) are billeted in one suburban Los Angeles home together, but through the magical art of movie makeup, undergo spontaneous race reversal. The whites become blacks; and vice versa. The families must live with these new "color" identities and countenance a very different world than the one they've experienced in the past.

In *Black. White.*, audiences meet African-Americans Brian, wife Renee, and son Nick, who are made "white." The white-family-turned-black consists of thick-headed ignoramus Bruno, his girlfriend Carmen, and daughter Rose.

The supposed dramatic point to this racial switch-eroo is simply to forge understanding about what it's like to see things from a different perspective; to reexamine racial prejudice and bias and even, preconceived notions. R.J. Cutler, a producer on the Morgan Spurlock documentary series *30 Days*, and rapper/movie-star Ice Cube are the two creative forces behind this six-week series, so one may harbor high hopes that this is genuine sociology and not crass, race-baiting commercialism.

Unfortunately—and even more so than many reality shows airing this year—the situations in *Black. White.* tend to appear forced and staged for maximum shock and "learning effect." For example, a white woman in "black face" attends an all African-American poetry/rap class. There, she gets a real education about being black.

Perhaps Robert Bianco, critic at *USA Today* said it best when he wrote that *Black. White.* is based on "two false premises, one more pernicious than the other: that you can understand someone of a different race simply by putting on makeup, and that you need that kind of understanding in order to treat people as the law and morality require. If inanity like *Black. White.* is what passes for racial dialogue these days, we'd all be better off if TV were encouraging us to talk less and behave better."[6]

Available on DVD.

BLADE: THE SERIES

(Spike)(CANCELED)(60minutes)(Wednesdays at 10:00pm EST; June 28, 2006-August 16, 2006) New Line Cinema/New Line TV/Marvel Films. Characters created by: Marv Wolfman. Executive Producers: Avi Arad, David S. Goyer, Jon Kroll, Jim Rosenthal. Produced by: Gordon Mark. Camera: Mark C. New. Film Editor: Leisa Lassek. Music: Ramin Djawadi. Written by: David S. Goyer, Geoff Johns, Barbara Nance, Chris Ruppenthal, David Simkins, Adam Targum, Daniel Truly. Directed by: Felix Enriquez Alcala Norberto Barba, Alex Chapple, John Fawcett, Peter O'Fallon, David Straiton, Brad Turner.

CAST
Kirk "Sticky Fingaz" Jones (Blade)
Jessica Gower (Chase)
Neil Jackson (Marcus Van Sciver)
Nelson Lee (Shen)
Jill Wagner (Krista Starr)

Blade—the African-American vampire slayer—appeared first in the comic book *Tombs of Dracula* (issue number ten, from Marvel) in 1972. A creation of Marv Wolfman, the cooler-than-cool superhero was drawn by artist Gene Colan garbed in a leather jacket and donning sunglasses. A "blaxploitation" hero of the disco decade, Blade dispatched creatures of the night with wooden stakes and plenty of 'tude.

More than two decades after his parturition in four-colors, actor Wesley Snipes brought the character to vivid and surly life in a trilogy of blockbuster films from New Line Cinema, *Blade* (1998), *Blade 2* (2002) and *Blade: Trinity* (2004). Snipes' version of the character was updated by writer/director David Goyer to be a more technological and taciturn avenger. To wit: the "Daywalker," as the half-vampire/half-human Blade was called by his enemies, deployed all kinds of gadgets, guns and steel weaponry to destroy villains ranging from Deacon Frost to the Council of the Vampire Nation.

In the summer of 2006, Goyer refashioned the myth of Blade as a summertime TV series called, appropriately, *Blade: The Series*. Although Snipes was reportedly offered the title role again, the actor turned it down, leaving the monosyllabic lead role instead to the rapper who goes by the handle "Sticky Fingaz."

Blade: The Series picks up exactly where the feature film trilogy leaves off: Blade is still combating the vampire nation, this time with the assistance of a new "tech" guy and sidekick named Shen (Nelson Lee). In the early episodes, Blade also meets and teams up with an Iraq war veteran, the beautiful Krista Starr (Jill Wagner), who—after being transformed into a vampire by the evil Marcus Van Sciver (Neil Jackson)—sides with the Daywalker and helps Blade defeat the evil vampires. Starr bears a personal grudge too: vampires played a role in the murder of her brother. Unlike the movies, which were set in Los Angeles, the TV series transfers the action to gritty Detroit, where Blade, Krista and Shen battle the various Vampire Houses, which boast names such as "Chthon," "Leichen," and "Armaya."

Various episodes reveal different aspects of this ongoing war between good undead and bad undead. In "Turn of the Screw," there's a search for Krista's mother. In "Death Goes On," a vaccine for the vampire "virus" is the object of a quest. In "Bloodlines," Blade contends with vampire outsiders and discontents (Bad Bloods) whom he grew up with and once fought side-by-side with. In "Sacrifice," further details of Blade's personal history are revealed, particularly the death of a surrogate father long ago.

Blade: The Series registered the highest Nielsen ratings of any original series premiere in the Spike channel's history, raking in a record 2.5 million viewers. After heavy curiosity viewing, however, that number dropped by more than fifty percent, and *Blade* was canceled.

Not yet available on DVD.

BONES

(FOX) (RENEWED) (60 minutes) (Tuesdays at 8:00 pm;
Wednesdays at 8:00 pm EST; September 13, 2005-May 17,
2006) Josephson Entertainment/Far Field Productions/20th
Century Fox Television. Created by: Hart Hanson. Executive
Producers: Hart Hanson, Barry Josephson, Stephen Nathan,
John Pontell. Co-Executive Producers: Dana Coen, Steve Beers.
Produced by: Greg Ball, Steve Blackman, Jim Chory, Dana
Coen, Kathy Reichs, Laura Wolner. Camera: Dermett Downs,
Cort Fey. Film Editors: Harry B. Miller III. Music: Crystal Method,
Peter Himmelman. Written by: Greg Ball, Stephen Nathan.
Directed by: Patrick R. Norris.

CAST

Emily Deschanel (Dr. Temperance Brennan)
David Boreanaz (Seeley Booth)
Eric Millegan (Zach Addy)
T.J. Thyne (Dr. Jack Hodgins)
Michaela Conlin (Angela Montenegro)
Jonathan Adams (Dr. Daniel Goodman)

Hart Hanson created this successful forensic thriller/
drama in the mold of *CSI*, but provided his new series a
structure more reminiscent of *The X-Files* (1993–2002),
with a scientist (a believer) and a skeptic (an FBI agent)
battling over cases while simultaneously falling in love.
After some schedule shuffling early in the season, *Bones*
turned out to be one of FOX's solid dramatic hits.

Bones is the story of Dr. Temperance Brennan (Emily
Deschanel), a forensic anthropologist working in Washington D.C.'s Jeffersonian Institute beside a group of
other geeks, including a computer expert named Angela
(Michaela Conlin), Dr. Hodgins (T. J. Thyne) and Zach
(Eric Millegan). Up until recently, Brennan's love life has
been troubled and she readily admits she found her most
"meaningful" relationships with dead people. All that
changes, however, when she meets handsome F.B.I. agent

Seeley Booth (David Boreanaz), a former sniper now
working in the Bureau. Booth works for the Homicide
Investigation Unit, and soon needs Brennan's expertise
on all kinds of cases involving the identification of murder victims. Booth taunts scientists in general as "squints"
and Brennan in particular as "Bones," (a name she hates)
but the pair nonetheless soon form a love-hate relationship as they solve various cases together.

The unlikely duo ends up hunting a terrorist in "The
Man in the S.U.V.," solve a Chandra Levy–style death
involving a Gary Condit–like Congressman ("Pilot"),
solve the murder of an ambassador's son on the grounds
of an exclusive private school ("A Boy in the Tree") and
identify the remains found in a nearby park ("A Boy in the
Bush"). On one occasion, Brennan and Booth attempt to
aid a man on death row and determine his innocence ("A
Man on Death Row").

Basically corpses show up *everywhere* and all are in
need of identification and forensic examination. Bones
turn up in the walls of dance clubs ("The Man in the
Walls"), inside bomb shelters ("The Man in the Fall-Out
Shelter"), in alleys ("The Superhero in the Alley") and
even in a refrigerator ("The Girl in the Fridge"). Basically,
there are skeletons in every closet.

As *Bones* grew more confident later in its good first
season, the series also began to stake out more personal
terrain. While out on a date, Brennan is targeted for a
revenge killing in "Two Bodies in the Lab," and another
tale, "The Soldier in the Grave" forces Booth to relive
memories of his stint as a sniper. Finally, the season finale,
"The Woman in Limbo," sees Brennan discovering secrets
about her dead parents, ones that call into question her
history and very identity.

Twenty-two hour-long episodes of *Bones* aired

throughout the 2005–2006 season, and the show shifted from Tuesday to Wednesday night at 8:00 pm in 2006. The series is famously "inspired" by the cases of a real-life forensic anthropologist named Kathy Reichs, which gives the show at least a modicum of plausibility. However, the real reason to watch is the chemistry between Boreanaz and Deschanel...which never fails to enliven stories that seem stolen right from the files of other criminal investigation series.

Critical opinion was mixed on *Bones*. Sid Smith of *The Chicago Tribune* found the dialogue and sexual tension "strictly canned and cutesy,"[7] whereas Ray Richmond of *The Hollywood Reporter* found that the series "hit the ground running" and was "instantly engaging."[8]

The first season DVD is available.

THE BOOK OF DANIEL

(NBC) (CANCELED) (60 minutes) (Fridays at 9:00 pm, EST; January 6, 2006–January 20, 2006) NBC Universal/Sony. Created by: Jack Kenny. Executive Producers: Jack Kenny, Flody Suarez, John Tinker. Co-Executive Producers: Alice West, James Frawley. Produced by: Tracey Stern, Harry Victor. Camera: Thomas Del Ruth. Film Editors: Paul Dixon, John Heath. Music: W.G. Snuffy Walden. Written by: Jack Kenny, Andrew Landis, David Simkins, Blair Singer, Julia Swift, Harry Victor. Directed by: James Frawley, Rob Thompson.

CAST

Aidan Quinn (Daniel Webster)
Susanna Thompson (Judith Webster)
Ellen Burstyn (Beatrice Congrave)
Garret Dillahunt (Jesus Christ)
Allison Pill (Grace Webster)
Ivan Shaw (Adam Webster)
Christian Campbell (Peter Webster)

Meet the Webster family. Here's the score card (and trust me, audiences will need one if they want to keep up). This series, which first aired as a two-hour special on NBC, introduces viewers to a pill-popping patriarch, Episcopal minister Daniel Webster (Aidan Quinn). He has a gay son, Peter (Christian Campbell), and an adopted Asian son too, Adam (Ivan Shaw).

Then there's Webster's daughter Grace (Allison Pill), who has been arrested for selling drugs (to make money to produce her manga comic), and Daniel's wife Judith (*Star Trek Voyager*'s former Borg Queen, Susanna Thompson), who enjoyeth the "occasional" martini too much, methinks.

Wait. I'm not finished.

There's also Daniel's mother, Catherine…who suffers from the worst case of TV Alzheimer's you're ever likely to see; meaning simply that she blurts out funny comments at the Sunday dinner table at just the right time but then—*every now and again*—says something incredibly poignant so you remember she's sick; like the touching interrogative to Daniel, "I'm your mother?"

Hold on. Still tallying here.

My notes indicate there's also Judith's brother-in-law, Charlie, who has left his wife and stolen over $3 million from Daniel's church (which, predictably, is in "crisis"). Meanwhile, Judith's sister seems engaged in a lesbian affair with Charlie's secretary.

And then there's Daniel's father (James Rebhorn), who is an intolerant bigot and doesn't realize that one of his grandsons is homosexual.

Oh, and I can't forget this: Ellen Burstyn is around too playing a supporting role as a well-dressed Church bishop who seems more like Martha Stewart than a pontiff.

Of course, there's also the requisite spiritual crisis of the week. For instance, in "Temptation," Daniel arbitrates a "sensitive" Terri Schiavo/euthanasia, end-of-life–type issue amongst his flock at St. Barnabus.

All this, and *The Book of Daniel* features a Buddy Christ too. Yep, Jesus Christ is one of the *dramatis personae*. The messiah materializes now and again to provide sage advice.

One would be hard-pressed to remember another drama/soap-opera so front-loaded with as many contrived elements as this short-lived experiment. Everything about the show is hackneyed, trite, and about as far from 21st century reality as anything currently airing on the SCI FI Channel (with the possible exception of *Mansquito*).

The result of so many dangling plotlines is that during its short life on broadcast, *Book of Daniel* wobbled and lurched from one quasi-meaningful "issue of the day" to another without really substantively focusing on *any-thing.* The template here appears to be *Desperate House-wives,* and *Book of Daniel* attempts to walk the same fine line of humor/melodrama as that popular ABC show.

Yet—and this is important—*Book of Daniel* is staggeringly unfunny. Near the end of "Temptation," for example, there's a scene set at a funeral in which an angry widow (Judith's sister) spots the mistress of her dead husband, and goes on a rampage in the cemetery. It should be funny, yet there's not a laugh or giggle to be found. It goes over like a lead balloon.

The Christian right wing also complained about the series' use of the "Buddy Christ" (a term coined in Kevin Smith's *Dogma*), and though I tend not to agree with these jokers, the movement had its reasons. If this character is supposed to really be Christ, and not a fantasy in Daniel's head, then the program is guilty of trivializing a figure that millions worship and revere…turning the savior into a sitcom character replete with catchphrases.

On the other hand, if the Buddy Christ in *Book of Daniel* is merely a fantasy, merely part of Daniel's interior dialogue with himself, then he's really just a self-righteous crutch of the lead character. Why? Because Jesus constantly soothes Daniel and makes him feel that his decisions are okay and acceptable. In other words, Daniel is rest assured in his self-righteousness, because Jesus is literally his copilot.

Ironically, Jesus Christ as depicted in *The Book of Daniel* doesn't object to the fact that the Webster family employs, essentially, an African-American manservant. One who has very few lines, and just gazes at the other characters with angelic disapproval and bemusement.

Even more to the point, Jesus doesn't object to a WASP-ish American family living in the lap of luxury in a wealthy community and huge house, while much of the outside world (and parts of America too) suffer from hunger and live in poverty. Nope, instead, Jesus is fully and enthusiastically engaged in the family's petty day-to-day drama. Should Grandpa be told that Peter is gay? Should Daniel just learn to "*talk to his daughter*"? Will geeks (not meeks) inherit the Earth?

Jesus as suburban friend and enabler reinforces the worst notions of modern American Christianity: that Jesus is perched on our shoulders, validating our personal, chosen lifestyle, instead of challenging it. By chosen, I refer to the choice to pursue the almighty dollar as the One True God. That is clearly the obsession of Daniel and his family here. And that's probably a worse sin than drug abuse, alcoholism or anything else. Because doesn't the Bible state that a "*rich man in heaven is like a camel through the eye of a needle*" (roughly paraphrased). So why is Jesus even bothering with Daniel and his family?

Let me put it this way: If Jesus is real, then the Websters are hellbound.

Here's a sample of Jesus's homespun wisdom on the series: "Life is hard for everyone, Daniel. That's why there's a nice reward at the end of it."

You know, that should be on a Hallmark card.

Only four episodes of *The Book of Daniel* aired on NBC before January 25, 2006, when the series was unceremoniously sent to TV Heaven. The AFA (American Family Association) claimed victory after protesting the series and allegedly writing over 600,000 e-mails to sponsors and the network. More than likely however, it was ratings—not Christian controversy—that killed this overloaded and absurd series.

Fans can have a rapture over the series all over again, following its release on DVD September 28, 2006.

BROTHERHOOD

(Showtime) (RENEWED) (60 minutes) (Sundays at 10:00 pm, EST; July 9, 200-September 17, 2006) Showtime. Created by: Blake Masters. Executive Producers: Blake Masters, Henry Bromell, Elizabeth Guber Stephen. Co-Executive Producers: Dawn Prestwich, Nicole Yorkin. Produced by: Donna Bloom. Camera: Ernest Holzman. Film Editors: Anthony Redman, Terry Keller. Music: Jeff Rona. Written by: Henry Bromell, Nicole Yorkin, Dawn Prestwich. Directed by: Ed Bianchi, Philip Noyce, Steve Shill.

CAST

Jason Isaacs (Michael Caffee)
Jason Clark (Tommy Caffee)
Annabeth Gish (Eileen Caffee)
Ethan Embry (Declan Giggs)
Stivi Paskoski (Pete McGonagle)
Kevin Chapman (Freddie Cook)
Fionnula Flanagan (Rose Caffee)

The best new drama of the 2005–2006 season is *Brotherhood*, a gritty drama that takes place in "The Hill," a blue collar neighborhood in Providence, Rhode Island. As the series makes plain, the Hill stands at an important crossroads between the past and the future; betwixt a time when neighborhood and community were important and today's 21st century, when big business rules the land and globalization threatens American jobs and the middle class.

In more personal terms, *Brotherhood* chronicles the experiences of the once tightly knit Caffee family. Tommy Caffee (Jason Clark) is an elected representative in the State House, attempting to bring money and prestige back to the economically devastated Hill, and also trying to make ends meet for his family.

Michael Caffee (Jason Isaacs) is Tommy's older brother, and as the series commences, this prodigal son returns to The Hill after five years. Unlike his politico brother, Michael is a gangster, and he promptly begins his own urban renewal policy in The Hill, which mostly involves muscling into ownership of local businesses such as a dilapidated movie theater, a convenience store, and a local bar. Michael also clashes with the town thug and crime lord, Freddie (Kevin Chapman), whose throne he ultimately desires.

While Tommy toils in political circles and struggles to keep Michael at arms-length—lest his reputation as a straight-shooter be compromised—Tommy's wife, Eileen (Annabeth Gish) faces her own personal apocalypse at home. A stay-at-home mom who takes care of her three girls, Eileen has been engaged in a sexual liaison with an old flame from high school and worse, has become addicted to drugs. In the series' early episodes, she faces clinical depression, the root cause of these destructive behaviors. She later confides in Michael's sister that she's had an affair.

Other regulars on *Brotherhood* include white-maned Fionnula Flanagan, who plays Tommy and Michael's lioness of a mother, Rose. Rose just lost the job she held at a local textile mill for over twenty years, and learns that the Union—which once attempted to protect employees—is now toothless. She also plays peacemaker between Tommy and Michael. "You either love your brother and take him at his word, or you don't," she warns a suspicious Tommy.

Pete McGonagle (Stivi Paskoski) is Michael's gangland enforcer, a surprisingly decent and sensitive man who has been on the wagon for two years…or at least until Michael returned to town. Ethan Embry plays Declan Giggs, a friend of the Caffee family turned local police detective. He's been tasked with bringing down Michael

Caffee…an assignment which becomes more problematic each passing day because of his partner's corruption and debt to Michael over a roadside shooting.

In basic terms, this summer series from Showtime gazes at the manner in which crime and politics are actually uncomfortably similar. Michael and Tommy both "hustle" in their own fashion to get things accomplished. Accommodations are made to get bills passed (or not passed), and the series reveals back room deals, insider trading, and so forth.

What remains most provocative about *Brotherhood*, however, is the populist tone it strikes in many episodes. In their own individual (and very different) ways, Tommy and Michael both want to preserve "The Hill" and the neighborhood. They fight battles to keep a highway out, are forced to deal with a new waste plant coming in, and so forth. They cling to the past, but the "progress" of globalization keeps changing the nature of the world—the neighborhood—they grew up in.

This is also Rose's battle. In one superlative installment, she grudgingly takes a job at a Wal-Mart, big-box type store and learns that the employees there have no rights, no health care…and no help. And without unions, they have no hope either. "Collective bargaining is the right of every American worker," she says, but her ideas—again ones relating to community and the way it is slipping away from us—are out of step in the "me first" 21st century America.

Sexy, gritty and never less than compelling, *Brotherhood* thrives as a terrific summer series, one that clearly understands the basic conceits behind politics and crime. Both "professions" are all about making compromises and being compromised.

The first season is available on DVD.

CLOSE TO HOME

(CBS) (RENEWED) (60 minutes) (Tuesdays at 10:00 pm; Fridays at 10:00 pm, EST; October 4, 2005–May 19, 2006) Jerry Bruckheimer Television/Warner Bros. Created by: Jim Leonard. Executive Producers: Jerry Bruckheimer, Jim Leonard, Jonathan Littman, Simon West. Produced by: Jill Lopez Denton. Camera: Michael Barrett, Rick Bota, Eric Schmidt. Film Editor: Kevin Krasney, Steven Lang. Music: Michael A. Levine, Jeanette Surga. Written by: Carol Barbee, Alfredo Barrios, Jr., Leo Geter, Jim Leonard, John E. Pogue, Lukas Reiter, Eric Shelton, Lindsey Sturman. Directed by: Charles Beeson, Steven De Paul, Kevin Dowling, Emilio Estevez, Karen Gaviola, Lewis H. Gould, Martha Mitchell, John Peters, Helen Shaver, Simon West, Alex Zarkrzewski.

CAST

Jennifer Finnigan (Annabeth Chase)
Kimberly Elise (Maureen Scotfield)
John Carroll Lynch (Steve Sharp)
Christian Kane (Jack Chase)

Close to Home is the not-particularly challenging or fresh story of new mother and tough prosecutor Annabeth Chase (Jennifer Finnigan), a so-called "superheroine who is making the world safe for motherhood,"[9] according to the *New York Post*. In the crime investigation drama, this trim blonde prosecutes criminals in suburbia, and the series "depicts appalling horrors perpetrated within seemingly normal American families."[10]

Annabeth has come off maternity leave; and her kindly and studly husband, Jack (Christian Kane) supports her return to the prosecutor's office. In Annabeth's absence, an ambitious prosecutor, Maureen (Kimberly Elise) has come on strong, hoping to advance her own career. This makes greater job pressure for Annabeth. Their boss is Steve Sharp (John Carroll Lynch).

Close to Home is another law enforcement/investigation show in the tried-and-true pattern of far too many other shows on TV these days. There's a righteous heroine who balances home life and a career, all while uncovering dirty secrets in neighbors' yards. It's surprisingly self-righteous and canned, a totally off-the-shelf drama. Or, as *The Boston Globe* noted, the series is "a contrived product."[11]

The lurid episodes make safe, wealthy suburbia appear a hot bed of deviancy and perversion. In the pilot, Annabeth prosecutes a woman who set fire to her own house, only to uncover a secret history of abuse. In "Suburban Prostitution," Annabeth goes after an illicit sex ring. You know the type—they just keeping popping up next door all the time like termites, right?

In "Meth Murders," a man stoned on meth commits a horrible crime, giving rise to lectures on drugs. Online predators come up in "Hot Grrl," and "The Rapist Next Door" involves a sex offender who moves into the neighborhood just as a rape occurs. It would be one thing if these lurid tales were played straight-faced without melodramatic bells and whistles, but the episodes tend toward histrionics, not true or authentic drama.

Close to Home achieved decent numbers when it premiered in October of 2006, about ten million viewers or so. However, canny CBS executives soon moved the female-friendly venture to Friday at 10:00 pm and shifted the lousy sci-fi drama *Threshold* into the less-desirable Tuesday slot. *Close to Home* was now paired with the equally preachy and treacly Jennifer Love Hewitt "inspirational" vehicle *Ghost Whisperer*. In its new slot, *Close to Home* drew nearly twelve million viewers, a considerable uptick in the ratings.[12] *Close to Home* has been renewed for a second season.

Not yet available on DVD.

THE COLBERT REPORT

(Comedy Central) (RENEWED) (30 minutes) (Week-nights at 11:30 pm, EST; October 17, 2005-Continuing) Busby Productions/Comedy Central. Created by: Stephen Colbert. Executive Producer: Stephen Colbert, Ben Karlin, Jon Stewart. Produced by: Jeff Cooperman. Camera: John Harrison, Torie Livia, John Meikeljohn, Dante Pagano. Film Editors: Jason Baker, Andrew Matheson, Josh Weinstein. Music: Cheap Trick. Written by: Michael Brumm, Rich Dahm, Eric Drysdale, Rob Dubbin, Glenn Eichler, Peter Gwinn, Laura Krafft, Frank Lesser, Tom Purcell, Allison Silverman. Directed by: Jim Hoskinson.

CAST
Stephen Colbert (Host)

Sometimes, a television series perfectly captures the mood of a time, the Zeitgeist. It's an unlikely (and infrequent) convergence of events that makes this synergy happen, but make no mistake, Comedy Central's *The Colbert Report*—a hit comedy from the makers of *The Daily Show with Jon Stewart*—is just such a program.

Five-and-a-half years into the second Bush Administration, with the War in Iraq a quagmire and New Orleans still in shambles after Hurricane Katrina, Americans are experiencing Bush fatigue "big time," and pundit fatigue too. The Bush Administration has relentlessly popularized its talking points with a two-fisted assault on the English language, providing citizenry with new and Orwellian terms such as "faith-based initiatives," "shock and awe," "metrics," "blame game," "flip-flop," "cut and run," "Clear Skies" initiatives and so forth.

Worse, the elephantine GOP echo chamber so thoroughly dominates the corporate-driven media of the 21st century that these terms and the Administration's talking points are endlessly shouted by angry, short-tempered pundits with names like Bill O'Reilly, Anne Coulter,

Laura Ingraham, Chris Wallace, and Brit Hume.

The noise had grown disconcertingly deafening until one man—a hero—punctured the balloon. Stephen Colbert, a comedian and former correspondent on *The Daily Show*, has almost singlehandedly shifted the dialogue in this country in a new and refreshing direction by crafting *The Colbert Report*: simultaneously a parody of talking-head programming like *The O'Reilly Factor* and a deconstruction of the ways they (deviously) get their points across.

On this half-hour "fake" news series, Colbert plays a blustering, arrogant, willfully ignorant O'Reilly–type, an unthinking cheerleader for everything the Bush White House does. But in assuming this role, Colbert actually exposes the talking points as ludicrous and the talkers for what they are: shameless self-promoters, parrots, and apologists for a corrupt government.

Structurally, *The Colbert Report* features several segments that are repeated frequently, including "Better Know a District," which introduces viewers to Congressmen and then slyly mocks the public servant.

There's also "All You Need to Know," which is the news reported through the crucible of Colbert's twisted mind, and the most popular segment of all: "The Word." In "The Word," Colbert introduces a word or term and explains why it is important and relevant. Meanwhile, on screen, bullet points about "the Word" appear beside him. Amusingly, these points seem to have been added by a subversive who realizes that the pundit Colbert plays is full of shit. Thus the bullets are ironic, or undercut the very point he's attempting to forge.

Famously, on his very first episode, Colbert used "The Word" to introduce the nation to a term he had invented. That word: "Truthiness." As we now know,

The truthiness shall set you free! It's Stephen Colbert, host of **THE COLBERT REPORT**.

truthiness is a word for something that "feels" accurate, but isn't actually truthful. It's "faith-based" knowledge, meaning that it sounds good but has no basis in fact. Colbert in fact, disdains facts, preferring to let his "gut" tell him what to think.

Another one of Colbert's words became famous in the summer of 2006. "Wikiality" relates to reality as it is defined at the online encyclopedia *Wikipedia*. Since the entries there can be edited by anyone, Colbert defines Wikiality as truth by consensus. In a world where corporations control a media biased towards conservative principles, *The Colbert Report* represents an assault on the prevailing wisdom, on assumption-based reporting, on "faith-based" truthiness, and on truth by consensus rather than by science or knowledge.

It also happens to be a damn funny show. In addition to his work on *The Colbert Report*, Stephen Colbert had a "Zeitgeist" moment this season when he brought his schtick to the annual White House Correspondents Dinner. There, Colbert took the podium, and with President George W. Bush just feet away, used comedy to speak truth to power. Ironically, the media did not at first report Colbert's speech, fearing that it was too incendiary.

Instead, mainstream sources including FOX News, MSNBC, and CNN reported only on the President's talk, which saw the Chief Executive pitted against a lookalike President Bush. But something funny happened and history was made. The Colbert speech took off on the Internet, and before long had registered almost 300,000 hits! Colbert and his persona were now a part of the American mainstream, despite the best efforts of the corporate media to deny him coverage.

The text of Colbert's speech is revolutionary. The comic used his "facts are bad" truthiness schtick to expose this President's flawed, simple-minded leadership. To wit, Colbert—in his Mark Twain moment—reported the following:

"I'm sorry, I've never been a fan of books. I don't trust them. They're all fact, no heart. I mean, they're elitist, telling us what is or isn't true, or what did or didn't happen. Who's Britannica to tell me the Panama Canal was built in 1914? If I want to say it was built in 1941, that's my right as an American! I'm with the president, let history decide what did or did not happen. The greatest thing about this man [President Bush] is he's steady. You know where he stands. He believes the same thing Wednesday that he believed on Monday, no matter what happened Tuesday. Events can change; this man's beliefs never will."[13]

Not yet available on DVD, but just Google Colbert's speech and revel in the truthiness.

THE COMEBACK

(HBO) (CANCELED) (30 minutes) (Sundays at 9:30 pm, EST;
June 5, 2005–September 4, 2005) Is or Isn't Entertainment/
Working Class Films/Warner Bros./HBO. Created by: Lisa Kudrow and Michael Patrick King. Executive Producers: Dan Bucatinsky, Lisa Kudrow, Michael Patrick King, and John P. Melfi.
Producer: Tim Gibbons. Camera: Nancy Schreiber. Film Editor:
David Rogers. Written by: Amy B. Harris, John Riggi, Michael
Schur, Linda Wallem. Directed by: Michael Lehmann, J. Clark
Matthis, Greg Mottoli.

CAST

Lisa Kudrow (Valerie Cherish)
Malin Akerman (Juna)
Robert Bagnell (Tom Peterman)
Lance Barber (Paulie G.)
Robert Michael Morris (Mickey)
Laura Silverman (Jane)
Damian Young (Mark Burman)

The Comeback is the highly amusing and—in some
cases—heartbreaking tale of washed-up TV actress, Valerie Cherish (Lisa Kudrow), once the star of a bad 1989–
1992 sitcom called "I'm It." That landmark series ran for
ninety-seven episodes but was unceremoniously dumped
right before magic episode number one-hundred. Why?
Audience backlash over an ill-conceived Rodney King
joke that came too soon after the Los Angeles riots.

It was either that joke that killed the show, or the fact
that a chimpanzee was added to the regular cast of the law
office ensemble comedy during the last season.

Anyway, thirteen years after "I'm It," the long out-
of-work Cherish is back with a vengeance, simultaneously
starring in a reality show entitled "The Comeback" and a
new network sitcom called "Room and Bored." The only
problem for Val is that the sitcom has suffered through
a drastic reimagining after the pilot. Instead of playing

an urbane architect who shares a condo with four thir-
tysomethings, Valerie has now been reduced to playing
bitter Aunt Sassy, an over-the-hill marmish-type whose
fashion sense runs to pastel jogging suits. Her costars are
all inexperienced but overtly horny twentysomethings,
and so Valerie feels out of place and past her prime.

Aunt Sassy's catchphrase on Room and Bored is "Note
to self: I don't need to see that!" and the pilot ridicules this
phrase mercilessly. There's a perfectly timed sequence—
captured in an overhead reality TV–style camera angle—
in which Valerie rehearses this insipidly unfunny phrase
(while simultaneously eating half a chocolate cake), and
it's wicked fun.

Co-created by ex-Friends star Lisa Kudrow, The
Comeback is filmed via the auspices of the mockumentary format popularized by Christopher Guest in such
films as Best in Show (2000) and A Mighty Wind (2003)
as well as such post-modern TV series such as The Office.
Therefore, Valerie spends an inordinate amount of time
in the series talking directly to the cameras. Her personal
and professional life thus unfolds in cinema verité before
our very eyes in a very naturalistic way. Essentially, it's a
slow-motion train wreck—and also extremely funny. The
series alternates between low humor and highbrow laughs
with great dexterity.

In The Comeback's pilot for instance, Valerie attempts
to make a touching confession in front of her personal
"video diary" camera, which is set up in her bathroom.
However, while Valerie attempts to craft art before the
camera, her husband Mark—just feet away—is (loudly)
using the toilet. The bursts of his thunderbucket punctu-
ate and interrupt Valerie's emotional moment.

In another episode, "Valerie Demands Dignity," Valerie is disturbed to learn (from Entertainment Weekly) that

reality TV is now considered dead. Her producers thus decide to couple her series with a new reality show, one starring an over-enterprising midget called "The Littlest Assistant." The sparks fly when this little person attempts to spice up Valerie's life for ratings gold. Valerie desperately desires to maintain her image as "nice" before the cameras, but before long she's reduced to hurling insults at the most annoying dwarf.

The Comeback is not only a triumphant return to series television for Kudrow, who gives an Emmy-worthy (and nominated) performance, but a blistering indictment of all things Hollywood. From insipid sitcoms and seedy reality shows that rely on sex and stunts, to star-sized egos, this series is razor-sharp in its observations about the entertainment industry. It requires great skill and a droll hand to go from poking fun at celebrity egos and Hollywood's obsession with youth to vetting cheerfully silly skits about reality shows, but *The Comeback* makes it all appear easy. Indeed, some of the clips of other TV shows airing on Valerie's network rival the very best of *Saturday Night Live*'s comedic commercials tradition.

For instance, there's a game show featured called "Take That" in which spouses earn points and money by literally bludgeoning each other with shovels and two-by-fours. Husbands get $200,000 for a blow to the wife's head.

Another show, "The Search for America's Next Great Porn Star" includes a gag involving a group of bubble-headed aspirants racing up a flight of stairs (trying to get to a vomit bucket) while "storing" *ahem* creamy material in their mouth. Whoever makes it to the roof without spitting up first is the winner.

Thirteen half-hour episodes of this very funny series were produced for HBO and began airing on June 5, 2005. The characters surrounding unfortunate Valerie Cherish include Jane (Laura Silverman), her much put-upon reality show producer; Mark (Damian Young), Valerie's clueless husband, who works outside the industry; Juna (Malin Akerman) the sexy but vapid star of *Room and Bored*, and Paulie G. (Lance Barber), the surly and sullen writer of the fictional sitcom.

Despite a brilliant premise and equally dynamic execution, HBO canceled *The Comeback* in late September after just one order of thirteen episodes, perhaps because the series failed to crack the 2.0 million viewer benchmark. In years to come, *The Comeback* is virtually guaranteed to be a cult hit amongst admirers of quality TV comedy.

The complete series is available on DVD.

COMMANDER IN CHIEF

(ABC) (CANCELED) (60 minutes) (Tuesdays at 9:00pm, EST; September 27, 2005-June 14, 2006) ABC/Battleplan Productions/Touchstone Television. Created by: Rob Lurie. Executive Producers: Steve Bochco, Marc Frydman, Dee Johnson, James Kiklighter, Rod Lurie. Co-Executive Producers: Allison Adler, Alison Cross, Geena Davis, Rick Wallace. Produced by: James Spies. Film Editors: Warren Bowman, Sarah Boyd, Khristal Khatib. Music: Larry Groupe. Written by: Allison Adler, Richard Arthur, Steve Cohen, Allison Cross, Anya Epstein, Joel Fields, Dee Johnson, James Kicklighter, Rod Lurie, Dahvi Waller. Directed by: Daniel Attias, Chris Long, Rod Lurie, Daniel Minahan, Vincent Misiano, Bobby Roth, Steven Shill, Rick Wallace, Greg Yaitanes.

CAST

Geena Davis (President Mackenzie Allen)
Donald Sutherland (Nathan Templeton)
Harry Lennix (Jim Gardner)
Kyle Secor (Rod Calloway)
Ever Carradine (Kelly Ludlow)
Matt Lanter (Horace Calloway)
Caitlin Wachs (Rebecca Calloway)
Jasmine Anthony (Amy Calloway)

Commander in Chief was one of the most anticipated and highly touted dramatic series of the fall of 2005, arriving on the airwaves just in time to rescue concerned political junkies who knew NBC's *The West Wing* was experiencing its last hurrah.

Even better, as the news stories in the mainstream media endlessly parroted, *Commander in Chief*—the inspirational story of a female POTUS played by Geena Davis—would prepare the nation for the inevitable coronation of Hillary Clinton in November 2008.

"This show will tap the thinking and heart of people about what it means to have a woman president and what it means to have a representative democracy," asserted Mary Wilson, founder of The White House Project and author of *Closing the Gap: Why Women Can and Must Help Run the World*, "I think it will get us closer than we have ever been."[14]

Unfortunately for Ms. Wilson and *Commander in Chief*, their candidate didn't exactly win the popular vote.

Commander in Chief was created by producer Rod Lurie, the same artist who developed the very fine year 2000 film *The Contender*, which starred Joan Allen as a female vice-president facing scandalous allegations from an opposition party (and being heckled by a Republican Congressman played by Gary Oldman). It's no coincidence that *Commander in Chief*'s Prez is named Allen after that very actress, an actress who, by the way, (along with Sigourney Weaver) apparently turned down the role.

The story of *Commander in Chief* goes as follows: A Republican President dies in office of a brain aneurysm, leaving his running mate, a political independent and—*gasp*—a woman, Mackenzie Allen, to ascend to his position. But Allen isn't going to have it easy as the Leader of the Free World. Her political nemesis is the dastardly and manipulative Conservative Speaker of the House, Nathan Templeton (Donald Sutherland).

Furthermore, at home, she must deal with her hapless spouse, "The First Husband," (Kyle Secor) and three troublesome children. It's the ultimate balancing act for this "career" woman. Allen must not only unite her family, but her country and—in times of crisis (like one brewing in Africa)—the whole world.

"My whole life has been about playing roles that women are excited to see and can identify with,"[15] Geena Davis noted, explaining the appeal of playing President of the United States on this series.

In its time on the air, *Commander in Chief* delved into

First Couple: Rod Calloway (Kyle Secor) and President Mackenzie Allen (Geena Davis).
From **COMMANDER IN CHIEF**.

all the political topics one would expect of a series focusing on the United States Presidency. In many instances a political story was sistered with a personal, family one.

In "First Choice," Mac had to select a Vice-Presidential nominee at the same time that her daughter's possibly damaging diary went missing. In "First Strike," Allen contended with a Latin American crisis while dealing with her kids' first day at public school. In "First Dance," Mac had to countenance her first international summit (with the Russian president) while her husband had to oversee his first state dinner.

Other subjects that came up in the eighteen-episode run of *Commander in Chief* included, a hurricane ("First Disaster"), terrorism ("First…Do No Harm"), preparations for a State of the Union address ("State of the Unions"), Mac's bout with appendicitis…which brought Templeton to the White House as Acting President because of rules of succession ("The Elephant in the Room"). There was even an attempt to resurrect the Equal Rights Amendment ("Unfinished Business").

All of this drama was fascinating, but nothing compared to the behind-the-scenes intrigue dominating *Commander in Chief*. Show runner and creator Rod Lurie was replaced early in the series' run by veteran *NYPD Blue* co-creator Steven Bochco when shooting allegedly fell behind (and ABC was forced to air a rerun).

Not much later, it was Bochco's turn to be impeached, and he in turn was succeeded by Dee Johnson for undisclosed reasons. Finally, another public controversy erupted just when *Commander in Chief* could least afford it. One episode concerned a riot in a D.C. suburb called Hyattsville, and the real-life residents there complained about their negative on-air depiction as criminals and scoundrels.

Note to President Allen: Try not to insult the Electorate.

Although it started out as the highest-rated drama of the 2005–2006 season with a whopping 16 million people tuning in for the debut, *Commander in Chief*'s ratings slipped as the season wore on. ABC pulled the series from the schedule for more than ten weeks in mid-season and then shifted it from its comfy Tuesday time slot to the more competitive Thursday at 9:00 time slot (where *Prime Time Live* had been stationed).

There, ratings were terrible (just 6.5 million viewers), and after two weeks, *Commander in Chief* was permanently removed from office. The series was canceled, despite the fact that the always-impressive Davis had won a Golden Globe for the role, as well as Emmy and SAG nominations.

The complete series is available on DVD.

CONVICTION

(NBC) (CANCELED) (60 minutes) (Fridays at 10:00 pm, EST; March 3, 2006-May 19, 2006) Wolf Films/NBC Universal. Executive Producers: Rick Eid, Walon Green, Peter Jankowski, Dick Wolf. Co-Executive Producer: Constantine Makris. Produced by: Laurie Arent, Carter Harris, Jane Raab. Camera: Ernest Holzman, John Thomas. Film Editor: Kevin Krasny. Music: Mark Post. Written by: Rick Eid, Walon Green. Directed by: Norberto Barba, Matt Reeves, Randy Zisk.

CAST
Eric Balfour (Brian Peluso)
Jordan Bridges (Nick Potter)
Milena Govich (Jessica Rossi)
Stephanie March (Alexandra Cabot)
Julianne Nicholson (Christina Finn)
J. August Richards (Billy Desmond)

After the unexpected failure in 2005 of the third tent pole in the formerly indomitable *Law & Order* franchise, *Trial By Jury*, skeptical voices in the entertainment industry began to whisper about the future. Was the franchise finally—*after umpteen years*—getting long in the tooth? Certainly the series were durable and performing well, but were they…sexy? Were they buzzworthy? And more to the point, could they continue to compete with that other police procedural franchise on CBS called *CSI*?

In response to such gossip, NBC rolled out a new product in the endless *Law & Order* line at the 2005–2006 mid-season point. Although *Law & Order* had been dropped from the series title (much as *Star Trek* had been dropped from the series *Enterprise* at one point in UPN history), *Conviction* was actually the fifth series in the proud lineage. Fred Thompson even put in a cameo appearance in the premiere to prove it.

Because the new series would focus on hotshot twentysomethings in the New York District Attorney's office, some critics saw *Conviction* as a blatant attempt to skew the property younger and sexier. Another creative decision also influenced that perception. Whereas the previous *Law & Order* series rigorously focused attention on the job at hand—on catching and prosecuting criminals, *Conviction* would be the first in the franchise to spend a great deal of time going home with the sexy young Assistant District Attorneys. Their love lives, their backstories became important in a way that personal narratives never had been in the other ventures.

Still, executive producer Dick Wolf insisted that—like his previous *Law & Order* shows—*Conviction* was truthful and accurate. "The actual bureau in New York has in the neighborhood of two- to three hundred people in their early twenties who spend fourteen, sixteen hours a day with each other and essentially have no other lives," he told *The Orlando Sentinel*, "There's a certain amount of pheromone in the air, and stuff's going to happen."[16]

Another effort to skew to a younger demographic was seen in NBC's marketing for the series premiere. *Conviction* played first not on television for the old fogies, but via computer downloads and iPods. Because—guess what—youngsters today like those contraptions! And that's the group the network desperately wanted to introduce the aging franchise to.

Conviction is set in the New York District Attorney's office, where Alexandra Cabot (Stephanie March) plays mother hen to a group of ambitious, hot-blooded ADAs. First on that list is Nick Potter (Jordan Bridges), an attorney who left corporate law to make fifty grand a year prosecuting crooks. Christina (Julianne Nicholson) is a newbie prosecuting her first big case, and so forth. Other personal stories in the series involve Christina becoming attracted to a star witness in a case, and going out on blind dates.

Even if the personal stories were hot, the crime angle of *Conviction* seemed like warmed-over porridge. "Break-up" involved a friend of Nick's getting busted for cocaine possession. "Indebted" was about the prosecution of a rap mogul accused of murder. "True Love" concerned a rape prosecution, and "Hostage" saw an attack on the court-house wherein many of the ADAs were held at gunpoint. How many times, and on how many different series (and in how many episodes of other *Law & Order* series?) have identical or similar tales been depicted?

Though undeniably economical (as a cost-saving measure it reused sets from *Trial By Jury*), *Conviction* failed to attract the number of viewers—of any age—that NBC sought, and it became the second *Law & Order* series to be canceled after a short run.

Next up: *Law & Order: Kindergarten Edition*! *Conviction: The Complete Series* is available on DVD.

Available on DVD.

COURTING ALEX

(CBS) (CANCELED) (30 minutes) (Mondays at 9:30 pm, EST; January 23, 2006–March 29, 2006) Touchstone Television/ Paramount Television. Created by: Fred Barron. Executive Producer: Rob Hanning. Co-Executive Producers: Eileen Conn, Seth Kurland. Produced by: Faye Oshima Belyeu, Jenna Elfman. Camera: John Simmons. Film Editor: Noel Rogers. Music: Greg Sill. Written by: Rob Hanning. Directed by: James Burrows, Pamela Frymar.

CAST
Jenna Elfman (Alex Rose)
Hugh Bonneville (Julian)
Dabney Coleman (Bill Rose)
Josh Randall (Scott Larson)
Jillian Bach (Molly)

An instantly forgettable mid-season addition to the 2005–2006 plate of quickly canceled sitcoms, *Courting Alex* initially looked like something else; perhaps it was built for long-term success after all. Veteran *Cheers* (1982–1993) director James Burrows was on board the project, as was *Dharma and Greg* (1997–2002) star Jenna Elfman and sitcom veteran Dabney Coleman (*Buffalo Bill*, 1983–1984). The series also started out strong in the ratings, cracking the top twenty shows on its first airing.

But *Courting Alex* did not have lasting power, and was canceled after just eight episodes aired. The problem? Lack of originality and passion, perhaps. There's just a feeling of inertia and been-there/done-that about the whole thing.

The situation comedy recounts the story of Alex Rose (Jenna Elfman), a buttoned-down attorney who takes a job at her father Bill's (Dabney Coleman) law firm. She falls for hunky Scott Larson (Josh Randall) while working legal cases, but Elfman underplays the lead role to an almost alarming degree. Maybe she wanted to prove she could be more than that free spirit, Dharma.

Or, as Tom Shales wrote in *The Washington Post*: "She's the wallflower at her own dance, the pooper of her own party. She's not bad, just flat; not annoying, just weak. Not that *Courting Alex* would be a bold comedy breakthrough with a livelier and funnier star (say, Teri Garr at her peak) present. It's a fairly standard proposition about a successful, single Manhattan lawyer named Alex Rose who, network publicity states, enjoys "everything life has to offer—except a life."[17]

Not currently available on DVD.

CRIMINAL MINDS

(CBS) (RENEWED) (60 minutes) (Wednesdays at 10:00 pm, EST; September 22, 2005-May 10, 2006) Touchstone Television/Paramount. Created by: Jeff Davis. Executive Producers: Ed Bernero, Mark Gordon. Co-Executive Producers: Jeff Davis, Judith McCreary, Peter Schindler, Deborah Spera. Produced by: Debra J. Fisher, Erica Messer, Peter R. McIntosh. Camera: Glenn Kershaw, Alex Nepomniaschy. Film Editors: Peter B. Ellis, Nina Gilberti, Jimmy Girtlian. Music: Mark Mancina, Steffan Fantini, Marc Fantini, Scott Gordon. Written by: Edward Allen Bernero, Jeff Davis, Judith McCreary, Erica Messer, Simon Mirren, Ed Napier, Andre Wilder, Aaron Zelman. Directed by: Félix Enriquez Alcalá, Kevin Bray, Guy Norman Bee, Matt Earl Beesley, Adam Davidson, Ernest Dickerson, Peter Ellis, Charles Haid, Chris Long, Gloria Muzio, J. Miller Tobin, Paul Shapiro, Richard Shepard, Andy Wolk, Thomas J. Wright.

CAST

Mandy Patinkin (Jason Gideon)
Thomas Gibson (Aaron Hotchner)
Lola Glaudini (Elle Greenaway)
Shemar Moore (Derek Morgan)
Matthew Gray Gubler (Dr. Spencer Reid)
A.J. Cook (Jennifer "JJ" Jareau)

To catch a criminal, you have to think like one. And to make a successful police procedural, you have to imitate lots of old TV shows.

Criminal Minds (originally *Quantico*) is the latest "get inside the head of a serial killer"-style series to come down the network pike. It bears more than a passing resemblance to FOX's much-mourned (and missed) cult-classic *Millennium* (1996–1998) in that it features a sensitive, mentally damaged but incredibly talented behavioral analyst as its lead character. No, it's not Lance Henriksen's Frank Black, but rather Mandy Patinkin's Jason Gideon.

In both cases, the protagonist in these series is recruited back to duty after a trauma. Here Gideon's last case (in Boston) went badly, and he's been on sabbatical and teaching ever since. When he's needed on a case in Seattle (where, not coincidentally, *Millennium*'s pilot was also set), he's back on the job and getting into the heads of serial killers.

Criminal Minds differs from *Millennium* because it (a) it's not nearly so clever or visionary. And (b) it surrounds its hero with a more likeable group of team members. Frank Black pretty much worked alone, save for Terry O'Quinn's Peter Watts, but Gideon is joined here by a large social circle.

Aaron Hotchner (Thomas Gibson) is the public face of the group, the socially skilled investigator and interviewer who gets along with everyone. Elle Greenaway (Lola Glaudini) is an expert in sex crimes. Derek Morgan (Shemar Moore) has a specialty in fixations and obsessive behavior like OCD. Matthew Gray Gubler plays the resident socially inept genius Dr. Spencer Reid, a stereotype also played by Brent Spiner on *Threshold* in the 2005–2006 season. And A. J. Cook is "JJ," the liaison between the crack team and the rest of the Bureau.

Like another newcomer to the season, *Killer Instinct*, *Criminal Minds* focuses on the most bizarre and perverse crimes imaginable, as Gideon and his team investigate them. In "Extreme Aggressor" the team goes after a serial abductor in Chicago who is responsible for four missing women. During this case, Gideon's first on the job, Hotchner is watching him for any signs of breakdowns. "Compulsion" takes the team to Arizona, where someone has been setting fires at a local university. "Won't Get Fooled Again" involves a bomber, "Plain Sight" a rapist in San Diego, "Broken Mirror" twins, "Derailed" a hostage situation on a train, "The Tribe" involves murders in New Mexico and so forth.

Like *CSI, Law & Order* and other investigation shows, *Criminal Minds* also boasts its own unique technojargon. Here unknown subjects are referred to as "unsubs."

Critics didn't warm up to *Criminal Minds* immediately, decrying the program's similarity to other crime/investigation series. "This may be the most gruesome, obnoxious, over-the-top crime drama yet," suggested *Newsweek's* Marc Peyser. "...everyone is competing with the folks on *CSI.* But the sneering Mandy Patinkin and his co-stars bring creepy robotic smugness to new and nauseating levels."[18]

Despite the derivative nature of *Criminal Minds,* the series cracked the top ten ratings in the late spring, once its super-sized competition, *Lost,* went into reruns.

The series has been renewed by CBS for a second season but is not currently available on DVD.

CRUMBS

(ABC) (CANCELED) (30 minutes) (Wednesdays at 9:30 pm, EST; January 12, 2006–February 7, 2006) Tollin Robbins Productions/Touchstone Television. Created by: Marco Pennette. Executive Producers: Marco Pennette, Brian Robbins, Michael Tollin. Produced by: Jason Fisher, Joel Stein, Shelley Zimmerman. Camera: Jim Roberson. Film Editor: Joe Berger, Peter Beyt. Music: Adam Cohen. Written by: Marco Pennette, Sung Suh, Regina Stewart, David Walpert. Directed by: Tim Wass.

CAST
Fred Savage (Mitch Crumb)
Jane Curtin (Suzanne Crumb)
Eddie McClintock (Jody Crumb)
William Devane (Billy Crumb)
Maggie Lawson (Andrea Malone)
Reginald Ballard (Elvis)

This sitcom from Marco Pennette, one of the writers of *Caroline in the City* (1995–1999) and the creator of another 2005–2006 train wreck (*Inconceivable*), involves an in-the-closet Hollywood screenwriter named Mitch played by former *Wonder Years* (1988–1993) star Fred Savage.

As the series opens, Mitch returns home to the heartland to take care of his dysfunctional "wild and crazy" family. Mitch's mother, Suzanne, played by *Kate & Allie* (1984–1989) and *Third Rock From The Sun* (1996–2001) star Jane Curtin, is just out of the sanitarium, driven there by the infidelity of her thoughtless husband, William Devane…whom she tried to murder. Suzanne doesn't know that Mitch is gay, either. She's also involved in a fling with an orderly at the institution, Elvis (Reginald Ballard).

Meanwhile, Mitch's brother Jody is a chef at the family restaurant, the Stone House Grill, and is resentful because Mitch has used elements of their family life (particularly a family tragedy in the past) to make it big in Hollywood.

Crumbs was a midseason replacement that carried high expectations with it. Gloria Goodale at *The Christian Science Monitor* predicted "it might just be the right vehicle for Jane Curtin's wonderful brand of suburban craziness."[19]

Unfortunately, that wasn't what happened. Instead, *Crumbs* lasted only a handful of episodes before cancellation. Furthermore, other reviews didn't register the same thoughts about the series' potential and saw the series as being overtly reminiscent of the critically acclaimed *Arrested Development*. Robert Bianco at *USA Today* wrote that "*Crumbs* is supposed to be about Mitch's attempt to reconnect with his family, but the family is so badly warped, you can't help thinking he'd be wiser to keep his distance."[20]

The New York Daily News noted that even though many of the situations on the situation comedy apparently arose from Pennette's real life, it didn't much matter. "Given the real-life scenarios Pennette had to draw from—his father left his mother for a younger woman; his mother tried to run the dad over and was sent to an institution for a while—this show doesn't live up to its potential."[21]

The series is not currently available on DVD.

DANE COOK'S TOURGASM

(HBO) (30 minutes) (Sundays at 11:00 pm EST; June 11, 2006-August 6, 2006) HBO/Superfinger Entertainment/The Jay & Tony Show. Created by: Dane Cook. Executive Producers: Jay Blumenfield, Dane Cook, Barry Katz, Tony Marsh, Brian Volk-Weiss. Produced by: Jay Chapman. Camera: Kirk Douglas. Film Editors: Jordan Beal, Pierre Dwyer. Music: Jeffrey Hepker. Directed by: Dane Cook.

CAST
Dane Cook ("The Leader")
Gary Gulman ("The Conflicted")
Robert Kelly ("The Instigator")
Jay Davis ("The Newbie")

This unscripted summer series from premium channel HBO is described (onscreen) as "30 Days, 20 Shows, 4 comedians, 1 bus." It's the story of popular young comedian Dane Cook (also executive producer and segment director)—who recently had a best-selling comedy CD called "Retaliation"—as he and three handpicked male comedians share an intense month on the road touring colleges.

"The ultimate road trip," this journey is a personal one as well as a professional opportunity, and the four men fight and quarrel endlessly on the bus, discussing everything from religion to porn (and the notorious "Red Tape"). Cook claims the tour is "about comedy," but also about "finding your voice" and showing the world "your light."

In the course of the nine-segment series, the smartaleck *Tourgasm* crew makes its way across country, stopping to play sold-out crowds at universities including Sonoma State (San Francisco), The University of Washington in Seattle, Kent State, Syracuse, and the University of Massachusetts. The eighth episode is a story about the comedians' backgrounds ("Back in the Day") and episode nine ("Tourgasm Curtain Call") is a reunion set 392 days after the end of the bus tour, which ended May 1, 2005.

The half-hour installments of *Tourgasm* also provide trenchant "Laws" of the road, a series leitmotif that serves as the lead-in to relevant tour segments. Among these "rules" are # 1: "No Bus, No Tour;" #7: "Work Hard at Play;" and # 69: "Good talk is porn talk."

In addition to highlighting regular life on the luxury bus, *Tourgasm* takes a page from other reality shows and features the four comedians involved in ludicrous group activities or contests. They play around as fighter pilots in one episode and engage in a mock, midair shootout. In another segment, they visit a school of culinary arts.

Overall, surprisingly little time is actually spent showing these men perform on stage. In the typical episode of *Tourgasm*, the TV audience hears only three or four jokes per comedian. The jokers (who readily admit their dysfunctional psychologies) occasionally get testy on *Tourgasm*, and one experiences a crisis and disappears from the tour for a time.

Watching the series one can't help escape the notion that all four men have been chosen to participate based on their relative youth, fitness, and good looks rather than the quality of their material…which (at least as shown on the series) lacks both genuine wit and humor. As critic Bill Frost writes: "If Tourgasm had spent more time on stage with Cook's standup buds and less time on the bus (it is a sweet ride, though), maybe we could have seen them land at least one punchline between 'em."[22]

Available on DVD.

DEAL OR NO DEAL

(NBC) (RENEWED) (30 minutes) (Various Nights; 8:00 pm, EST; December 19, 2005-June 5, 2006) Executive Producer: Scott St. John. Producers: Judy C. Helm, Brian and David Veskosky. Film Editors: Cas Casey, Bryan Eber, Paul Frazier, Christian Hoffman. Music: Brad Chiet. Directed by: R. Brian Di Pirro, Bob Levy.

CAST
Howie Mandel (Host)

Every few years, network TV experiences a resurgent "game show" craze. Back in 2000 and 2001, ABC fed the craze with *Who Wants to Be A Millionaire* (every… bloody…night…of…the…week!), as did NBC with the vitriolic *The Weakest Link.*

Now the cycle's come around yet again, and 2005's *Deal or No Deal*—which sounds suspiciously like the Monty Hall classic, *Let's Make a Deal*—is the latest thing. It also happens to be a surprise phenomenon, one of the most unexpectedly popular efforts of the year.

And as it turns out the comparison to *Let's Make a Deal* isn't even particularly apt. *Let's Make a Deal* featured colorful guests in crazy costumes enthusiastically guessing about the prizes hidden behind numbered doors. *Deal or No Deal* is a different breed all together. Reflecting the *gravitas* of our age, this effort from the producers of *Fear Factor* and *Extreme Makeover* is a serious, no-frills business that feels like an anxiety-provoking meeting with mortgage lenders or other high-powered pressure-cooker rather than genuine fun.

Everybody and everything looks great on this series. The host and the contestants are decked out in sharp suits and beautifully lit. The primary set is a multistory affair, opulently illuminated, and it effortlessly displays the wealth of American culture. As for the game play itself, it is basic and streamlined, and the stress level of the contestants appears quite high. The fun inherent in the enterprise is seeing when or if a contestant will crack, then cave.

The premise of *Deal or No Deal* is simply this: host Howie Mandel—now entirely shorn of his once trademark curly hair—invites up to the podium a new contestant. One evening, it was a Las Vegas S.W.A.T. officer. Anyway, to paraphrase Mr. Mandel, there are "*no crazy stunts, no trivia, no skill*" involved in the ensuing game, just an answer to the simple question "deal or no deal?"

Thus this is a perfect game for the age of accidental celebrities like Paris Hilton. The contestants don't need to be intelligent, well-read or talented. They just have to show up and bear the pressure.

Anyway, to get the game started, twenty-six supersexy models who look like they were hatched from Robert Palmer's cloning facility, descend onto an imposing staircase holding twenty-six suitcases. In each suitcase is a denomination of money ranging from one penny to a million dollars. The contestant picks a briefcase in hopes that it contains big money, and then has to watch—in torturous slow-motion and between commercial breaks—as he is asked to open up the other cases, a few at a time, to determine how much cash he wins.

Every now and then, a shadowy, Darth Sidious-type figure ominously called "*the Banker*" makes an offer from a dark booth high above the stage, attempting to play the odds and keep the contestant from winning too much money. In a bit of theatrical melodrama, the banker telephones down to the stage and makes offers that the contestant can either accept or reject. Hence a deal. *Or no deal.*

As matters get increasingly hairy, the contestant is allowed to bring a team of supporters on stage. And then, when things get really rough, an "expert" comes up for moral support and professional advice. In a splendid bit of cross-promotion for *The Apprentice*, that expert was Donald Trump on one occasion. Trump first advised the police officer contestant to "*go for it*," but when the money got up to $359,000 the Don wisely admonished the contestant to "*take the money.*"

He did.

To make the game interactive, *Deal or No Deal* also offers viewers a chance to win money at home. Audiences can win $10,000 if they get up off the sofa and text message a "guess" about which of six briefcases contains the money.

Game shows have a long and storied history on television (anybody else remember *Whew!*?), and they're occasionally diverting, especially if you're stuck at home taking heavy flu medication. But unlike many of its more loosely paced brethren, *Deal or No Deal* is tension city. Also, a word to the wise: if you want to get on any quiz show as a contestant, *Deal or No Deal* seems like the ideal choice since prospective contestants won't need to study geography, science, history, sports and leisure, entertainment trivia, or anything else.

At least when *Jeopardy*'s over, viewers will have learned a thing or two about a thing or two, and won't feel like they've wasted a half hour of their lives. That might just be the deal breaker on *Deal or No Deal*. My best "offer" to NBC? They should play this thing out fast. Of course, that's just my interpretation.

Because so far, the series has been huge, and the craze surrounding it exhibits no signs of abating. As late as June 2006, *Deal or No Deal* was ranking as the number one series to air on network television, destroying impressive competition such as ABC's NBA Finals. This game show has even—on occasion—challenged, if not defeated, competition as big as FOX's *American Idol*.

No wonder bald Howie looks so smug up there on stage: *Deal or No Deal* made a triumphant, two-hour return to television on September 18, 2006.

Not available on DVD.

Who's got the big money?
Howie Mandel (foreground) hosts **DEAL OR NO DEAL**, while a bevy of models (background) watch.

DOCTOR WHO

(SCI FI Channel) (RENEWED) (60 minutes) (Fridays at 9:00 pm, EST; March 26, 2005–June 18, 2005) BBC. Executive Producers: Russell T. Davies, Julie Gardner, Mal Young. Produced by: Phil Collinson. Film Editors: Liana Del Giudice, Mike Jones, John Richards, Graham Walker. Original Theme Music: Ron Granier. Written by: Paul Cornell, Russell T. Davies, Mark Gatiss, Janes Hawes, Steven Moffet, Robert Shearman. Directed by: Joe Ahearne, Keith Boak, Brian Grant, Euros Lyn.

CAST
Christopher Eccleston (The Doctor)
Billie Piper (Rose)

The original BBC science-fiction series *Doctor Who* (1963–1989) ran for an unmatched (and glorious) twenty-six years (and 159 multipart half-hour serials) before airing its last tale, "Survival" in 1989. Although American television attempted to resurrect the popular British series in an ill-advised 1996 FOX TV movie (starring Paul McGann as the titular character), that attempt failed, leaving fans of the mysterious Doctor—an alien known as a "Time Lord"—in the lurch.

But in 2005, producer Russell T. Davies, a fan of *Buffy the Vampire Slayer* (1997–2003) and Joss Whedon, succeeded in doing what had once been deemed impossible: resuscitating the Doctor and remaking the new series in the adult but sharp-witted image of Whedon's postmodern efforts.

On March 16, 2006, a full year after the series aired in England, The SCI FI Channel began airing the thirteen hour-long serials comprising the first season of the "new" Doctor Who. The new series stars Christopher Eccleston as the ninth incarnation of the mysterious renegade alien with a fetish for helping Earthlings, and Billie Piper as his lovely and acerbic human companion, a 21st century London girl named Rose.

As before, the series boasts an elastic, flexible format, meaning the Doctor, a time traveler, can go anywhere in time and space in his odd vessel, the TARDIS (Time And Relative Dimension in Space). As longtime admirers are aware, the TARDIS resembles a phone booth and is larger on the inside than on the outside, making it the most bizarre spacecraft in entertainment history.

In an effort not to confuse newbies discovering *Doctor Who* for the first time, the first season of this popular BBC series sees the Doctor remaining relatively close to Earth. The inaugural segments witness him combating deadly plastic automatons called The Autons in "Rose," traveling to the destruction of Earth's sun in the year five billion A.D. ("End of the World"), and visiting Wales in 1869 ("The Unquiet Dead"), but never actually leaving the solar system.

Other notable episodes serve as valuable social commentary, with "The Long Game" concerning a future Earth in which an outpost called Satellite 5 controls the entire human media…and is rather biased in presentation of stories (just like FOX News). "Dalek" resurrects a popular alien foe from the original series, a pepper-pot shaped mechanoid villain bent on "exterminating" all life that is different from itself. This genocidal creature, a Dalek, is—like the Doctor himself—the victim of an enigmatic (and universal) holocaust known as "The Time War."

Another *Doctor Who* episode, "Father's Day" concerns a temporal paradox. To wit, Rose travels back in time and prevents her father's death…which means she's changed her own past! By doing so, she rips open a tear in time, allowing ravenous dragon monsters to swoop into our corrupted reality and destroy it!

Fans and new viewers alike reacted warmly to this classy and faithful updating of the British science-fiction legend, but were soon in for a rude awakening. Christopher Eccleston, who plays the Time Lord (here the last of his race), announced his decision to depart from the role after one season, meaning that yet another incarnation of the Doctor would be required for future installments.

David Tennant accepted that assignment, and his Season Two episodes of the new *Doctor Who* were also acquired by The SCI FI Channel for airing in September, 2006. The Christopher Eccleston season of the new *Doctor Who* was released on DVD during the summer of 2006.

Available on DVD.

E-RING

(NBC) (CANCELED) (60 minutes) (Wednesdays at 9:00 pm, EST; September 21, 2005–August 5, 2006) Jerry Bruckheimer Television/Warner Bros. Created by: David McKenna, Ken Robinson. Executive Producers: Jerry Bruckheimer, Jonathan Littman, David McKenna. Produced by: David Barrett, Taylor Hackford, Paul Moen, Erik Oleson. Camera: Marvin Rush, Tom Yatsko. Film Editors: Joshua Butler, Scott Lerner, Todd E. Miller, Sean Albertson. Music: Trevor Morris. Written by: Laurie Arent, Ken Biller, David Gerken, Lauren Gussis, Karen Hall, David McKenna, Erik Oleson, Michael Ostrowsk, J. Scott Reynolds, Ken Robison. Directed by: David Barrett, Craig R. Baxley, Taylor Hackford, Perry Long, Tim Matheson, Gloria Muzio, John F. Showalter, Dean White, Alex Zakrzewski.

CAST

Benjamin Bratt (Major Jim Tisnewski)
Dennis Hopper (Colonel Eli McNulty)
Aunjanue Ellis (Major Sergeant Jocelyn Pierce)
Kelsey Oldershaw (Angie Aronson)
Kelly Rutherford (Sonny Liston)
Joe Morton (Steve Algazi)

E-Ring is a military drama from megaproducer Jerry Bruckheimer (*CSI*) that gazes at the goings-on inside the Department of Defense, and in particular, the Pentagon.

E-Ring is the chronicle of patriot Major Jim Tisnewski (Benjamin Bratt), a former Special Forces operative who has been assigned to the Pentagon's "E" division ("*the outer and most important ring of the Pentagon*") after a tour in Afghanistan. In his new capacity, Jim is assigned to monitor international hot spots and to make preparations and plans for war. He must simultaneously navigate DoD politics and international crises.

Jim's superior officer on *E-Ring* is tough-as-nails Colonel McNulty, played by counterculture icon and movie star, Dennis Hopper. "McNulty's a nasty piece of work,"

Hooper told *Entertainment Weekly* reporter Josh Rottenberg. "He's crusty and a bit mad, but his intentions are right on."[23] McNulty is a Vietnam veteran whose wife left him while he was a prisoner of war.

Other characters on the series include Jocelyn Pierce (Aunjanue Ellis), an officer and widower who keeps an eye on McNulty and Tisnewski when they threaten to go off half-cocked. There's also beautiful "Sonny" Liston (Kelly Rutherford), the legal officer for the DoD and Jim's former girlfriend. Joe Morton plays an assistant secretary of Defense, Steven Algazi, who harbors political aspirations.

Twenty episodes of this hour-long series were filmed for the fall season, and various stories involve hunky Tisnewski interfacing with political hotspots around the world. The rescue of a spy in China is integral to the plot in the series pilot. Tisnewski travels to the Middle East and Iraq to learn more about America's involvement with Iran in "Escape and Evade," and genocide is the issue of the day in "Tribes." *E-Ring* also circles topical issues such as prejudice against Muslims in the United States, and sexual misbehavior in the Marine Corps. ("Weekend Pass") On hand are all the action tropes one would expect of a military drama, including episodes about a biological plague ("Breath of Allah") and the ferreting out of a spy in the Pentagon ("Five Pillars.")

Variety's critic Brian Lowry called *E-Ring* "rather static" and noted that "Bratt's character has become a desk jockey, meaning he watches a monitor and tries to look pensive—while somehow still keeping his biceps flexed—as other execute the orders."[24] Audiences seemed agreed with this assessment and *E-Ring* didn't fare well in the ratings against ABC's powerhouse *Lost*.

Not yet available on DVD.

EMILY'S REASONS WHY NOT

(ABC) (CANCELED) (30 minutes) (Monday at 9:00 pm, EST; January 9, 2006) Pariah/Sony TV. Created by: Carrie Gerlach. Executive Producers: Allison Adler, Vivian Cannon, Bill Diamond, Emily Kapnek, Gavin Polone, John Sakmar, Robin Schiff. Co-Produced by: James Weiss. Camera: Checco Varese. Film Editor: Steven Rasch. Music: Jared Faber. Written by: Carrie Gerlach, Cynthia Greenberg, Emily Kapnek, Craig Zisk. Directed by: Michael Patrick Jann.

CAST
Heather Graham (Emily Sanders)
Nadia Dajani (Reilly)
Khary Payton (Josh)
Smith Cho (Glitter)

Emily's Reasons Why Not is the 2005–2006's most high-profile network disaster. The ABC series was heavily promoted on billboards and on air on both coasts (reputedly to the tune of $5 million), and the central notion was promising: movie star Heather Graham (*Boogie Nights*) headlining a sitcom about sex and dating. The show was gifted a tough time slot, it's true, in that FOX's *24* had already established a fervid audience on Monday nights at 9:00 pm, but *Emily's Reasons Why Not* tanked even before the fifth season premiere of the Kiefer Sutherland drama. So that's not an excuse.

Emily's Reasons Why Not is the familiar story of twentysomething Emily (Heather Graham), an attractive young woman who works in the publishing industry (on self-help books) and blames the failure of her most recent romantic relationship on the fact that she ignored the little voice inside warning her about it. Basically, she ignored her instincts, the ones that told her "why not" to do certain things.

As the series commences, Emily is determined to adhere to her internally voiced reasons "why not" to do things, and episodes suggest this leitmotif with titles such as "Why Not to Date Your Gynecologist," "Why Not to Date a Twin," and "Why Not to Cheat on Your Best Friend."

The supporting cast includes Emily's best girlfriend, a bitter pill named Reilly (Nadia Dajani), and her gay best friend, Josh (Khary Payton). Smith Cho plays Emily's workplace foil, Glitter, a one-time protégée who has turned to the dark side and is always firing-off zingers.

The pilot episode—the only episode that aired—focuses on Emily's dead-on-arrival relationship with a co-worker named Stan (Victor Webster), whom she suspects may be gay. Naturally, her chorus of friends have humorous thoughts about that, and Emily must resolve the situation (in twenty-two minutes, no less).

Emily's Reasons Why Not was canceled after one broadcast (January 9, 2006), and the numbers explain why ABC was in such a hurry to pull the plug. The Graham comedy lost 36 percent of the audience held by its lead-in, the reality show *Wife Swap* and—adding insult to injury—it registered numbers reflecting a 22 percent drop from the previous year's mid-season show in that slot, *The Bachelorette*.[25]

"It's a shame," reported executive producer Gavin Polone regarding the quick cancellation. "A lot of people were working really hard and the show kept improving. Sony spent a huge amount of money and were very supportive. I can't fault ABC, though: they promoted it like crazy and when the audience stays away in this super competitive environment, quick decisions are made."[26]

This high-profile failure of *Emily's Reasons Why Not* caused other industry watchers to take note, and

Newsweek commented that "no one has ever bombed as badly as Heather Graham," while maintaining "a show that focused on Graham's inability to find a man isn't funny. It's just laughable."[27]

Other observers saw the failure of *Emily's Reasons Why Not* in more basic (and less personal terms). *A big star does not a good show make.* "Regardless of what name you put in there, the audience still wants to see a great show," according to Ryan Martin, from the Agency for the Performing Arts.[28]

Well said.

Not available on DVD at this time.

She has good reason to look worried. Heather Graham stars in
EMILY'S REASONS WHY NOT ... which survived only one episode on the air.

EPITAFIOS

(HBO) (Limited Run) (60 minutes) (HBO on Demand) Pol-Ka Producciones/HBO. Created by: Marcelo and Walter Slavich. Executive Producers: Luis F. Peraza, Adrian Suar. Co-Executive Producer: Fernando Blanco. Produced by: Diego Andrasnik, Victor Tevah. Camera: Guillermo Zappino. Film Editors: Alejandro Alem, Alejandro Parysow. Music: Ivan Wyszogrod. Written by: Marcelo and Walter Slavich. Directed by: Alberto Lecchi, Jorge Nisco.

CAST

Julio Chavez (Renzo Marquez)
Paola Krum (Dr. Laura Santini)
Cecilia Roth (Marina Segal)
Antonio Birabent (Bruno Costas)
Villanueva Cosse (Marco Marquez)
Luis Luque (Jimenez)

Epitafios, or "Epitaphs" is the harrowing, highly disturbing multipart (thirteen episode) tale of a diabolical and obsessive serial killer who has spent the last four years of his life developing an intricate plan to bring justice to those authority figures who botched a delicate hostage situation at a Buenos Aires university years earlier. In that situation, four young students died (in a fire) when a rescue attempt went horribly wrong.

This lunatic (whose identity is cloaked from the viewer for the first several episodes of the series) inscribes "epitaphs" on specially designed grave stones for those whom he plans to "judge" guilty (meaning: *kill*). These epitaphs are wordy and mysterious, their meanings unfathomable until final justice is rendered, like this example: "Here Lies He Who Turned Deception into A Game."

It's left to a balding, retired policeman-turned-cab-driver, Renzo (Julio Chavez) and the gorgeous psychologist he once loved, Dr. Laura Santini (Paola Krum) to catch the killer before he strikes again. This case is very personal, however, since it was Renzo and Santini who botched that hostage situation at the college years earlier. In particular, one headstone is marked with both their names…so they realize the killer is coming for them soon.

The bread and butter of the highly cinematic *Epitafios* is the notion that a fine line separates revenge and justice; and it's a line based entirely on personal, subjective perspective. However, viewers may find themselves in love with the stunning, lush visualizations and compositions more than the admittedly deep thematic strands. Filled to the brim with gruesome, inventive (and gory) death scenes *Epitafios* is perhaps the most cinematic venture to appear on television in some time.

In some regards, this Spanish language series represents a lengthy variation on David Fincher's 1995 film noir, *Seven*, in particular because *Epitafios* is filmed (by DP Guillermo Zappino) in such sterling fashion. It's a world of rain-soaked streets, off-kilter close-ups, and revealing angles. In short, the series is simply beautiful to gaze upon; and the mise en scène is the best featured on a TV show since *The X-Files* (1993–2002).

In the first three episodes, audiences witness corpse pieces strewn across a house that represents an externalization of the killer's mind, see vicious dogs ripping out a detective's throat (in a tense sequence that makes fine use of quick cross-cutting), and watch as a penny-pincher's mouth is stitched into an open, agape position while coins are hurled down her throat (and the camera actually travels down her esophagus and tilts down into her stomach). Most horribly of all, there's a scene involving a beautiful leather fetish model stretched to death on a rack…before acid is poured on her face. Then one hand is amputated.

Their love affair could get them killed. Dr. Laura Santini (Paola Krum) and Renzo (Julio Chavez) steal a romantic moment in the gory film noir, **EPITAFIOS**.

Then, when you think it's over...well, you get the idea...

The (wide) suspect pool in *Epitafios* consists mostly of the relatives of those hostages from years back...parents, ex-lovers, etc., who somehow might desire revenge, but this series skillfully alternates "current" murders with flashbacks of the University siege (which ends disastrously in flames), as well as fine character development.

On the latter front, Renzo quit the force over the siege, then fell in love with Santini, who spurned him. Now he's hooked on expired antidepressants (provided to him by a transvestite taxi passenger) and still desperate to be romantically involved with Santini.

Meanwhile, the killer has communicated with the psychologist and demanded that she become *intimate* with Renzo, lest her son be killed. It's all fascinating thriller material, and the best part is how the characters learn and develop. At first, Renzo and Santini are behind the eight ball, confused by their nemesis. By the middle of the series, however, they are catching up quick, and coming closer to foiling the killer's plan. One episode features a nailbiting chase through an airport (ending in the men's room), as both killer and Renzo close in on a victim at the same time. Will Renzo save him, or will the killer win? I won't tell, but set-pieces like that make *Epitafios* a viewer's delight.

Released internationally in 2004, HBO acquired *Epitafios* in 2005 and began running the series in the autumn of that year.

The series is available on DVD.

EUREKA

(SCI FI Channel) (RENEWED) (60 minutes) (Tuesdays at 9:00 pm, EST; July 18, 2006-August 29, 2006) The SCI FI Channel/NBC Universal. Created by: Andrew Crosby, Jaime Paglia. Executive Producers: Andrew Crosby, Jaime Paglia. Co-executive producer: Kirk Schaefer. Consulting Producer: David Greenwalt. Produced by: Robert Petrovicz. Director of Photography: Rick Maguire. Film Editor: Michael Stern. Music: Mark Mothersbaugh. Written by: Don E. Fesman, Harry Victor, Andrew Crosby. Directed by: Peter O'Fallon, Jefery Levy, Jeff Woolnough.

CAST

Colin Ferguson (Sheriff Jack Carter)
Salli Richardson (Allison Blake)
Jordan Hinson (Zoe Carter)
Joe Morton (Henry)
Erica Cerra (Deputy Jo Lupo)
Ed Quinn (Dr. Nathan Stark)

This high-rated summer series aired on the SCI FI Channel and concerns an odd little burg in the Pacific Northwest. In the first episode of the hour-long sci-fi drama, Marshall Jack Carter (Colin Ferguson) and his delinquent daughter, Zoe (Jordan Hinson) are *en route* to California when they end up in Eureka, a community of scientists that was created by the U.S. government after World War II and doesn't appear on any map. In fact, only the Pentagon knows it exists.

Eureka, it turns out, is a community of geniuses and scientists, a place where the best thinkers in America can send their children to school, receive the finest health care, and live in a comfortable middle-class utopia. The only problem is that sometimes, the populace's technology-advancing schemes and experiments go badly wrong, jeopardizing the town, and—on occasion—the world itself.

After helping out on one such crisis, Carter becomes the new sheriff of Eureka, and he and Zoe move in. He's assisted on the job by a gorgeous deputy named Jo (Erica Cerra), but Carter's heart belongs to Allison Blake (Richardson), the town's liaison to the DoD and the Pentagon. Unfortunately, Allison is still entangled with Dr. Nathan Stark, her former husband…who has yet to grant her a divorce. Stark (Ed Quinn) won the Nobel Prize in Mathematics, but is an acerbic, difficult man to get along with. He runs Eureka's underground "Advanced Research Facility" a giant installation consisting of five levels that looks like something out of *The Andromeda Strain* (1971).

In a typical episode, Carter must juggle town "business" (as weird as it gets) with his role as Zoe's parent. The episode "Dr. Nobel" involves Carter escorting Zoe to the local nursing home where she can fulfill her community service time, and then heading off to the Advanced Research Facility where a doomsday weapon from the 1960s is on a countdown to activation.

It turns out that the man behind that weapon (which involves "ionosphere particle weapons" and mirrors positioned on the Moon) is elderly and demented Eureka resident Irvin Thatcher, who long ago nearly won a Nobel Prize himself for his theory of "Mutually Assured Destruction." Now, Irvin lives in the very nursing home where Zoe is pitching in, and Carter must undergo a dangerous experiment to help the senile old man recall the weapon's deactivation procedure. This is easier said than done, however, because Thatcher's dementia stems from a personal tragedy. When he lost the Nobel Prize in 1962, he turned inward on himself, never proposed to the love of his life, and lost all connection to the outside world. Now, with just seven hours till the weapon fires,

Carter, Stark, Blake and the others must stage a "Nobel Prize" ceremony for the old man and set the path of his life straight.

As the preceding summary makes plain, *Eureka* is a series with a sense of whimsy. It's not dark and angst-ridden like so many sci-fi series today. Instead, it is reminiscent of the CBS small-town drama *Picket Fences* (1992–1996) or other dramas wherein characters and humanity come before technology.

Eureka has thus far drawn high ratings on The SCI FI Channel, with its premiere two-hour pilot pulling over 4 million viewers to the tube. This is a high number for basic cable, and one which landed *Eureka* in the top ten roster for cable that week. Also, *Eureka* is now part of the technology vanguard and new media of 2006. To wit, the SCI FI Channel has been posting "webisodes" (Internet-based installments) of a *Eureka* spin-off called "Hide and Seek."

Not yet available on DVD.

EVERYBODY HATES CHRIS

(UPN) (RENEWED) (30 minutes) (Thursdays at 8:00 pm, EST; September 22, 2005–May 6, 2006) Chris Rock Entertainment/3 Art Entertainment. Created by: Chris Rock, Ali Le Roi. Executive Producers: Dave Becky, Howard Gerwitz, Ali Le Roi, Chris Rock, Michael Rotenberg. Co-Executive Producers: Aron Abrams, Rodney Barns, Jim Michaels, Gregory Thompson, Kriss Turner. Produced by: Alyson Fouse. Camera: Mark Doering-Powell. Film Editors: Courtney Carrillo, Earl Watson, James Wilcox. Music: Marcus Miller. Written by: Aron Abrams, Rodney Barnes, Lance Crouther, Alyson Fouse, Howard Gerwitz, Felicia D. Henderson, Ali Le Roi, Courtney Lilly, Chris Rock, Kriss Turner, Gregory Thompson. Directed by: Tamra Davis, Denni Gordon, Reginald Hudlin, Eric Leneuville, Jeff Melman, Linda Mendoza, Chris Rock, Matt Shakman, Lev L. Spiro, Ken Whittingon.

CAST
Terry Crews (Julius)
Vincent Martella (Greg)
Tichina Arnold (Rochelle)
Tequan Richmond (Drew)
Imani Hakim (Tonya)
Tyler James Williams (Chris)
Chris Rock (Himself/Narrator)

This is a delightful and sharp-edged situation comedy "inspired" by comic Chris Rock's "life as a kid," according to the series' promotional materials. Although the title clearly suggests *Everybody Loves Raymond*, and the nostalgia factor of an adult man remembering his childhood (narrator Rock), evokes *The Wonder Years*, *Everybody Hates Chris* is a thoroughly original and charming sitcom, as well as one of the few programs on network television that earns the right to be called funny.

Everybody Hates Chris is set in Bedford-Stuyvesant in 1982, as a teenage Chris (Tyler James Williams) attends a mostly white (and Italian) school, and grapples with his two younger siblings, Drew (Tequan Richmond) and Tanya (Imani Hakim). Chris's parents, Julius (Terry Crews) and Rochelle (Tichina Arnold), try to keep the house (and children) on track, but are overworked. Greg (Vincent Martella) is Chris's friend at school.

Every episode follows the misadventures of Chris, and features the gimmick of having a title beginning with the phrase "Everybody Hates…" In "Everybody Hates Basketball," Chris makes the basketball team. In "Everybody Hates the Laundromat," a trip by the siblings to do the family laundry ends with chaos. A broken hot water heater spoils the holidays for the financially strapped family in "Everybody Hates Christmas," and Chris's grandfather passes away in "Everybody Hates Funerals."

In addition to being raucously funny, especially the Mom character, Rochelle, *Everybody Hates Chris* is also enjoyable purely from a nostalgia point of view. One episode involves the 1980s Atari game "Asteroids" and other shows evoke funny, idiosyncratic memories of the bygone Reagan Decade.

Everybody Hates Chris faced a challenging time slot in its freshman season, battling it out with *Survivor* on CBS, *The O.C.* on FOX, and the *Friends* spinoff *Joey* on NBC, yet nobody (critics nor audiences) hated *Chris* and the series was picked up when UPN and the WB merged to create the CW.

New episodes were slated to begin airing in October of 2006 on Sunday nights at 7:00 pm, and Whoopi Goldberg had even scheduled a guest appearance.

Available on DVD.

THE EVIDENCE

(ABC)(CANCELED)(60 minutes)(Wednesdays at 10:00 pm, EST; March 22, 2006-July 1, 2006) John Wells Productions/Warner Bros. Television. Created by: Sam Baum, Dustin Thomason. Executive Producers: Sam Baum, Dustin Thomason. Produced by: John Wells. Camera: David Geddes, Kramer Morganthau. Film Editor: Padraic McKinley. Music: Doug De Angelis. Written by: Sam Baum, William N. Fordes, Gary Glasberg, Dustin Thomason. Directed by: Guy Bee, Stephen Cragg, Ernest Dickerson, Gary Fleder, Lesli Glatter and Nelson McCormick.

CAST
Martin Landau (Dr. Sol Gold)
Orlando Jones (Cayman Bishop)
Rob Estes (Sean Cole)

ABC briefly gave this new crime-drama *Invasion*'s time slot in the spring of 2006, at Wednesdays at 10:00 pm; following powerhouse *Lost*. The crime investigation series is set in San Francisco and involves two cop buddies Bishop (Orlando Jones) and Cole (Rob Estes) investigating homicides. They often rely on important evidence, and information from medical examiner Dr. Gold, played by Oscar winner and *Space:1999* (1975–1977) star Martin Landau. A continuing subplot involves the unsolved murder of Cole's wife. Cole and Bishop also share a bantering, funny relationship, which enlivens many of the episodes.

Only eight episodes of *The Evidence* were produced (and four aired), and each installment involved the discovery of a dead body and the attempt to solve the murder. A boxer ("Down for the Count"), pharmacist ("Pilot"), and paramedic ("Stringers") were among the featured deceased.

The visual "hook" or gimmick in *The Evidence* is that each show opened with a voiceover by veteran Landau and focused on close-up insert shots of the evidence that would prove vital to the solution of the week's central crime.

Not currently available on DVD.

EXTRAS

(HBO) (RENEWED) (30 minutes) (Sundays at 10:30 pm, EST; July 21, 2005-August 25, 2005) BBC/HBO. Created by: Ricky Gervais and Stephen Merchant Executive Producer: John Plowman. Producer: Charlie Hanson. Camera: Martin Hawkins. Film Editor: Nigel Williams. Written and directed by: Ricky Gervais and Stephen Merchant.

CAST
Ricky Gervais (Andy Millman)
Ashley Jensen (Maggie Jacobs)

Ricky Gervais and Stephen Merchant's follow-up to the break-out BBC sitcom *The Office* (2001–2003) ditches that series' much-imitated mockumentary format, yet the show's feel is still improvisational and spontaneous. Gervais again firmly holds center stage, this time playing hapless Andy Millman, a disgruntled "background artist" (or movie extra) on an endless quest to get a "real" line in a movie and hence graduate to the role of actor. The British series follows his often cringe-inducing misadventures from movie set to movie set as Andy attempts to ingratiate himself with famous actors, producers, directors, and the like—universally with unfortunate results.

According to Gervais, he was inspired to create *Extras* because fame fascinates him. "It makes me laugh," he told *Entertainment Weekly's* Dalton Ross, "the things people are willing to do just to get on telly. There was a show in England where B-list celebrities work on a farm and one of them masturbated a pig! It fascinates me, this desperation."[29]

Writing and directing partner Merchant plays Gervais's sleepy, lassitude-filled agent on this HBO/BBC collaboration in what amounts to a wonderful recurring character bit, but perhaps more notably, Gervais has been joined on *Extras* by a partner equally as clueless and

pitiable as his underachieving Millman. Ashley Jensen plays Maggie, a fellow "extra" and clearly the Ethel to Millman's Lucy. Maggie boasts a terrible knack for saying offensive things in uncomfortable social situations, and in one episode, refuses to date a fellow who was born with one leg longer than the other. In the process, she makes an unwelcome comment about his Herman Munster–sized shoe. In the episode that guest stars Samuel L. Jackson, Maggie attempts to prove she isn't a racist and tells Jackson she loved him in *The Matrix*.

Of course, that was Laurence Fishburne...

Perhaps the finest moment in this very funny series arises in the first episode. Kate Winslet is the celebrity guest star. She plays herself, and joins Maggie and Millman on the set of a World War II/Holocaust–themed film (so she can win an Oscar, the actress cynically reveals). Anyway, Winslet kindly provides Maggie advice about how to spice up her telephonic sex skills. Later in the show, Maggie's boyfriend is on set, and behind his back, the celebrated star of *Titanic* proceeds to make all manner of obscene gestures and comments. In the midst of Winslet's outrageous and vulgar pantomime—*with her tongue hanging out one side of her mouth, and one hand tweaking her bosom*—she gets caught by the boyfriend. It's a hilarious turn from an A-list level movie star and just one reason why *Extras* proves such a blast.

The first season of *Extras* includes six half-hour episodes. In addition to Kate Winslet and Samuel L. Jackson, *X-Men's* Patrick Stewart shows up for an amusing turn. The series' second episode provides a meaty role for comedian Ben Stiller, also playing himself...only as a maniacal, self-involved director. In this story, Stiller is attempting to make a "prestige" movie about the Bosnian War of the mid-1990s, and goes on egotistically—at some length—about the cathartic value of his cinematic oeuvre, including *Dodgeball* (2004).

By narrowing its focus to the movie industry and by boasting celebrity cameos, *Extras* joins Lisa Kudrow's *The Comeback, Curb Your Enthusiasm*, and *Entourage* in gazing at (and satirizing) the world of contemporary Hollywood. Critical response to *Extras* was generally mixed, with some reviewers feeling it was less successful than *The Office*, and a rehash in terms of characterization for Gervais. Other critics disagreed, however. Writing for *The New York Daily News*, David Bianculli noted that "it's a rarity for someone to come up with two different brilliant series," and he noted that *Extras* is "fabulously funny."[30]

A second season has been commissioned, and the first season is now available on DVD.

FALCON BEACH

(ABC Family) (RENEWED) (60 minutes) (Mondays at 9:00 pm, EST; January 5, 2006–April 8, 2006) Insight Production Company Ltd/Original Pictures Inc. Created by: Shannon Farr, John Murray. Executive Producers: Barbara Bowlby, John Brunton, Kim Todd. Produced by: Shannon Farr, John Murray, Ellen Rutter. Camera: Alwyn Kumst. Film Editors: Robert Lower, Ron Wisman. Music: Brian Carson. Written by: Elizabeth Stewart, Theresa Beaupre, Daegan Fryklind, Grant Sauve. Directed by: Norma Bailey. Bill Corcoran, Drew Potter.

CAST

Steve Byers (Jason Tanner)
Jennifer Kydd (Paige Bradshaw)
Devon Weigel (Tanya Shedden)
Morgan Kelly (Lane Bradshaw)
Allison Hossack (Ginny Bradshaw)
Ted Whittall (Trevor Bradshaw)
Lynda Boyd (Darlene Shedden)
Jill Teed (Peggy Tanner)

Filmed in Canada, this original dramatic series occurs in the waterfront town of Falcon Beach, in New England. It's the story of a young man, Jason Tanner (Byers), whose father tragically died when he was fourteen, and who now works at the local marina with his mother.

Tanner is a good-looking athletic young blond, a "bronzed" beach god who rides a motorcycle and loves water sports. In the course of the soap opera, he's confronted with a specific problem regarding romance. In particular, there are two women vying for his affection. One is Tanya (Devon Weigel), the other is a rich girl who hates Falcon Beach but who slowly warms up to it once the summer begins, Paige Bradshaw (Jennifer Kydd). Much of this triangular romance involves the class warfare inherent in the town and community. There's always an influx of wealthy homeowners in the summer, whereas the townies live there all year long. But when summer comes, there's tension…

The ad lines also promised that once the "summer starts" "innocence ends" in promoting *Falcon Beach*, and the series certainly delivered hot young bodies in spades. Ironically, many of the series' plot lines were also not that far removed from the innocent beach films of Frankie Avalon and Annette Funicello in the 1960s.

One episode involves the breakdown of Jason's boat, and the re-opening of a local dance hall ("Getting to Know You"), a chestnut that could have been a subplot in *Beach Blanket Bingo* (1965).

The series is not yet available on DVD.

FOUR KINGS

(NBC) (CANCELED) (30 minutes) (Thursdays at 8:30 pm, EST; January 5, 2006-March 16, 2006) Ko Mut Entertainment/Warner Brothers Television. Created by: David Kohan and Max Mutchnick. Executive Producers: David Kohan, Max Mutchnick. Co-Executive Producers: Julie Anne Larson, Lester Lewis. Producers: Katy Ballard, Bill Daly. Camera: Tony Askins. Film Editor: Peter Chakos. Music: Scott Clausen, Christopher A. Lee. Written by: Neil J. Deiter, Dan Fybel, Jonathan M. Goldstein, Laura Gutin, Daniel Hsia, David Kohan, Gabe Miller, Max Mutchnick. Directed by: Barnet Kellerman.

CAST
Seth Green (Barry)
Josh Cook (Ben)
Todd Grinnell (Jason)
Shane McRae (Bobby)

Four Kings is the all-too familiar story of four buddies, the four self-named "Kings of New York." Together, they make the unusual life-choice to live together in a ritzy apartment after it is willed to Ben, the nicest of the bunch, by his dead grandmother.

Barry (Seth Green) is the short, jealous friend, who thinks Ben, a magazine writer, gets everything he wants. Bobby (Shane McRae) is the slacker, and Jason is the type-A aggressive personality. Together, these four "kings" joke about dating and try to perfect the one night stand. They go out on blind dates, and do all the silly things sitcoms require of upstanding young people these days.

The talents behind the very-successful *Will & Grace* created this short-lived sitcom. In concept, *Four Kings* was designed to recrown NBC as ratings royalty on its slipping Thursdays night (formerly known as "Must See TV"). *Four Kings* was even heir to the cushy slot between *Will & Grace* (in its last season) and the new hit *My Name Is Earl*. But it was all to no avail: the show was only broadcast a half-dozen or so weeks before NBC dethroned it in March of 2006. *U.S. News and World Report* was just one periodical that suggested the series was nothing more than "a tired attempt at another *Friends*."[31]

Here's an interesting in-joke, however. Seth Green, star of *Four Kings* later appeared on an episode in the third season of HBO's *Entourage* as himself. He commented on the premise (and failure) of *Four Kings*, claiming that no one could believe that four adult straight men would choose to live together. Of course, that concept is also the premise for *Entourage...*

Not available on DVD.

FREDDIE

(ABC) (CANCELED) (30 minutes) (Wednesdays at 8:30 pm, EST; October 12, 2005-April 12, 2006) Mowhawk Productions Inc./Warner Bros. TV. Created by: Bruce Helford, Conrad Jackson, Bruce Rasmussen. Executive Producers: Bruce Helford, Conrad Jackson, Debora Oppenheimer, Bruce Rasmussen. Co-executive producers: Tom Hertz, Lori Kirkland Baker. Produced by: Lou Fusaro, Conrad Jackson. Camera: Peter Smokler. Film Editor: Larry Harris. Written by: Lori Kirkland Baker, Andy Berman, Paul Ciancarelli, David Dipietro, Kristin Marvin Hughes, Conrad Jackson, Steve Molaro, Dailyn Rodriguez. Directed by: Gerry Cohen, Bob Koherr, John Pasquin.

CAST

Freddie Prinze Jr. (Freddie Moreno)
Jacqueline Obradors (Sofia)
Brian Austin Green (Chris)
Jenny Gago (Grandma)
Chloe Suazo (Zoey)
Madchen Amick (Allison)

Supposedly inspired by the life of its star, Freddie Prinze Jr., *Freddie* is an ABC situation comedy concerning the young twentysomething owner of a restaurant in Chicago, Freddie Moreno (Freddie Prinze Jr.).

After a family crisis—including the death of his brother—Freddie's sister-in-law, Allison (Madchen Amick), her adolescent daughter Zoey (Chloe Suazo), and non-English-speaking Grandma (Jenny Gago) move into his fancy apartment with him and quickly turn the bachelor's life upsidedown. Brian Austin Green plays Freddie's next door neighbor, best friend, and occasional romantic competitor, Chris, in this situation comedy.

A fairly standard sitcom, *Freddie* dovetails around such topics as the vicissitudes of dating, ("Rich Man, Poor Girl"), and utilizes the restaurant as a location to generate humorous predicaments. In "Food Critic," for instance,

Freddie realizes that the critic reviewing his establishment is person he beat up a long time ago.

Freddie Prinze Jr. had an eventful year on his first regular TV series. Rumors flew (and were just as quickly denied by publicists) that the show was causing a rift with his actress wife, Sarah Michelle Gellar. Then one day, (October 5, 2005) Prinze reported to work with mysteriously broken ribs, which were later attributed to the talent eating too much Chinese food(!).

In addition, Prinze also found the grind of starring in a sitcom difficult. "Everybody said [creating] a half-hour would be so easy," he explained. "And that you go in at 10 [a.m.] and you're out at 5 [p.m.]. They just lied so badly! I'm already tired all the time. They just completely lied!"[32]

Freddie was also touted as being part of an all-Latino comedy block, since the series followed George Lopez's show on ABC's Wednesday night…even though "Freddie didn't really make a name for himself as a Latino performer"[33] according to Alex Nogales, president of the National Hispanic Media Coalition.

Even Freddie Prinze Jr.'s status as teen icon ultimately worked against this now-defunct series, because female fans at the live taping would reportedly hiss at co-star Green during scenes of conflict between the two male characters. "We have like a rule and I feel bad saying this," noted Prinze, "but we couldn't have like young, young girls there [taping] because they're not coming to the sitcom to laugh, they're coming to [see me]."[34]

Not currently released on DVD.

FREE RIDE

(FOX) (CANCELED) (30 minutes) (Sundays at 9:30 pm, EST; March 1-April 9, 2006) Fox 21. Created by: Rob Roy Thomas. Executive Producer: Rob Roy Thomas. Co-Executive Producer: Michael Binkow. Produced by: Joe Revello. Camera: Steve Ackerman. Film Editors: John W. Carr, Noriko Milyaka, Jason Rosenfield. Music: Mark Wike. Written and directed by: Rob Roy Thomas.

CAST
Josh Dean (Nate Stahlings)
Erin Cahill (Amber)
Dave Sheridan (Dove)
Loretta Fox (Margo Stahlings)
Allan Harvey (Bob Stahlings)
Dan Wells (Steve Moss)

Free Ride is a partially improvised situation comedy from creator Rob Roy Thomas, and one that could have had half-a-chance if it had stayed in its post-*American Idol* berth, rather than moving to Sunday nights. It was actually that rarity on television these days: a funny sitcom.

Free Ride focuses on Nate (Dean), a young man or, in the parlance of the day, *a slacker,* who leaves UC Santa Barbara and returns home to Johnson City, Missouri ("Missouri Loves Company"). When he gets there, however, he discovers that his room has been converted into a gym, and that his parents (Loretta Fox and Allan Harvey) are endlessly bickering.

After moving into the garage, Josh runs into a friend from high school, Amber (Erin Cahill) and realizes that he's in love with her. The only problem is that Amber is engaged to be married to Steve Moss (Dan Wells) in just five months, unless Josh can work his *mojo* on her. He tells his parents he plans to stay in town just five months...in other words, until his girl gets married. Dove (Dave Sheridan) is the series' trademark "wacky" character, a party animal (and Christian rocker) who works at the local big box store, here called Kash Kutters. Dove becomes Josh's new best friend.

In the course of the six thirty-minute episodes of *Free Ride* that made it to air, Nate seeks a job in construction, only to discover he'll be building the house of the would-be happy couple, Steve and Amber ("Procrastinating"). He also attempts to get close to Amber through her brother ("Amber Alert"), and ends up taking his dad to the hospital ("Colon Blow to the Head") for a crazy ordeal.

The 2005–2006 season was a vicious one for situation comedies, and unfortunately, *Free Ride* didn't get a free ride, or even a fair hearing. Like *Arrested Development*, another fine comedy, it was cast aside by FOX before it had the opportunity to prove itself long-term.

Not currently available on DVD.

GHOST WHISPERER

(CBS) (RENEWED) (60 minutes) (Fridays at 8:00 pm, EST; September 23, 2005-May 5, 2006) Sanders/Moses Productions/Touchstone Television. Created by: John Gray. Executive Producers: John Gray, Kim Moses, Ian Sander. Co-Executive Producer: James Van Praagh. Producer: Jennifer Love Hewitt. Camera: James Chressanthis. Film Editors: John Duffy, Scott Vickrey. Written by: John Belluso, Catherine Butterfield, Emily Fox, John Gray, Lois Johnson, Jed Seidel, Rama Stagner. Directed by: John Belluso, James Chressanthis, James Fralwey, John Gray, Kevin Hooks, David Jones, Joanna Kerns, Eric Laneuville, Bill L. Norton, Peter O'Fallon, Peter Werner.

CAST
Jennifer Love Hewitt (Melinda Gordon)
Aisha Tyler (Andrea Moreno)
David Conrad (Jim)

This supernatural TV program, hilariously titled *Ghost Whisperer* (as in *The Horse Whisperer* or *The Dog Whisperer*) airs on CBS Friday nights at 8:00 pm and exists to satisfy all those gullible viewers still in mourning over the cancellation of syrupy fare like *Touched By An Angel* (1994–2003), or *Highway to Heaven* (1984–1989).

In other words, that broad swath of Christian conservative middle America that includes, predominantly, overweight, middle-aged women who collect angel figurines. It's a series that, like the aforementioned *Touched By An Angel*, "separates red state and blue state viewers,"[35] as *Ventura County Star* reviewer Joel Brown noted.

Ghost Whisperer focuses on gorgeous young Melinda, played by Jennifer Love Hewitt, a young woman (like Allison Dubois on NBC's *Medium*) capable of communicating with the dead. Though the series sometimes gets creepy in its pursuit of afterlife specters, the primary angle here is to help the dead escape the guilt of their past

and move on to greener pastures on The Other Side. The concentration is on "inspirational" stories of healing and forgiving, not *X-Files*–type scares.

Melinda is married to a hunkish paramedic (and a very patient man) named Jim (David Conrad), who relentlessly and endlessly dotes on her. Each week, Melinda and her token African-American friend, Andrea (Aisha Tyler)—who run a fancy upscale boutique together—talk about the ramifications of the latest ghost incursion and help each other understand Melinda's unusual gifts.

Ghost Whisperer comes from the auspices of "psychic" James Van Praagh (author of the popular memoir, *Living with Dead*) and is reportedly based on the story of Mary Ann Winkowski, a show consultant and real life ghostbuster. "Mary Ann is someone who specializes in earthbound spirits," reported Van Praagh, "which means that when we leave the body at the time of death, most of us are going to the other side, if you will. There's a light for every single person."[36]

Melinda, like her real-life counterpart, helps people find the light. In "On Wings of a Dove," for instance, she communicates with a shirtless, vaguely Hispanic-looking ex-con ghost who died in her husband Jim's ambulance and has "latched on" to him. This makes him act cranky. At first, Melinda thinks Jim's just not that into her anymore, but then realizes hubby's got a monkey (er, ghost) on his back. She learns from the spirit that he needs forgiveness from the parents of a man he accidentally killed. When that doesn't work out, Melinda realizes the spirit can "pass on" to the next world only if he makes peace with his own family: a wife and young son. With Jim's help, she facilitates the spirit's ascent to the afterlife.

In "The Voices," a teenager steals Jim and Melinda Gordon's SUV for a joyride. But when the Gordons get the vehicle back, Melinda finds the radio is transmitting EVP or White Noise…the voices of the dead! Worse, her cell phone and answering machine are also malfunctioning. The result—Melinda starts to experience bad headaches. It's as though she's on overload, receiving messages from those who can't cross over. Turns out, the car thief's mother died in the woods recently (during an adulterous tryst), and wants to contact her juvenile delinquent son and tell him—*wait for it*—that she *loves* him. She's giving Melinda the headaches trying to get her important message through.

And so it goes on, one of the most plastic-looking, fake, and overlit series ever to land on dramatic television. The series creators realize they are catering to an audience that can't countenance the least bit of ambiguity or reality; thus Melinda's world is a perfect, protected, affluent consumer bubble of designer clothes, streetside cafes, boutiques, and high-end furniture. It's overdesigned; America as Pier One store. In storytelling, *Ghost Whisperer* devotes itself almost primarily to navel-gazing and popcorn philosophy: earnest Jennifer Love Hewitt's angst-ridden "grappling" with her unusual gift.

Many supernatural programs on television are bad (see: *Supernatural*), but not a one of 'em so blatantly reduces matters of life, death, and spirituality to something so safe and boring as the equation stewed up in *Ghost Whisperer*, an unholy hodgepodge of New Age "forgiveness" and Christian afterlife principles. The prevailing wisdom seems to be that the dead remain in our world because they somehow failed to live up to a Christian moral code in life; once they pass on their messages of "acceptance," "forgiveness," and the like, they can just hop an elevator straight up to Heaven.

Alas, *Ghost Whisperer* is also a total vanity production for Hewitt. The series is dominated by close-up shots of the actress, granting the audience seemingly endless—*even slow-motion views*—of the performer's face. Watching the unending string of close and medium shots targeted at Hewitt's face, one begins to obsess. Is that a real mole under her right eye, or an affectation? And then one might become entranced by her hair. It appears to literally change styles in almost every shot. Just how many hairstyles is Ms. Hewitt afforded per episode? My guess is at least four…which seems excessive, even for a *Ghost Whisperer*.

In cynical Hollywood fashion, *Ghost Whisperer* also exploits some sort of basic, deep-seated female wish-fulfillment syndrome. Hewitt is married to an understanding and gorgeous husband, who spends the bulk of every episode tending to her every need, fretting over her constantly. Why, there's even a scene in "The Voices" where Ms. Hewitt is made up to resemble a little girl, replete with pig tails! She sits in bed and her hubby delicately and lovingly spoon-feeds her chicken soup. All because those meanie ghosts are giving her bad headaches. Aww! *Ghost Whisperer* is attempting to win the hypochondriacal/stay-at-home Mom demographic. It seems to be succeeding. The series has been renewed for a second season, though Aisha Tyler will not be returning as Andrea.

Though audiences apparently eat this drivel up, the critics have been merciless. "The sooner this series passes into the light, the better,"[37] suggested *The South Florida Sun-Sentinel*. Brian Lowry at *Variety* called it "a cloying, my-heart-(and-soul)-will-go-on drama" and a "shamelessly sentimental hour."[38]

Available on DVD.

A HAUNTING

(Discovery Channel) (RENEWED) (60 minutes) (Fridays at 10:00 pm, EST; October 28, 2005-August 24, 2006) New Dominion Pictures. Executive Producer: Tom Naughton. Co-Executive Producer: Nicolas Valcour. Producers: Liza Douglas, Joseph Maddrey, Larry Silverman. Camera: Ray Brown, David Haycox, Gregoire Valcour. Film Editors: Kevin Anderson, Andrew Monument. Music: Ed Smart. Directed by: Vernon Guinn, David Halcox, Stuart Taylor, Joe Wiecha.

"Between the world we see and the things we fear… nightmares become reality. These are the true stories of the innocent and the unimaginable."

The quote above is an abbreviated version of the grave-voiced narration which opens each and every hour of the Discovery Channel's new series, *A Haunting*. As described by episode producer Joseph Maddrey, the series' mission is "first and foremost, to scare the audience."

The "true stories depicted in each episode," he says "were chosen with that goal in mind…Many of the cases in the first season episodes are locally famous, and have inspired books or short segments on other television series…"

Controversially for some critics, *A Haunting* deploys many of the prevailing reality-show styles popular today to tell its far-fetched tales of haunted houses. In other words the series manipulates the "real" or "true story" approach of the *Blair Witch Project* (1999), coupled with the currently in-vogue documentary format audiences have enjoyed in mainstream theatrical hits such as *Fahrenheit 9/11* (2004), *Supersize Me!* (2005), and *March of the Penguins* (2005). In essence this an expedient for getting audiences viscerally involved with the story. Most recently, *The Exorcism of Emily Rose* brought the "true story" card out of mothballs.

Despite attempts to suggest these stories are real (as well as interviews with the real participants in the case studies), *A Haunting*, as Maddrey indicates, is designed to scare the pants off viewers. It is edited and constructed with a tip of the hat to (and a thorough understanding of) the last fifty years of horror cinema history. And that means you've got your P.O.V. subjective shots (from the viewpoint of the spook!), you've got your high-angle shots (which mean doom and entrapment), and you even have the classic "Stay Awake!" shot (wherein a character—after suffering a nightmare—bolts up in bed, sweating profusely). It's all on *A Haunting*, combined to create an experience some folks might mistake for fact…if they're very, very gullible.

A typical installment of *A Haunting* is "Echoes from the Grave" which tells the story of Ron and Nancy Stallings in the year 1965. They believe they've found the perfect house, a historic home built in 1920 near Baltimore. But when they move in with their six children, things start to go mysteriously awry. A faucet spigot opens by itself. Heavy footsteps are heard in the hallways at night. Nancy's cousin Bill, an attorney, feels an *"overwhelming sense of dread"* when he tries to walk to the second floor. A priest comes to bless the house, but inconveniently forgets to bless the porch (*D'oh!*)

The ghostly presence(s) continue to raise a ruckus, at one point animating a little tricycle. These activities spur Nancy to call on the services of renowned paranormal investigator Hans Holzer (from Austria) and his *"transmedium."* Perhaps the most disturbing information comes from a notation Bill sees at the Hall of Records: every previous family living in that house has seen a loved one *die* there before escaping…

The episode's climax is a laundry list of horror movie

techniques as Ron and Nancy (Hey, Ron and Nancy? What kind of joke is that?) prepare to leave the haunted house at last, when Nancy inconveniently forgets something important in one of the upstairs bedrooms. Of course, she goes back into the house alone, and the evil spirits terrorize her with two minutes of unremitting scares. Faucets turn on and off. Windows lock and unlock. Doors slam and open. A chair races across the floor of its own volition. This is a crazy, inspired, nearly Raimi-esque moment of horror and not what one would expect from a series that promises to tell "true stories."

Viewed as a spooky anthology about haunted houses, *A Haunting* is fun, but one wonders how the creators of this show can adhere to a fairly limited format over time. The story structure is a familiar one to fans of haunted house movies. Let me diagram the paradigm: There's the honeymoon stage, wherein a happy couple buys a "fixer upper" that they shouldn't be able to afford. Then there's the uncertainty stage, wherein the family moves into the haunted house and begins to experience feelings of apprehension, nightmares, and a general sense of wariness. Then there's the recognition stage, where the occult is acknowledged and steps are taken to get help (either moving out, conducting research at the Hall of Records, or bringing in an expert). Finally, the beleaguered family achieves a sense of safety after escaping from the house, in the Let's-All-Take-A-Deep Breath Stage.

"We're trying to strike a delicate balance between documentary and drama," Maddrey explains further. "On one hand, it can be very difficult to create dramatic tension—which relies so much on pacing and acting—within a format that uses narration and interviews to convey information. On the other hand, these shows have the potential to be scarier specifically because we are continually reminded that this is someone's real-life story. Many of the participants in these episodes agreed to be interviewed because they want others to know that hauntings are real. They believe that a program like this may help people in similar situations to cope with the unexplainable. We are giving them a voice."

Coupled with Discovery Channel's cheesy new series *I Shouldn't Be Alive*, *A Haunting* makes part of a potent and sensational contribution to the network's prime-time, original programming lineup.

The series has already been renewed for additional seasons, but is not yet available on DVD.

Russell Shultz (Adam Goldberg) and Jason Payne (Chris O'Donnell) forge a new friendship in the short-lived **HEAD CASES**.

HEAD CASES

(FOX) (CANCELED) (60 minutes) (Wednesdays at 9:00 pm, EST; September 14, 2005-September 21, 2005) 20th Century Fox Television. Created by: Bill Chais. Executive Producers: Bill Chais, Barry Josephson. Co-Executive Producer: Chris Mundy. Produced by: Harry V. Bring, Gary Law. Co-Producer: Chris O'Donnell. Camera: Lloyd Ahern, Michael Trim. Film Editors: Lauren Schaffer, William Scharf. Music: Lisa Coleman, Wendy Melvoin. Written by: Bill Chais. Directed by: Andrew Fleming, Craig Zisk.

CAST
Chris O'Donnell (Jason Payne)
Adam Goldberg (Russell Shultz)
Rhea Seehorn (Nicole Walker)
Rockmond Dunbar (Dr. Robinson)
Krista Allen (Laurie Payne)
Jake Cherry (Ryan Payne)

What is *Head Cases?* Well, *Head Cases* is the answer to a trivia question. *What was the first cancellation of the 2005–2006 season?* This series by creator Bill Chais aired only twice before FOX pulled the plug on the legal drama… even though it starred movie star Chris O'Donnell.

Head Cases is the personal story of Jason Payne (O'Donnell), a high-powered attorney who buckles under the pressure and ends up going to a mental institution after a row with his wife. When he leaves the facility and returns to normal life, however, Payne can't get his old job at the law firm back and must relent to working with another mentally unstable lawyer, the dangerously unpredictable Shultz (Goldberg). Together, they represent unusual, down-on-their-luck and bizarre clients in need of legal assistance. In concept, the series is not that far removed from the WB's superior *Just Legal*, which also plumbs the notion of an unconventional law partnership.

Although six episodes of *Head Cases* were produced, FOX didn't waste time pulling the plug on this sometimes drama/sometimes comedy. When *Head Cases'* second airing (on September 21) drew only 3 million viewers—giving it a ranking of 104th out of 115 series—it lost all future appeals.[39] *Head Cases* was unceremoniously replaced on the schedule by episodes of *Nanny 911*.

Not currently available on DVD.

HEIST

(NBC)(CANCELED)(60 minutes)(Wednesdays at 10:00 pm, EST; March 22, 2006-April 19, 2006) Hypnotic/NBC Universal/ Sony. Executive Producers: Mark and Rob Cullen, David Bartis, Bernie Brillstein, Doug Liman, Peter Safrian. Co-Executive Producer: Natalie Chaidez. Produced by: Sean Ryerson. Camera: Jamie Barber. Film Editor: Juan Carlos Gaza. Written by: Mark and Rob Cullen, Chris Mundy, Evan Reilly. Directed by: Ed Bianchi, Doug Liman, Any Wolk.

CAST
Dougray Scott (Mickey O'Neil)
Steve Harris (James Johnson)
Seymour Cassel (Pops)
Marika Dominczyk (Lola)
David Watton (Ricky)
Michele Hicks (Amy Sykes)
Reno Wilson (Tyrese Evans)
Billy Gardell (Billy O'Brien)

The 2005–2006 season saw the arrival of three TV dramas concerning crooks attempting to pull off elaborate cons or heists. In all cases, the crooks were pretty much depicted as the protagonists. There was this NBC effort, *Heist*, AMC's *Hustle*, and FX's *Thief*. *Thief* (starring the superb Andre Braugher) is the gritty dark version of the genre, *Hustle* is the consummate brainteaser and "team" show, and *Heist* is…

Well, *Heist* is the one show that viewers apparently decided they could afford to miss; and did miss. The series was canceled by NBC after five episodes aired.

It's surprising that *Heist* would prove the weak link in the "crooks and cons" sweepstakes of 2005–2006. After all, it boasts the talents of writers Rob and Mark Cullen, who had created the fun FX series, *Lucky*, as well as those of Doug Liman, the director of such feature film hits as *Mr. and Mrs. Smith* (2005), *The Bourne Identity* (2004) and *Swingers* (1996). With that kind of behind-the-scenes talent, expectations were high.

Heist recounts the tale of Mickey (Dougray Scott), an affable and charming criminal on the verge of embarking on his biggest job yet: a triple-jewelry story robbery that could net him and his crew half-a-billion dollars. Unfortunately for Mickey, Detective Amy Sykes (Michele Hicks) of the LAPD gets wind of something illicit going down after investigating a robbery in Beverly Hills. Mickey tries to get to know his new nemesis, but ends up falling for her…and therein lies the tale.

Steve Harris (*The Practice*) plays James, Mickey's sidekick, and Sykes is saddled with two bickering police partners, played by Gardell and Wilson. None of this material is particularly memorable or sharp, and because it aired on a major network, *Heist* feels a lot more generic and less interesting than either of its cable brethren.

Not available on DVD.

HEX

(BBC America) (CANCELED) (60 minutes) (Thursdays at 9:00 pm EST; September 18, 2005-December 18, 2005) Shine/Sony Pictures TV International. Executive Producers: Dean Hargrove, Sara Johnson, Elisabeth Murdoch. Produced by: Johnny Capps, Julian Murphy. Camera: Geoffrey Wharton. Film Editors: Belinda Cottrell, Adam Recht, John Richards, Matthew Tabern. Music: James Brett. Written by: Julian Jones, Lucy Watkins. Directed by: Brian Grant, Andy Goddard.

CAST
Jemima Rooper (Thelma Bates)
Christina Cole (Cassie)
Laura Pyper (Ella)
Michael Fassbender (Azazeal)
Colin Salmon (David Tyrel)
Amber Sainsbury (Roxanne)
Jamie Davis (Leon)

Described as a "supernatural coming of age series," the scintillating adolescent drama *Hex* began airing on BBC America early in summer of 2006. Although the series had premiered in England (on Sky One) in 2004, BBC America aired all eighteen episodes of the first two seasons in one 2006 sortie.

Hex is set at a countryside boarding school/high school in rural England, called Medenham. There, a beautiful (and promiscuous) blond student named Cassie (Christina Cole) learns that she's actually the reincarnation of a powerful, historic witch. Her roommate, a lesbian named Thelma (Jemima Rooper) is killed in a terrible scene and then becomes Cassie's constant companion and guardian…as an incorporeal ghost (who can only change her fashions by stealing the clothes off corpses). Now Thelma can watch Cassie shower, but she can never touch her; an arrangement that vexes the spirit.

Meanwhile, Cassie falls in love with a sultry and dangerous bad boy named Azazeal (Michael Fassbender), but he's actually a mythological creature called a "Nephilim," a fallen angel who hopes to breed with a human and launch a new crusade against Heaven. Guess who Azazeal's selected to be the mother of his child? Yep, it's Cassie. Worse, as Thelma soon learns, these events have apparently repeated over and over again through history, with the women in Cassie's role all suffering horrible deaths.

In one episode of *Hex*, Cassie is briefly possessed by a demon and in that compromised state has sexual intercourse with Azazeal, an act which effectively brings about the End of Days. After an accelerated pregnancy, she gives birth to a son, Malachai, who—once grown—can release two hundred Nephilim monstrosities from their supernatural prisons. The only way to stop this pending apocalypse is by killing Malachai, but that's understandably difficult for Cassie, the boy's mother. Another problem: if the baby dies, order in the universe is restored and Cassie will no longer be able to communicate with the ghostly Thelma.

Soon, another student, Ella (Laura Pyper) arrives at Medenham. She's a witch hunter determined to stop Azazeal, and hellbent on murdering Malachai. Other cast members on *Hex* include Roxanne (Amber Sainsbury), a ravenous schoolgirl trying desperately to deflower a handsome instructor at the school who also happens to be Azazeal's minion. And Leon (Jamie Davis) is Ella's confused boyfriend, also doomed to some unpleasant "growing pains."

Critic W.M. Stephen Humphrey at *The Portland Mercury* termed *Hex* "*Buffy the Vampire Slayer* crossed with late-night Cinemax,"[40] because the series boasts graphic sex scenes with plenty of female nudity. As for the

Buffy metaphor, it is appropriate for abundant enough reasons. Cassie's relationship with a hulking, brooding, 200-plus year old "monster," dramatically recalls Buffy's relationship with the sometimes good/sometimes soulless vampire, Angel.

Fans will also remember that Buffy's witch friend, Willow became a lesbian in later seasons, and here Rooper—a similar friend and supporting character, also plays a lesbian. Maneater Roxanne is also heavily reminiscent of Charisma Carpenter's selfish Cordelia character, concerned only with fashion, sex, and herself. There's even a strong accent on comedy and wisecracks, so *Hex* could—at least on first glance—be aptly termed a clone of the more popular American series.

"Everybody was expecting a second *Buffy,* which did nothing but help us," said producer Brian Grant. "It brought a whole pile of people to the table who might not have come. When they realized it wasn't *Buffy*—cause it's nothing like *Buffy* really—it still brought an audience who went 'Oh, what a surprise.' [It's the] biggest audience [that Sky's] ever had—we can't complain!"[41]

Indeed *Hex* is more frankly and openly sexual, and in some terrible sense, much darker than its American cousin. The characters here are frequently faced with terrible decisions (such as aborting a child that could destroy the world). They also act more selfishly and unheroically than the more likable *Buffy dramatis personae.* In one episode, for instance, Thelma makes an alliance with Azazeal to get something she desperately desires, and this accommodation nearly kills Ella.

Also, without revealing too much, *Hex* brazenly pulls a *Psycho*-style trick midway through its second season, killing off a main character and throwing the entire series into disarray and chaos. This move will leave faithful viewers reeling. Finally, *Hex* features fewer and less impressive special effects than *Buffy the Vampire Slayer* did, but as characters fumble and fight and darkness encroaches inevitably on mankind, the series becomes more and more compelling; particularly as a statement about tomorrow's generation heading over a precipice.

Unfortunately, *Hex's* viewing numbers dropped precipitously in the UK in 2005, spurring an eventual cancellation in 2006. The viewing numbers went from over a million to just 200,000.

"*Hex* was an exciting, original idea that captured the attention of critics and audiences alike," said Sky One executive Richard Woolf. "We're extremely proud of the series, but feel that it's come to a natural end."[42]

Not yet available on the DVD format.

HOT PROPERTIES

(ABC) (CANCELED) (30 minutes) (Fridays at 9:30 pm, EST; October 7, 2005–December 30, 2005) Interbang Inc./Warner Bros. Created by: Suzanne Martin. Executive Producer: Suzanne Martin. Co-Executive Producers: Andy Gordon, Chuck Ranberg, Jay Daniel. Producers: Valerie Ahern, Christian McLaughlin. Camera: Nick McLean. Film Editor: John Fuller. Music: Jeff Rona. Written by: Suzanne Martin, Valerie Ahern, Andrew Gordon, Sebastian Jones, Christian McLaughlin, Patrick Ribon, Chuck Ranberg. Directed by: Andy Ackerman, Jeff Melman.

CAST

Stephen Dunham (Dr. Charlie Thorpe)
Evan Handler (Dr. Sellers Boyd)
Amy Hill (Mary)
Christina Moore (Emerson Ives)
Gail O'Grady (Ava Summerlin)
Nicole Sullivan (Chloe Reid)
Sofia Vergara (Lola Hernandez)

This ABC sitcom about the lives and loves of four Manhattanite real estate agents had the poor luck to appear on TV the self-same season that a similar concept (four professional women sharing a condo) was thoroughly ridiculed and roasted as "Room and Bored" on the pilot of the Lisa Kudrow satire, *The Comeback.* Once you've watched how that clever HBO series systematically skewers ensemble sitcoms like *Hot Properties*, it's tough to take the real thing seriously.

Created by Suzanne Martin, *Hot Properties* follows the adventures of four beautiful and neurotic women. There's Chloe (Nicole Sullivan), a woman with bad luck dating. Her last serious fling was with a man she nicknamed "Ambassador cross dresser." There's Ava Summerlin (Gail O'Grady) a 41-year-old woman who has married a 25-year-old aspiring actor, Scott, and wants to have children with him. There's Lola Hernandez (Sofia Vergara), a hot-blooded Latina with a ridiculously thick accent who finds herself continually falling for gay men and thus being "the Latina Liza." Finally, we have Emerson Ives (Christina Moore), a spoiled rich girl who has never before left her parents' overbearing stewardship and receives a $20,000-a-month stipend.

These women work together in their lush real estate office and share building space with a bald psychologist, Dr. Boyd (Evan Handler) and a slick, womanizing dermatologist, Dr. Thorpe (Stephen Dunham). Mary (Amy Hill) is the put-upon building receptionist, always at the ready with a quip or a bottle of whiskey when times get rough.

Like so much on TV in the twenty-first century, *Hot Properties* is not actually a bad show, just a tragically familiar one. The central situation was a bit too familiar and cliched, and the jokes are generally weak. For instance, one episode "Sex, Lies, and Chubby Chasers" tries to eke out a laugh from the pronunciation of "Van Gogh," and fails rather miserably. Another episode, "It's a Wonderful Christmas Carol on 34th Street" is that old sitcom chestnut: the mawkish Christmas tale.

Occasionally a joke hits the mark, such as the occasion when Chloe, describing her chubby-chasing boyfriend Craig, notes to her gal pals: "*To him, the cellulite on my ass is like Angelina Jolie's lips.*" However that silly quip is the exception rather than the rule. Still, the cast is enthusiastic and gorgeous, and one can see how the series might have improved and sharpened if given time.

Hot Properties premiered October 7, 2005 at 9:30 pm and was coupled with the very similar "chick" sitcom, *Faith & Hope*, until its order of thirteen episodes ran out on December 30 and the series was canceled by ABC.

Not available on DVD.

HOW I MET YOUR MOTHER

(CBS) (RENEWED) (30 minutes) (Mondays at 8:30 pm, EST; September 19, 2005-May 15, 2006) 20th Century Fox. Created by: Carter Bays, Craig Thomas. Executive Producers: Carter Bays, Rob Greenberg, Craig Thomas. Produced by: Randy Cordray. Camera: Steven V. Silver. Film Editor: Kirk Benson. Music: Tree Adam. Written by: Carter Bays, Maria Ferrar, Suzy Greenberg, Chris Harris, Brenda Hsueh, Kourtney Kay, Gloria Calderon Kellett, Phil Lord, Sam Johnson, Chris Marcil, Chris Miller, Ira Ungerleider. Directed by: Pamela Frydman.

CAST

Josh Radnor (Ted Mosby)
Jason Segel (Marshall)
Cobie Smulders (Robin)
Neil Patrick Harris (Barney)
Alyson Hannigan (Lily)

How I Met Your Mother is a breath of fresh air in terms of the sitcom format. It's one of those increasingly rare birds: a situation comedy that's actually funny, though viewers could certainly do without the laugh track. The sitcom's story is vetted as a flashback of sorts. In the year 2030, a guy named Ted (voiced by Bob Saget) explains to his kids how he came to meet their mother.

Flashback to present. Ted (Radnor) is a young man, a 27-year-old architect living in an apartment with his buddy, Marshall (Jason Segel). Marshall has just proposed to his girlfriend of almost a decade, a vivacious (and silly) kindergarten teacher named Lily (Alyson Hannigan). This turn of events gets Ted thinking about his romantic situation and he quickly realizes he desires the same thing: to find the right woman, fall in love and settle down. Ted believes he might be able to experience just such a relationship with a woman he's fallen in love with: Robin (Cobie Smulders).

Neil Patrick Harris, formerly Doogie Howser, plays the series' wild-and-crazy guy character (replete with a catchphrase; "Suit up!"), named Barney. Barney is only too happy to lend Ted the benefit of his knowledge and experience when it comes to women.

In the twenty-two episodes of this inventive and frequently amusing sitcom, Ted embarrasses himself (and others) over his devotion to Robin. In "Purple Giraffe," he invites her to a party he's throwing. She doesn't show up…so he throws another party in hopes that she will. And on it goes.

Later in the first run of shows, he dates a girl named Victoria, but by the end of the season, Robin is back on his radar. In "Nothing Good Happens After 2:00 am," Ted gets a late night call from Robin and rekindles feelings about the relationship. In the season finale, Ted attempts to convince Robin to abandon a camping trip so she can hang out with him instead. Other episodes include "Game Night," in which each of the *dramatis personae* is encouraged to recount their most embarrassing moment.

Sitcoms about lovelorn young men are a dime a dozen, especially in 2005–2006, but *How I Met Your Mother* is quirky and fun, and most importantly, well-cast. Lines that are only borderline amusing become laugh-out funny in the mouths of vets like Hannigan and Harris. Truly, these two talents are the series' most valuable players, and they grant the enterprise a sense of professionalism and pace that many sitcoms don't acquire until later seasons (if ever). The series "introduces a level of unpredictability not usually found in comedies,"[43] wrote Barry Garron for *Hollywood Reporter*, and that may be part of the charm.

Much more unusual and unpredictable than the

sometimes familiar plot lines, is the manner in which this comedy is shot and assembled. *How I Met Your Mother* is a series that uses multi-camera coverage but the "editing and cutaways" of a single-camera show. That offensive laugh track is added later with a post-taping audience. "It's harder to launch a sitcom these days," says co-creator Craig Thomas in describing the series. "People are a little bored with the purely traditional form of it, but were huge fans of *Cheers* and *Seinfeld*. If you could do that sitcom and just update it a little bit and have it be a little quicker and with a different narrative storytelling device, it would feel familiar enough but exciting enough that people might want to watch it."[44]

The stellar ratings have borne out Thomas's theory. *How I Met Your Mother* returns September 18, 2006 on CBS.

Available on DVD.

HOW TO GET THE GUY

(ABC) (CANCELED) (60 minutes) (Mondays at 10:00 pm, EST; June 12, 2006-July 3, 2006) Deacon Productions/Scout Productions. Executive Producers: David Collins, David Metzler. Co-Executive Producers: Don Morando. Produced by: Kevin Finn, Jennifer Herschko, Susan McGinn, Brian Robel, Joy Hryniewicz. Camera: Sam Ameen. Film Editors: Richie Edelson, Kevin Finn, Sam Mussari, Michael Polakow. Music: Rob Cairns. Directed by: Ricki Kim.

CAST
J.D. Roberto
Teresa Strasser

This hour-long series is sort of like a reality show version of the Will Smith movie, *Hitch*…only taken from the female perspective.

From the makers of *Queer Eye for the Straight Guy* (2003–   ) arrives this ABC series about life, love and finding Mr. Right. In *How to Get the Guy*, life coaches J.D. Roberto and Teresa Strasser guide four lovelorn women in their thirties through the perils of finding new and rewarding relationships, an endeavor set against the scenic backdrop of San Francisco. The women are Alissa ("The Dreamer"), Anne ("The Girl Next Door"), Kris ("The Party Girl"), and Michelle ("The Career Girl").

These coaches help the women through the "terrifying" romantic holiday, Valentines' Day, and enroll them in a "Love Lab." Among the clever advice dispensed by these lovelife gurus: "get in the game," "keep it light," "volume date" and—naturally—"let him pay."[45]

Unfortunately—on this TV show—it's the viewer who pays.

How to Get The Guy, never really got in the ratings game and regularly lost about "forty percent of the viewers who were watching *Supernanny* in the hour preceding it."[46] A summer series, the program aired just four times on ABC (from June 12 to July 3, 2006), and was part of that network's disastrous summer lineup, which also included the low-rated reality series, *The One: Making a Music Star*.

Whether or not you get the guy, you can't get the DVD: it's not available at this time.

HUSTLE

(AMC) (RENEWED) (60 minutes) (Saturdays at 10:00 pm, EST; Wednesdays at 10:00 pm, EST; January 14, 2006-August 2, 2006) Kudos Films/BBC. Created by: Tony Jordan, Bharat Nalluri. Executive Producers: Simon Crawford Collins, Jane Featherstone, Gareth Neame. Produced by: Lucy Robinson, Karen Wilson. Camera: Balazs Boylgo, Gordon Hickie, Kieran McGuigan, Jake Polonsky, Adam Suschitzky, Sean Van Hales. Film Editors: Victoria Boydell, Andrew McClelland. Music: Magnus Fiennes, Simon Rogers. Written by: Steve Coombs, Matthew Grahalm, Tony Jordan, Ashley Pharoah, Howard Overman, Julie Rutherford. Directed by: Robert Baily, Otto Bathurst, Colm McCarthy, Bharat Nalluri, Alrick Riley, Minkie Spiro, John Strickland.

CAST

Robert Vaughn (Albert Stroller/"The Roper")
Adrian Lester (Mickey Stone/"The Inside Man")
Jaime Murray (Stacie Monroe/"The Lure")
Robert Glenister (Ash Morgan/"The Fixer")
Marc Warren (Danny Blue/"The Wild Card")

This BBC series had aired for three seasons and eighteen episodes in Britain (where it was still going strong), but the 2004 series *Hustle* was picked up for airing in America in January of 2006.

Hustle is a crime caper series. Although AMC's promotional material strives to compare it to such recent cinematic efforts as *Snatch* (2000) and *Ocean's 11* (2001), the vibe is more clearly the 1960s team espionage series, *Mission: Impossible* (1966–1973). Only here, the team is not on the side of the angels'. That doesn't mean that the team consists of bad guys, it just means that they're criminals. The point of the comparison is that *Hustle* boasts as many twists as turns as *Mission: Impossible* and its complex plots (with delightful, ironic solutions) recall the intelligence of that brilliant American effort.

Hustle follows the adventures of ex-con Mickey Stone (Adrian Lester) as he's released from prison and teams up with an old mentor, grifter Albert Stroller (Robert Vaughn). Soon, they are contemplating and executing complex "long cons" against enemies. On the team is Ash, the "fixer," and the beautiful Stacie, the "Lure." The team is joined by Danny Blue (Marc Warren), the aptly named "wild card," who could foul up or save a con in a cold minute.

Episodes feature the gang conning "bad guys" who, quite frankly, deserve the humiliation. The team uses a fake painting to bilk an arrogant gallery owner in "Picture Perfect." In "Touch of Class," a divorcee is the "mark." An avaricious property developer gets the business in "Gold Mine" and in the second season finale, "Eye of the Beholder," the team decides to go after the Crown Jewels!

Gorgeous, smart, fast-paced, and requiring much rewinding, *Hustle* is a brilliant bit of business, and one of the very best dramas on TV. Hosannas to AMC for picking it up. The series has been called "hyperkinetic"[47] and a good turn of phrase for the well-cast drama. *The New York Times* hails *Hustle* as a "refreshing throwback to 1960s caper movies and series like *The Avengers*. It's slick, clever and playful: it offers a Cool Britannia that doesn't exist in real life in Britain or on television on either side of the Atlantic."[48]

Salon notes that along "with snappy dialogue and slick little scenes, what stands out the most about *Hustle* is how beautifully it's filmed. Every shot is an inventively lit, expertly framed work of art...worth watching for that reason alone."[49]

Hustle plays and feels like a feature film every week, and like other unconventional fare such as *Epitafios*, stylishly resuscitates the crime genre. Most importantly, *Hustle* is whip-smart and funny as hell.

Available on DVD.

I SHOULDN'T BE ALIVE

(The Discovery Channel) (RENEWED) (60 minutes)
(Fridays at 9:00 pm, EST; October 28, 2005-continuing) Darlow Smithson Productions/Channel 4 Television/Discovery Communications. Executive Producers: Adalene Alani, Nick Copus, Jack Smith, John Smithson. Produced by: Ben Bowie, Alex Marengo, David Wheeler, Holly Wingens. Camera: Jeremy Hewson. Film Editors: Mark Davies, Ben Laster. Music: Andy Bush, Dave Gale, Dave Hewson. Written by: Nick Copus, Jaime Smith, John Smithson. Directed by: Ian Barnes.

Airing Friday nights before *A Haunting*, *I Shouldn't Be Alive* forms part of The Discovery Channel's "harrowing" reenactment double bill. Unlike *A Haunting*, which focuses on the supernatural, *I Shouldn't Be Alive* is a survival reenactment series about "the extraordinary resilience of the human spirit," according to the series' promotional material and executive producer John Smithson (creator of the 2003 film *Touching the Void*).

Each hour of *I Shouldn't Be Alive* features dramatic (and sometimes cheesy) reenactments of a terrible tragedy…often in an unusual, exotic and picturesque location. The people who actually survived these frightening events are also brought on screen to be interviewed about their near-death experiences, much like the survivors of haunted houses on *A Haunting*.

I Shouldn't Be Alive has thus far featured a group of explorers lost in the Amazon and at the mercy of an untrustworthy guide ("Escape from the Amazon"); showcased a drama about a terrified family (including a little baby) trapped in a blizzard ("Soldier in the Snow"); recounted the tale of a storm at sea in which sailors are forced to survive for days in shark-infested waters ("Shipwrecked Sailors"); and more.

Characters depicted on the series have been captured by guerillas ("Kidnapped by the Khmer Rouge"), and faced terror by water ("Kayakers"), and land ("African Safari"). If one is susceptible to these kind of extreme stories, the series engenders a sort of "there but for the grace of God" atmosphere. The only problem is in knowing how much is true and how much is tarted up for drama's sake.

Not currently on DVD.

IN JUSTICE

(ABC) (CANCELED) (60 minutes) (Fridays at 9:00 pm EST; January 1, 2006-March 31, 2006) Touchstone Television. Created by: Michelle King, Robert King. Executive Producers: Stu Bloomberg, Michelle and Robert King. Camera: Tom, Szentgyorgyi. Film Editor: Paul Dixon, David Dworetzky. Written by: Michelle and Robert King, Marc Guggenheim, Terri Kopp. Directed by: Steven De Paul, Paul Holahan, Mick Jason.

CAST

Jason O'Mara (Charles Conti)
Kyle MacLachlan (David Swain)
Marisol Nichols (Sonya Quintano)
Constance Zimmer (Brianna)
Daniel Cosgrove (Joe Lemonick)

A midseason replacement, *In Justice* is a would-be familiar lawyer series turned upside down. During its brief run between January and March of '06, *In Justice* gazed at the mostly unexplored "other side" of the American justice system. Where so many series, including the defunct *NYPD Blue* (1993–2005) or *Law and Order* (1990–present) focus on cops solely as heroes who put away villainous criminals, glorifying the police in a sense, *In Justice* faces a more unpleasant truth; in particular, that many innocent people are wrongly convicted in this country and serving time in prison.

In Justice is the story of David Swain (Kyle MacLachlan), an eccentric corporate attorney who earns nearly $700 an hour and yet still finds himself feeling unfulfilled. So Swain utilizes his personal fortune to create the National Justice Project and runs the new operation out of an old hotel. There, Swain and his investigators, including a former cop, Charles Conti (Jason O'Mara) and a trio of young (and—*naturally*—attractive) attorneys (Marisol Nichols, Constance Zimmer, Daniel Cosgrove) peer into

suspect old cases and help prove to new juries that these men and women were wrongly convicted…sometimes deliberately so.

In one case, "Badge of Honor," the attorneys help free a policeman convicted of killing another policeman. In another, a junkie convicted of murder is redeemed ("Brothers and Sisters"). The lawyers help a black man escape from death row execution in one story (how many times have we seen that?!), and in another tale, they prove that a man is not a despicable baby killer.

Like so many programs these days, *In Justice* boasts an unusual visual hook or technique that attempts to separate it from the crime investigation pack. Here, each program opens with a "flashback" revealing a crime as it was presented to the juries originally. In other words, inaccurately. Later, as Swain and his ace team of do-gooders discover the truth, the same crime featured earlier in the hour is re-parsed demonstrating what *actually* happened, not what prosecutors and judges believe happened.

In Justice may have been a hard sell for those in middle America, who are accustomed to seeing staple good guys like detectives "win." That didn't happen here, as critic Debra Watson noted. "In the initial episodes of the series, we have seen a top FBI official led off in handcuffs, a prosecutor admitting to illegally coaching witnesses to get a homicide conviction and a lawyer/politician attempting to cut a deal to cover up his firm's criminal activity…The program has offered us lying witnesses, incompetent "experts" and federal law-enforcement officials willing to send innocent men to life in prison in pursuit of their law-and-order agenda. Cops interrogate children in the most brutal fashion so they can get false confessions and wrap up their cases."[50] Take that, *Law & Order!*

Not available on DVD.

INCONCEIVABLE

(NBC) (CANCELED) (60 minutes) (Fridays at 10:00 pm, EST; September 23, 2005-September 30, 2005) Tollin-Robbins Productions. Created by: Marco Pennette. Executive Producers: Joe Davola, Oliver Goldstick, Marco Pennette, Brian Robbins, Michael Tollin. Co-Executive Producers: Alison Cross, Chris Long, Alice West. Produced by: Shelley Zimmerman. Camera: Jamie Anderson, David J. Miller. Film Editors: David Crabtree, Scott K. Wallace. Warren Bowman. Music: Jeff Martin. Written by: Oliver Goldstick, Marco Pennette. Directed by: Chris Long.

CAST

Ming-Na (Dr. Rachel Lu)
Jonathan Cake (Dr. Malcolm Bowers)
David Norona (Scott Garcia)
Reynaldo Rosales (Angel Hernandez)
Joelle Carter (Patrice Locicero)
Mary Catherine Garrison (Marissa Jaffee)
Angie Harmon (Dr. Nora Campbell)

The goings-on at the Family Options Fertility Clinic were the subject matter for this short-lived soap opera/medical series that aired on Friday nights.

Dr. Rachel Lu (Ming-Na) and womanizer Dr. Malcolm Bowers (Jonathan Cake) run the busy infertility clinic—where something dramatic is always happening, either with the staff or the clientele. In the pilot, for instance, a set of Caucasian parents get the shock of their lives when the surrogate mom under their employ gives birth to an African-American baby. Wacky fun, no?

Another plot strand involves a gay couple that wishes to start a family and pursues a plan to do so. This is the most touching portion of the show. It's not handled frivolously and is a genuine advance in the treatment of homosexuals on television. "There's so much evolving for domestic partnerships and gay families," noted producer Goldstick, "I thought it would be great if a lawyer was gay and having a child. We just feel that this is another family that needs to be seen on television. These are our lives, and we want something that reflects the lives we are seeing."[51]

Yet another strand on *Inconceivable* involves the veteran widower who wants to use his deceased spouse's egg to conceive a child. Finally, a minister and his wife visit the clinic in hopes of solving their infertility problem. The minister's wife is so desperate to be a parent she would just as soon use another man's sperm.

Inconceivable is Marco Pennette's second series of the 2005–2006 season (the other being the sitcom, *Crumbs*), and unfortunately, neither effort saw much good luck while on the air. *Inconceivable* aired only twice (in late September, 2005) before NBC pulled it from the schedule. Worse, only 5.5 million viewers sampled *Inconceivable* originally. In its second week, it drew what *Daily Variety* terms "near record-low numbers."[52]

When NBC slipped a rerun of *Law & Order: Criminal Intent* in *Inconceivable's* Friday slot the following week, the repeat actually drew a higher number, 7 million viewers! Although NBC had previously promised to return *Inconceivable* to its slot, the rerun's higher numbers symbolized a death knell for an interesting series that wasn't exactly like everything else on the tube.

Not currently available on DVD.

From left to right, the ensemble cast of **INCONCEIVABLE**:
Hank Harris, Kevin Alejandro, Joelle Carter, Jonathan Cake, Ming-Na, Alfre Woodard,
David Norona, Mary Catherine Garrison.

INVASION

(ABC) (CANCELED) (60 minutes) (Wednesdays at 10:00 pm, EST; September 21, 2005-May 17, 2006) Shaun Cassidy Productions/Warner Bros. Created by: Shaun Cassidy. Executive Producers: Shaun Cassidy, Thomas Schlamme. Co-Executive Producers: Michael Berns, Becky Hartman-Edwards, Lawrence Trilling. Producer: Timothy Marx. Camera: Jeff Jur. Film Editors: Matthew Colonna, Timothy Good, Kristin Windell. Music: Jason Derlatki, John Erlich. Written by: Michael Alaimo, Michael Berns, Shaun Cassidy, Charlie Craig, Becky Hartman Edwards, Michael Foley, Julie Siege. Directed by: Ernest Dickerson, Bill Eagles, Rod Holcomb, Michael Nankin, Thomas Schlamme, Steve Shill, Lawrence Trilling, Harry Winer.

CAST

William Fichtner (Sheriff Tom Underlay)
Eddie Cibrian (Russell Varon)
Kari Matchett (Dr. Mariel Underlay)
Lisa Sheridan (Larkin Groves)
Tyler Labine (David Groves)
Alexis Dziena (Kira Underlay)
Evan Peters (Jesse Varon)
Ariel Gade (Rose Varon)
Aisha Hinds (Mona Gomez)

Invasion is a dramatic science fiction series from *American Gothic* (1995–1996) creator Shaun Cassidy. It's the television equivalent of the 1950s and 1970s classic film tale, *Invasion of the Body Snatchers*.

The action on *Invasion* begins in a small American town, Homestead, Florida. A whopper of a hurricane named Eve is bearing down on the little tropical paradise, and nervous families are buttoning down for the inevitable interruption of power and services. Tom Underlay (William Fichtner), who miraculously survived an airplane crash ten years earlier, serves as the town sheriff and is busy making preparations for the hamlet as he cares for his daughter, Kira (Alexis Dziena) and his new wife, the

beautiful physician, Mariel (Kari Matchett).

At the same time, Mariel's ex-husband, Russell Varon (Eddie Cibrian), a Cuban emigre and forest ranger, prepares his family for the deluge. His second wife, a TV news reporter named Larkin (Lisa Sheridan) is *very* pregnant, making the storm all the more terrifying. Russell's children with Mariel are also visiting his house in the woods at the time of the storm: surly teenager Jesse (Evan Peters) and little cherub Rose (Ariel Gade). The Varons also live with David (Tyler Labine), Larkin's conspiracy-minded brother and expert blogger.

But something strange happens when Hurricane Eve strikes Homestead. Rose, who is standing by the water in the eye of the storm, sees translucent yellow tear-drop-shaped lights descend from the sky and land gently into the lake. And Mariel, *en route* home to Tom and Kira after checking on Jesse and Rose—disappears. She is found near the water, days after the hurricane...naked and apparently suffering from amnesia.

In fact, dozens of Homestead citizens are waking up after the storm in this unusual fashion: with no clothes, and no memory about what occurred. Their families began to whisper about their oddly transformed loved ones. "*She didn't come back the same...*"

As *Invasion* progresses, Russell, Larkin, and David investigate the strange phenomenon and conclude that extraterrestrials of some variety used Hurricane Eve as cover to establish a beachhead on Earth. And worse, these water-bound aliens have physically bonded with the compromised human survivors of the storm. Now, Mariel and others are actually "hybrid" creations in brand new, incredibly strong (and bullet-resistant) bodies. These survivors also feel a strange, inexplicable attraction to water, and begin to congregate together. Sheriff Tom is apparently both the leader and vanguard—the advance scout—for this invasion on American soil.

The aliens are well-placed to infiltrate our society, as the creepy, deliberately paced series makes clear. The local priest is among their number, and he organizes a "Hurricane Survivor's Group" for the amnesiacs…really a gathering place for the affected. There, Tom asserts his authority and explains the changes to the hybrids. "I emerged stronger and with a clearer purpose…"Tom tells the flock gathered around him about his transformation, "and that's the gift Hurricane Eve gave you." By his way of thinking, they've all been "*chosen*" to rebuild the community "*as they rebuild themselves.*"

His word can be interpreted two ways. Either Tom's encouraging others who have seen tragedy in their lives, or, he's rallying the alien troops for the impending colonization. Guess which is the right answer?

Larkin's network boss is also amongst the compromised; appropriately played by the venerable Veronica Cartwright…the only actress whose character survived the 1978 version of *Invasion of the Body Snatchers*. Anyway, Cartwright's exec is actively suppressing TV stories that might alert the outside world to the strange happenings in Homestead. And Tom wants to declare martial law in the battered town, further isolating it from the rest of America. As *Invasion* continues and the aliens grasp for more and more power, terminating a Navy air man found in the Everglades in one episode and destroying (or at least stealing) some unusual skeletal remains that would reveal their nature, *Invasion* lands on surer and surer footing. The structure of this dramatic series is surprisingly solid. The background of two families, joined by divorce and remarriage—suspicious of one another—proves tremendously effective in ramping up the paranoid aspects of the plot. Is Mom acting strangely because the kids don't like her new husband (the sheriff), or because she's been compromised by an alien? Answering that question allows room for internal, emotional conflicts (resentments, jealousies, etc.) and external, life-threatening ones (an alien invasion!) to intermingle.

It was only many weeks into *Invasion* that the physical form of the aliens and the disgusting process of hybridization were revealed in all their glory. At first, the creators only showcased the aftermath of the "joining" (some nasty punctures and bite marks), and then they showed pieces of the alien biology (a stinger or claw of some sort). Finally, *Invasion* revealed how the aliens would attack humans in the water, with the yellowish lifeforms collapsing around the human form like a folding umbrella, and inserting strange, glowing tubes into the rib cage.

"The Cradle" finally lays bare the truth that Mariel and the others were somehow physically *re-created* by the aliens in new bodies. She boasts the same memories as the real Mariel, but the human Mariel is actually at the bottom of a pond somewhere…rotting. In one of *Invasion's* most terrifying moments, Mariel goes out for a moonlit swim, looks down beneath the placid, glassy water…and sees her own decaying corpse staring back at her.

Before long on *Invasion,* the battlelines are drawn. On one side is Russell and the CIA, which has learned that previous incursions by this species went horribly wrong in Brazil and Cuba. On the other side is Tom, who is building an army of hybrids on an island just off the coast of Florida. Mariel bridges the gap. She still loves her children (whereas most hybrids hate their human children) and she struggles to retain her humanity. She's the link between the warring factions.

Anyway, this two-families-forced-together aspect of the series remains its greatest strength; the thing that kept viewers watching even when individual installments feel slow or deliberately opaque. The "blended family" drama raises the stakes a bit. Russell and Mariel are supposed to share responsibility for their children; but it's also clear that neither really trusts the other. Plenty of divorces get this ugly even without aliens, don't they? The paranoia about "the ex" is always high, but add a mysterious hurricane, some orange lights in the water, and, you've got Anxiety Central here. It's a classy setup. Children endangered? Check! Jealous "new" spouses? Check! One-upmanship among families? Check! See how nicely all that works side-by-side with the alien "body snatchers" drama?

"The scariest movies for me are the movies that play on our real primal fears," Shaun Cassidy said in the press, "*Rosemary's Baby* wasn't about the monster. It was about, is my baby ok? *The Exorcist* was about a mom making sure her kid was ok. Our show is about a dad trying to protect his family, about a sheriff trying to protect his family in his greater community against a threat. You don't need an alien. A hurricane, a tsunami, can be pretty devastating. Divorce can be pretty devastating."[53]

Cassidy also pointed out that the division in Homestead reflects a division in America. Not along species lines, but political ones. "The country is at war," he told *Broadcasting and Cable*. "There's a red country and a blue country out there. There's very clearly drawn lines of divisiveness in the world, and who's an alien is kind of a subjective thing. I'm not making a political statement with the show. But it is certainly in the air and in my head and heart, and that's going to come out on the page."[54]

During its time on the air, *Invasion* suffered its share of controversy. It began airing just weeks after Hurricane Katrina destroyed New Orleans, and over 1,000 Americans died. As the series concerned the aftermath of a similar storm, ABC was accused of insensitivity for airing the spot. ABC responded to the outcry by pulling commercials for *Invasion* off the air. The network quickly went into damage control mode and sent out a press release: "First and foremost, our thoughts go out to all those affected by this tragedy. As with anything as serious as this, we are taking great efforts to assess sensitivities with regard to our series. We are currently looking at all our programming and marketing efforts with this in mind."[55]

Finally, ABC decided to air a "viewer advisory"[56] before the premiere episode of the series and ultimately the controversy was a tempest in a teapot. Although *Invasion* garnered decent ratings and a rabid fan following, with great regret ABC canceled the series (which ended on a cliffhanger).

The complete series is currently available on DVD.

JUST LEGAL

(WB) (CANCELED) (60 minutes) (Mondays at 9:00 pm, EST; September 19, 2005-October 3, 2005) Jerry Bruckheimer Television/Warner Bros. Television. Created by: Jonathan Shapiro. Executive Producers: Jerry Bruckheimer, Jonathan Littman, Jonathan Shapiro. Co-Executive Producer: Rama Stagner. Produced by: Merri Howard. Camera: Charlie Lieberman, Stephen St. John. Film Editor: Peter Basinski, Todd Fulkerson, Steven Lang, Thomas J. Nordberg, Scott J. Wallace. Music: Atli Orvarsson. Written by: Jonathan Shapiro, Rob Bragin. Directed by: John Badham, Andrew Davis, Dwight Little.

CAST

Don Johnson (Grant Cooper)
Jay Baruchel (David "Skip" Ross)
Jamie Lee Kirchner (Dee)

Just Legal is a series created by Jonathan Shapiro, a former writer on David E. Kelley "law firm" series such as *The Practice* (1997–2004) and *Boston Legal* (2004–present). It boasts the unwelcome distinction of being the *second* series canceled in the 2005–2006 season (following hot on the heels of another unconventional legal series, *Head Cases*). *Just Legal* aired a mere three times on Monday nights before the WB pronounced sentence on the series.

Just Legal is the story of a 19-year-old legal prodigy named David "Skip" Ross (Jay Baruchel). Skip (named so because he "skipped" several grades in school) suffers from ageism in reverse: no reputable law firm in town will hire him because he's too young. Fortunately, Ross finds employment in the beachfront office of a dissolute middle-aged lawyer named Grant Cooper, played with boozy charm by Don Johnson. Cooper is an old cynic, made so by years of working in the tangled legal system (and one big case that went bad), but his association with young Skip soon rekindles his idealism, as well as his love affair with the law. Another regular, Dee (Jamie Lee Kirchner) is an ex-con on parole who soon becomes Cooper and Ross's assistant and receptionist.

In the pilot episode, Cooper and Ross defend a woman in court against charges of gang activity and murder. In "The Runner," a black man is accused of a robbery because of his skin color, and Cooper plays the race card with unexpected results. In the last episode aired, "The Limit," Cooper and Ross take on a civil case: suing a plastic surgeon after he's bungled a patient's stomach surgery. Much of the interpersonal fireworks from week-to-week involve Cooper's inherent slackness, and his willingness (and desire) to plead cases out, rather than go to court. Of course, Ross wants to take every case to trial…

Writing for *The Hollywood Reporter*, Barry Garron wrote that *Just Legal* was an "absorbing, well-paced legal drama with both heart and attitude, not to mention cinematography good enough to carry the Jerry Bruckheimer imprimatur,"[57] but even with accolades like that as Exhibit A, audiences didn't seek the series out.

Not available on DVD.

KILLER INSTINCT

(FOX) (CANCELED) (60 minutes) (Fridays at 9:00 pm; September 23, 2005-December 2, 2005) Regency Television. Created by: Josh Berman. Executive Producers: Charlie Craig, Ed Zuckerman. Produced by: Joseph Patrick Finn, Augie Hess, Erin Maher, Kay Reindl, Luke Schelhaas. Camera: David Hennings, Philip Linzey. Film Editing: Ken Bornstein, Augie Hess, Kevin D. Ross. Music: Mark Morgan. Written by: Josh Berman, Charles Grant Craig, Carla Kettner, Robert Lieberman, Erin Maher, Kay Reindl, Luke Schelhaas. Directed by: James A. Contner, Robert Lieberman, Bryan Spicer, David Straiton.

CAST

John Messner (Detective Jack Hale)
Kristin Lehman (Detective Danielle Carter)
Chi McBride (Lt. Matt Cavanaugh)
Steven Chang (Yimang)

Known first as "Deviant Behavior" and then "The Gate,"[58] *Killer Instinct* is the account of a detective named Jack Hale (John Messner), who—as the series begins— returns to San Francisco's Deviant Crime Unit from a six month hiatus following the death of his partner. At the DCU, Hale goes after the most perverse and sick killers imaginable.

At first (in the pilot), Hale is teamed with Detective Ava Lyford (Marguerite Moreau), but she's replaced in the second episode by Kristin Lehman's character, Detective Danielle Carter, a forensic expert and rookie. Chi McBride, late of *Boston Public*, appears as Hale's typically wrong-headed and worried superior officer on the police force.

Killer Instinct aired in *The X-Files'* original time slot and dutifully follows Hale and Carter as they solve the strangest and most violent crimes imaginable. The series is a gory and over-the-top version of *CSI*, with a slice of *Millennium* thrown in for good measure.

The series pilot involves women who appear to be dying in their sleep…but who are really the victim of… spiders. "We're gearing these crimes to almost be popcornish," said Peter Ligouri, the entertainment president at FOX. "You know, suffering from arachnophobia myself, yes, I cringed also when I saw it. But the intent here is actually to create creative, fun crimes."[59]

Nice. Well, if not truly fun (and how many crimes are?), the other vicious acts investigated by Hale and Carter were—at the very least—unique. Someone was stealing donated organs in "Five Easy Pieces," twins were murdered in "O Brother, Where Art Thou?" and Egyptology played into the resolution of a crime in "Die Like An Egyptian." Depending on one's point of view, these morbid tales were either extremely inventive or just further evidence that the police procedural format had become severely exhausted.

Only nine episodes aired before FOX pulled the series. Not currently available on DVD.

Detective Danielle Carter (Kristin Lehman) and Det. Jack Hale (John Messner)
are on the case—and looking hot!—in **KILLER INSTINCT**.

Too many chefs spoil the broth?
Jack (Bradley Cooper, left), Seth (Nicholas Brendon, center), and Steven (Owain Yeoman)
star in the canceled **KITCHEN CONFIDENTIAL**.

KITCHEN CONFIDENTIAL

(FOX) (CANCELED) (30 minutes) (Mondays at 8:30 pm, EST; September 15, 2005-December 5, 2005) Darren Starr Productions/New Line Television/20th Century Fox. Created by: David Hemingson. Executive Producers: David Hemingson, Darren Star. Co-executive producers: Richard Appel, Dan Sterling, Joshua Sternin, Jeffrey Ventimilia. Producers: Jeff Morton, Lesley Wake Webster. Camera: Tim Ives, Bruce M. Pasternack. Film Editor: John Axness. Music: Daniel Licht. Written by: Dean Lopata, Lesley Wake Webster. Directed by: Victoria Hochberg, Fred Savage.

CAST

Bradley Cooper (Jack Bourdain)
Nicholas Brendon (Seth Richman)
John F. Daley (Jim)
Jaime King (Tanya)
Frank Langella (Pino)
Bonnie Somerville (Mimi)
Owain Yeoman (Steven Daedalus)

This comedy set in the fast-paced world of a restaurant kitchen comes from producer Darren Starr (*Sex and the City*, 1998–2004) and starred Bradley Cooper (formerly of *Alias* 2001–2005), as Jack Bourdain, a character based on the real life New York chef Anthony Bourdain, whose memoirs were also called *Kitchen Confidential.*

In *Kitchen Confidential*, Jack is riding out a bad spell in his career as a chef until, with the help of his girlfriend, he gets the call to captain the cooking squad at Nolita's, a ritzy Italian restaurant preparing for a grand reopening.

The catch is that Jack has only forty-eight hours to assemble a kitchen team and whip everyone into shape.

This won't be easy, especially since Jack has a reputation as a hard-drinking, fun-loving party animal...and most of his friends expect him to still be "that guy."

At the new restaurant, Jack immediately clashes with the manager, Mimi (Bonnie Somerville), but brings aboard his old friends Seth (*Buffy the Vampire Slayer*'s Nicholas Brendon), an artist with desserts, and Steven (Owain Yeoman), whose specialty is concocting seafood entrees to die for. Frank Langella plays Pino, the restaurant owner (and adulterer), and luscious Jaime King is on hand to play Tanya, a hostess.

Fast-spaced, energetic and shiny with staccato dialogue and nice dramatic flourishes (including whiz-bang flashbacks and actors addressing the camera head-on) *Kitchen Confidential* inarguably evidenced a great deal more verisimilitude than the average half-hour situation comedy. The actors played their parts with a strong dose of reality, the sets appeared three-dimensional and authentic rather than stagey and the stories were for the most part enormously witty and engaging.

Unfortunately, *Kitchen Confidential* drew lousy numbers on FOX (along with other new dramas such as *Reunion* and early casualty *Head Cases*). These failures sparked comments from the network that it could not be the number one broadcast network with such underperformers...a bad sign. Despite the enormously appealing cast and outstanding production values, *Kitchen Confidential* was canceled in December of 2005.

Not currently available on DVD.

KYLE XY

(ABC Family) (ABC) (RENEWED) (60 minutes) (Mondays at 8:00 pm, EST; June 26, 2006-August 28, 2006) Touchstone Television. Executive Producers: Eric Bress, J. Mackye Gruber, David Himelfarb, J.C. Spink, Erich Tuchman. Produced by: Charlie Gogolak, Julie Plec. Film Editor: Shannon Murphy. Music: Michael Suby. Written by: Steve Lilien, Michael Oates Palmer, Elle Triedman, Bryan Wynbrandt. Directed by: Guy Norman Bee, Michelle MacLaren, Michael Robison, Patrick Williams.

CAST
Matt Dallas (Kyle)
Marguerite MacIntyre (Nicole Trager)
Bruce Thomas (Stephen Trager)
April Matson (Lori Trager)
Jean-Luc Bilodeau (Josh)
Chris Olivero (Declan McManus)

Kyle XY is another science fiction/mystery dramatic series along the lines of ABC's *Lost,* or more aptly, FOX's canceled *John Doe* from the 2002–2003 season. As *Kyle XY* commences, an adolescent boy, with no name and no memory of his identity, is found wandering in the forest by the police. He's taken to juvenile hall where it's discovered the boy lacks a belly button! Still, kindly Seattle social worker, Nicole Trager (Marguerite MacIntyre) agrees to let the boy—now named Kyle (Matt Dallas)—live in her house with her family.

Kyle slowly adjusts to living with the Trager family, which includes Nicole's suspicious husband, Stephen (Bruce Thomas), attractive daughter and love interest Lori (April Matson) and younger brother, Josh (Jean-Luc Bilodeau), who suspects Kyle is an alien. The whole world is new to Kyle; everything from emotions to relationships is a question mark. Where did he come from? Who is he? Why is he here? These are among the questions the series raises.

In the first season of this Vancouver-based series, *Kyle XY* explores Kyle's sleepwalking ("Sleepless in Seattle"), his first day of high school ("This is Not a Test"), and the boy encounters people claiming to be his real parents ("Overheard"). Mysteries develop as the season goes on, especially when it looks as though the innocent-seeming Kyle may be involved in a murder.

Matt Dallas, who has become a breakout star thanks to the series, had another idea about its genesis and source material. He told *TV Guide*: "My manager said 'You're coming in to play this alien boy who doesn't really speak English. And you have an hour to prepare.' I just thought 'He's like *Edward Scissorhands*,' where he was coming into society and experiencing all this stuff."[60]

ABC Family had a bonafide summer hit with *Kyle XY,* and when an episode aired on its parent network, ABC, the show drew healthy numbers there too, in the range of 5 million viewers. Such success has spurred ABC to renew the series for a second season of thirteen episodes.

The first season is not yet available on DVD.

THE LOOP

(FOX) (RENEWED) (30 minutes) (Wednesdays at 9:30 pm; Thursdays at 9:30 pm, EST; March 15–April 13, 2006) Olive Bridge Entertainment/Wounded Poodle Productions/Fox. Executive Producers: Pam Brady, Will Gluck. Co-Executive Producer: Ira Ungerleider. Produced by: Victor Hsu, John Ziffren. Camera: Steven B. Poster, Michael A. Price. Film Editors: Christopher Cooke, Matt Friedman, John Murray. Music: Brad Segal. Written by: Pam Brady, Will Gluck. Directed by: Jay Chandrasekhar, Dennie Gordon, Betty Thomas, Rawson Marshall Thurber.

CAST
Bret Harrison (Sam)
Philip Baker Hall (Russ)
Amanda Loncar (Piper)
Sarah Mason (Lizzy)
Erich Christian Olsen (Sully)
Joy Osmanski (Darcy)
Mimi Rogers (Meryl)

In the 2005–2006 season, the broadcast networks really went after one demographic for their situation comedies: twentysomething slackers. There were shows with titles like *Four Kings, Free Ride*, and this series, *The Loop*. Most were decidedly interchangeable—not to mention unfunny—yet this is the one that survived. Which is too bad, because *Free Ride* was better.

The Loop dramatizes the life of (yawn) a slacker named Sam (Bret Harrison) who is the first among his friends to hold down a real job. He is the youngest executive ever at a cutthroat airline business in Chicago. His boss is Russ (Philip Baker Hall), and Sam works with a sexually carnivorous piranha named Meryl (Mimi Rogers), whom he constantly evades. This is an unrealistic plot point, because what red-blooded American male wouldn't want to sleep with Mimi Rogers at least once?

Meanwhile, Sam's overqualified administrative assistant, Darcy (Joy Osmanski), hates him. But work is only "half" Sam's life, as *The Loop* endlessly point out. At home, he lives in an apartment with a gaggle of fellow slackers. Piper (Amanda Loncar) is a med student and roommate that Sam has a crush on. Sully (Erich Christian Olsen) is his older brother, who works odd jobs and just wants to make it with the ladies, and Lizzie is a roommate, a gorgeous bartender (Sarah Mason).

According to the series' press material, *The Loop* concerns "the daunting challenges of real life," meaning balancing career and personal lives. But mostly, it's just the same old hat about superficially diverse youngsters living together and trying to date. It's actually a series that hedges it's bets, since it's half *Friends* (about personal lives) and half workplace ensemble comedy, like *The Office*.

So far, the seven episodes of the series involve the impact of Sam's drinking on work ("Jack Air") and his attempts to win over Piper. *The Loop* has been renewed by FOX, and is slated to return as a midseason replacement, in January 2007.

The series is not available on DVD.

LOVE INC.

(UPN) (CANCELED) (30 minutes) (Thursdays at 8:30 pm, EST; September 22, 2005–May 11, 2006) Chase TV/Littlefield Co./Berg/Koules Productions/Paramount. Executive Producers: Mark Burg, Adam Chase, Oren Koules, Warren Littlefield. Co-Executive Producers: Maggie Bandur, Andrew Secunda. Produced by: Mark H. Ovitz, Laurie Parres. Camera: Mikal Neiers. Film Editor: Robert Bramwell. Written by: Maggie Bandur, Sean Conroy, Michael Curtis, Sarah M. Fitzgerald, Clarence Livingston, Laurie Parres, Robert Peacock, Andrew Secunda. Directed by: Henry Chan, Sheldon Epps, Katy Garretson, Ellen Gittelsohn, Arlene Sanford, Rob Schiller, Steve Zuckerman.

CAST
Busy Phillips (Denise)
Vince Vieluf (Barry)
Reagan Gomez-Preston (Francine)
Ion Overman (Viviana)
Holly Robinson Peete (Clea)

This UPN sitcom focuses on a "full service dating consulting firm" [61] in the City, created by a woman named Clea (Holly Robinson Peete). She has staked the business's success on her own happy marriage of almost a decade. Unfortunately, in the series premiere, Clea's husband leaves her, relegating Cleo to the singles scene and threatening business.

Fortunately, Clea has a lot of help at her company, particularly from Denise (Busy Phillips), a vivacious, socially adroit woman who can make any match stick…

she's that good. Sadly for Denise, however, her miraculous powers don't seem to work for her, and she's caught in one bad relationship after another.

This is a workplace ensemble company, and the remainder of the cast includes Viviana (Ion Overman), the outrageous receptionist, a tech staff member named Francine (Reagan Gomez-Preston) and the only male on hand, Barry (Vince Vieluf). Together, they play matchmaker to odd clients.

And it's a tough group too. In "Mad About You," they deal with an obsessive, high-maintenance client. In "Bosom Buddies," they get their first lesbian client. In "Amen," it's an ex-priest. Before long, Love Inc. is catering to geeks ("Three's Company"), and even agorophobes ("Anything but Love"). At the same time, Denise tries to help Clea get over the pain of her failed marriage ("Living Single").

The ardent TV watcher will dutifully note that all these episode titles take their names from popular sitcoms. Other titles include: "Curb Your Enthusiasm," "Family Ties," and "Major Dad."

In all, twenty-two episodes of *Love Inc.* were aired in the 2005–2006 season, but the comedy did not survive the UPN's transition to the CW. One bit of trivia about *Love Inc.*: *Beverly Hills 90210* (1990–2000) star Shannen Doherty played the role of Denise in the original pilot.

Not available on DVD.

LOVE MONKEY

(CBS/VH1) (CANCELED) (60 minutes) (Tuesdays at 10:00 pm, EST; January 17, 2006-February 7, 2006; April 11, 2006– May 16, 2006) Beyahibe Films/Thirty-Four Films/Paramount/ Sony. Based on the novel by: Kyle Smith. Executive Producers: Mark Johnson, Michael Rauch, John Wirth. Co-Executive Producer: Melissa Rosenberg. Produced by: Tom Cavanagh, Don Kurt, Bryan Seabury. Camera: Tom Houghton, Richard Rutowski. Film Editors: Russ Denore, Susan Graef, Deborah Moran. Music: John Bissell, Alan Lazar, Didier Rachou. Written by: David Handelman, Jonathan Moskin, Michael Rauch, Melissa Rosenberg, Justin Tanner, Elyzabeth Gregory Wilder, John Wirth. Directed by: Jace Alexander, Tamra Davis, John Fortenberry, Ken Girotti, Don Kur, Jerry Levine, Ron Lagomarsino, Wendy Stanzler.

CAST

Tom Cavanagh (Tom Farrell)
Jason Priestley (Mike)
Katherine La Nasa (Karen)
Larenz Tate (Shooter)
Christopher Wiehl (Jake)
Judy Greer (Bran)
Ivana Milicevic (Julia Hixon)

Based on the best-selling novel by Kyle Smith, *Love Monkey* is the tale of Tom Farrell (*Ed*'s Tom Cavanagh), a single record executive who gets fired from his job in the record industry and is dumped by his girlfriend the same day. Tom is a passionate sort who believes music should be about quality, a tenet which puts him at odds with his bosses and others.

Tom is soon working for True Vinyl Records, a company where he hopes to find a talented up-and-coming new artist and restore his luster in the industry. He's surrounded by a circle of Manhattanite friends including Mike (Jason Priestley), who's married to his expecting sister, Karen (Katherine La Nasa), and Shooter (Larenz Tate). He's also buddies with a former athlete turned sportscaster, Jake (Christopher Wiehl) and has a non-romantic relationship with the attractive Bran (Judy Greer). Meanwhile, he lusts after his perfect woman: Julia (Ivana Milicevic).

If this sounds a wee bit familiar, it should, since it's very close to the plot and premise of the other one-hour dramedy of the 2005–2006 season, *What About Brian*. It also boasts some similarities with the situation comedies *Free Ride*, *Teachers*, and *The Loop*, only skewing into the thirties instead of twenties.

Episodes of *Love Monkey* involve Tom's attempt to find that one music star that can catapult him back to the big time. He represents his ex-girlfriend's band in "The One Who Got Away," and corrals a raucous rock act in "The Window." A funeral leads to an unexpected discovery in "Opportunity Knocks" and Tom considers buying the catalog of a once-famous singer who crashed and burned after a promising first album in "Mything Persons."

Bolstering several episodes, real music industry insiders such as Aimee Mann, John Mellencamp, and LeAnn Rimes show up in various installments.

CBS canceled *Love Monkey* after just three airings, but music network VH1 picked up the series. It began airing the unseen episodes on April 11, 2006.

In spite of its distinctive title, the most significant problem with *Love Monkey* is that it looks and feels uncomfortably similar to many hour-long or half-hour comedy shows of the year. It attempts to be a hybrid of workplace ensemble and *Friends*-style comedies, as if it can't decide which audience it would like to draw. Cavanagh is always a pleasure to watch, but this is a much less satisfying, authentic and original effort than his previous series, the splendid *Ed* (2000–2004).

Not available on DVD at this time.

LUCKY LOUIE

(HBO) (CANCELED) (30 minutes) (Mondays at 10:30 pm, EST; June 11, 2006-August 20, 2006) HBO Independent Productions. Created by: Louis C.K. Executive Producers: Dave Becky, Mike Royce, Vic Kaplan. Producer: Andrew D. Weyman. Film Editor: Brian Schnuckel. Written by: Kit Boss, Louis C.K., Mary Fitzgerald, Greg Fitzsimmons, Don Mintz. Directed by: Andrew D. Weyman.

CAST

Louis C.K. (Louie)
Pamela S. Adlon (Kim)
Mike Hagerty (Mike)
Laura Kightlinger (Tina)
Jim Norton (Rich)
Rick Shapiro (Jerry)
Kimberly Hawthorne (Ellen)
Jerry Minor (Walter)
Kelly Gould (Lucy)

Videotaped before a live audience, *Lucky Louie* starring comedian Louis C.K. is a sitcom that views itself as the heir to such blue collar classics as *The Honeymooners* and *All in the Family* (1971–1979). The series concerns a working class American family run by hapless Louie, living in a tiny, rundown apartment building in an urban setting. The primary sets on this HBO series include a dilapidated hallway (with dents and paint scrapes in plain view), a garish kitchen, and a tiny bedroom. If the Kramdens were around in the 21st century, this might be their environs.

Louie is a dopey, overweight, working class Joe raising his smartaleck daughter, Lucy (Kelly Gould), who in one episode asks him "why?" endlessly. Louie is also engaged in a constant state of war with his wife, an attractive brunette nurse named Kim (Pamela S. Adlon). Louie doesn't understand Kim, and so his friends at the muffler shop where he works, including Mike (Mike Hagerty), offer sage advice about women. Tina (Laura Kightlinger) is Kim's friend, performing essentially the same function, only in reverse. The next-door neighbors are Walter (Jerry Minor) and Ellen (Kimberly Hawthorne), a well-to-do African-American couple. Walter and Ellen wear nicer clothes and own nicer furniture…which raises the practical question of why they're living in the same rundown urban building with Louie's on-the-edge-of-poverty family.

In the course of the series, Louie forsakes frequent masturbation sessions when Kim wants more sexual intercourse…a ruse, in fact, for her to become pregnant again ("Pilot"). Another episode, "Kim's O" revolves around Louie's wife experiencing her first real orgasm at age thirty-seven…after seven years of marriage! Most plots revolve around domestic issues, and occasionally, ones involving modern city life, like "A Mugging Story," wherein Kim goes ballistic after losing her pocket book in a duel with a teenage mugger.

Lucky Louie comes straight from the mind of C.K., who has honed this working-class material for years. "When I started writing this stuff, I didn't know it would be successful," he told reporter Ed Condran. "When I said that 'I now understand why babies get thrown in the garbage,' I was surprised that Middle America got it. Soccer moms in Cincinnati told me how hilarious the 'baby in the garbage' joke was to them."[62]

That anecdote brings up a reason why many are of two minds regarding *Lucky Louie*. The kind of meanspirited humor of "babies thrown in the garbage" is part of the series' problem. Although *Lucky Louie* attempts to shatter sitcom stereotypes by featuring close-up simulated sex ("Kim's O"), full-frontal male nudity ("A Mugging

Story"), and scatological language (the word "fuck" is used on a regular basis), the underlying tenor here is crass and crude, and rather unpleasant. Married life is depicted ruthlessly, which is an interesting perspective, yet the characters are all despicable and selfish. Nor do they express themselves cleverly. Instead swearing is a crutch for bad writers. All this more aptly makes *Lucky Louie* an heir to *Married with Children* (1987–1997) rather than *All in the Family* or *The Honeymooners*.

Also, *All in the Family* revolved around blue collar people confronting issues like racism, sexual harassment, rape, infidelity, and menopause. The stories didn't just bring up an issue as a source of humor; new thoughts were vetted. There's no genuine overarching social value or message in *Lucky Louie*, as the characters don't engage the outside world in any meaningful way and remain stubbornly stupid and fail to grow.

However, it is impossible not to appreciate the audacity of *Lucky Louie*. It doesn't buy into Hollywood myths about America, and that is refreshing…even liberating. The American dream of prosperity has never looked so unattainable on a TV show…or at least not attainable in a very, very long time, as Neil Swidey writes in *The Boston Globe*: "Lots of sitcom sets looked this working-class in the '70s, in the era of *Good Times*, before we were all asked to swallow the notion that coffee-house waitresses could afford spacious Greenwich Village apartments with skyline views."[63]

Somewhere, deep down, *Lucky Louie* may be onto something.

The series is not yet available on DVD.

MASTER OF CHAMPIONS

(ABC) (CANCELED) (60 minutes) (Thursdays at 8:00 pm, EST; June 22, 2006–July 20, 2006) Y27 Entertainment. Executive Producers: Tim Crescenti, Yoshira Yasuoka, Isao Zatsu, Jonas Larsen, Anthony Ross. Produced by: Brian De Esch, Sean M. Kelly, Scott Larson. Film Editors: Mark Andrew, Shawn Gutierrez, Frankie Le Nguyen, Marcelo Sansevier, Reggie Spangler.

CAST
Chris Leary (Host)
Lisa Dergan-Podsednik (Host)
Steve Garvey, Oksana Baiul, Jonny Moseley
(Panel of Champions)

CONTESTANTS
Princess Elayne, Chris Florin, Billy Matsumoto, Rick Smith, Mike Winters.

Master of Champions ran for five weeks in the summer of 2006 on ABC. It's a reality show in which six competitors of unique "talent" strive to see their names added to a "Wall of Champions," and therefore must run a gauntlet of competition before facing the studio audience for approval. After three contestants are eliminated, the final three contestants then go before a "panel of champions" including sports figures Baiul, Moseley, and Garvey.

Master of Champions featured bizarre events like "International Human Fireworks," pizza tossing, a unicycle obstacle course, urban freestyle dancing, yo-yos, and bottle flipping, among other things. It's based on a Japanese game show, but Americans didn't take to this latest bit of bread and circuses.

Not released on DVD.

MASTERS OF HORROR

(Showtime)(RENEWED)(60 minutes)(Fridays at 10:00 pm, EST; October 25, 2005-January 27, 2006) IDT Entertainment/Industry Entertainment/Nice Guy Productions. Created by: Mick Garris. Executive Producers: Keith Addis, Andrew Deane, Mick Garris. Produced by: Lisa Richardson, Tom Rowe. Camera: Jon Joffin, Attila Szalay. Film Editors: Andrew Cohen, Mark L. Levine, Patrick McMahon. Music: Ed Shearmur. Written by: Don Coscarelli, Mick Garris, Matt Greenberg, Sean Hood, Richard Christian Matheson, Drew McWeeny, Dennis Paoli, Stephen Romano, David Schow, Scott Swan, Steven Webber Directed by: Dario Argento, John Carpenter, Larry Cohen, Don Coscarelli, Joe Dante, Mick Garris, Stuart Gordon, Tobe Hooper, John Landis, William Malone, Lucky McKee, John McNaughton.

This anthology series from Showtime is a veritable "who's who" of horror legends. Created by Mick Garris, *Masters of Horror* each week (and in hour-long installments) showcases the work of a famous genre director. The lineup for the first season is impressive. Dario Argento (*Suspiria,* 1977), John Carpenter (*Halloween,* 1978), Larry Cohen (*It's Alive,* 1973), Don Coscarelli (*Phantasm,* 1979), Joe Dante (*Gremlins,* 1984), Stuart Gordon (*The Reanimator,* 1985), John Landis (*An American Werewolf in London,* 1981), John McNaughton (*Henry: Portrait of a Serial Killer,* 1989), and Tobe Hooper (*The Texas Chain Saw Massacre,* 1974) are among the auteurs recruited to horrify and chill audiences.

What may be most fascinating about *Masters of Horror,* however, is the fact that most of the directors don't tread into obvious or empty horror conventions, but instead vet stories that serve as social commentary on our times.

Joe Dante's entry, "Homecoming" is a perfect example, a segment that artfully crosses zombie films with political science. Since George A. Romero's *Night of the Living Dead* (1968) was released nearly forty years ago, many critics have interpreted the ghoulish dead rising from their graves in symbolic fashion; as a kind of protest of the Vietnam War; a return of the dead soldiers to menace the homeland that let their deaths occur in an unjust conflict. "Homecoming" makes that concept literal, when—on a talk show that resembles CNN's *Larry King Live* (only here it's *Mandy Clark Live*)—a political operative for a Bush-like president named Shelly trades commentary with a Gold Star mother (just like Cindy Sheehan) who has seen her boy die in the Iraq War and wonders what it was all for. This conservative operative, David Murch (Jon Tenney) says that if he had just one wish, it would be that all the dead soldiers could come back to life…so they could testify about how proud they are to have given their lives for this President.

The president likes that sound bite so much, he actually uses it in his convention speech as Election Day draws near. Meanwhile, the sound bite also wins Murch the not-very-tender sexual affections of an Ann Coulter knock-off named Jane Cleaver (Thea Gill). The episode's satire works particularly well in this aspect of the tale: there's a photo of Jane on her new book cover that mirrors the famous "distorted" legs photo of Coulter from *Time Magazine* in 2005.

Anyway, Murch's wishes do come true. Dead veterans of "this engagement" arise from the dead…and the only way to stop them is to let them vote in the upcoming election. At first, the Karl-Rove-like Kurt Rand (Robert Picardo) believes that this development will be the perfect propaganda for a President running as a war hero (even though he never served in a war), and the Religious Right (led by a Falwell lookalike) quickly notes that the zombies are giving the President "a stamp of heavenly approval" for his war. Things don't quite turn out as the conservatives would like, however…

Another socially conscious installment is "Dance of the Dead," from surrealist Tobe Hooper, a director who always champions breaking the rules and the shattering of accepted decorum. His segment is simultaneously an antiwar parable and a metaphor for teenage movies of the 1950s.

"Dance of the Dead" arrives courtesy of a short story by Richard Matheson (adapted by Richard Christian Matheson). It's the disturbing story of a girl named Peggy, who *on her seventh birthday* witnesses a devastating terrorist attack on the country. This assault is depicted in frightening and upsetting terms: the sky goes gray and dark all of a sudden, and then chunks of flesh begin to peel off the partygoers, curling up like crispy potato skins.

Flash forward ten years. The world is a vastly changed place. *Especially in America.* Peggy works at a local diner with her restrictive, conservative Mom, and lives a sheltered life. She knows nothing of life outside the town boundaries. Nonetheless, a new "death culture" consumes the youngsters broaching adolescence in a USA where California doesn't exist anymore. This death culture, by the way, is a reflection and extension of the 1980s punk rock ethos. Nihilism, self-destruction, no empathy…real dark stuff.

Then, one day, a handsome bad boy named Jak comes to town, and takes Peggy to the forbidden local hot spot in Meskeet, a city where a night club called "The Doom Room" revels in human (or is it inhuman?) depravity. Robert Englund portrays the emcee at the Doom Room, and introduces a show that features a zombified dancer jerking and spasming on the stage. She's kept on her feet by thugs with cattle prods. That undead dancer, it seems,

is Peggy's long lost sister. Sold into slavery by her Mom some years back, when the girl got into drugs and Mom didn't want to deal with her anymore…

Drug use, the sex trade, thugs stealing blood ("we're just in it for the red"): "Dance of the Dead" portrays an America turned upside down by a weapon of mass destruction. A terrifying aftermath has been extrapolated in this post-apocalyptic world, and it ain't pretty. Yet, in some freaky, bizarre way, the episode also plays as a parody/homage of 1950s "teenager" movies. You know the type of film: a motorcycle gang rides into town, and the leader romances a pretty, virginal townie. She's innocent and wide-eyed, and her parents are terrified she'll lose her virtue to the twin demons of Harley-Davidson and rock 'n' roll. In the end, the parents learn a little bit about tolerance, and the kid learns a little more about the world. Either that, or there's wall-to-wall violence and a generational culture clash.

Only here, in "Dance of the Dead," the teenage culture really is obsessed with death. The music *is* hateful, the drugs *are* destructive, and the "truth" out there in the world is that Mom is no compassionate, Christian conservative. She's a really, really bad person. Other episodes aren't quite so revolutionary, but depend instead on good characterization and solid thrills. "Incident On and Off a Mountain Road" is directed by Don Coscarelli, the genius who gave the world *Bubba Ho-tep* (2003). *Phantasm's* Tall Man himself, Angus Scrimm, guest stars in this episode, which also features Bree Taylor and a pumped-up Ethan Embry. The source material is Joe K. Lansdale's short story, adapted by Coscarelli and Stephen Romano.

This episode deals with a motorist named Ellen, who—on a cold and dark road in the middle of nowhere—

runs into a terrible speed trap set by what appears to be a ghoulish mountain man (replete with metal teeth). This pale, bald monstrosity chases her through the woods and forests of the nearby mountain terrain, but Ellen is steeled to fight back by her (mostly bad) relationship with her former husband, Bruce (Ethan Embry).

Even while pursued by this strange local devil, Ellen hears the voice and words of her survivalist husband. "I believe anything can happen to anyone at at any time, in any place," he warns in the first memory, featured as a flashback. "Crazy always works," he advises, when things get rough for Ellen. And "When all else fails, try anything," that inner voice suggests in the moment of greatest crisis and least hope.

So what audiences get is a grueling, harrowing hour of *Deliverance*-style drama that resembles 1970s savage cinema, as Ellen tries to claw, scratch and bite her way to freedom. This becomes especially important after she is captured and taken to the mountain man's house, where he straps his victims to a table and carves out their eyes with a drill.

Alas, *Masters of Horror*—despite the above-mentioned high-water marks, remains very hit or miss. John Landis's segment, "Deer Woman" is a tongue-in-cheek segment involving a half-woman/half-deer who lures unsuspecting men to their deaths with the promise of sex. Stuart Gordon, a director who has so memorably directed Lovecraft-inspired material before contributes "Dreams in the Witch House," a confusing and overlong episode about a physics student from Miskatonic University who rents a room in a creepy, sleazy boarding house. He's working on a theory about the intersection of universes, and soon realizes *from the scratching noises in the wall* that this very house represents one such nexus.

In fact, an evil witch and her familiar, a talkative rat with a human face, go to and from dimensions willy-nilly, stealing away human babies for ritual sacrifice. The witch seduces the physics student because she needs a male to perform the ritual, and plans to use him as her "arms" for the next murder, of a lovely neighbor's child, Danny.

Although the story is pure Lovecraft, it's slow and repetitive. How many times do viewers need to see the protagonist fall asleep and wake up in a different locale, before understanding the concept? The episode suffers from flaws that dominate many episodes. They'd work much better at a half-hour but at almost sixty minutes feel padded and dull.

Individual episodes have been released on DVD, and a second season of the anthology has been commissioned by Showtime.

MEERKAT MANOR

(Animal Planet) (RENEWED) (30 minutes) (Fridays at 8:00 pm EST; June 9, 2006-August 25, 2006) Oxford Scientific Films. Executive Producers: Mark Wild, Simon Willock. Produced by: Lucinda Axelsson, Chris Barker. Camera: John Brown. Film Editor: Caroline Hawkins.

CAST
Sean Astin (Voiceover Narrator)

In the summer of 2006, American television watchers fell in love with this new Animal Planet series, a documentary about…mongooses. For the uninitiated, meerkats are tiny (adorable) mammals who stand sometimes on their hind legs and are very, very funny.

Meerkat Manor focuses on one large family of the furry critters, a group nicknamed "the Whiskers" who live in the Kalahari Desert in South Africa. This group of the social animals (who live in brush, holes and burrows) has been observed for ten years by British documentary filmmakers, and each of the thirteen half-hour-long episodes deals with a crisis in the animal kingdom that in some way turns out to mirror our own human "animal" existence.

The Whiskers family consists of several very individual meerkats including Flower, Zaphod, Youssarian, Mozart, Tosca, and Shakespeare. The family encounters snakes ("A Family Affair") and must deal with illness when one of their number is bitten. The family countenances mean neighbors (a rival pack of meerkats) in a battle over territory ("Love Thy Neighbor"), and attempt to move a slow child out into the world as an adult ("Childhood's End"). The Whiskers also face the birth of a new baby (or in this case, litter) in "Flower Power."

The season finale of *Meerkat Manor* aired on August 25, 2006, and a second and third season of the series had already been announced when this book went to press.

Not currently released on DVD.

THE MIRACLE WORKERS

(ABC) (60 minutes) (Mondays at 10:00 pm, EST; March 6, 2006–April 3, 2006); Renegade 83 Entertainment/Dreamworks TV. Executive Producers: David Garfinkle, Jay Renfroe, Darryl Frank, Justin Falvey. Co-Executive Producers: Scott Jeffress. Produced by: Jon Cornick, Dennis Principe Jr. Camera: Jung Johann, Andre Martinez, Joel Schwartzenberg, Matt Valentine. Film Editors: Jeff Becko, Mike Benson, Alex Katz, West Paster. Music: Lee Sanders. Directed by: Gary Shaffer.

CAST

Redmond Burke (Host)
William Cohn (Host)
Janna Bullock (Host)
Tamara Houston (Host)

This unscripted medical series ran for five episodes in the spring of 2006, and for once, a reality show didn't appeal to the lowest common denominator. It's true that *Miracle Workers* is a sob story each and every week, but it's also a "feel good" show that—for the most part—turns out happy.

Two cardiologists (Redmond Burke and Billy Cohn) and two nurses (Janna Bullock and Tamara Houston) are the hosts of this reality series, which concerns "real people overcoming insurmountable odds with the help of an elite team of medical professionals"[64] according to the press kit.

Each episode usually involves a team of doctors helping two patients. The show is thorough and impressive in that it follows these patients from explanation of the problem (meaning first-person talking head interviews with the family), to the doctor consultations, to surgery and ultimately through recovery itself. Often, "cutting edge" special effects (meaning CG animations) are marshaled on the series to make the byzantine medical procedures seem more clearly understandable.

Less graphic than a show about surgery might be, *Miracle Workers* is sponsored by CVS Pharmacies and is an emotional humdinger each and every installment.

The so-called "Miracle Workers" in the course of the series help Todd Heritage, a blind man; Vanessa Slaughter, a 47-year-old woman suffering from degenerative bone and joint disease who has already had five unsuccessful surgeries; Emily Bresly, a 19-year-old suffering from a severe case of Tourette's syndrome; Adrian Keller, a 4-year-old with a fatal condition called Vater's Association (a lump in his chest); Jack Brown, a house painter in Lake Worth, Florida with a shattered heel; Charles Valentino, a 53-year-old former Broadway dancer living in Los Angeles and suffering from osteoarthritis. The doctors also help Mesquite Nevada's Charlene Lustig battle her Parkinson's Disease, and work to save little Felipe Arcila, a 4-year-old who lacks a left ventricle in his heart, and who could die in mere days.

At the time of this book's writing, ABC had not yet scheduled further episodes of *Miracle Workers*, but had not announced the cancellation of the series, either.

Not available on DVD.

MODERN MEN

(WB) (CANCELED) (30 minutes) (Fridays at 9:30 pm, EST; March 17–April 28, 2006) Jerry Bruckheimer Television/Warner Bros. Executive Producers: Jerry Bruckheimer, Jonathan Littman, Marsh McCall. Co-Executive Producer: Aaron Peters. Camera: Julius Metoyer Jr. Film Editors: Brent Carpenter, Kenny Tintorri. Music: John Adair, Steve Hampton. Written by: Craig Doyle, Aaron Peters, Mike Tevenbaugh. Directed by: Terry Hughes.

CAST

Eric Lively (Doug Reynolds)
Josh Braaten (Tim Clark)
Max Greenfield (Kyle Brewster)
Marla Sokoloff (Molly Clark)
George Wendt (Tug)
Jane Seymour (Dr. Victoria Stangel)

This WB sitcom only survived a month or so on the air in the Spring of 2006, and was heralded by critics as being one of the worst programs of the season. *San Francisco Chronicle* critic Tim Goodman opined of *Modern Men* that "it's stupid and annoying and a retread of countless other stupid and annoying, totally unoriginal WB sitcoms."[65] Ouch!

Modern Men is the witless story of three guy friends (no, not four kings) in their young adulthood who experience perpetual bad luck with women. Basically, they suffer from the three Ds of dating: Tim's (Josh Braaten) been dumped; Doug (Eric Lively) is divorced; and Kyle (Max Greenfield) is stuck on meaningless dalliances…in full-on one-night-stand mode. However, these issues keep the guys from ever being happy, or ever finding a truly suitable partner.

Tim's sister Molly (*The Practice*'s Sokoloff) intervenes and suggests a cure-all for their woes: a life coach who can help them evolve beyond their current wretched state.

Surprisingly, the guys actually take the advice and into the scene walks the gorgeous and leggy Dr. Victoria Stangel (Jane Seymour), who promptly realizes the level of Neanderthal nitwits she's dealing with. Her sage advice? *Be honest with women.*

In later episodes she also stresses emotional bonds over physical intimacy ("Sexual Healing") and tries to teach the men to listen in "Timmy Can You Hear Me?"

Cheers (1982–1994) veteran George Wendt appears as Tim's father in the short-lived series.

Not available on DVD.

MY NAME IS EARL

(NBC) (RENEWED) (30 minutes) (Tuesdays at 9:00 pm, EST; Thursdays at 9:00 pm, EST; September 20, 2005-May 11, 2006) Amigos de Garcia Productions/20th Century Fox. Created by: Gregory Thomas Garcia. Executive Producers: Marc Buckland, Gregory Thomas Garcia. Co-Executive Producers: Bobby Bowman, Barbie Adler. Produced by: Henry J. Lange Jr., Jason Lee, Michael Pennie. Camera: Eyal Gordan, Victor Hammer. Film Editors: Lance Luckey, William Marrinson. Music: Danny Lux. Written by: J.B. Cook, Victor Fresco, Zack Friedman, Greg Garcia, John Hoberg, Michael Pennie, Timothy Stack, Hilary Winston.. Directed by: Mark Buckland, Tamra Davis, Chris Koch, Lev L. Spiro, Victor Nelli Jr.

CAST
Jason Lee (Earl Hickey)
Ethan Suplee (Randy Hickey)
Jaime Pressly (Joy)
Nadine Velazquez (Catalina)
Eddie Steeples (Darnell)

NBC found comic gold in the charming *My Name Is Earl*, a one-camera situation comedy that focuses on the esoteric subject of…karma.

My Name Is Earl tells the tale of sloppy, low-functioning Earl Hickey (Jason Lee), a dopey but earnest man who buys a $100,000 dollar lottery ticket only to lose it when he is struck by a car and consequently rushed to the hospital. Earl later recovers the ticket, but that's only because his life has been transformed by a new thought. While in the hospital, you see, he happens to see star Carson Daly on television talking about this mysterious notion of karma; the idea that what you put out in the universe comes back to you. Earl starts to realize that he's been pretty awful to a lot of people in his life, and so crafts a list of all the bad things he's done in his time on this mortal coil. Crossing off names and numbers on

that list becomes his new prime objective, and getting the money from that lottery ticket helps him accomplish his mission.

My Name Is Earl follows Hickey on his quest to get square with karma. He's joined on this assignment by his simpleton, overweight brother, Randy (Ethan Suplee), and a gorgeous Latino maid named Catalina (Nadine Velazquez), who works at the run-down motel where they've taken up residence. Joy (Jaime Pressly) is Earl's white-trash (but hot!) ex-wife, who is sometimes his nemesis because she thinks she's entitled to the lottery money. Sometimes, however, she's the very person Earl must get right with. Darnell (Eddie Steeples) is Joy's new husband and because he works at the local crab shack, Earl calls him "Crabman." Earl and Randy's parents are also recurring characters. Beau Bridges plays Earl's disappointed, perpetually irritated father, Nancy Lenehan, his mom.

Various half-hour episodes depict the specifics of Earl's quest to get right with the universe. In one episode, he might need to make right with a boy he bullied in high school; in other he countenances the idea that the very lottery ticket which changed his life might belong to someone else.

In "Randy's Touchdown," Earl realizes it's his job to help Randy relive the football glory he stole from him in high school. In "Cost Dad the Election," Earl recalls how his dad once ran for Mayor, and how Earl's public misbehavior threw the vote to his opponent. In another episode "Broke Joy's Fancy Figurine," Earl realizes there are amends to be made with Joy, and he stages the very beauty pageant she had wanted to win as a child.

"Half the fun of the show is watching Earl and his band of merry morons try to get a toe back inside the door of polite society, from which they've been exiled so long that they barely remember the concept," suggested *The Miami Herald*, "In deadpan innocence, they rampage over just about every societal restriction short of cannibalism."[66]

With good notices and good ratings, the funny, brash and good-hearted *My Name Is Earl* very quickly became the breakout comedy hit of the 2005–2006 season, earning it a quick full season pickup from NBC. In midseason, NBC pulled *My Name Is Earl* and its 8:30 pm companion, *The Office*, over to Thursday nights from their original time-slots on Tuesdays in an attempt to resurrect the "Must See TV" buzz of the *Seinfeld* and *Friends* era.

Available on DVD.

Karma has its way with brothers Randy (Ethan Suplee, left) and Earl (Jason Lee, right) in the break-out hit **MY NAME IS EARL**.

THE NEW ADVENTURES OF OLD CHRISTINE

(CBS) (RENEWED) (30 minutes) (Mondays at 9:30 pm, EST; March 13, 2006-May 22, 2006) Warner Brothers Television. Executive Producers: Kari Lizer, Andy Ackerman. Produced by: Lisa Helfrich Jackson. Camera: Gregg Heschong, Wayne Kennan. Film Editor: Pat Barnett. Music: Matter. Written by: Steve Baldikoski, Bryan Behar, Adam Barr, Daniel Evenson, Kari Lizer, Katie Palmer. Directed by: Andy Ackerman.

CAST
Julia Louis-Dreyfus (Christine)
Clark Gregg (Richard)
Hamish Linklater (Matthew)
Trevor Gagnon (Ritchie)
Emily Rutherfurd (New Christine)
Tricia O'Kelley (Marly)
Alex Kapp Horner (Lindsay)

Seinfeld curse? What *Seinfeld* curse? Julia Louis-Dreyfus, who spent so many years playing New Yorker Elaine on that famous NBC series, actually had a strong return to television with *Watching Ellie.*

But audiences didn't come, and so there's *The New Adventures of Old Christine*, a very funny sitcom that proves the old situation comedy format isn't quite dead. In fact, the wince-provoking behavior (and verbal flights of fancy) by Christine will leave one thinking of HBO fare like *Curb Your Enthusiasm* or *The Comeback* rather than the typically shallow brand of broadcast network sitcom.

The premise of *The New Adventures of Old Christine* is that Christine (Julia Louis-Dreyfus) has been living busily if happily post-divorce. She's still pals with her husband, Richard (Clark Gregg), she's raising her nine-year-old son, Ritchie (Trevor Gagnon), and even running her own business, a thirty-minute work-out gymnasium

for women who do too much with too little time.

All is well until Christine learns that Richard now has a girlfriend, also named Christine. Hence, Old Christine and New Christine (Emily Rutherfurd). This sends the neurotic Old Christine into a tailspin. In early episodes she rushes into the sack with a man the mothers at Ritchie's new school call "Sad Dad" (a hysterical Andy Richter), just to prove that she hasn't lost it.

Old Christine has a way of making simple things go horribly wrong. That's why the series represents such a star turn for Dreyfus, who again proves herself a ballerina of physical comedy. The episodes are typical sitcom grist. You've seen the concepts a million times already, and yet Dreyfus—leaner, meaner and funnier than you've seen her in years—provokes gasps and cackles with her numerous faux pas, tongue-tied exaggerations, and missteps.

One episode involves Old Christine being set up on a blind date after she realizes that her best friends introduced Richard to New Christine ("Open Water"). In "Exile on Lame Street," Christine makes a fool of herself after her husband takes Ritchie to a Rolling Stones concert, and she has second thoughts about permitting it. In "Teach Your Children Well," Ritchie's ninth birthday goes awry, and in "A Fair to Remember," Christine harbors doubts about breaking up with a boyfriend when she finds out that he—just like Richard—is dating someone else. She just can't catch a break.

In a year in which literally dozens of sitcoms bit the dust or just plain sucked, *The New Adventures of Old Christine* is a fresh of breath air. There's life in that old sitcom yet…and audiences agree in overwhelming numbers. The first season averaged 12.6 million viewers[67] and was renewed for the fall '06 season.

Not yet available on DVD.

NIGHTMARES AND DREAMSCAPES:
FROM THE STORIES OF STEPHEN KING

(TNT) (60 minutes) (Wednesdays at 9:00 pm EST; July 12, 2006-August 2, 2006) An Ostar Production. Executive Producer: Bill Haber. Produced by: Brett Popwell, John McMahon, Jeffrey Hayes, Mike Robe. Directors of Photography: Ben Nott, John Stokes. Film Editors: Michael Ornstein, Scott Vickrey, Michael Weissman. Music: Jeff Beal. Based on short stories by: Stephen King. Written by: Lawrence Cohen, Mike Robe, April Smith. Directed by: Mikael Salomon, Mike Robe.

TNT termed this horror anthology "the four-week television event of the summer" in its advertisements, and for good reason. Horror writer Stephen King is not only a brand name in movies and television going as far back as the 1970s, but this hour-long series is superbly cast with top stars such as William Hurt, William H. Macy, and Samantha Mathis turning in guest appearances.

Like *Masters of Horror* on Showtime, *Nightmares and Dreamscapes* is a collection of unusual horror stories sans voiceover or narrator. Instead, there is simply an "umbrella" of unity holding the various episodes together. On *Masters of Horror*, that umbrella is the inclusion of the cinema's finest horror directors. Here it's tales (or short stories) of the macabre from Stephen King, still horror's most successful novelist.

The stories on *Nightmares and Dreamscapes* run an impressive gamut of styles. "Autopsy Room #4" stars Greta Scacchi and Richard Thomas, and concerns a man wheeled into the morgue at a South Carolina hospital after he's suffered an apparent fatal heart attack on a golf course. Turns out, the corpse (Thomas) isn't so dead after

all…he was bitten by an unusual snake and left paralyzed. The audience hears his desperate thoughts throughout the episode as the doctors come perilously close to cutting him up.

Yes, this is the old chestnut (seen on *Alfred Hitchcock Presents* [1955–1962] and in Wes Craven's film *The Serpent and the Rainbow*, 1988) about a man who appears dead, but is conscious, alert, and feeling *everything* as he is about to be dissected or buried alive. In previous stories, what's saved the poor wretch's life is a biological reflex action: a tear rolling down his cheek at just the right instant. Since this is Stephen King, and this master of horror boasts a wicked sense of humor, the reflex in "Autopsy Room #4" is something quite different and unexpected. Just as he is about to be cut open, Thomas experiences an…erection for all to see.

"You Know They Got a Hell of a Band" is a totally different sort of entry. Here, a bickering married couple played by Steven Weber and Kim Delaney take a trip through the Pacific Northwest and make a very wrong turn…into a Norman Rockwell town called "Rock and Roll Heaven." There, Janis Joplin is a waitress in a local diner, Ricky Nelson is the short-order cook, Otis Redding is the town sheriff, and Elvis Presley is the mayor.

Turns out there's no escape from this corner of the *Twilight Zone*…oops, I mean "nightmares and dreamscapes," and the couple is doomed to an unending rock performance by the genre's greats. This is a fairly disappointing and nonsensical story, and one that fails to scare in the slightest. One reason why "You Know They Got a Hell of a Band" fails so egregiously is that the writers (scenarist King and writer Mike Robe) fail to make any connection between the personalities of the "victims" and their eventual fate…trapped in rock limbo. In classic

Twilight Zone episodes such as "Nick of Time," which finds a superstitious William Shatner held in thrall to a fortune telling machine, there's a clear connection between personal foible and ironic twist of fate. No such relationship is forged here, and so the episode is without real suspense or dynamic character interest. In fact, it comes off campy and ludicrous.

More genuinely thoughtful is "The End of the Whole Mess," a stirring story that asks pertinent questions about human nature and the times we live in. Ron Livingston plays Howard Fornoy, a man spending his last minutes alive recounting for a camera (in a video journal) how the world is going to end. He tells the invisible audience the life story of his brother Bobby (Henry Thomas), a child prodigy—a Da Vinci or Einstein—who finds his "true north" in curing the ultimate human disease. No, not cancer or AIDS. Instead, he hopes to cure "mean-

ness" and develops a calmative that suppresses human aggression and makes people unwilling or unable to fight. Bobby calls his invention "*pacifist white light*" and is able to deliver it to the world with catastrophic results. See, there's a side effect he didn't reckon on. The calmative also causes early Alzheimer's…and so the whole population is doomed.

Because it airs on basic rather than premium cable, *Nightmares and Dreamscapes* is less gory and graphic than *Masters of Horror*, but the stories are at approximately the same middling level. Some entries are stirring, but most are simply run of the mill. And very few actually scare. These two series are nice to have around in the age of pabulum like *Supernatural*, but watching both anthologies, it's clear that the ironic touch of Rod Serling is missing. And missed.

Not yet available on DVD.

NIGHT STALKER

(ABC) (CANCELED) (60 minutes) (Thursdays at 9:00 pm, EST; September 29, 2005–November 11, 2005) Big Light Productions/ Touchstone Television. Created by: Jeffrey Grant Rice. Executive Producers: Daniel Sackheim, Frank Spotnitz. Co-Executive Producers: John Peter Kousakis, Michelle MacLaren. Produced by: Robert P. Cohen, Gary La Poten. Camera: Rick Maguire, Clark Mathis, Robert Primes. Film Editors: Christopher Cook, Marta Evry, Jimmy Hill, Sunny Hodge. Music: Michael Wandmacher. Written by: Adam Armus, Norma Kay Foster, Thoms Schnauz, Frank Spotnitz, Gregory Storm, Adam Sussman. Directed by: Daniel Sackham, Tony Wharmby.

CAST

Stuart Townsend (Carl Kolchak)
Gabrielle Union (Perri Reed)
Eric Jungmann (Jain McManus)
Cotter Smith (Tony Vincenzo)

When a TV movie (based on an unpublished novel by Jeffrey Rice) called *The Night Stalker* premiered on January 11, 1972, it generated surprisingly strong ratings. In fact, the ratings were downright scary. The story of a down-on-his-luck reporter, Carl Kolchak battling a vampire in modern-day Las Vegas earned a staggering 33.1 rating and a 48 share of the audience. These numbers made it the highest rated TV movie of all time, a title it held for decades. A second TV-movie starring Darren McGavin, *The Night Strangler*, soon followed and repeated the first film's success.

And then came series television. *Kolchak: The Night Stalker* premiered on September 13, 1974…and ratings soon dropped precipitously. The series was canceled by ABC after just twenty hour-long episodes…but fans remembered it; in many cases with a passion. The original program has been credited as the inspiration for *The X-Files,* among other productions.

In 2005, after an absence of thirty years, Carl Kolchak returned to prime-time television for the more tersely titled *Night Stalker*, a reimagination of the franchise from the mind of Frank Spotnitz, a writer and producer on *The X-Files*. On the original series, nothing was known of Carl's backstory, including his family relationships. Instead, as played by McGavin, Kolchak was a mystery (and definitely a character) as he battled very distinctive monsters of the week; creatures like a succubus ("Demon in Lace"), a shape-shifting Rakshasa ("Horror in the Heights"), witches ("The Trevi Collection"), and even Helen of Troy ("The Youth Killer").

On the new series, these elements were altered. Kolchak became a young, handsome reporter, played by Stuart Townsend, and he eschewed the old Kolchak's uniform (a seersucker suit and straw hat). The character was granted a new backstory. In particular, his wife was murdered under unusual circumstances on the road, and Kolchak was considered by some to be the culprit. In fact, this backstory is highly reminiscent of one featured on a British supernatural series from 1979, called *The Omega Factor*.

Regardless, Kolchak's backstory isn't the only thing that had changed in thirty years. The monsters changed too. Now Kolchak didn't face mythological beasts like werewolves, vampires, and succubi but rather weird half-seen creatures often created from dark human emotions like guilt. He was also paired with a beautiful partner, Perri Reed (played by Gabrielle Union).

The only nod to the original series, besides the name and central premise of the new *Night Stalker*, was a cameo in the first episode by Darren McGavin himself. Of a sort, anyway. Twenty-five-year-old footage of the actor as he was in 1975 was digitally enhanced and combined

Where's Darren McGavin when you need him?
Kolchak (Stuart Townsend) and Perri Reed (Gabrielle Union) investigate a creepy crime scene in the remake,
NIGHT STALKER.

into fresh newsroom footage with the new cast.

Despite such changes from the cherished source material, *Night Stalker* strove to create a unique aura that would separate it from television's storied supernatural pack (meaning The *X-Files*, *Supernatural*, *Poltergeist: The Legacy*, *Millennium* and so on). With all the lovely night-time shots of city lights, gleaming silver skyscrapers, isolated cars speeding on asphalt highways, and quick cuts to lonely, strange perspectives (a rattling wind chime, a gently swaying swing on a playground), one could strongly feel the aura of an isolating, dehumanizing metropolis; a place where plenty of people dwell…but they don't connect and don't help one another. It's a frightening phantasm of modern urban America, a place where people see, but don't do anything. Where people close their eyes and choose not to believe something that is unbelievable.

This a different view of life than *Kolchak: The Night Stalker* evidenced. The original series was born in post-Watergate America, when Woodward and Bernstein were still national heroes. Yet, the new show is faithful in the sense that it still offers a vision that upholds the original's conceit of the little guy vs. City Hall. In the 1974 progenitor, Kolchak was a nobody, just a fly in the ointment, but here, it's even worse. This Kolchak is actively despised and persecuted by the establishment. When media pundits suggest newspaper editors should be tried as traitors, this new show oddly fits the times.

For instance, an episode entitled "The Source" involves Kolchak (Stuart Townsend) in a case that could cost him his career. If the author doesn't reveal his sources on the story of a drug cartel murder, an FBI agent will have him locked up in jail. Right as this episode was airing, it was reflecting the national discourse. In the Valerie Plame/CIA leak case, a Federal prosecutor sent reporter Judith Miller to jail for refusing to divulge her source. In its own fashion, the series was reflecting reality and grappling with current events.

The burgeoning subtext on *Night Stalker*, often brought out in Kolchak's cleverly written narrative voice-overs, was that monsters are born out of human sin, and that concept alone gives this series a leg up on less intellectual fare such as the WB's competition, *Supernatural*.

"In this show, evil really does have supernatural forces at its command. Good does not," said producer Spotnitz, "Good has to operate through human beings. That is so interesting to me."[68]

Still, audiences apparently didn't feel the same way. Original series fans found the Townsend incarnation of their hero bland, boring, and too good looking for their tastes. Furthermore, the stories were mostly derided as leftover *X-Files* or *Millennium* episodes. *Night Stalker*, after initially receiving promising ratings, was pulled off the air after just seven weeks. The remaining three episodes of the series were later broadcast for the first time on the SCI FI Channel.

A historical footnote: *Night Stalker* was also one of the first three programs (along with *Desperate Housewives* and *Lost*) that ABC made available for download to wireless devices like iPods.

A DVD release in the summer of 2006 followed *Night Stalker*'s run on the SCI FI Channel.

Available on DVD.

THE ONE:
MAKING A MUSIC STAR

(ABC) (CANCELED) (Tuesdays, 9:00–11:00 pm; Wednesday 8:00-9:00 pm; EST; July 18, 2006–July 26, 2006) Pulse Creative/Endemol Entertainment. Executive Producer: Matt Kunitz. Co-Executive Producers: Michael Dempsy, Rick Ginbakk, Produced by: Joe Coleman, Rebecca Shumsky. Film Editors: Paul Coyne, Mark Markley. Directed by: Alan Carther, J. Rupert Thompson.

CAST
George Stroumboulopoulos (Host)
Kara DioGuardi (Judge)
Andre Harrell (Judge)
Mark Hudson (Judge)

CONTESTANTS
Nick Brownell, Austin Carroll, Michael Cole, Aubrey Collins, Caitlin Evanson, Scotty Granger, Jaydyn Maria, Adam McInnis, Jackie Mendez, Syesha Mercado, Jeremiah Richey

The One: Making a Music Star is a short-lived summer series based on a popular Spanish-language program entitled *Operacion Triunfo*. Set at "The One" Academy, the reality series was designed to follow a group of aspiring young singers for ten weeks (and twenty episodes) as they honed their skills with the help of a vocal coach, a choreographer, a personal trainer and other "professors."

What was to separate the series from the infinitely more popular *American Idol* was that the show served as a backstage drama too, filled with the relationships and rivalries of the young singers.

In each installment, after the singers performed (à la *American Idol*), a panel of "experts" would then offer their opinion about who should stay, and who would be eliminated from the competition. Sound familiar?

Also—and again like *American Idol*—the results were to be announced on a separate results program in an attempt to squeeze out ratings gold. ABC even scheduled the show on Tuesdays and Wednesdays...just like *Idol!* George Stroumboulopoulos was the host of the series, filling the Ryan Seacrest role.

The highly derivative *The One* quickly proved a ratings debacle for ABC and was canceled after just two rounds of performances and eliminations. The series boasted "the weakest premiere of any reality show on any network" in history and took a second honor, as "the lowest-rated series premiere in ABC history."[69]

The dramatic failure of the American *The One* quickly scuttled plans for a Canadian spinoff the series, which was to have aired on the CBC.[70]

The series is not available on DVD.

ONE OCEAN VIEW

(ABC) (CANCELED) (60 minutes) (Mondays at 10:00 pm, EST; July 31, 2006-August 7, 2006) Executive Producers: Jonathan Murray, Joey Caron. Co-executive Producers: Laura Karkoian, Dana De Mars. Camera: Jack Reichert.

CAST
Miki Agrawal
Radha Agrawal
John Healy
Heather Lutz
K.J. Nies
Usman Shaikh

Eleven gorgeous, upwardly mobile twentysomethings briefly shared a beach house (and exchanged bodily fluids) on *One Ocean View,* a short-lived ABC reality series from the creators of MTV's *The Real World.*

Set on Fire Island, *One Ocean View* aired briefly in the summer of 2006, and followed the adventures of Generation Y up-and-comers: Heather Lutz, a Playboy model and *MySpace* star; John, a Wall Street broker; Usman, *another* Wall Street lawyer and quite the Lothario, and Miki and Radha, the owners of an organic pizzeria.

"In keeping with the usual reality-show rules, everyone comes to One Ocean View with a personal agenda—in this case, it's the quest for summer love," writes *Globe and Mail* journalist Andrew Ryan. "All the twentysomethings are unattached and a few recently divorced. Some are seeking a soul mate; others are just looking for a good time."[71]

That description just about sums up this extremely shallow series about hooking up at the beach. *One Ocean View* drew a paltry 2.8 million viewers to the tube, and was promptly replaced after just two episodes by *Supernanny.*

One Ocean View joins ABC summer failures *How to Get The Guy* and *The One: Making a Music Star* as among the lowest rated series of the year.

Not available on DVD.

OUT OF PRACTICE

(CBS) (CANCELED) (30 minutes) (Mondays 9:30 pm, EST; Wednesdays at 8:00 pm, EST; September 19, 2005–March 29, 2005) A Knotty Entertainment/Picardon Productions/Paramount. Executive Producers: Joe Keenan, Christopher Lloyd. Co-Executive Producers: Bob Daily, Michael Jamin, David Litt. Co-Producer: Tony Knick. Produced by: Alec Barnow, Maggie Blank. Camera: Maggie Blank. Film Editor: Ron Volk. Music: Bruce Miller. Written by: Alex Barnow, Tucker Cawley, Marc Firek, Joe Keenan, D.J. Nash. Directed by: Mark Cendrowski, Scott Ellis, Sheldon Epps, Kelsey Grammer, Bob Koherr, James Widdoes.

CAST

Christopher Gorham (Dr. Benjamin Barnes)
Paula Marshall (Dr. Regina Barnes)
Ty Burrell (Dr. Oliver Barnes)
Jennifer Tilly (Crystal)
Henry Winkler (Dr. Stewart Barnes)
Stockard Channing (Dr. Lydia Barnes)

Out of Practice is a sitcom about the Barnes family, a family of doctors. Dad Stewart (Henry Winkler) is a gastroenterologist. Mom (Stockard Channing) is a renowned cardiologist. Lesbian sister Regina (Paula Marshall) is an ER physician, and brother Oliver (Ty Burrell) is a plastic surgeon with an eye for the ladies. The series focuses on the other brother, Ben, however, a counselor…and therefore not a real "M.D." like the rest of his family. He symbolizes the "soft" science of psychology instead.

Turns out, Ben's counseling abilities are much needed. Although his mom is a cardiologist, she knows nothing of the heart and is still wounded over her estrangement from Stewart, who recently divorced and is now sleeping with his assistant, Crystal (Jennifer Tilly). Making matters more complex, Crystal also happens to be one of Ben's patients! Ben is married, though his wife is never seen in the series: she's a progressive warrior always out fighting the good fight, on some kind of environmental crusade.

The crazy family dynamics of *Out of Practice* are familiar to long-time sitcom watchers (and even ones just tuning in to such 2005–2006 fare as *Arrested Development* and *Crumbs*), but the difference here is that veteran producer/writer Christopher Lloyd (*Frasier*, *Wings*) and Kelsey Grammer (*Cheers*, *Frasier*) are on board in creative capacities, and the Fonz himself, Henry Winkler, makes a terrific showing as the series' patriarch. Still, episodes are fairly familiar in terms of concepts.

Mom needs to be set up for a date in "The Heartbreak Kid," Ben is set up on a blind date ("The Truth About Nerds and Dogs"), and so forth. One of the most amusing episodes was called "Thanks" and it reveals how Thanksgiving is a bad time for the Barneses. That's when the children learned of the parents' separation, and one year it was also the occasion of Regina's coming out.

Although *Out of Practice* drew strong ratings initially, even cracking the top twenty, CBS pulled the half-hour situation comedy from the schedule in March of '06, before all twenty-two episodes had aired.

Not currently released on DVD.

PEPPER DENNIS

(WB) (CANCELED) (60 minutes) (Tuesdays at 9:00 pm, EST; April 4, 2006–July 4, 2006) Two Presbyterians/Twenty-One Laps Entertainment/20th Century Fox. Executive Producers: Gretchen J. Berg, Aaron Harberts, Jason Katims, Shawn Levy. Produced by: David M. Burrs, Liz Heldens, Adele Lim, Kelly A. Manners, Matt McGuinness, Katie O'Hara. Camera: Peter Lyons Collister, Bruce M. Pasternack, Joe Pennella. Film Editors: Stuart Bass, Matt Friedman, Scott Gamzon, Kevin D. Ross. Written by: Gretchen J. Berg, Christopher Fife, Aaron Harbert, Liz Heldens, Jason Katims, Adele Lim, Katherine Lingenfelter, Matt McGuinness, Lisa Parsons. Directed by: Robert Berlinger, Allison Leddi-Brown, Paul Laver, Shawn Levy, Arlene Sanford, Oz Scott, Lev L. Spiro.

CAST

Rebecca Romijn (Pepper Dennis)
Josh Hopkins (Charlie Babcock)
Brooke Burns (Kathy Dinkle)
Lindsay Price (Kimmy)
Rider Strong (Chick)

Pepper Dennis is a one-hour "career comedy" following in the tradition established by sitcoms such as *The Mary Tyler Moore Show* (1970–1977) and the more recent hour-long drama, *Ally McBeal* (1997–2002).

Pepper Dennis is the adventure of an ambitious and beautiful local TV reporter in Chicago, played by Rebecca Romijn. In the series' first episode, she sleeps with a handsome man named Charlie, who ends up getting the position for news anchor at her station. Dennis must also contend with her sister, Kathy (Brooke Burns), who has just left her husband after six years of marriage, and moves in with the reporter. Other cast members include Pepper's makeup gal, Kimmy (Lindsay Price) and the news room camera operator, Chick (Rider Strong).

Various episodes of *Pepper Dennis* follow the journeys of the newswoman on "the beat" and each installment title ends with the line "Film at Eleven." In "Frat Boys May Lose Their Manhood—Film at Eleven," Pepper sees a psychologist and also covers a story about fraternity hazing. In "Pepper Dennis Behind Bars—Film at Eleven," Pepper goes to jail for not revealing a source...a popular story seen in the 2005–2006 season on other series including *Night Stalker*, and no doubt a reflection of the Valerie Plame CIA leak case. In another story, Pepper Dennis deals with the disappearance at the altar of a woman who may be a runaway bride...or not ("Heiress Bridenapped—Film at Eleven").

Although *Pepper Dennis* received mostly positive notices, the WB canceled the series in the summer of 2006. It would not be making the leap to the new CW Network, despite the fact that the dozen or so episodes that did air had begun to develop an avid fan following.

Not yet available on DVD.

PRISON BREAK

(FOX) (RENEWED) (60 minutes) (Mondays at 8:00 pm, EST; August 29, 2005-May 15, 2006) Adelstein-Parouse Productions/Original TV/Rat Entertainment/Twentieth Century Fox. Created by: Paul Scheuring. Executive Producers: Marty Adelstein, Neal H. Moritz, Matt Olmstead, Dawn Parouse, Michael Parone, Brett Ratner, Paul Scheuring. Produced by: Garry A. Brown. Camera: Robert La Bonge, Chris Manley. Film Editors: James Coblentz, Etienne Des Lauriers, Scott Eilers, Kaya Fehr, Mark Helfrich. Written by: Zack Estrin, Matt Olmstead, Nick Santora, Paul Scheuring, Karyn Usher. Directed by: Jace Alexander, Guy Ferland, Sergio Mimica-Gezzan, Brad Lachman, Dwight Little, Brett Ratner, Bobby Roth, Brad Turner, Michael Watkins, Dean White, Greg Yaitanes, Randall Zisk.

CAST

Dominic Purcell (Lincoln Burrows)
Wentworth Miller (Michael Scofield)
Robin Tunney (Veronica Donovan)
Peter Stormare (John Abruzzi)
Amaury Nolasco (Fernando Sucre)
Marshall Allman (L.J. Burrows)
Wade Williams (Brad Bellick)
Paul Adelstein (Paul Kellerman)
Robert Knepper (T-Bag)
Sarah Wayne Callies (Dr. Sara Tancredi)
Muse Watson (Charles Westmoreland)
Lane Garrison (Tweener)
Stacy Keach (Warden Henry Pope)

Pardon the expression, but *Prison Break* is the "breakout" hit of the 2005–2006 season and also the epitome of the "high concept" television notion, or "*Lost*" Factor. In creating this series, Paul Scheuring has thought in unconventional terms, thereby creating a worthy companion-piece to such high-tension programming as *24*. Already, his style is being aped in the 2006–2007 season with serialized programming such as *Vanished*, which aired briefly on FOX before a hasty cancellation.

Prison Break is one hell of a rollercoaster ride, and the tale of young Michael Scofield (Miller), a brilliant Chicago architect who believes that his brother, Lincoln Burrows (Purcell) has been framed for murder. Accordingly, Scofield devises an intricate (and I mean *intricate*) plan to free Lincoln from Fox River Prison where's he incarcerated…and due to be executed. For Michael, that escape plans involves: (1) having his entire torso inked with a tattoo that's really a blueprint of the prison; (2) getting himself arrested and sent to Fox River himself; and (3) winning the affections of a woman there he's never even met.

Once inside the prison, Scofield methodically acquires the supplies he needs to make the escape possible. Before long, he's dismantled the toilet in his cell and opened up a corridor to another building, but in the process he is forced to take into his confidence his cellmate, Sucre (Amaury Nolasco).

Which brings up a point. Michael is a brilliant thinker, an intellectual. But putting his plan into practice requires that he be a social thinker, and that means contending with people. In this endeavor, Michael is less successful, and indeed frequently gets tripped up. His encounters with an incarcerated Mafioso, Abruzzi (Peter Stormare) results in the amputation of a toe. His inability to garner the confidence of another inmate, Westmoreland (Muse Watson)—who could be the legendary D.B. Cooper—could scuttle the scheme. Before the big escape, Michael inadvertently assembles a dirty dozen of miscreants that he's now obligated to help. The most despicable is a child molester named T-Bag (Robert Knepper).

Part of Scofield's plan involves gaining access to certain sections of the prison at the right moment, and he befriends the prison's warden, Henry Pope (Stacy Keach);

getting time in Pope's office to construct a replica of the Taj Mahal as an anniversary gift for Pope's wife. Michael also makes regular visits to the prison infirmary and lovely Dr. Sara Tancredi (Sarah Wayne Callies), the daughter of the governor. They form a tight bond, especially after Michael saves Tancredi's life during a riot. As much as is the tattoo on his back and chest, Tancredi's friendship is a necessary element of the plan.

Highly suspicious of Michael is Officer Bellick (Wade Williams), the prison guard captain and a corrupt thug. He recruits an inmate named Tweener (Lane Garrison) to spy on Scofield, and Michael—again making an error when it comes to "human intelligence"—takes him in.

Outside the prison, *Prison Break* also follows the lives of several characters peripherally related to Scofield. As it turns out, Burrows truly has been framed for murder, and the person behind the conspiracy is the Vice President of the United States, played by Patricia Wettig. She assigns a covert agent to tie up the loose ends of the plot, which involves killing Lincoln's ex-wife and teenage son, L.J. (Marshall Allman). When that plan goes awry, L.J. is accused of the murder and left to flee. Helping both L.J. and Lincoln while ferreting out the details of the conspiracy is lovely Veronica Donovan (Robin Tunney), an attorney in love with Lincoln.

Each episode of *Prison Break* ups the ante at Fox River State Penitentiary, as the day of Lincoln's execution looms closer. Many episodes end on a cliffhanger note, but in the end the first season culminates with eight men (including Michael and Lincoln) escaping the walls of the prison.

Season two of *Prison Break* involves the manhunt, and already Michael Scofield has a new and worthy adversary, a Federal agent portrayed by *Invasion*'s William Fichtner. The premiere of *Prison Break*'s second season also involves the murder of a series regular, just to keep viewers off-balance.

Critics have been quick to note that *Prison Break* is sometimes farfetched and that it requires viewers to "chuck their disbelief off the watch tower."[72] That may be true, but the characters and situations are so interesting, the tension so nailbiting, that such a complaint almost seems like nitpicking. The series is "an entertaining, big-narrative concept"[73] according to *People*'s Tom Gliatto. Critics should be championing this serial for what qualities it does boast: namely a brawny, daring imagination, a fine cast, and a breakneck pace.

The first season is available on DVD.

PSYCH

(USA) (RENEWED) (60 minutes) (Fridays at 10:00 pm, EST; July 7, 2006-August 25, 2006) Tagline Productions. Executive Producers: Steve Franks, Chris Henze, Kelly Kulchak. Co-Executive Producers: Jack Sakmar, Kerry Lenhart, Mel Damski. Produced by: Paulo De Olveira, Wendy Belt Wallace. Camera: Michael McMurray, Greg Middleton. Film Editors: David Crabtree, James Ilecic, Allan Lee, Gordon Rempel. Music: Adam Cohen, Brandon Christie, John Wood. Written by: Andy Berman, Anupan Nigam. Directed by: Michael Engler.

CAST
James Roday (Shawn Spencer)
Corbin Bernsen (Henry Spencer)
Dule Hill (Gus)
Maggie Lawson (Juliet O'Hara)
Tim Omundson (Carlton Lassiter)

In the spirit of the USA Network's quirky detective series *Monk* comes this wildly entertaining detective series that spoofs "psychic" network hits such as *Ghost Whisperer* and *Medium*. *Psych's* amusing tagline? "Fake psychic. Real detectives."

Psych depicts the adventures of Shawn Spencer (James Roday), a slacker who retains such a keen and finely developed sense of observation that he can solve a murder just by reading body language and gestures of suspects appearing on television. He knows that the police won't believe his "remote" crime-solving abilities are genuine, so to help them out, he instead pretends to be psychic. In truth, he's just picking up on tangible clues; if only others would look closely enough.

Spencer is joined on his mystery-solving escapades by his friend and sidekick Gus (Dule Hill), and his Dad (Corbin Bernsen) is the man who taught him (as a boy) how to study and observe human behavior; but who is now somewhat disenchanted with Spencer's "gimmick" (faking psychic powers).

In its first amusing season, this hour-long mystery takes Shawn and Gus all over Santa Barbara solving crimes. The duo must solve a murder at a spelling bee ("The Spelling Bee"), at a Civil War reenactment ("Weekend Wariors") and even a boy's disappearance at a comic convention! Other stories involve the duo crashing a wedding ("Speak Now or Forever Hold Your Piece") and a mystery in which the only useful witness to a murder is a cat who belonged to the corpse ("9 Lives").

The creators of this series must have felt "psyched" when they saw the ratings. In its premiere installment, *Psych* drew a impressive six million viewers, actually improving on the ratings of its lead in, *Monk*.[74]

The series is not yet available on DVD.

THE REAL HOUSEWIVES OF ORANGE COUNTY

(Bravo) (RENEWED) (60 minutes) (Tuesdays at 10:00 pm, EST; March 21, 2006-May 2, 2006) Dunlop Entertainment/ Kaufman Films. Created by: Scott Dunlop. Executive Producers: Scott Dunlap, Kevin Kaufman, Patrick Moses, David Rupel. Produced by: Brad Isenberg. Camera: Steve Korkis, Roger Roddy. Film Editors: Derek McCants, Lorraine Salk.

CAST
Kimberly Bryant
Jeana Keough
Vicki Gunvalson
Jo De La Rosa
Lauri Waring
Matt Keough
Shane Keough

The press release from the unscripted series *The Real Housewives of Orange County* states that this reality program "will follow five sophisticated women and their families who lead glamorous lives in a picturesque Southern California gated community where the average home has a $1.6 million price tag and residents include CEOs and retired professional athletes. Orange County 'housewives' Kimberly, Jeana, Vicki, Lauri and Jo are used to the good life and will do everything they can to hang on to it. The women each have their own personal story to share, and they've granted Bravo an all-access pass into their lives, families, friendships, careers, and homes. From diamond parties to Botox sessions to the stress of having a high-powered career, the women take viewers along for the ride and into their real-life dramas that show how life isn't always perfect behind the gates. Just what lies beneath the surface of this 'perfect' community?"[75]

In other words, it's *Desperate Housewives*...for real. Even Bravo's president Laura Zalaznick was brazen about the comparison "From *Peyton Place* to *Desperate Housewives* viewers have been riveted by the fictionalized versions of such lifestyles on television. Now, here is a series that depicts real-life 'desperate' housewives with an authentic look at their compelling day-to-day drama."[76]

Considering all the references to the ABC series, maybe it's not really the housewives who are desperate; maybe it's the network executives.

As the press release indicates, this series track the lives of five rich women inside the hallowed gates of Coto de Caza. Kimberly is the trophy wife. Jeana Keough is the former Playboy playmate married to a major league ballplayer. Jo is the young one of the bunch. Lauri is recently divorced and therefore forced to cut back on the finer things in life. Finally, Vicki is a self-made woman who claims to be a devout Christian. This, despite the fact she's divorced and on her second marriage.

In essence, this reality series is about rich white women who have nothing better to do than spend money and get plastic surgery. It's a travesty, a blight upon television and humanity. Which doesn't mean it isn't occasionally fun to watch...in the same way a train wreck or auto accident would be.

At *Slate*, Troy Patterson wrote that *The Real Housewives of Orange County* is "a craftily presented slice of America that makes room for guns, silicone, status anxiety, and sibling rivalry....But what makes the show something better than a guilty pleasure is the way that, after introducing its subjects as borderline-reprehensible cartoons, it allows them flickers of self-awareness or shows them trying their damnedest to be terrific parents."[77]

Bravo announced a renewal for the series on July 14, 2006, though the series is not yet released on DVD.

RELATED

(WB) (CANCELED) (60 minutes) (Wednesdays at 9:00 pm, EST; October 5, 2005-March 20, 2006) Class IV Productions/ Warner Bros. Executive Producer: Marta Kauffman, Steve Pearlman, Andrew Plotkin. Produced by: Robert Lloyd Lewis. Camera: Paul Maibum, Charles Minsky. Film Editors: Barry L. Gold, Brady Heck, Martin Nicholson, Mark Schweib. Music: Blake Neely. Written by: Maggie Friedman, Jennifer Maisel, Kath Lingenfelter, Alex Taub, Liz Tuccilo. Directed by: Arvin Brown, Martha Coolidge, James Frawley, Elodie Keane, Joanna Kern, Michael Lange, Patrick Norris, Lee Rose.

CAST
Jennifer Esposito (Ginnie Sorelli)
Kiele Sanchez (Ann Sorelli)
Lizzy Caplan (Marjee Sorelli)
Laura Breckenridge (Rose Sorelli)
Callum Blue (Bob)
Dan Futterman (Danny)
Tom Irwin (Dad)
Christine Ebersole (Renee)

This WB series follows in the tradition of drama comedies (or, in the vernacular, "dramedies") such as *Love Monkey* and *What About Brian*. *Related* is the saga of the Manhattan-based Sorelli family, deli owners, and it commences as the widowed patriarch of the family (Tom Irwin) announces to his four very different daughters that he is getting engaged to a woman named Renee (Christine Ebersole), a personality that the daughters don't particularly like.

In birth order, the four Sorelli daughters include the following: eldest daughter, Ginnie (Jennifer Esposito), a Type-A personality who's very organized and who is married to a goofy husband named Bob (Callum Blue). Ginnie soon finds out she's pregnant and that revelation sends Bob, a software engineer, reeling.

Next in the pecking order is Ann (originally to be played by Laura San Giacomo), portrayed by Kiele Sanchez. She's a therapist dating a restaurateur named Danny. In proceeding hour-long episodes of the series, they break up ("Hang in There, Baby"), and she deals with the fallout and depression of the relationship's end ("Cry Me A Sister").

Then there's Marjee (Lizzy Caplan), a flighty flibbertigibbet and event planner who wants to move in with Dad. Finally, the baby of the group is Rose (Laura Breckenridge), the indulged and directionless sister. She was enrolled at NYU studying to be a doctor, but as *Related* begins, she starts taking drama courses. In subsequent episodes, she dates a fellow acting student, and then lands her first gig ("The Naked Truth").

Related generally averaged about 2.5 million viewers per episode, which in the final analysis wasn't enough to grant it a berth in the new (and tight) CW schedule. After one season on the air, the Sorelli soap opera came to an abrupt end.

The series is not available on DVD.

ROME

(HBO) (RENEWED) (60 minutes) (Sundays at 9:00 pm, EST; August 28, 2005-November 20, 2005) BBC/HD Vision Studios/HBO. Executive Producers: Frank Doelger, Bruno Heller, William J. MacDonald, John Milius, Gareth Neame, Anne Thomopoulos. Produced by: Todd London, Robert Papazian, Marco Valerio Pugini, Frank Yablans. Camera: Martin Kenzie, Maro Pontecaro, Alik Sakharov. Film Editors: Glenn Farr, Sidney Wolinsky. Historical Consultant: Jonathan Stamp. Written by: Bruno Heller. Directed by: Michael Apted, Allen Coulter, Julian Farino, Alan Poul, Mikael Saloman, Steve Shill.

CAST
Kevin McKidd (Lucius Vorenus)
Ray Stevenson (Titus Pullo)
Kenneth Cranham (Pompey)
Lindsay Duncan (Servilia)
Tobias Menzies (Brutus)
Kerry Condon (Octavia)
Karl Johnson (Cato)
Indira Varma (Niobe)
David Bamber (Cicero)
Max Pirkis (Octavius)
James Purefoy (Marc Antony)
Ciaran Hinds (Julius Caesar)
Polly Walker (Atia)
Lee Boardman (Timon)

HBO and the BBC co-produced this lush and impressive period piece shot in Bulgaria and Italy at a price of $70–100 million[78]…and every single dollar is up on the screen.

Rome is the tumultuous and highly compelling story of Julius Caesar's rise to power. The visually stunning endeavor—which truly makes viewers feel they "are there"—opens in Ancient Gaul, where a plotting Caesar (Ciaran Hinds) has been conquering barbarians for years and is finally ready to make a triumphant journey home. At his side is Marc Antony (James Purefoy), a playboy soldier with designs on power.

Meanwhile, back in Rome, inept ruler Pompey (Kenneth Cranham) and many of the senators, including Cato (Karl Johnson), fear that Caesar has grown so popular with the common man that he will seize control of the state and transform the Republic into an Empire, bringing tyranny to the long-established democracy. These fears prove justified, and before long, Caesar indeed crosses the Rubicon to take his place as Rome's only ruler.

Hinds is splendid as the avaricious Caesar, and the writing makes clear the contradiction inherent in this legendary historical figure: he is both bent on consolidating his power AND improving the lot of the common man. He is both corrupt politician and magnanimous man-of-the-people, if that duality is at all possible.

Rome boasts splendid production values and special effects, and closely follows the dynamic conflict between Pompey and Caesar from Rome to Greece to Egypt. Splendid battle sequences appear along the way, though actual warfare is not the series' point. To the contrary, social warfare and positioning is the order of the day as Caesar's family, led by the scheming, maniacal Atia (sexy Polly Walker), seeks to dominate Roman city life at the expense of everybody else. She manipulates her daughter Octavia's (Kerry Condon) marriage, expresses outrage that son Octavius (Max Pirkis) has not yet "penetrated" a woman, and interferes in the lives of everyone she comes in contact with.

Also among those featured in *Rome*'s ensemble are Servilia (Lindsay Duncan), Caesar's spurned mistress, who grows into a real threat, and Brutus (Tobias Menzies), Servilia's son and the man destined to kill a tyrant.

The first series of *Rome* ends its twelve-episode run with the very bloody assassination of Caesar in the Senate… at the hand of Brutus (and at the urging of Cassius) in "Kalends of February."

Although *Rome* focuses on the big political players, the true value of this program arises from its gritty, believable depiction of the Roman street. In particular, the series often adopts the viewpoint of two average Joes, two low-ranking Roman soldiers attempting to make their way in the cruel world. Vorenus (Kevin McKidd) and Pullo (Ray Stevenson) are these Roman "everymen," and their experiences contrast effectively with those of consuls, queens, senators, and nobles.

Vorenus and Pullo keep *Rome* grounded in reality rather than overblown political opera, and illuminate what daily life must have been like all those years ago. These characters are also funny as hell, going from battlefield to business; traveling from land to land; being shipwrecked and even having interludes with Cleopatra. Vorenus rises through the ranks of Caesar's administration after first dismissing him as a tyrant, and Pullo descends into a life of crime before becoming a hero of the gladiatorial games ("Spoils").

Calling a spade a spade, *Rome* is also a rampant, over-the-top sex-fest. Everybody is having sex with *everyone* in the series. Sex is used as a political weapon, as a power play between Cleopatra and Caesar. There are homosexual relationships depicted (Servilia and Octavia) and suggested (Octavius and Caesar); incestuous sex (siblings Octavia and Octavius), good old-fashioned sex among the common married folk (Niobe and Vorenus) and even interclass sex between the scheming noblewoman Atia and her underling, Timon.

It would be tempting to state that there's so much sex going on in that you'll forget the details of the complex plot, but that's not likely. *Rome* is brilliantly scripted and the sex is only one aspect of the impressive and varied tapestry. At times, *Rome* also proves unrelentingly gory, especially in the episode wherein Vorenus comes to Pullo's aid in the arena, and various limbs are chopped off as blood decorates the Roman sands. But one leaves the series contemplating not the sex nor the violence, but that times have not changed so much. Politicians still cling to power; men still ease into corruption to save their families; and wars for territorial and political domination are still waged.

Critic Hal Boedeker hailed *Rome* as "the best new drama of the fall" of 2005 and said it was the *Spartacus* "for the TV-MA"[79] generation, as it features full-frontal nudity. *Multichannel News* noted that "those tuning in will get an eyeful," not just of "rich" scenery and sets but also "bloodletting."[80]

Audiences were more than intrigued, and *Rome* became the highest rated program on HBO since the fourth season premiere of *Six Feet Under* in June 2004. *Rome,* which built "momentum" with HBO subscribers and "critics"[81] has been renewed for a second season to begin airing in January 2007. The long delay is partially due to the fact that some series sets in Bulgaria were flooded.

The first season is now available on DVD.

REUNION

(FOX) (CANCELED) (60 minutes) (Thursdays at 9:00 pm, EST; September 8, 2005-December 15, 2005) Class IV Productions/Warner Bros. Created by: John Harmon Feldman, Sara Goodman. Executive Producers: John Harmon Feldman, Steve Pearlman, Andrew Plotkin. Co-Executive Producer: Gina Fattore. Producers: Kathy Gilroy-Sereda, Jennifer Johnson. Camera: David Maxness. Film Editors: Clay Cambern, Joshua Charson, Mark S. Manos, Adam Weiss. Written by: John Harmon Feldman, Gina Fattore, Mark Goffman, Sara Goodman, Jennifer Johnson, Edgar Lyall, Bruce Zimmerman. Directed by: John Amiel, Lou Antonio, Milan Cheylov, James Frawley, Michael Katleman, Michael Lange, Rick Rosenthal.

CAST

Dave Annable (Aaron Lewis)
Alexa Davalos (Samantha Carlton)
Will Estes (Will Malloy)
Sean Faris (Craig Brewster)
Chyler Leigh (Carla)
Amanda Righetti (Jenna Moretti)
Mathew St. Patrick (Detective Marjorino)

The 2005–2006 season was the year of high concept TV with programs such as *Prison Break, Surface, Invasion,* and *Threshold.* One very promising high-concept series, but one which ultimately didn't make grade the viewers, was the soap-opera/mystery serial, *Reunion.*

Reunion is the story of six friends who graduate from Bedford High School in 1986. These buddies are inseparable, but by 2005 something terrible has occurred: one friend has murdered another. *Reunion* begins in the year 2005 with the funeral of the "victim," and the beginning of the subsequent investigation by Detective Marjorino (Mathew St. Patrick), who also hides a secret. Marjorino starts peering into the past of each of the five surviving "friends" of the deceased, and each new episode gazes at one year (following 1986) in their tumultuous lives.

The major *dramatis personae* in *Reunion* are: blue-collar Will (Will Estes), best friend of wealthy slacker, Craig (Sean Faris), and who eventually becomes a Catholic priest. Will is also in love with Craig's girlfriend, Sam (Alexa Davalos), a gorgeous medical school student who is pregnant with Will's baby in 1986, but then gives the child up for adoption in London.

There's also Carla (Chyler Leigh), a quiet, smart girl who has never left quiet Bedford, but who becomes a manipulative vixen over the twenty-year span of the series. Then there's Jenna (Amanda Righetti), an insecure and promiscuous young woman hoping to start a career in the movies. Future tycoon Aaron (Dave Annable) is in love with Jenna, but Carla is in love with Aaron, so that's another love triangle.

All the trouble starts in *Reunion* on the night of a party in 1986, shortly before high school graduation. On a beer run, Will and Craig are involved in a car accident in which the driver of the other car dies. Craig was driving, but he convinces Will to take the rap, so he can go to school at Brown. Will acquiesces, and eventually spends a year in jail for a crime he didn't commit. From there, things spiral out of control…and lead to murder.

One of *Reunion*'s first episodes was preempted for a prime-time presidential address, and that loss of momentum seems to have cost this fascinating and complex series dearly. Ratings dropped and FOX pulled the series after nine episodes…leaving unresolved the identity of the killer.

When *Reunion* was canceled, the series had only reached the year 1998, leaving many fans waiting for a DVD release of the series…which has yet to materialize.

Not yet available on DVD.

SAVED

(TNT) (RENEWED) (60 minutes) (Mondays at 10:00 pm, EST; June 12, 2006-August 28, 2006) Fox 21/Imagine Television/TNT. Created by: David Manson. Executive Producers: David Manson, David Nevins. Produced by: Shawn Williamson. Camera: Barry Donlevy, Kramer Morganthau. Film Editor: Peter C. Frank. Music: Dave Porter. Written by: Kira Arne, Joseph Dougherty, Ann Hamilton, John Mankiewicz, David Manson. Directed by: Arvin Brown, John David Coles, Stephen Kay, Dean White, Alex Zakrwewksi.

CAST

Tom Everett Scott (Wyatt Cole)
Omari Hardwick (Sack)
Elizabeth Reaser (Alice)
Michael McMillian (Harper)
Tracy Vilar (Angela)
David Clennon (Dr. Leon Cole)

Saved is the tale of a young "slacker" in Portland, Oregon named Wyatt Cole (Tom Everett Scott). Wyatt's got a gambling addiction that's out of control, and he doesn't know what he wants to do with his life. Over the objections of his father, Dr. Cole (David Clennon), Wyatt quits medical school and decides to become a paramedic. The high-risk, high-speed action in a rocking-and-rolling ambulance is just like the rush of adrenalin he feels while gambling. He never knows what's going to happen next…

This summer series from TNT (which gave the world *The Closer* the previous summer) follows Wyatt's escapades riding shotgun in an always-speeding ambulance, and evocatively captures the feeling of the road, particularly in the way it deploys music like Creedence Clearwater Revival's "Bad Moon Rising" for atmosphere. The soundtrack is like an ambulance radio turned permanently "on."

Other characters in the series include Sack (Omari Hardwick), ambulance jockey and Wyatt's partner. Sack has a family at home, and during the course of the series' hour-long episodes must contend with mounting costs in health care and education.

Alice (Elizabeth Reaser) is an Emergency Room doctor in the local hospital and Wyatt's ex-girlfriend. Naturally, he's still in love with her. Harper (Michael McMillian) and Angela (Tracy Vilar) are another ambulance team, another odd-couple of sorts, the former being a newbie on the job (and a Mormon to boot) and the latter being an all-business-all-the-time type.

The premiere of *Saved* aired commercial-free on TNT, and garnered the best ratings for a scripted cable series of the year. The episodes themselves move at warp speed.

"A Day in the Life" sees Wyatt and Sack dealing with the aftermath of a drunk driving incident. "Lady and the Tiger" involves a priest with epilepsy. "The Living Dead" occurs on a full moon, when all the lunatics come out to make problems for the paramedics. An emergency C-section spawns threats of a lawsuit in "A Shock to the System," and "Family" deals more explicitly with Wyatt's relationship with his father on the day of his sixtieth birthday.

Although some critics have compared *Saved* to *Bringing Out the Dead*, a movie starring Nicolas Cage as a paramedic, the TNT series has a feel all its own. It's unique and one of the more promising dramas to premiere in the 2005–2006 season.

Not available on DVD.

SEX, LOVE & SECRETS

(UPN) (CANCELED) (60 minutes) (Tuesdays at 9:00 pm, EST; September 27, 2005-October 11, 2006) Axelrod/ Edwards/Paramount Television. Executive Producers: Jonathan Axelrod, Daniel Cerone, Kelly Edwards. Co-Executive Producers: Michael Gans, Richard Register. Produced by: James Hilton, Robert M. Rolsky, Elle Triedman. Fcamera: Tom Burston. Film Editors: Armen Minasian, Stewart Schill. Written by: Daniel Cerone, Michael Gans, Michael Platt, Richard Register, Barry Safchik, Elle Triedman. Directed by: Allison Leddi Brown, David Straiton, Rachel Talalay.

CAST
Denise Richards (Jolene)
Eric Balfour (Charlie)
Lauren German (Rose)
Omar Miller (Coop)
Tamara Taylor (Nina)
James Stevenson (Hankd)
Lucas Bryant (Milo)

Former Bond Girl and ex-Mrs. Charlie Sheen, Denise Richards headlined this Generation Y soap opera that aired on UPN four times before it was canceled due to low ratings.

The provocatively titled *Sex, Love & Secrets* is a drama that focuses on a group of twentysomethings living affluent lives in trendy Silver Lake, California. All of them boast secrets about, well, love and sex. The ad line promised that the only thing that could tear this group apart...*was the truth!*

Richards played a maneating publicist named Jolene who was causing trouble for Hank (James Stevenson), who only wanted to marry Rose (Lauren German). Eric Balfour, who appeared in two canceled series during the 2005–2006 season (the other being *Conviction*), played Charlie, a hairdresser and womanizer who had slept with his best friend Coop's (Omar Miller) girlfriend.

Hoping to land somewhere between *Beverly Hills 90210* and *Melrose Place*, *Sex, Love & Secrets* apparently pleased no demographic and was gone from prime time by Halloween of 2005.

Not available on DVD.

SEXUAL HEALING

(Showtime) (60 minutes) (Friday at 10:00 pm, EST; July 21, 2006-August 25, 2006) Life in Progress Production/Showtime. Executive Producers: Harry and Joe Gantz, Dr. Laura Berman, Sam Chapman. Produced by: Colleen Kaman, Steven Dunning, Evie Shapiro, MJ Rizk. Camera: Bradley Sellers. Film Editors: Nina M. Gilberti, Victor Livingston. Music: David Baerwald, Timothy Fitzpatrick.

CAST
Dr. Laura Berman

In her plush sky rise offices in Chicago (in a building named for her...), lovely Dr. Laura Berman dispenses much-needed therapy to troubled couples. That's the premise of this sometimes riveting reality series that premiered on Showtime July 21, 2006 and ran for a six-episode season.

In each hour-long episode, Berman tends to two or three couples experiencing intense sexual difficulties in their relationships. Surprisingly, Berman's advice and guidance is neither cheesy nor over the top. Instead, this therapist and earth mother proves a reserved, thoroughly professional presence who projects an aura of calm and kindness into proceedings that might otherwise descend into histrionics. Berman's a strong anchor for the series and gives the enterprise an air of legitimacy.

As the title suggests, *Sexual Healing* concerns sex, and each client couple is often given homework assignments by Dr. Berman (like "surrender dates"). Berman will often assign an exercise that involves "*touch and body communication, a sense of sexuality, and slowing down with no expectations of sexual arousal,*" for instance. This is done to help couples reacquaint themselves with their partner's body.

Also, on one occasion, Berman shows up to a therapy sessions with sexual toys as gifts, such as vibrating underwear activated by remote control. Despite such gimmickry, Berman doesn't ham it up. Instead, she conducts often tearful and intimate individual therapies with her clients. Histories of infidelity and sexual abuse are frequently raised, as are explicit sexual fantasies (involving dominance, for instance). Still, Berman's approach is one of restraint and exploration. For instance, she sends one woman for a medical exam after learning of her lack of sexual appetite. It turns out Berman was right to do so: the woman was perimenopausal and probably in need of hormone therapy.

On another episode, Berman sends a particularly combative couple to tantric sexual healing courses to avert the husband's predilection for premature ejaculation. The teachers of this course proceed to demonstrate relaxation techniques using a crystal phallus and a pillowy prop vagina.

Later in the same show, night vision cameras capture the couple "practicing" in their hotel room bed, though nothing untoward is actually depicted on camera.

Dr. Berman's therapy is for all people; black, white, Latino, gay and straight, and although there's certainly a prurient aspect to this series, it's highly likely that any couple could learn a thing or two from Berman's ministrations.

The series is not available on DVD.

SLEEPER CELL

(Showtime) (RENEWED) (60 minutes) (Various nights; 10:00 pm, EST; December 11, 2005-December 18, 2005) Showtime. Created by: Ethan Reiff and Cyrus Voris. Executive Producers: Ethan Reiff and Cyrus Voris. Producer: Janet Tamarao. Camera: Matthew Jensen, Robert Primes. Film Editors: Lance Anderson, Rob Kuhns, Tony Solomons. Music: Mike Grene, Paul Haslinger. Written by: Michael C. Martin, Kamran Pasha, Ethan Reiff, Janet Tamaro, Cyros Voris, Alexander Woo. Directed by: Ziad Doueri, Guy Ferland, Nick Gomez, Leon Ichaso, Clark Johnson, Leslie Libman, Rick Wallace.

CAST
Michael Ealy (Darwyn)
Oded Fehr (Farik)
James LeGros (Ray Fuller)
Alex Nesic (Christian)
Melissa Sagemiller (Gayle)
Blake Shields (Tommy)

This harrowing dramatic series from Showtime concerns an African-American FBI agent who infiltrates (in Los Angeles) a cabal of Islamic militants, fanatical "holy warriors" bent on repeating the horrors of 9/11 to put "steel in the spine of the Muslim nation."

Sleeper Cell stars the charismatic Michael Ealy as the FBI protagonist, a gentle Muslim named Darwyn. That's a good choice of names, because one immediately senses this sensitive man—isolated deep under cover—will indeed need to prove fit (not to mention nimble) to survive life inside a terrorist cell. His boss in the bureau, Ray Fuller (James Le Gros) is a friend and a supporter, but even Ray can't help Darwyn when push comes to shove. And—unfortunately—Fuller comes to a bloody end midway through the series' run of ten hour-long episodes.

In the first episode of *Sleeper Cell*, Darwyn is released from the Federal Penitentiary at Lompoc (a ruse to gain the trust of radicals), and is contacted at a synagogue by an Islamic terrorist named Faris-al-Farik (a very menacing, charismatic Oded Fehr). Darwyn is soon taken into the group's confidence on a first mission while at the same time falling in love with one terrorist's neighbor, a single mom named Gayle (Melissa Sagemiller). Among the other members of the cell are a mad-dog Frenchman named Christian (Alex Nesic) who is angry that his wife is planning to leave him, and Tommy (Blake Shields), a spoiled American rich boy who wants to get back at his mother.

A compelling cross between *24* and *Prison Break*, *Sleeper Cell* is beautifully photographed and packed with moments of pulse-pounding anxiety; such as the disturbing instance wherein a terrorist named "Bobby" (Abdullah Habib) is punished by his fellow jihadists for boasting about their upcoming mission to a relative in Egypt. The other terrorists bury the guy up to his neck in desert sands…and then throw rocks at his skull until the battered man is dead. Nice.

Each episode follows Darwyn as he attempts to learn the particulars of the cell's plot against America, maintain his own belief in Islam as a peaceful religion, and at the same time prove his loyalty to the cutthroat terrorists. Early on (episode #2), there's a plan to release weapons-grade anthrax into a shopping mall's air conditioning unit (a plotline mirrored on *24* this season), but it is just a rehearsal for the bigger attack.

In a later installment, Darwyn is enlisted to help the cell raise money for its attack, because—as one villain points out—"waging holy war on American soil is cost effective…but it isn't free." This mission leads Darwyn and the others to Mexico and murky moral territory where they unwittingly become involved with child prostitutes and make a choice about how to help them.

Friends or foes?
Faris-al-Farik (Oded Fehr, left) and Darwyn (Michael Ealy, right) plot terror in Showtime's
SLEEPER CELL.

Yet another compelling narrative involves the terrorist cell murdering a scholar who has been attempting to deprogram Al-Qaeda sympathizers and who considers radical Islam "cultist." The series finally culminates in nailbiting fashion with Farik's attack on Dodger Stadium, "home to America's favorite pasttime." His plot involves releasing a cloud of deadly phosgene gas into the stadium where the death toll could be over 100,000.

With only minutes before the attack, Darwyn is on his own to stop the terrorists and save the day…

In general, critics appreciated *Sleeper Cell*. It was deemed "involving enough to be a sleeper hit"[82] and termed "pounding excitement."[83]

However, it's not just a compelling action-ride like *24*. *Sleeper Cell* is also groundbreaking. It's the first series in American history to feature a practicing Muslim as the central protagonist; both an action hero and a romantic figure. In the series, Darwyn wrestles with his faith and is ultimately reaffirmed in it.

The show is available on DVD.

Watch out for Tonya Harding!!!
Kristy Swanson and partner Lloyd Eisler take the crown in **SKATING WITH CELEBRITIES**.

SKATING WITH CELEBRITIES

(FOX) (RENEWED) (60 minutes) (Wednesdays at 9:00 pm, EST; January 18, 2006–March 2, 2006) A. Smith & Co. Productions. Executive Producers: Arthur Smith, Kent Weed. Co-Executive Producer: Rob Dustin. Produced by: Terry Coyle, Jordan Beck, Faye Stapleton. Film Editors: Roger Bartlett, Dave Basinki, Chad Dickman, Bryan M. Horne, Marc Markley, Rick Weis. Directed by: Kent Wood.

CAST
Scott Hamilton (Host)
Summer Sanders (Host)
Dorothy Hamill (Judge)
Mark Lund (Judge)
John Nicks (Judge)

CONTESTANTS
Tai Babilonia, Todd Bridges, Bruce Jenner, Dave Coulier, Nancy Kerrigan, Deborah Gibson, Kurt Browning, Jillian Barberie, John Zimmerman, Kristy Swanson, Lloyd Eisler.

Starting in January 2006, FOX began airing the unscripted reality series *Skating with Celebrities* to capitalize on the unexpected (and inexplicable…) popularity of *Dancing with the Stars* and *So You Think You Can Dance*. Only this time, all the performing would—naturally—take place… on ice. Olympic Gold Medalist winner Scott Hamilton was assigned to cohost this circus with Summer Sanders, and then it was just a matter of teaming up famous skaters with "stars" and watching the bruises form.

For seven weeks, America tuned in as celebrities took spills on the ice and their skills gradually improved. There were six teams on the show competing against each other, each one coupling a skater with a celebrity (or what passes for celebrities on reality shows). *Full House* (1987–1995) star Dave Coulier coupled with clubbed skater Nancy Kerrigan; seventies icon Bruce Jenner (a gold medalist in the decathlon) doubled with Tai Babilonia; faded pop star Debbie Gibson teamed with Kurt Browning; Jillian Barberie worked with John Zimmerman; *Diff'rent Strokes* (1978–1986) former child-star Todd Bridges kept it real with Jenni Meno; and film's *Buffy the Vampire Slayer* Kristy Swanson teamed with Lloyd Eisler.

The skating teams were assessed by a panel of three judges (sound familiar?): nice Dorothy Hamill, mean British-sounding fellow John Nick, and bland Mark Lund. The basis was two criteria: technical difficulty and artistic merit. Each week, the skaters also had to perform according to a carefully selected theme. These were "music from the movies," the 1970s (meaning, inevitably, disco) and songs from the current Top 40. One team was eliminated each week until the final episode, which pitted the Barberie duet against Swanson's team.

In the end, Swanson and Eisler were victorious, and so was FOX, which aired *Skating with Celebrities* right after powerhouse *American Idol*.

The series is not currently available on DVD.

SONS & DAUGHTERS

(ABC) (CANCELED) (60 minutes) (Tuesdays at 9:00 pm; March 7, 2006–April 6, 2006) Broadway Video/NBC Universal. Created by: Fred Goss. Executive Producers: Jo Ann Alfano, Fred Goss, Nick Holly, Lorne Michaels. Produced by: Andrew Singer. Camera: Jeff Ravitz. Film Editors: Blue, Jon Corn, Bradley Warden. Music: Adam Gorgoni, William J. Berry. Written by: Jordana Arkin, Julie Bean, Will Calhoun, Fred Goss, Nick Holly, Tom Huang. Directed by: Dan O'Conner, David Steinberg, Anson Williams, Lorie Zerweck.

CAST

Fred Goss (Cameron Walker)
Gillian Vigman (Liz Walker)
Jerry Lambert (Don Fenton)
Alison Quinn (Sharon Fenton)
Max Gail (Wendel Halbert)
Dee Wallace (Colleen Ahalbert)
Amanda Walsh (Jenna Halbert)
Desmond Harrington (Wylie Blake)
Greg Pitts (Tommy White)

Fred Goss, the mastermind behind the improvised cable comedy *Significant Others*, brought his unique brand of humor to ABC for a short-lived series about a large, dysfunctional family, in *Sons & Daughters*.

The series starred Goss as Cameron, married to his second wife, Liz (Gillian Vigman) and raising three children; one from a previous marriage. He also had to contend with his sister, Sharon (Alison Quinn), his half-sister Jenna (Amanda Walsh), and his mother's (Dee Wallace) new husband, Wendel (Max Gail).

Goss explained how the series was created in improv form. "Instead of just being this raw improv from the actors, it's more like we're all writing it on the fly, both in front of the camera and behind it," he told *Blogcritics.org*, "There are no jokes in the script. There's no dialogue in the script. What we'll do is we'll write the basic story first, so everything makes sense and we know what the drive is. Then we go through and we start to analyze what can you possibly do to get comedy out of this. Then we'll do another pass where we go through and say 'let's work in a couple of good physical bits.'"[84]

Despite such an interesting way of crafting a family sitcom, *Sons & Daughters* suffered from a lack of originality in terms of plotting. In fact, many of the narratives featured on the series were already old when *I Love Lucy* and *The Honeymooners* were on. In one episode, "Surprise Party," Cameron doesn't tell anyone he's been laid off because he doesn't want to spoil his 40th birthday party for the family. In another episode, "The Homecoming," his long-estranged father returns to dredge up old, uncomfortable emotions.

A family get-together goes comedically and horribly wrong in "BBQ Therapy," and Cameron feels guilty after a fight with Colleen causes her to experience chest pains in "Hospital Visit." As these brief synopses reveal, there's nothing original or forward-looking in the actual material.

The ratings were not kind to *Sons & Daughters*. The series aired opposite the popular FOX drama *House*, and then—even worse—had to face head-to-head an ascendant *American Idol*. ABC canceled the series after just a half-dozen episodes.

Not currently available on DVD.

SOUTH BEACH

(UPN) (CANCELED) (60 minutes) (Wednesdays at 8:00 pm, EST; January 11, 2006-February 22, 2006) Flame Televison/Nuyoricon Productions/Paramount. Created by: Matthew Cirulnick. Executive Producers: Simon Fields, Tony Krantz, Philip Levens, Jennifer Lopez. Co-Executive Producer: Matthew Cirulnick. Produced by: Terry Miller, Antoinette Stella. Camera: Tom Priestly. Film Editors: Shawn Paper, Michel Schultz. Music: Michael Wandmacher. Written by: Matt and Greg Cirulnick, Melody Fox, Peter Hume, Scott Kaufer, Phillip Levens. Directed by: John Ensler, Tim Hunter, David Jackson, Peter Medak, Whitney Ransick.

CAST

Vanessa Williams (Elizabeth Bauer)
Marcus Coloma (Matt Evans)
Chris Johnson (Vincent)
Lee Thompson Young (Alex Bauer)
Odette Yustman (Arielle Casta)
Giancarlo Esposito (Robert Fuentes)
Adrianne Palicki (Brianna)

"Even paradise has a dark side," warned the advertisements for this ill-fated soap opera from executive producer, J.Lo. It was bad enough that the series filmed in Miami during Hurricane Season 2005—the worst ever, but the ratings were terrible from the start. The much-heralded two-hour premiere on UPN tanked, and things never got better for *South Beach*.

South Beach is a bikini-clad, beach series about two guys from New York, Vincent (Chris Johnson) and Matt (Marcus Coloma), who give up life in the frozen north and head to South Beach. Matt is making the trip because he wants to hook up with his former girlfriend, an aspiring model named Arielle (Odette Yustman). When he arrives, however, he discovers that Arielle is dating Alex (Lee Thompson Young), the owner of South Beach's hottest nightclub, Nocturnal.

While Vincent gets embroiled in the seedy criminal world of Miami, working for a crime lord named Fuentes (Giancarlo Esposito), Matt gets a job at The Hotel Soleil, an exclusive resort owned and operated by Alex's hot-to-trot mother, Elizabeth (Vanessa Williams)...a woman with a well-known penchant for younger men. Brianna (Adrianne Palicki) is another model, and therefore both friend and competitor to Arielle.

Rife with nubile young flesh, this soap opera followed these characters as they tried to make a go of life in South Beach. They dealt with rappers, corrupt cops, crime, and Miami's renowned "Fashion Week." The primary settings were the Soleil, Nocturnal and—of course—the beach.

South Beach earned particularly savage reviews and the final episode title reflected the thoughts of many critics. "It Looked Like Somebody's Nightmare."

Not currently available on DVD.

SUPERNATURAL

(WB) (RENEWED) (60 minutes) (Tuesdays at 8:00 pm, EST; September 13, 2005-May 4, 2006) Kripke Enterprises/Wonderland Sound & Vision/Warner Bros. Created by: Eric Kripke. Executive Producers: Eric Kripke, McG, David Nutter, Robert Singer. Co-Executive Producers: Richard Hatem, Kim Manners, John Shiban. Produced by: Peter Johnson, Cyrus Yavneh. Camera: Serge Ladouceur. Film Editors: David Ekstrom, Paul Karasick, Anthony Pinker. Music: Jay Gruska. Written by: Terri Hughes Burton, Bill Coakley, Sera Gamble, Richard Hatem, Eric Kripke, Ron Milbauer, John Shiban, Raelle Tucker. Directed by: Guy Bee, Peter Ellis, Kin Girotti, David Jackson, Allan Kroeker, Kim Manners, Robert Duncan McNeill, David Nutter, Robert Singer.

CAST
Jared Padalecki (Sam Winchester)
Jensen Ackles (Dean Winchester)

The new horror series *Supernatural* is the season's second variation on the tried-and-true *The X-Files* format (the first being ABC's short-lived *Night Stalker*). The only significant difference is that *Supernatural* clearly skews younger. Tom Shales aptly described the series as "essentially the Hardy Boys go Ghost busting" and *USA Today* noted that *Supernatural* is "*Route 66* meets the *X-Files* and *Star Wars* at a truck stop," because of the series' road setting.

Supernatural follows the spooky adventures of two twentysomething brothers, sensitive Sam (*Gilmore Girls* alum Jared Padalecki) and wiseacre Dean (*Dark Angel* alum Jensen Ackles) Winchester, as they—in their own terminology—"hunt" for the mysterious and malevolent otherworldly forces that murdered their mother twenty years ago. The Winchesters are also hot on the heels of their missing father (Jeffrey Dean Morgan), who has

made this hunt his life's quest and who has disappeared; conveniently leaving behind map coordinates and clues in a journal that his sons can interpret and follow. They do so in their hot rod, meeting new ghosts (and new love interests like *Angel's* Amy Acker) at each new exit.

In *Supernatural's* pilot episode, Sam and Dean imitate Federal Marshals to investigate a town where a manifestation called a "Woman in White" (i.e. a "Lady in White") lures unfaithful men to unpleasant ends. The second adventure, "Wendigo," involves the brothers coming to the aid of campers under assault by a carnivorous Native American manifestation of evil. Later episodes such as "Phantom Traveler" posit ghostly terror on a jetliner, deal with urban legends ("Hook Man"), and resuscitated Japanese movie (*The Ring; Grudge*) "revenge from the grave" horror ("Dead in the Water").

Although renewed for a second season (where it appears on the new CW Network) *Supernatural* started strong and then went downhill quickly. Following in the tradition of several great horror films, the series begins with what this author terms the "deadly preamble" or crime in the past, in this case the unusual and terrifying murder of the Winchester matriarch.

Here, the show is at its creepy best as mom awakens in the middle of darkest night to the sound on the baby monitor of Sam crying. When she goes to his crib, she spots a lurking, shadowy figure (one that she mistakes for her husband) who urges her to be silent. She nods sleepily and heads downstairs, only to realize her husband is asleep in front of the TV and that the dark figure with her child is an intruder…or something worse. David Nutter directed the pilot and this *X-Files* veteran knows precisely how to make a vignette like this one a frightening, self-contained "scare sequence."

"Pull my Finger!" Dean (Jensen Ackles, left) and Sam Winchester (Jared Padalecki, right) confront the supernatural in... **SUPERNATURAL**.

Despite a strong opening, the pilot quickly fails to live up to potential; as do most followup episodes. The Winchester boys inevitably follow in their father's footsteps since he's left them a map of his travels, and routinely encounter the supernatural. They do so without flinching, without goose bumps, and mostly without skepticism.

Worse, for a show meant to blend *Route 66* with *The X-Files*, there is no actual sense of "the road" in the series. No sense of being trapped for long hours in a car on the highway, fighting road hypnosis, sleeping, trying to locate an obscure spot on map; being in a strange location trying to get ones' bearings. There's no atmosphere like that at all. The Winchester boys inevitably reach their destination comfortably, feel right at home, vanquish the supernatural forces, and go on their way. They might as well be beamed down into each haunted spot for all the atmosphere on the show.

The X-Files was so scary that it kept a generation of horror movie fans at home on Friday nights, yet *Supernatural* treats the unknown almost as the Mafia...an evil organization out to whack the Winchester boys. There is no prevailing world view on *Supernatural* (for instance, belief vs. science) and therefore no uncertainty, no sense of mystery. Furthermore, the boys have very little curiosity about their "enemy." Basically, their research about the supernatural comes down to checking their dad's notes, and one begins to wonder why—other than capturing

the young demographic—the series doesn't concern him rather than these two representatives of callow youth.

The running character gags on *Supernatural* are mostly lame too. Since Sam and Dean don't have the FBI behind them (like Mulder and Scully), they routinely pretend to be officials like marshals and forestry agents. They pick names like "Crockett and Tubbs" or "Han and Luke" for this charade but in reality, their ruse would fool no one; certainly not the town sheriffs and authority figures they cow with such obvious jokes. For one, their youth should set off suspicion. For another, it seems like nobody but Dean and Sam have ever watched a movie or TV show, or is aware of the pop culture.

Writing for *The Chicago Tribune*, Maureen Ryan enunciated the series' flaws: "What *Supernatural* lacks," she suggested "is the rich mystery and moral complexity of truly great horror fare such as *Rosemary's Baby*. Genre fans used to the emotional depth and extraordinary storytelling of *Buffy the Vampire Slayer* and *Angel* will find that this show is not even remotely in *Buffy's* or *Angel's* league."[85]

Despite flaccid, hackneyed storytelling and the lack of compelling *dramatis personae*, *Supernatural* proved one of the WB's few freshman hits during the 2005–2006 season. When genre shows such as *Threshold, Night Stalker, Surface*, and *Invasion* all went down, *Supernatural* survived.

The first season is available on DVD.

SURFACE

(NBC) (CANCELED) (60 minutes) (Mondays at 8:00 pm, EST; September 19, 2005-February 6, 2006) NBC Universal. Created by: Jonas and Josh Pate. Executive Producers: Jonas and Josh Pate. Co-Executive Producer: Jeffrey Reiner. Produced by: Jay Beattie, Dan Dworkin, Darcy Meyers, Ed Mikovich. Camera: John Aronson, Cary Capo, William Wages. Film Editors: Louise Innes, Leon Ortiz-Gil, Steve Polivka. Music: W.G. Snuffy Walden, Joseph Williams. Written by: Jason Cahill, Jonas and Josh Pate. Directors: Felix Enriquez Akala, Aaron Lipstadt, Josh and Jonas Pates, Jeff Woolnough.

CAST

Lake Bell (Dr. Laura Daughtery)
Jay R. Ferguson (Rich Connelly)
Carter Jenkins (Miles Bennett)
Ian Anthony Dale (Davis Lee)
Leighton Meester (Savannah Bennett)
Eddie Hassell (Phil Nance)

Surface is one of the most unusual and flat-out entertaining TV series to come down the pike in the 2005–2006 season. Notice that I didn't write that it was "original." Yes, it's unique for television (another high concept program), but *Surface* (originally called *Fathom*) cribs liberally from the greatest movie blockbusters of the modern era. That's almost okay though: the Spielberg-ian *Surface*—a TV series about giant reptilian sea monsters—plays like a summer movie each and every week, only serialized. If viewers dig old monster movies and the Spielberg canon…this effort is like manna from Heaven.

In *Surface*, something strange is happening under the water (just like in *Jaws,* 1975). Diverse characters, including a gorgeous marine biologist, Dr. Laura Daughtery (Lake Bell), a working-class Southern dude in an unhappy marriage, Rich (Jay R. Ferguson), and a precocious teenager named Miles (Carter Jenkins) become entangled with a rapidly expanding mystery. They all experience *ahem* close encounters with heretofore unknown sea creatures. *Giant* sea creatures.

Each character reacts differently to the discovery. Laura wants to learn more. She's an obsessed scientist who believes that exposing this new life form will make a career for her and change biology as we understand it. Rich is clearly the Richard Dreyfuss character from *Close Encounters* (1977). His brother gets killed by one of the creatures while they're on a dive in the ocean, and Rich becomes obsessed. He experiences visions of a strange light at the bottom of the ocean; just the way Dreyfuss' character in Spielberg's classic fixated on Devil's Tower.

As for Miles, he encounters one of the baby monsters, whom he names Nimrod. He promptly decides to bring Nim home and keep him as a pet. Yes, this is the *E.T.* (1982) scenario regurgitated, as a little boy befriends an "outsider"/alien with unusual abilities.

The stories of Laura, Rich, and Miles all join up (eventually) on *Surface*, but the series also plays like an extended disaster film, with diverse characters in different cities all sharing part of the same crisis or mystery, but from different perspectives. The monsters, of course, represent that mystery. They're giant sea lizards who can generate electromagnetic shifts and pulses; and whose presence is killing off ocean life by the ton. Worse, the beasts are actually reforming the Earth's surface to be more to their liking. If they succeed and survive, they'll ascend to the apex of the food chain and human beings will be in real trouble. Just imagine a Godzilla roaming in every city…

Generally, each episode of *Surface* also features a signature "monster" moment that generates shock and awe or laughter, depending on the success of the special

Glamorous Dr. Laura Daughtery (Lake Bell) muses about giant sea monsters in **SURFACE**.

effects, which prove variable. *Surface* episodes feature a boat attack on the waters of Australia as a sea monster breaks the surf and swallows a fishing boat in one gulp. Another episode opens with a whirlpool vortex opening up on Lake Travis in Texas. A small motorboat with a teenybopper aboard gets sucked into it while a parasailer watches in terror and dismay above, tethered to the doomed craft. Another "teaser" moment depicts a small jet breaking up in midair during a fierce storm caused by the traveling monster herd. One of the best special effects moments occurs at the bottom of the sea, where the monsters dwell inside volcanoes (they're immune to heat), and the shot of these giant things rolling around and luxuriating in lava is terrific.

On the other hand, some effects in *Surface* appear ridiculous. The sequence involving Old Faithful exploding in Yellowstone National Park is terrible…some of the worst process work I've seen on TV since *Babylon 5* (1993–1999). Also, the closing images of the series—a CGI pullback revealing that Wilmington, North Carolina, and indeed the whole Southeast seaboard, has been devastated in a "tele"-tsunami (caused by the giant sea monsters)—are laughably fake.

Surface proceeds along two distinct plot lines after Rich and Laura team up. In their plot line, they construct a makeshift submarine and pilot it to the bottom of the ocean to videotape images of the sea creatures laying eggs. The trip goes badly, and they're trapped at the bottom of the sea with diminishing air. Eventually, through their own resourcefulness (and a little push from the beasties) they return to the surface with videotape in hand.

After they're rescued at sea by a helicopter, Laura and Rich hitchhike to San Francisco and peddle their videotape to a reporter who works for NBC (cross-promotion synergy!!!). Their footage of the "American Nessie" airs on MSNBC's "Countdown" starring Keith Olbermann (who guest stars on the show), but Laura is discredited and made to look a fool on national TV. At least she can comfort herself by the knowledge that only a couple of hundred thousand people watch MSNBC each night. Anyway, this prime-time appearance gets the duo tagged by armed operatives of the "Agency for Strategic Intelligence," and they flee their hotel room. Really and truly fugitives now, Rich and Laura manage an escape (and Rich steals a gun) but are contacted by a secret benefactor, one utilizing technology outside "the public domain."

Consequently, Laura visits the secret headquarters of "Mr. Big," their hidden ally. Turns out Mr. Big is a Mrs., a scientist (played by Martha Plimpton) who once worked for a nameless Corporation ("a shell within a shell within a shell") to alter "RNA Enzymes." The short story: she (and about 2,500 other scientists) engineered the sea creatures now making mincemeat of the food chain. Laura seems disappointed by this discovery because she wanted the creatures to be naturally occurring "creations" rather than designed by the hand of man. She asks the Plimpton character why anyone would design these ravenous sea monsters, and Mrs. Big's response is the classic line from any overreaching scientist in a monster movie: "Because we could."

While all this is occurring, far away in North Carolina, young Miles lands himself in deep legal trouble after stealing a car to protect the baby monster, Nimrod, and ultimately must send his scaly little buddy back to the ocean. However, Nimrod returns with a school of his cohorts and Miles fears that little Nim has murdered a fisherman. Turns out instead that a bunch of the little critters are living in the shallows near an appetizing electrical cable (which the creatures feed on).

Miles nearly dies after being attacked by the sea monsters in the shallows. The bite, however, instead grants Miles some sort of "communion" with Nimrod, and he also possesses some of the lizard's abilities. His hands don't prune after being in water (!) and more importantly, Miles now appears capable of affecting nearby electrical fields. Eventually, Miles became a sort of pied piper to Nim and the other critters, leading them out to sea.

Surface ends after fifteen hour-long episodes with Laura Daughtery's portentous declaration, *"It's a New World."* She states this from a vantage point atop a church steeple in a modern American city on the flooded East Coast of America…now overrun by green sea monsters. By climaxing on this catastrophic and apocalyptic note, *Surface* proved to have the courage of its nutty convictions. It would have been tempting to end on an easier, less-expensive note, one that wouldn't turn the universe of *Surface* upside down. But instead, the writers and creators of this series (The Pate Brothers) selected the hard way, and followed through with the logical outcome, which involves irrevocable damage to our environment.

It would have been great if NBC had renewed the nutty *Surface*, but low ratings precluded a second season.

The complete series is available on DVD for all those who love sea monsters and cheesy disaster movies.

TEACHERS

(NBC) (CANCELED) (30 minutes) (Tuesdays at 9:30 pm; March 28, 2006–May 2, 2006) Two Soups Productions/NBC Universal. Executive Producers: Matt Tarses, Bill Wrubel. Produced by: Matthew Nodella. Camera: Bill Berner. Film Editor: Peter Chakos. Music: Rick Cowling. Written by: Will Calhoun, Michael Lisbe, Robin Shorr, Matt Tarses. Directed by: James Burrows, Gail Mancuso, Bill Wrubel.

CAST
Justin Bartha (Jeff)
Sarah Alexander (Alice)
Deon Richmond (Calvin)
Phil Hendrie (Dick)
Sarah Shahi (Tina)
Kali Rocha (Principal Emma Wiggins)
Matt Winston (Mitch)

Another dead-on-arrival sitcom, *Teachers* is a tepid remake (like *The Office*) of a popular British series...only without the wit, humor, or subtlety of the original venture. *Teachers* follows the adventures of another young slacker, this time Jeff (Justin Bartha) a teacher employed at a New Jersey High School. His buds are Calvin (Deon Richmond) and Dick (Phil Hendrie), fellow teachers and partners in crime. Brit Sarah Alexander plays Alice, another fellow educator and the focus of Jeff's unrequited attention and love.

Yes, it's actually *another* series about a young man hopelessly and blindly in love with a woman who doesn't want to give him the time of day. Kali Rocha portrays Jeff's foil, Principal Wiggins, and Mitch (Matt Winston) is the obnoxious, run-to-the-principal teacher who doesn't cotton to Jeff's unconventional methods and manner.

This situation comedy ran for six episodes in the spring of 2006 and drew poisonous reviews. *The Boston Globe* called it a "slavishly dopey comedy," and that was about the best grade *Teachers* could hope for. Various episodes hammered home the tired notion of Jeff being in love with Alice. In "Substitute," the series premiere, he hit on a hot substitute, Tina (Sarah Shahi) in an attempt to make Alice jealous. In "Prom," Jeff asked Alice to the prom as a fellow chaperone, and in "Schoolympics" he tried to impress her with his coaching/training skills during the annual battle against a rival school, Caulfield Prep.

For a series set at a school as "the workplace," *Teachers* bore precious little resemblance to any real school in history, and the plots concerning school issues seemed almost secondary. In "Field Trip," Jeff raised the ire of a parent's association after taking his class to see *Romeo and Juliet*. Yes, an acknowledged Shakespeare classic—taught in American high schools since time immemorial—was the unlikely source of the tussle. Couldn't the series have actually utilized a genuinely controversial play instead, such as *Angels in America,* or *The Vagina Monologues*? Nope, because someone in Kansas or Oklahoma might not have heard of those dramas, I guess.

Everything about *Teachers* is prepackaged, rote and woefully generic. The biggest crime of all? Before being canceled by NBC, *Teachers* still earned higher ratings than the brilliant but lowly rated *Scrubs*, which functioned as its lead-in.

Not available at this time on DVD.

THIEF

(FX) (CANCELED) (60 minutes) (Thursdays at 10:00 pm, EST; March 28, 2006–May 2, 2006) Regency Television. Executive Producers: David Manson, Norman Morrill, Gavin Polone. Produced by: Penny Adams, Iain Paterson. Camera: Uta Brieswitz, Peter Sora. Film Editors: Conrad Gonzalez, Paul Trejo. Music: Richard Marvin, John Van Tongeren. Written by: Rafael Alvarez, Norman Morill, David Manson. Directed by: John David Coles, Paul McGuinan, Dean White.

CAST
Andre Braugher (Nick Atwater)
Malik Yoba (Elmo)
Yancey Arias (Gabo)
Clifton Collins Jr. (Jack)
Mae Whitman (Tammi)
Will Yun Lee (Vincent)
Michael Rooker (Detective John Hayes)
Clayne Crawford (Izzy)
Dina Meyer (Wanda)
Bitty Schram (Lila)
Linda Hamilton (Roselyn)

This six-episode series from FX is so harrowing and gut wrenching that it just might dissolve your stomach lining. Like life, the series *Thief* has an uncanny way of turning suddenly, horribly wrong just when one least expects it. On the surface, it's a crime drama about a big heist, but *Thief* is also a gorgeously shot character piece; and a study in probability—of what *can* happen to the best laid plans of mice and men.

Set in New Orleans, *Thief* follows a character named Nick Atwater. He's brought to life in fascinating shades by ex-*Homicide* star Braugher, who won an Emmy for his portrayal. Nick's a thief and a crook, and—as he soon finds out—he's also going to have to act the role of father for his teenage stepdaughter, Tammi (Mae Whitman) following the death of his wife, Wanda (Dina Meyer). This is easier said than done.

Meanwhile, Nick gathers his gang of thieves, including a tech man named Izzy (Clayne Crawford), a fence, Roselyn (Linda Hamilton), and his old friend Gabo (Yancey Arias). This time they all have their eyes set on a $30 million payday, but to get it they'll have to steal the dough from a plane *en route* to Colombia (and controlled by the U.S. government). Worse, as fate would have it, several opponents are already triangulating on Nick, including a crooked cop, Hayes (Michael Rooker) and a Chinese assassin, Vincent (Will Yun Lee).

In tense, uncompromising terms, *Thief* follows the progression of the heist. "Flight" dramatizes the day of the operation, a day when things go horribly awry for Nick and the others. There's a Judas amongst the group, and Tammi picks that day to run away. The final episode of the series, "In the Wind" is all about the heist's aftermath, as the survivors of the heist try to escape New Orleans with their booty.

Make no assumptions about who lives and who dies in *Thief*. It's cutthroat, surprising and gritty in its depiction of a world that spirals out of control.

Not yet available on DVD.

30 DAYS

(FX) (RENEWED) (60 minutes) (Wednesdays at 10:00 pm, EST; July 26, 2006-August 30, 2006) Actual Reality Pictures/ Borderline TV/Reveille Productions. Executive Producers: Mala Chapple, R.J. Cutler, Dave Hamilton, Nick McKinney, Howard Owens, Benjamin Silverman, Morgan Spurlock, Angela Victor. Produced by: Sebastian Doggart, Alan LaGarde, Mark Landsman, Blake Levin, Monica Martino, Patrick McManamee, Chris Nee, Fred Richel. Camera: Brian Danitz, Mike Desjarlais, Steve Hollis, Sarah Levy, John Mans, Bob Maraist, Amanda Micheli, Gary Russell. Film Editors: Doug Abel, Poppy Das, Greg Finton, Andy Robertson, Azin Samari. Music: Jeff Cardoni. Directed by: Morgan Spurlock.

CAST
Morgan Spurlock (Host)

Morgan Spurlock's 2005 celebrated documentary, *Super Size Me* not only took on McDonald's and the fast food industry in contemporary America, it was nominated for a gaggle of awards, including an Academy Award for Best Documentary Feature. That movie followed producer and director Morgan Spurlock on a month-long investigation of American eating habits as he charted the effects of eating nothing but food from the McDonald's menu for an agonizing thirty days. What he found on this quest was astonishing: nearly thirty pounds gained in four weeks, a decreased sexual appetite, and most frightening of all…liver damage (i.e. "pickling") on a scale with alcoholism.

Spurlock brought the same format (a month-long or "30-day" investigation of one topic) to television for the FX cable channel during the dog days of summer in 2005. The series produced six hour-long episodes of varying quality that each gazed at an important topic (such as alcoholism, religion, sexual orientation) in our daily lives. *30 Days'* finest installment from the first season is also the first one produced and aired, entitled "Minimum Wage."

In this episode, Morgan and his vegan girlfriend, Alex, try to make a go of life making just $5.15 an hour. It's a long, desperate haul and the documentary exposes how expensive life in America has become. And how, unfortunately, even two people working two full-time minimum wage jobs simply can't survive for long, especially when one factors in health care, children, and transportation. It's a shocking, illuminating hour, very much in the progressive spirit of *Super Size Me.*

Alas, the remainder of *30 Days* plays a bit more like the unscripted series *Black. White.* as the scenarios became increasingly exploitive and less educational. Followup episodes from the initial season find a straight man moving into the gay community in San Francisco for a month ("Straight Man in a Gay World") and a Christian moving into the Muslim community in Michigan for thirty days ("Muslims and America"). The nadir of the series is an episode involving a mother's plan to go toe-to-toe with her daughter's binge drinking, entitled "Binge Drinking Mom." Morgan, how could you?

30 Days second season dealt with ideas such as immigration, the Atheist/Christian divide, outsourcing and the hot-button issue of abortion (pro-life versus pro choice.) The second season began airing on FX in late July of 2006.

Only the first season has been released on DVD.

THREE WISHES

(NBC) (CANCELED) (60 minutes) (Fridays at 9:00 pm, EST; September 23, 2005-December 9, 2005) Glassman Media/June Road Productions/NBC Universal. Executive Producers: Andrew Glasman, Jason Raff. Co-Executive Producers: Lewis Fenton, Grant Julian, Lillian Lim. Produced by: Tim Graydos, Mike Aho, Nate McIntosh, Emily Sinclair. Camera: Guido Frenzel. Film Editors: Jeff Bartsch, Avi Fisher, Michael Friedman. Music: Bob Thiele, Jr. Directed by: Tony Croll, Andrew Glassman, Jason Raff.

CAST

Amy Grant (Host)
Carter Oosterhouse (Carpenter)
Diane Mizota
Eric Stromer (Contractor)
Amanda Miler (Designer)

Five time Grammy Award–winning Christian singer Amy Grant was the host of this short-lived attempt to capture some of the *Extreme Makeover: Home Edition* demographic. In *Three Wishes*, Amy and a team of talented builders and specialists descend upon a town and seek out the most heartwrenching cases. *"If you could wish for one thing, what would it be?"* The show asked, and then—often under the radar of the wisher—Amy and her team would make it happen. In each episode, Amy's crew would grant three individuals their wishes, and Amy would take time to sing an inspirational song or two.

"When I heard about this show, I was extremely moved by NBC and the production company's concept to provide incredibly positive changes in the lives of different people," host Grant noted. "Seeing the initial prep work the producers had done for the pilot episode gave me reason to look at my own life—and remind myself, once again, to never underestimate the impact that one life can have on another."[86]

In the ten episodes that aired between September and December of 2005, the *Three Wishes* crew traveled the United States. In Sonora, California the team made sad people happy by providing a poor school with a new football field, helping a child be adopted by his beloved stepfather, and aiding an athlete injured in a car accident get an expensive surgery that would enable her to play sports again.

In Brooking, South Dakota, the crew came to the aid of a man dying of an inoperable brain tumor, and helped him stage a family reunion. In Covington, Georgia, a woman seeking her biological mother was one of the recipients of the good deeds.

Three Wishes is a maudlin, tear-provoking show, and yet how can anybody complain too strenuously about a series that exists simply to do nice things for people (and feature lots of corporate product placement)? Or, as Amy Grant noted in *TV Guide*, "Real fulfillment is found in proportion to how we invest in each other's lives."[87]

Although NBC unconventionally promoted the show by marketing primarily in smaller Red State cities including Des Moines, Nashville, and Salt Lake City, *Three Wishes* regularly placed only third in its Friday time slot, making it a midseason casualty.

It has not been released on DVD.

Amy Grant (right) makes dreams come true on the feel-good reality series **THREE WISHES**.

THRESHOLD

(CBS) (CANCELED) (60 minutes) (Fridays at 10:00 pm, EST; Tuesdays at 10:00 pm, EST; September 16, 2005-November 22, 2005) Braga Productions/Heyday Productions/Paramount. Created by: Bragi F. Schut. Executive Producers: Brannon Braga, David S. Goyer, David Heyman. Co-Executive Producers: Anne McGrail, Dan O'Shannon, Marc Rosen., Bragi F. Schut. Producers: Andre Bormanis, David Livingston, Karen Moore. Camera: Steve Bernstein, Frank Byers. Film Editors: Heather MacDougall, Conrad Smart. Music: Ramin Djawadi, Steve Jablonsky. Written by: Amy Berg, Andre Bormanis, Brannon Braga, Andrew Colville, David S. Goyer, Anne McGrail, Barbara Nance, Dan O'Shannon, Bragi F. Schuti. Directed by: Peter Hymans, Bill L. Norton, David S. Goryer, David Jackson, Tim Matheson.

CAST
Carla Gugino (Dr. Molly Anne Caffrey)
Brian Van Holt (Sean Cavennaugh)
Brent Spiner (Dr. Nigel Fenway)
Robert Patrick Benedict (Lucas Pegg)
Peter Dinklage (Arthur Ramsey)
Charles S. Dutton (J.T. Baylock)

Of all the alien invasion and supernatural series bowing during the 2005–2006 season, *Threshold* ranks as the worst and most absurd; or more aptly, the most disappointing. The sci-fi series arises from the auspices of Brannon Braga, who produced the last several years of UPN's *Star Trek Voyager* (1995–2001) and *Enterprise* (2001–2005), and David Goyer, the writer/director from the prominent *Blade* movie franchise. These credentials promised at least a modicum of intelligence and wit, but both attributes proved to be in woefully short supply before CBS pulled the series due to low ratings.

Threshold is the tale of an alien invasion in contemporary, post-9/11 America. An alien signal has arrived on Earth and infected a ship at sea…causing insidious effects on the ship's crew and threatening the entire human race. If the signal's telepathic powers spread from the ship's crew to other humans, it will mutate rank-and-file people into alien "sleepers"—a metaphor for Al Qaeda—and the war is lost. Fortunately for mankind, fast-talking scientist Molly Ann Caffrey (Carla Gugino) has drafted a plan for just such an eventually, called "Threshold."

That plan, *unfortunately*, involves a phobic geek (Robert Patrick Benedict), a womanizing midget (Peter Dinklage), a divorced scientist (Brent Spiner), and a hulky, gun-toting agent (Brian Van Holt) slowly tracking down the alien signal wherever it pops up and hoping they can squelch it in time.

Glad to know the government is prepared for a crisis…

Each week on *Threshold,* the nefarious alien "signal," which can rewrite the genetic pattern of any material on Earth, organic or inorganic, is almost released. Then it is stopped at the last instant, while everyone breathes a sigh of relief in the finale.

In one episode of *Threshold*, called "Blood of the Children," the alien infection passes into a Military Academy, and the *Threshold* team must determine which cadet is compromised. The alien plan in this episode is one of the most ridiculous: the sleeper agent wants to gain access to the Internet and upload the genetics-altering signal to the World Wide Web, where 33 percent of the country's population would be infected in hours, at least according to Molly, who uses the spread of the "Paris Hilton sex tape" as her statistical model. Fortunately, the right cadet, Jenklow, is fingered, and the nefarious plan is stopped.

Okay, so viewers are asked to believe that these evil aliens—who are so powerful that they can rewrite human DNA from afar with one signal—*can't manage to upload a file on the Internet?* That their entire plan depends on getting one agent to upload one file onto the Net? Why do they choose a Military Academy, where (conveniently for the writers) only one room is wired with Internet access? Why not go somewhere else to upload the signal, say—to any home computer, a public library, or any dorm room on any college campus?

Another problem is that the aliens never attempt this plan again. Never attempt to send out three infected agents simultaneously and have all of them attempt the upload at the same time. Why? Just because the *Threshold* team stops it once doesn't mean the plan is a bad one, right?

The cast of **THRESHOLD**. Top: Brent Spiner (Dr. Fenway); middle: Charles S. Dutton (Baylock), Robert Patrick Benedict (Lucas); bottom: Brian Van Holt (Cavennaugh), Carla Gugino (Caffrey), Peter Dinklage (Arthur).

Unfortunately, *Threshold* is a series rife with this kind of narrative inconsistency. The worst example is an episode entitled "Pulse." The plot is basically the same, except substitute a cell phone network and iPods for the Internet. Those rascally aliens are back to their uploading tricks, and this time they get even closer to success…their signal threatens all of Miami. So what does the *Threshold* team do? They detonate an electromagnetic pulse over the city and shut down all networks, thus stopping the invasion. The coda of the episode is unintentionally hysterical. The boss of the *Threshold* unit, Baylock, notes happily that the Corps of Engineers is already deployed in Miami and will "have the power grid back up by nightfall." What?!

Audiences are supposed to swallow the idea that in the post-Katrina, post-9/11 age, the U.S. government response will be so effective and so quick as to fix an entire city in one night? That there were would be no American casualties? No looting in a major metropolis like Miami if it were rendered totally dark and totally incapacitated? In real life, the Corps of Engineers would take a week to prepare for their stint in Miami and there would be lawlessness in the meantime. And an electromagnetic pulse would take out cars, microwaves, ATMs, cell phones, everything! Hospitals would have no equipment, there would be no television. Buses wouldn't run, and that would mean no evacuation. *That's all going to be fixed overnight?* Who pays to repair all the cars?

The problem with *Threshold* is that the writers blithely pulse an entire American city and then end the episode on a happy note as if everything's okay. You could get away with that in a perfect universe, like *Star Trek*'s, but in 2006 America? Someone needs a reality check.

Secondly, the pulsing of Miami basically destroys the credibility of all future *Threshold* episodes. Because every time the alien signal is about to break loose, we know what to do now, don't we? Just pulse the whole damn city! Or the country even! Hell, it worked in Miami (and the Corps of Engineers had the power grid up within a day!). How grave would any future alien threat on *Threshold* truly prove since in the fourth episode the team had already gone to the option of last resort, and not only did the EMP defeat the aliens, it caused no serious harm to the populace?

Note to would-be "sci-fi" writers: aliens who can't upload files to the Internet or a calling-circle on their cell phones (yet can transmit a bio- and techno-altering signal across lights years of space) just aren't very scary. Or believable.

Threshold originally aired on Friday nights at 9:00 pm, but when ratings quickly proved underwhelming, CBS moved *Close to Home* into its time slot and transferred *Threshold* to Tuesdays at ten. The ratings didn't improve, and CBS quickly "pulsed" *Threshold*, thereby pulling the plug on one of the most poorly conceived science fiction TV shows in the history of the medium.

Ironically, the cast of *Threshold* was very strong, featuring movie stars Caffrey and Dutton as well as *Next Gen* icon Spiner. Yet in every case, these talented actors were forced to play stereotypes and vet ridiculous, hole-ridden plots. It's no wonder that audiences stopped the signal sooner rather than later.

The last three episodes of *Threshold* never aired on network television, but were made available for download on the Internet by CBS. In August 2006, it was announced that the SCI FI Channel had acquired the rights to rerun the entire series.

The complete series is also available on DVD.

TREASURE HUNTERS

(NBC) (RENEWED) (60 minutes) (Sundays at 9:00 pm, EST; June 18, 2006–August 21, 2006) Magical Elves Productions/ Imagine Television/Madison Road Entertainment/NBC Universal. Executive Producers: Dan Cutforth, Jane Lipsitz, Brian Grazer, Davia Nevins, Tom Mazza, Danica Krislovich, Jak Severson. Co-Executive Producers: Rick Ringbakk, Richard Buhrmann, Gunnar Wettesberg. Produced by: Noel A. Guerra, Tony Sacco, Craig Spirko, Javier Winnik. Camera: Marc McCrudden, Gretchen Warthen. Film Editors: Marc Clark, Michael Friedman, Noel A. Guerra, Tenna Guthrie, Robbie Paramour, Claire Scanlon. Music: Sean Callery. Directed by: Tony Sacco.

CAST
Laird Macintosh (Host)

CONTESTANTS
Team Air Force, Team Brown Family, Team Ex-CIA, Team Fogal Family, Team Geniuses, Team Grad Students, Team Southie Boys, Team Wild Hanlons.

This unscripted reality "contest" series from the producers of *Project Runway* was sometimes derided by critics as a needlessly complicated variation on *The Amazing Race* formula.

Treasure Hunters premiered on NBC television in two-hour form (from 8:00 to 10:00 pm) just a month after producer Grazer's *The Da Vinci Code* debuted in movie theaters and made a killing. Like that film, *Treasure Hunters* is a series about deciphering puzzles and secrets, and following clues to unearth mysteries and ultimately…prizes. There's a little bit of American history here, a pinch of puzzle-solving or code breaking, and—of course—the interpersonal strife that is part and parcel of the reality show format.

In the ten episodes of *Treasure Hunters*, ten teams of three contestants each zip back and forth across the United States (and Europe) to locations such as Mount Rushmore in South Dakota in search of booty and the key to unlocking a "cryptex." In one episode, the teams go to a mine in Montana (following in the footsteps of Lewis & Clark, according to promotional materials). Another episode finds them in Brooklyn, yet another in Savannah, GA.

Five teams began their *Treasure Hunters* quest in Hawaii, the other five in Alaska, and the units bear names like "Ex CIA," "Grad Students," "Air Force," "Young Professionals," "Team Miss USA," "Geniuses," "The Southie Boys," "The Brown Family," and so forth. Each week, one team gets eliminated from the contest, narrowing the number of souls in search of the "treasure."

The series is not available on DVD.

TUESDAY NIGHT BOOK CLUB

(CBS) (CANCELED) (60 minutes) (Tuesdays at 10:00 pm EST; June 13, 2006-June 20, 2006) The Jay and Tony Show. Executive Producers: Jay Blumenfield, Tony Marsh. Co-Executive Producers: Brianna Bruderlin. Produced by: Patrick Bachmann, Susie Delava, Dean Ollins. Story Producers: Barbara Bonds, Erin Camerford, Erin Paullus, Maria Schwartz, Melanie Switzer. Camera: Mark Lynch. Film Editors: Pierre Dwyer, Jon Emerson, David Harris, Richard Kreitman, Tyrone Tomke, Eric Torres, Ted Woerner. Music: Christopher Brady. Directed by: Tony Sacco.

Seven suburban women get together every Tuesday at their Scottsdale, Arizona book club to share their marital and romantic woes in this unscripted, short-lived summer series from CBS. The women in the series are branded by the producers with labels or "handles," which they either live up to or down to, depending on perspective, and books hardly enter the picture. I'm not even sure all the women can read.

The women in the series are Tina ("The Divorced Mom"), Cris ("The Loyal Wife"), Jenn ("The Trophy Wife"), Jamie ("The Conflicted Wife"), Lynn ("The Newlywed"), Kirin ("The Doctor's Wife") and Sara ("The Party Girl"). Individually and *en masse* they complain about all the reality show standards: infidelity, alcoholism, divorce, etc. Meanwhile, they share secrets about their husbands and their sex lives.

Only two episodes of *Tuesday Night Book Club* aired on CBS before the axe fell. The episodes "What Happens in Book Club Stays in Book Club" and "How Long Have You Been Having An Affair?" did not please critics, who complained that many of the events and confrontations in the series appeared staged and acted, rather than spontaneously experienced. Audiences didn't care much to join the club either. *Tuesday Night Book Club* aired opposite the NBA Basketball Finals and got trounced.

The series is not available on DVD.

TWINS

(WB) (CANCELED) (30 minutes) (Fridays at 8:30 pm, EST; September 16, 2005-March 3, 2006) KoMut Enterprises/ Warner Bros. Executive Producers: David Kohan, Max Mutchnick. Co-Executive Producer: Chris Kelly. Camera: Gregg Heschong. Film Editor: Art Kellner. Music: Paul Buckley, Jack Diamond. Written by: Hillel Abrams, Daisy Gardner, Wendy Goldman, Chris Kelly, Dana Klein, Adam Lorenzo, Mike Sikowitz, Christopher Vane, Barry Wernick. Directed by: James Widdoes.

CAST
Sara Gilbert (Mitchee)
Molly Stanton (Farrah)
Melanie Griffith (Lee)
Mark Linn-Baker (Alan)

The WB doesn't have a good track record crafting situation comedies and *Twins* is no exception. It's the story of sisters Mitchee (Sara Gilbert) and Farrah (Molly Stanton). Mitchee is smart, and takes after her dad, Alan (Mark Linn-Baker). Farrah is dippy but gorgeous, and takes after her mother, Lee (Melanie Griffith), a model. It's an Odd Couple scenario as Mitchee and Farrah work together to run their parents' lingerie shop, Arnold Undergarments.

Now ask yourself: why, oh why—*just once*—couldn't the smart sister have taken after the mother? And the dumb but good-looking one take after the Dad? Why is the mother always burdened by looks and no brains? When will TV series stop reinforcing ancient stereotypes?

All right, so anyway, while Lee and Alan bicker, Mitchee and Farrah also bicker. They bicker about men, about how to run the business, you name it. In "Fruit of the Lunatics" the girls attempt a truce, but end up fighting over the design of a new product (meaning underwear). In "Model Student," both women get traffic tickets AT THE SAME TIME (what a coincidence, huh?) and must attend a remedial driving class together. It's too cute by half, and any relation to the way human beings actually relate is purely coincidental.

Instead of making the move to CW, *Twins* was (mercifully) axed after one season of eighteen half-hour installments.

It is not available on DVD.

UNAN1MOUS

(FOX)(CANCELED)(60 minutes)(Wednesdays at 10:00 pm, EST; March 22, 2006-May 10, 2006) Three Ball Productions. Executive Producers: John Foy, Lincoln Haitt, Todd A. Nelson, J.D. Roth. Co-Executive Producers: Robin Feinberg, Adam Greener. Producer: Adam Paul. Story Producer: Matt Assmus. Music: Jeff Lippencott, Mark T. Williams. Written by: Rob Cohen, David Wollock.

CAST
J.D. Roth (Host)

CONTESTANTS
Adam, Jameson, Jamie, Jonathan, Kelly, Richard, Steve, Tarah, Vanessa.

This strange eight-episode reality/game show series aired in the winter of 2006 on FOX, following the ratings-grabbing *American Idol* results show on Wednesday nights.

In the course of *Unan1mous*, nine contestants of diverse backgrounds are plunked down in an underground bunker to see who will win a kitty of $1.5 million. The only drawback is that the decision on the identity of the winner must be…*unanimous*. Oh and—of course—contestants cannot vote for themselves. That kind of negates the whole idea of unanimity…right? There's at least one holdout.

These edicts regarding game play essentially mean that—following in the grand history of reality shows—the nine strangers backbite and manipulate each other to win the money. Another difficulty: if the strangers can't settle on a winner, their pot of gold drains away before their eyes, the loot becoming progressively less sweet. Indeed, the winner of the series, a designer named Tarah, came out of the game with just $362,000!

The contestants on *Unan1mous* were Richard (a writer), Jameson (a gay activist), Kelly (a Christian minister), Jamie (a choreographer), Jonathan (a womanizer), Tarah (the designer), Steve (a truck driver and conservative Christian), Vanessa (a left-wing atheist) and Adam, a poker player. They seemed chosen specifically for the fact that they wouldn't get along, and indeed that was the case. J.D. Roth was the host overseeing the interpersonal circus, which often saw barbs between those of diverse beliefs (conservatives vs. gays; conservatives vs. liberals, etc.) at each other's throats.

Even though *Unan1mous* benefited from a dream slot following *American Idol*, it was trounced on a regular basis by ABC's *Lost*, as well as by *Criminal Minds*. Critics were also—*dare I say it*—unanimous in their disdain for the series, which many compared unfavorably to *Big Brother*. *TV Guide* gave it a jeer for "taking reality TV to greedy new lows," and complained that "in order to gain sympathy, one player lied about having testicular cancer…Our verdict on this is *Unan1mous: It's Unforg1vable.*"[88]

Not available on DVD.

THE UNIT

(CBS) (RENEWED) (60 minutes) (Tuesdays at 9:00 pm, EST; March 7, 2006–May 16, 2006) David Mamet Chicago/ MiddKidd Productions/20th Century Fox/CBS. Created by: David Mamet. Based on the book "Inside Delta Force" by: Eric L. Haney. Executive Producers: Carol Flint, David Mamet, Shawn Ryan. Co-Executive Producers: Paul Redford, Vahan Moosekian. Produced by: Sharon Lee Watson. Camera: Krishna Rao. Film Editor: David Greenberg, David Koeppel. Music: Robert Duncan. Written by: Carol Flint, Eric L. Haney, David Mamet, Lynn Mamet, Paul Redford, Shawn Ryan. Directed by: Felix Enriquez Alcala, Stephen De Paul, Guy Ferland, Steve Gomez, Davis Guggenheim, Ron Lagomarsino, Bill L. Norton, Oz Scott, J. Miller Tobin.

CAST

Dennis Haysbert (Jonas Blane)
Regina Taylor (Molly Blane)
Robert Patrick (Colonel Tom Ryan)
Audrey Marie Anderson (Kim Brown)
Max Martini (Mack Gerhardt)
Abby Brammel (Tiffy Gerhardt)
Michael Irby (Charles Grey)
Demore Barnes (Hector William)
Scott Foley (Bob Brown)
Alyssa Shafer (Serena Brown)

From award-winning playwright David Mamet and the author of *Inside Delta Force*, Eric L. Haney, comes this compelling CBS drama that gazes at the men in a top secret American Special Forces Team, the so-called "Unit" of the title.

However, this is no cut-and-dry action series about Americans wiping out terrorists in a post-9/11 world. On the contrary, *The Unit* bifurcates the drama beautifully. Roughly half the show concerns the men of the Unit on their dangerous globe-hopping adventures, and the other half occurs on the "homefront," as their spouses deal with real life. Things like money, bills, affairs, etc.

Rewardingly, the scripts are punctuated by Mamet's trademark snappy dialogue and character exchanges. What's more genuinely fascinating, especially for a television program, is *The Unit*'s stunning visual design scheme. The "battle" or "mission" scenes involving the Unit appear washed out, with many greens and olives (reflecting the military aspect) overriding the other colors of the spectrum. In these sequences, the camera is shaky and handheld, and sometimes it takes a few seconds to find focus…which is a brilliant way of suggesting life unfolding before our eyes, not some kind of canned drama.

By contrast, the homefront sequences, the scenes involving the wives, adopt a different palette. These domestic moments are almost deliberately cartoonish and fake. There's gaudy straw blond hair, loud pink blouses, golden-mustard appliances in the kitchen, baby blue wallpaper and the like dominating these sequences. The subtle (and implicit) suggestion of this is that the Unit—living in a harsh world of camouflage and khakis—protects the America we know: the one of bright pastels and basic colors.

It also appears the camera exposure is set differently in the combat and suburban scenes, capturing motion in different ways, and that grants *The Unit* even more visual appeal, as well as thematic clarity. This is clearly one of those rare occasions in which a TV series' look reflects its content and enhances the depiction of the subject matter.

Because *The Unit* is a David Mamet series, it's not black-and-white in the sense that the narratives don't often boast easy or pat resolutions. Characters struggle and act in a human, recognizable fashion. Therefore lead actor Dennis Haysbert, playing Unit squad captain

They man **THE UNIT**.

Left to right: Jonas Blane (Dennis Haysbert) and Bob Brown (Scott Foley) face down an FBI agent.

Jonas Blake, can be the action hero of the hour, and also go home and yell at his wife. It's a fascinating blend.

The Unit involves Jonas Blake (Dennis Haysbert) leading top secret missions around the world with his team, which includes a newbie, Bob Brown (Scott Foley), Mack (Max Martini), and Hector (Demore Barnes). They are given their marching orders by Colonel Tom Ryan (Robert Patrick), who is having an illicit sexual affair with Mack's wife, Tiffy (Abby Brammel), at least until he gets married. This is a troubling development, because inside the Unit, the team's code of ethics require that anyone fooling around with another member's wife be killed!

Meanwhile, Blake's wife, Molly (Taylor) wants a better life: more things and more security. She's tired of Jonas risking his life for meager pay, and is desperate to find a way to render the family economically free from the Unit. In one episode, a real estate scheme goes badly and she loses $40,000. In another, she tries to push Jonas into taking a new job.

In its first season, *The Unit* takes its military characters around the world. They go on a mission to Indonesia ("200th Hour"); to Afghanistan (to assassinate a new Taliban leader) in "Dedication"; and to Yugoslavia to bring down a warlord (with the assistance of UN Forces) in "The Wall." Their secret ops involve not just assassination, but battling terrorists, retrieving top secret technology and data (like a Chinese spy satellite in "Stress"), and bugging the Iranian Embassy in an episode called "Security" that looks at growing tension with Iran, and the fear that other major powers such as the former Soviet Union are helping the Islamic nation build weapons of mass destruction.

The Unit is one of the highlights of the 2005–2006 season, a cleverly constructed and interesting drama… especially for those who mourn FX's *Over There*, a summer series from 2005 that also looked at soldiers (in Iraq) and their spouses back home.

The Unit has been renewed for a second season.

The first season was made available on DVD starting September 19, 2006.

THE WAR AT HOME

(FOX) (RENEWED) (30 minutes) (Sundays at 8:30 pm, EST; September 11, 2005–April 30, 2006) Acme Productions/ Rob Lotterstein Productions/Warner Bros. Created by: Rob Lotterstein. Executive Producers: Suzan Bymel, Michael Hanel, Rob Lotterstein, Mindy Schultheis. Produced by: Darin Henry, Al Lowenstein. Camera: Don Morgan, Mike Perlin. Film Editor: Andrew Chulak. Music: W.G. Snuffy Walden, Joseph Williams. Written by: Stephen Engel, Jennifer Glickman, Darin Henry, Bill Kunstler, Rob Lotterstein, Phil Osterr, Matthew Salsberg. Directed by: Andy Cadiff, Matthew Salsberg.

CAST

Michael Rapaport (Dave)
Anita Barone (Vicky)
Kyle Sullivan (Larry)
Kaylee Defer (Hillary)
Dean Collins (Mike)

This raunchy family sitcom inherited the slot held by another popular TV family—*Malcolm in the Middle. The War at Home* was lucky in its placement (after *The Simpsons*). Except for some occasional visual flourishes this is typical sitcom fodder.

This is the story of a family with apparently no last name. Dave (Michael Rapaport) is the rough-around-the-edges dad, who frequently laments how tough parenting is these days, and how much it has changed since he was a kid. Vicky (Anita Barone) is Dave's long-suffering wife. Together they share the responsibility of raising three children.

The eldest is daughter Hillary (Kaylee Defer), a 16-year-old who is expressing too much interest in dating, sex, drugs, and other adult things. Dave is terrified she's going to start having sex.

Their middle child is Larry (Kyle Sullivan), an unpopular 15-year-old who expresses interest in musicals and taking baths. Dave's fear? His son could be gay.

Finally, there's 13-year-old Mike (Dean Collins), an adolescent treading that difficult line between childhood/ manhood. Should he be interested in video games or girls? Dave, as *People Magazine* noted, "isn't mean, just stupid in a brutish way and clumsily insensitive about hot-button topics like homosexuality and interracial dating."[89]

Dave fights his children every week, trying to maintain the status quo at home, and just get his kids out of the house without getting pregnant or ending up in jail. In "Guess Who's Coming to BBQ" Dave holds a barbecue for Hilary's latest boyfriend…an African-American, and ends up accusing the boy's father of racism. In "High Crimes," Dave is worried first that Kim is having sex, and then—secondly—concerned that she's found his stash of weed. In "The West Palm Beach Story," we meet Dave's parents and get some insight into why he is the way he is. None of these stories tread new ground, but *The War at Home* replaces originality with raucous humor, and sometimes it works.

Sometimes it doesn't, because the jokes are cruel and stereotyped…especially the ones about only gay men appreciating musicals. In one episode, Larry tries out for the high school musical, *Annie Get Your Gun*. Series producer Lotterstine told *The Advocate* that "a homo sensibility is all over this otherwise traditional sitcom,"[90] but one would be hard pressed to prove that the sensibility is anything other than good, old-fashioned gay bashing and pandering to stereotypes. Also, gee whiz, a "homo" sensibility? How about saying a "gay" sensibility? Another stereotype and one offensive to me personally as a new father: WASP dads are all blundering, rough-edged hypocrites out-of-touch with their emotions and the needs of their families.

Not currently available on DVD.

WEEDS

(Showtime) (RENEWED) (30 minutes) (Mondays at 10:00 pm, EST; August 7, 2005–October 10, 2005) Lions Gate TV/Titled Productions. Created by: Jenji Kohan. Executive Producer: Jenji Kohan. Co-Executive Producers: Roberto Benabib, Craig Zisk. Camera: Bobby Bukowski, Feliks Parnell. Film Editors: Lisa Bromwell, David Helfland. Music: Malvina Reynolds. Written by: Jenji Kohan, Michael Platt, Barry Sufchik, Matthew Salsberg, Shawn Schepps. Directed by: Brian Dannelly, Tucker Gates, Lee Rose, Arlene Sanford, Burr Steers, Craig Zisk.

CAST
Mary-Louise Parker (Nancy Botwin)
Elizabeth Perkins (Celia Hodes)
Kevin Nealon (Doug Wilson)
Justin Kirk (Andy Botwin)
Tonye Patano (Heylia James)
Romany Malco (Conrad Shepard)
Hunter Parrish (Silas Botwin)
Alexander Gould (Shane Botwin)
Renee Victor (Lupita)
Allie Grant (Isabelle Hodes)

Weeds is the comedic tale of Nancy Botwin, a suburban soccer mom whose life is suddenly turned upside down when her Jewish husband, Judah (Jeffrey Dean Morgan of *Supernatural*) dies of a heart attack. Nancy has two sons, Silas (Hunter Parrish) and Shane (Alexander Gould), and suddenly, she isn't certain she can even afford to keep them in school, much less continue employing a maid (Renee Victor) and living in the cookie-cutter upscale California community of Agrestic.

Nancy's method of solving the money flow problem is unconventional. She becomes Agrestic's only marijuana dealer, skirting the law and serving the needs of the suburban population. Among her customers is dopey Doug Wilson, a city council official played by Kevin Nealon. Nancy buys her stash from a cranky African-American businesswoman named Heylia (Tonye Patano), and has begun to fall in love with Heylia's cousin Conrad (Romany Malco), a man just aching to start his own organic marijuana business. But he needs seed money.

Other regulars on *Weeds* include Andy (Justin Kirk), Nancy's trouble-prone brother-in-law, an unemployed pot smoker who in the course of the series is arrested for possession. The arrest puts Andy on "the grid" and before long he's in danger of being shipped to Iraq because he once signed up for the Armed Forces. Andy's way out of the Army involves training as rabbi.

Nancy's best friend is Celia Hodes, played by the Emmy-nominated Elizabeth Perkins. Celia is unceasingly cruel to her overweight (and possibly lesbian) daughter, Isabelle (Allie Grant), but her focus soon shifts when Celia is diagnosed with cancer.

In the course of *Weeds'* first season, Nancy learns the "ropes" of dealing pot. She employs a network of dealers herself, including Sanjay, a smitten Valley State Student, and opens up a bakery as a front business (which she calls a "fakery"). On one occasion, Nancy loses $14,000 in weed to a competitor on the college campus only to have Conrad rush in to save her.

While dealing with these problems, Nancy handles her increasingly troubled children. Shane is her youngest boy, and he bites a kid during a karate tournament, shoots a mountain lion in the backyard, creates a terrorist beheading video, starts a fire at school, and begins writing gangsta' rap. Meanwhile, Nancy's older boy, Silas, dates a deaf girl, starts having sex, and begins experimenting with Ecstasy.

A social satire that pokes wicked fun at the "little boxes" of gated communities and America's Starbucks Coffee culture, *Weeds* is a brilliantly written and performed highlight of the 2005–2006 season. The final episode of the year was a cliffhanger that saw Nancy forming a new coalition of customers, dealers, and legal assistance to jumpstart Conrad's business. That triumph was quickly overturned, however, in the episode's final scene, which found Nancy in bed with her new boyfriend…who just happened to be a DEA Agent.

In addition to Elizabeth Perkins, the first season of *Weeds* was nominated for four other Emmy Awards. The first season is available on DVD.

Weed Woman: Nancy Botwin (Mary-Louise Parker) makes dealin' pot look good in **WEEDS**.

WHAT ABOUT BRIAN

(ABC) (RENEWED) (60 minutes) (Mondays at 10:00 pm; April 16, 2006-May 8, 2006) Touchstone Television/Bad Robot/Free Cheese. Created by: Dana Stevens. Executive Producers: J.J. Abrams, Bryan Burk, Jeff Judah, Gabe Sachs, Thom Sherman, Dana Stevens. Co-Executive Producers: Dan Lerner. Produced by: Kate Angelo, David Graziano, Carol Trussel. Camera: Russ Alsobrook. Film Editors: Sue Blainey, Louis A. Innes. Music: Michael Giacchino, Grant Lee Phillips. Written by: Jeff Judah, James Kicklighter, Sheila Lawrence, Raven Metzner, Gabe Sachs, Dana Stevens, Stu Zicherman. Directed by: Dan Lerner.

CAST

Barry Watson (Brian)
Matthew Davis (Adam)
Sarah Lancaster (Marjorie)
Rick Gomez (Dave)
Amanda Detmer (Deena)
Rosanna Arquette (Nic)
Raoul Bova (Angelo)

Dana Stevens, the screenwriter behind the 1999 feature, *For the Love of the Game*, created this drama about a circle of friends that aired on ABC for five weeks in the spring of 2005.

What About Brian centers on Brian (Barry Watson), a decent and kind 34-year-old surrounded by a wide circle of friends. Yet he is the only one among six buddies that remains a bachelor.

Brian's calling circle includes his older sister Nic (Rosanna Arquette), a woman in her forties who is attempting to conceive a baby and is having fertility issues. She's newly married to a much younger man named Angelo (Raoul Bova). Brian is also close with a married couple, Dave (Rick Gomez) and Deena (Amanda Detmer). They're so settled in their rote life that their sex lives have grown boring. Finally, Brian is in love with his friend, Marjorie (Sarah Lancaster), who has just become engaged to Brian's best buddy, the handsome but lascivious Adam (Matthew Davis). In the first episode, Brian realizes that he has no social life because he's been pining away for Marjorie. Simply put, no other women can compare.

In "Two in Twenty-Four," Brian's friends urge him to try to sleep with two different women in a twenty-four-hour period and the bored Deena contemplates the idea of an open marriage when she grows sexually attracted to an acquaintance. In "Moving Day," Brian helps Marjorie move into a place with Adam in anticipation of their nuptials, and it's an occasion to reexamine their relationship. In "The Importance of Being Brian," everybody is looking for Brian because it's the weekend, but he's trying to make a go of it with a new girlfriend. The final episode was called "Sex, Lies, and Videotape" and brought all the plot points to a climax. Nic's fertility, Deena's desire for sex outside of marriage, and Brian's friendship with Marjorie were all on the table.

The reviews were not very strong for *What About Brian.* "The dialogue ranges from ridiculous to tiresome,"[91] noted *USA Today.* The series also drew distinctly undistinguished ratings during its month on the air, but in a surprise move, ABC renewed the series and put it on its fall 2006 schedule. The renewal may have come about over a matter of clout. One of *What About Brian's* executive producers is none other than *Lost* co-creator J.J. Abrams, and perhaps—if you'll forgive this suggestion—ABC wanted to maintain a strong relationship with him.

Not currently available on DVD.

WHO WANTS TO BE A SUPERHERO?

(SCI FI Channel) (RENEWED) (60 minutes) (Thursdays at 9:00 pm, EST; July 27, 2006-August 31, 2006) POW! Entertainment/Nast Entertainment. Executive Producers: Gill Champion, Andrew Jebb, Stan Lee, Scott Satin. Co-Executive Producer: Rick Telles. Produced by: Carrie Brown, Tess Gamba, Yuka Kobayashi, Jenna Smith. Camera: Bruce Ready. Film Editors: David Dean, Joe Miale. Music: Scooter-Pietsch. Directed by: Rick Telles.

CAST
Stan Lee (Host)

CONTESTANTS
Matthew "Feedback" Atherton, Steel "Iron/Dark Enforcer" Chambers, Tonya "Creature" Kay, Jonathan "Rotiart" Finestone, Tonatzin "Lemuria" Mondragon, Darren "Nitro G" Passarello, E. Quincy " Ty'Veculus" Sloane, Mary "Monkey Woman" Votava, Chris "Major Victory" Watters, Chelsea "Cell Phone Girl" Weld, Nell "Fat Mama" Wilson.

The SCI FI Channel launched this summer series with Marvel comics legend Stan Lee as host. Lee is renowned as the creator of superheroes such as Spider-Man, The Hulk, and The Fantastic Four, and here he shepherds eleven finalists through six one-hour episodes as he searches for a "real" life (costumed) superhero from among the ranks of regular Americans.

In each episode of *Who Wants to be a Superhero?*, the finalists (ensconced in a secret lair) take their marching orders and participate in trials of endurance (and character) selected by the series producers. After individual missions, the participants are judged by Lee (seen on a monitor) and either advance to the next round, or are eliminated and must torch their costumes. Two contestants are eliminated every week.

Among the "heroes" vying to be the champion are men and women with handles such as Feedback, Creature, Major Victory, Lemuria, Levity, Monkey Woman, Fat Mama, Cell Phone Girl, and the villainous Dark Enforcer. The grand prize on this odd unscripted series is actually threefold. The winners will get a real comic book (by Stan Lee, no less) created about their character, the SCI FI Channel will produce an original movie about their exploits, and they will make a public appearance at Universal Studios Orlando.

Although—like many summer series in 2006—*Who Wants to be a Superhero?* is an unscripted reality show and therefore faced the possibility of exploitation and lowest-common-denominator behavior, the series gained a following among some genre fans because of the program's concentration on what it *means* to be a superhero. It's not the superpowers, silly, as the individual episodes make clear; it's the heart inside that matters. Courageous, inventive Stan Lee is thus the perfect host and judge to make this point clear (and he often does so) Lee reminds viewers and contestants alike that superheroes represent goodness, community and justice, not darkness or selfishness.

Excelsior!

RETURNING TV SERIES

ACCORDING TO JIM

(ABC) (RENEWED) (30 minutes) (Tuesdays at 8:00 pm, EST; September 20, 2005-May 2, 2006) Touchstone Television/Brad Grey Television/Suzanne Bukinik Entertainment. Executive Producers: Warren Bell, Jim Belushi, Suzanne Bikinik, Marc Gurvitz, Howard J. Morris, Bob Nickman, Jonathan Stark. Co-Executive Producers: Nastaran Dibai, Tracy Gamble, Jeffrey B. Hodes. Produced by: John D. Bech, Ron Hart, Bob Heath. Music: Rich Ragsdale. Written by: John D. Beck, Daniel Egan, David Feeney, Harry Flanagan, John Hart, Howard J. Morris, Christopher J. Nowak. Directed by: James Belushi, Gary Cohen, Leonard R. Garner Jr., Steve Zuckerman.

CAST
Jim Belushi (Jim)
Courtney Thorne-Smith (Cheryl)
Kimberly Williams-Paisley (Dana)
Larry Joe Campbell (Andy)
Taylor Atelian (Ruby)
Billi Bruno (Gracie)
Conner Rayburn (Kyle)

All TV is wish-fulfillment to one degree or another. As audience members, we can experience life as a doctor, a lawyer, an astronaut, or—as in the case of *According to Jim*—an obnoxious family man. This long-lived ABC situation comedy is the story of a wrong-thinking, chubby, balding, and wholly irritating guy named Jim (Jim Belushi) who evidences bad behavior constantly. He's uncommunicative and difficult, and yet he's married to the most gorgeous woman imaginable, Cheryl (Courtney Thorne-Smith) and she absolutely loves him, in spite of his many, many character flaws.

This is a comedy about suburban life and Jim works in the construction business (at Ground Up) with Cheryl's brother Andy (Larry Joe Campbell). Meanwhile, this blustery, meat-and-potatoes man also raises three kids: Ruby (Taylor Atelian), Gracie (Billi Bruno) and the youngest, Kyle (Conner Rayburn). Adding spice to the mix is Dana (Kimberly Williams-Paisley), Cheryl's sister, who gets married in the fifth season of the show.

Each episode revolves around smarmy Jim misbehaving in one way or another. He plays hooky with Kyle on the boy's first day of school so he can go see the Cubs play ball in "Foul Ball." He enters a marathon he can't possibly win in "The Race" to prove a point about machismo to the boy. He enters his wife into a charity contest (without her knowledge) where the prize is a visit to the Playboy Mansion ("Charity Begins at Hef's"). He provides Andy dating advice that backfires in "The Chick Whisperer," and so on.

Really, what does Cheryl see in this guy? He's not handsome; he's not bright; and he's not really a very nice guy, either. And clearly, he lacks common sense. But one supposes that all the balding, fat, misbehaving guys who watch TV need to believe that they can be appealing to beautiful women too. The series has been renewed for a sixth season by ABC.

The series has not yet been released on DVD.

ALIAS

(ABC) (CANCELED) (60 minutes) (Thursdays at 8:00 pm, EST; September 29, 2005–May 22, 2006) Touchstone Television/ Bad Robot. Executive Producers: J.J. Abrams, Jesse Alexander, Jeff Pinkner. Produced by: Chad Savage. Film Editors: Anthony Miller, Fred Toye, Kristen Windell. Written by: Jesse Alexander, Josh Applebaum, Jeffrey Bell, Monica Breen, Andi Bushnell, Breen Frazier, Andre Nemec, J.R. Orci, Alison Schapker. Directed by: James Babbit, Jeffrey Bell, Richard Coad, Tucker Gates, Karen Gaviola, Ken Olin, Donald E. Thorn, Jay Torres, Fred Toye, Robert M. Williams.

CAST
Jennifer Garner (Sydney Bristow)
Victor Garber (Jack Bristow)
Ron Rifkin (Arvin Sloane)
Michael Vartan (Michael Vaughn)
Carl Lumbly (Marcus Dixon)
Kevin Weisman (Marshall Flinkman)
Rachel Nichols (Rachel Gibson)
Elodie Bouchez (Renee)
Balthazar Getty (Thomas Grace)

While *Alias* and *Lost* creator J.J. Abrams went off to shoot *Mission: Impossible 3* (2006) with Tom Cruise, and to negotiate to produce and direct *Star Trek XI*, his TV superspy drama on ABC, *Alias* passed the important milestone of 100 episodes.

Unfortunately, *Alias*'s move to Thursday nights at 8:00 pm opposite the CBS reality series *Survivor: Guatemala*, also spelled the end for secret agent Sydney Bristow's (Jennifer Garner) international espionage career, and the series, which had commenced in Fall of 2001, was canceled.

Although ABC Entertainment President Stephen McPherson promised the series would not wind down but rather "rev up" and be "the event it deserves to be"[1] the network added insult to injury by scheduling the final episode of the drama opposite the season finale of the more-popular spy drama on FOX, Kiefer Sutherland's *24* and it was consequently destroyed in the ratings.

Gazing back at the final seventeen episodes (an abbreviated season, at ABC's behest), one can see how the series attempted to walk two lines simultaneously. Before the cancellation came down from ABC, it was known that star Jennifer Garner was expecting a baby with husband Ben Affleck, and would likely not return for further seasons, or would—at the very least—be forced to take a sabbatical. So, in an effort to keep the series alive, a batch of young new characters were added to the mix. Rachel Nichols played Rachel Gibson, a young spy protégée for Sydney, who even experienced her own adventure in "Solo." Also, Balthazar Getty was added as a new hunky young male agent, Thomas Grace, following the surprise death of series hero (or was he a double agent?) Michael Vaughn, played by Garner's ex-boyfriend, Michael Vartan. Vaughn had apparently died in a car accident, even as Sydney was carrying his unborn child, a plot device to explain Garner's growing baby bump.

When ratings slipped and the decision to cancel *Alias* was cemented, the fifth season took a sharp turn and began tying up all the loose ends established in previous seasons by bringing back various series characters. Lena Olin, who plays Sydney's villainous mother in 2002–2003, returned for "Mother Instinct" and the series finale, and Bradley Cooper (who had seen his own series, *Kitchen Confidential* canceled in 2005–2006) returned for an episode as reporter Will Tippit ("There's Only One Sydney Bristow"). Series villain Sloane (Ron Rifkin) was also featured heavily in the last season, attempting to cure his daughter, Nadia of a deadly disease. This subplot dovetailed with the solution of a series-long mystery involving the ancient inventor named "Rambaldi" and his unusual/metaphysical contraptions. As *Alias* wound down, the episodes increasingly turned to the discovery and possession of the Rambaldi Sphere, a special device that ensure the owner power beyond imagination.

Alias ended with the eternal entrapment of villainous Sloane and the death of both of Sidney's parents, Irina and good guy Jack Bristow (regular Victor Garber). A final coda revealed Sydney and Vaughn (who was not really dead) raising their daughter, Isabelle, years after the end of the series.

The fifth and last season became available on DVD November 24, 2006.

ALL OF US

(UPN) (RENEWED) (30 minutes) (Mondays at 8:30 pm, EST; September 19, 2005–March 15, 2006) Overbrook Entertainment. Created by: Betsy Borns, Jada Pinkett Smith, Will Smith. Executive Producers: Betsy Borns, James Lassiter, Jada Pinkett Smith, Will Smith. Produced by: Leo Clarke, Stacy A. Littlejohn, Dan Signor. Camera: Mikel Neiers, John Simmons. Film Editor: Michael Wiclox. Music: Mare Kinchen, Paulette Maxwell, Kevin Scott. Written by: Jared Bush, Rod J. Emelle, Chad Drew, Arthur Harris, Lori Lakin, Stacy A. Littlejohn. Directed by: Debbie Allen, Chip Hurd, Ted Lange, Alfonso Ruberio, Leslie Kolins Small, Steve Zuckerman.

CAST

Duane Martin (Robert James, Sr.)
Lisa Raye (Neesee James)
Khamani Griffin (Robert James, Jr.)
Tony Rock (Dirk)

When *All of Us* premiered in the autumn of 2002, the big "buzz" was that the sitcom was "loosely" based on the lovelife of film stars Will Smith and wife Jada Pinkett Smith. That alone made it appointment TV. When folks tuned in, they saw the story of a man named Robert James, Sr. (Duane Martin), who is in love with one woman, Elise Neal's Tia, while still attempting to maintain a relationship with his ex-wife, Neesee (Lisa Raye), the mother of his son, Bobby Jr. (Khamani Griffin). In this relationship, it was assumed that Neal was playing the Pinkett character; Martin the Will Smith character.

So audiences must have felt incredibly confused when the third season of *All of Us* began in the fall of 2005 and star Elise Neal (and her character, Tia) were missing in action. The actress had left the series (or had been let go, according to some allegations), and now the focus of the sitcom was Duane and Lisa getting back together to raise their son.

Wow, I didn't know Will Smith and Jada Pinkett Smith broke up and Mr. Smith got back with his first wife! Did you?

Anyway, in its third season *All of Us* is no longer the same series as it once was, and—in fact—it's even kind of insulting since Elise Neal played such a charming character and Neesee was clearly designed to be the foil.

Whatever.

This season saw Neesee and Duane edging closer together. In the appropriately titled season premiere, "Starting Over," Robert is truly in a bad place. He's mysteriously sans girlfriend, he's lost his job…and Neesee has moved in with him because her apartment burned down. They aren't together, but the vibe is there, even as in future episodes (like "Kiss, Kiss, Pass") Robert starts dating again. Also in this season: Duane's crazy, horny friend Dirk (Tony Rock) continues to make a mess of things.

Another running plot on *All of Us* involves Neesee and Duane attempting to raise young Bobby. In one episode, "Don't Make My Brownies Blue," Bobby wants to be a rapper. In "The N Word," an installment directed by Will Smith, Bobby does the unthinkable and uses the N-word in front of company.

The series is not currently available on DVD.

THE AMAZING RACE

(CBS) (RENEWED) (60 minutes) (Tuesdays at 9:00 pm, EST; September 27, 2005-December 13, 2005; February 28, 2006-May 17, 2006) Jerry Bruckheimer Television/Touchstone Television/Earth View Productions/Flashback Productions/World Race Productions. Created by: Elise Doganieri, Bert Von Munster. Executive Producers: Jerry Bruckheimer, Jonathan Littman, Bert Van Munster, Hayma Washington. Co-Executive Producers: Amy Chacon, Scott Einziger. Produced by: Missy Bania, Jennifer Basa, David C. Brown, Jarratt Carson, Allison Chase, Curtis Culden, Al Edmonston, Lisa Ely, Andrew Fran, Paul Frazier, Shannon McGinn, Bob Parr, Bill Pruitt, Alex Rader, Ben Samek, Brian Tanke. Camera: Tom Cunningham. Film Editors: Jon Bachmann, Steven Escobar. Music: John M. Keane. Directed by: Bert Von Munster.

CAST
Phil Keoghan (Host)

2005 CONTESTANTS
The Aiello Family, The Black Family, the Bransen Family, the Gaghan Family, the Godlewski Family, the Paolo Family, the Schroeder Family, the Weaver Family.

2006 CONTESTANTS
BJ and Tyler, Danielle and Dani, Dave and Lori, Eric and Jeremy, Fran and Barry, John and Scott, Lake and Michelle, Ray and Linda, Joseph and Monica, Ray and Linda, Wanda and Desiree.

The premise of the popular *The Amazing Race*, which has been on the air since 2001, is that twelve teams of two set out on a race with the same set of advantages and disadvantages. During the race, the teams receive tasks or "challenges" in race envelopes, and must solve riddles or succeed in seemingly treacherous physical events (like crossing a dangerous suspension bridge). Those who can't keep up lose, with one team eliminated per episode. The prize is one million dollars.

Seasons eight and nine of the unscripted "game" show *The Amazing Race* aired during the span covered by this book. From September to December of 2005, CBS aired a version of *The Amazing Race* subtitled *The Family Edition*. Beginning with a two-hour season premiere (starting the race at the Brooklyn Bridge), this variation of the tried-and-true formula was first to feature team members that were all related. The winner of the event was the Linz Family.

From February to May of 2006, *The Amazing Race* returned for a season of ten additional hour-long episodes back in its old, more familiar formula. This race ended at Flushing Meadows Park, New York City, and saw best friends Rob and Brennan beat separated parents Frank and Margarita as well as life partners Joe and Bill for the $1 million prize.

The first and seventh seasons are available on DVD.

AMERICA'S MOST WANTED

(FOX) (RENEWED) (60 minutes) (Saturdays at 9:00 pm, EST; January 7, 2006-August 19, 2006) 20th Century Fox. Produced by: Kenneth A. Carlson, Alissa Collins, Peter G. Gillespie, Lance Heflin, Cord Keller, Greg Klein, Evan A. Marshall, Cindy Miller, Sam Rath, Todd Robiinson, Karen S. Shapiro, Paul C. Simpson, Sedgwick Tourison, Kurt Uebersax. Camera: Jeremy Settles. Film Editor: Gary Myers. Music: Lorne Ralf, Julie Greaux, Craig Sharmat, Jeremy Sweet, Bill Wandel.

CAST
John Walsh (Host)

America's Most Wanted is legendarily one of the earliest and most successful examples of the reality series format. Fox tried to kill the crime series in 1996, but audiences, law enforcement officials, and politicians all complained about the move. After a six-week hiatus, the series was back on the air. It's never been off since, and in the year 2006, *America's Most Wanted* celebrated its eighteenth season hunting down fugitives and bringing criminals to justice.

John Walsh, who lost his son Adam to a violent predator in 1981, is the committed and much-honored host of this series ("where America fights back!"), which searches for dangerous fugitives and missing children. Usually two fugitives and one missing child are profiled in reenactments in each hour-long episode. The series has been called exploitive by some, since it features those dramatic enhancements of terrible crimes, but it's difficult to argue with success.

To date, *America's Most Wanted* has been deemed responsible for bringing a whopping 900 criminals to justice.

The series has not yet been released on DVD.

AMERICA'S NEXT TOP MODEL

(UPN) (RENEWED) (60 minutes) (Wednesdays at 8:00 pm, EST; September 21, 2005-December 7, 2005; March 1, 2006-May 17, 2006) 10 x 10 Entertainment. Created by: Tyra Banks. Executive Producers: Tyra Banks, Anthony Dominici. Produced by: Allison Chase, Joe Coleman, Barry Hennessey, Justin Lacob, Maggie Zeltner. Camera: Paul Starkman. Film Editor: Michael Polakow. Directed by: Luis Baneto, Guido Verweyen.

CAST
Tyra Banks (Judge)
Twiggy (Judge)
J. Alexander (Judge)
Nigel Barker (Judge)
Jay Manuel (Judge)

2005 CONTESTANTS
Ashley Black, Lisa D'Amato, Diane Hernandez, Kyle Kavanagh, Nicole Linkletter, Nik Pace, Sarah Rhoades, Jayla Rubinelli, Bre Scullark, Kim Stolz, Ebony Taylor, Cassandra Whitehead, Coryn Woitel.

2006 CONTESTANTS
Nnenna Agba, Sarah Albert, Furonda Brasfield, Gina Choe, Jade Cole, Joanie Dodds, Danielle Evans, Mollie Sue Steenis-Gondi, Kathy Hoxit, Leslie Manola, Kari Schmidt, Brooke Staricha, Wendy Wiltz

Two cycles of this popular UPN reality series ran during the full 2005–2006 season. Cycle 5 aired from September to December 2005; Cycle 6 from March to May 2006. Each boasted twelve hour-long episodes.

In *America's Next Top Model*, thirteen beautiful young women compete to become a successful model. The grand prize is a contract for management by the Ford Model company, a $100,000 contract with Cover Girl, and an *Elle* Magazine cover with Tyra. To win, each aspiring model runs a gauntlet of tasks. They must select the right hair, the right costumes, walk on a moving platform without falling, and learn poise, all while living together in a Bel Air Mansion.

The contestants are selected by judges, including series creator and supermodel Tyra Banks. In Cycle 5, a 19-year-old from North Dakota named Nicole was crowned the next top model; and in Cycle 6 the winner of the contest was Little Rock, Arkansas babysitter, Danielle.

America's Next Top Model survived the blending of UPN and the WB and returned for the late-2006 season on CW.

The first season of the series is available on DVD.

AMERICAN IDOL

(FOX) (RENEWED) (60 minutes) (Tuesdays at 9:00 pm; Wednesdays at 9:00 pm; January 17, 2006-May 24, 2006) Executive Producers: Simon Fuller, Cecile Frot-Coutaz, Simon Jones. Produced by: Jennifer Bresnan, Billy Cooper, Ron De Shay, John Entz, Nicola Gaha, Tarvenia Jones Patrick Lynn, Simon Lythgoe, Beth McNamara, Andy Meyer, Megan Michaels. Camera: Jack Messit, Dave Rutherford. Film Editors: George W. Ball, Bill De Ronde, Sharon Evereitt, Kevin Finn, Spencer Keimon, David Michael Maurer, William Morris, Ryan Polito, Julius Ramsay, Dora Rosas, Patrick Sayers. Music: Cathy Dennis.

CAST
Ryan Seacrest (Host)
Simon Cowell (Judge)
Paula Abdul (Judge)
Randy Jackson (Judge)

FINALISTS
Melissa McGhee, Kevin Covais, Lisa Tucker, Mandisa Hundley, Bucky Covington, Ace Young, Kellie Pickler, Paris Bennett, Chris Daughtry, Elliot Yamin, Katharine McPhee, Taylor Hicks.

In its fifth season, the talent show *American Idol* continued to prove a ratings juggernaut. It triumphantly emerged (again) as the number one show on television.

The terrible triumvirate (left to right): Simon Cowell, Paula Abdul, and Randy Jackson rate talent (and nontalent) in the juggernaut **AMERICAN IDOL**.

Amazingly, ratings were up well over the series' fourth season, with a whopping 36 million viewers tuning in for the season finale aired in May 2006. This was the network's largest entertainment programming audience in its history."[2] The series logged more views than the "old" big three (ABC, CBS, NBC) combined.

Although a behind-the-scenes lawsuit threatened the series' delicate chemistry in November 2005, and nearly stole away its primary asset, talent judge Simon Cowell, who had argued with series creator Simon Fuller over the format of his own talent show, *The X Factor*, ultimately all was well, as would-be singers auditioned from across the country, from Chicago and Denver to Greensboro, North Carolina and San Francisco, Las Vegas to Austin, Texas.

As in previous seasons, *American Idol* aired on two nights each week. Tuesday night was the performance night wherein young talents would strut their stuff and viewers had the opportunity to call in their votes. Wednesday night offered the "results" show, in which the votes were tallied and broadcast, and the less-successful singers eliminated. Host Ryan Seacrest crowed on one occasion in the fifth season that more Americans had voted in the talent contest than had exercised their right to vote in a presidential election.

This year, there was one notable change in the *American Idol* format: the male and female performers were separated into two groups, and the "elimination round" leading up to a top twelve contestants included one for each group, ostensibly so there would be more balance between male and female talents.

As in previous seasons, there was also theme night on *American Idol*, and this year saw songs of the 1950s performed, as well as a Stevie Wonder night. There were rumors throughout the year that pop-star Prince would step into the fray, but ultimately the Purple One didn't appear.

The finalists at the Kodak Theater in *American Idol's* fifth season included Melissa McGhee, Kevin Covais, Lisa Tucker, Mandisa Hundley, Bucky Covington, Ace Young, Kellie Pickler, Paris Bennett, Chris Daughtry, and Elliot Yamin.

The final combatants—the top two—were Katharine McPhee, a 22-year-old from Los Angeles, and the salt-and-pepper-haired 29-year-old Birmingham, Alabama native, Taylor Hicks. Hicks emerged the winner in the finale (and was soon named *People Magazine*'s "hottest bachelor"). McPhee didn't do too badly herself either: she soon had a number one hit with her version of "Somewhere Over the Rainbow."

In the summer of 2006, McPhee revealed to the press that she was struggling with an eating disorder.

Several compilation sets *The Best of American Idol* are available on DVD.

Season-by-season box sets are not available yet.

THE APPRENTICE

(NBC)(RENEWED)(60 minutes)(Thursdays at 9:00 pm, EST; Mondays at 9:00 pm, EST; September 22, 2005–December 15, 2005; February 27, 2006–June 6, 2006) Trump Productions LLC/Mark Burnett Productions. Created by: Mark Burnett. Executive Producers: Jay Bienstock, Mark Burnett, Donald Trump. Co-Executive Producers: Kevin Harris, Conrad Riggs. Produced by: James Canniffe, Seth Cohen, Patrick Costello, Rob La Plante, Rene Nosser, Bill Pruitt, Katherine Walker. Camera: Tom Cunningham, Scott Duncan, Derek Hoffman, Alan Piera, Matt Sohn, Gretch Warthen. Film Editors: David Cutler, Steven Escobar, Barry Gold, Janet Swanson. Music: Jeff Lippencott, Mark T. Williams. Directed by: Bob McKinnon.

CAST
Donald Trump (The Boss)
George Ross (Judge)
Carolyn Kepcher (Judge)

2005 CONTESTANTS
Kristi Caudell, James Dillon, Marshawn Evans, Markus Garrison, Melissa Holovach, Adam Israelov, Rebecca Jarvis, Mark Lamkin, Clay Lee, Brain Mandelbaum, Felisha Mason, Toral Mehta, Jennifer Murphy, Randal Pinkett, Josh Shaw, Chris Valletta, Jennifer Wallen.

2006 CONTESTANTS
Lee Bienstock, Leslie Bourgeois, Theresa Boutross, Brent Buckman, Jose Diaz, Bryce Gahagan, Charmaine Hunt, Allie Jablon, Andrea Lake, Michael Laungani, Tarek Saab, Stacy Schneider, Tammy Trenta, Lenny Veitman, Roxanne Wilson, Sean Yazbeck, Summer Zervos.

Like *The Amazing Race*, two seasons of NBC's sturdy reality series, *The Apprentice* actually aired during the span covered by this book, one from September to December 2005, and one from February to June of 2006, comprising seasons four and five of the series, respectively.

The Apprentice follows a group of eighteen prospective employees as they undergo tasks to become assistant to businessman Donald Trump and win a million dollars. In both series, fifteen hour-long episodes ensue in which the contestants complete tasks and battle it out. The losers are dismissed from The Board Room with Trump's terse "You're Fired."

In Season Four, an African-American man named Randal Pinkett became the fourth apprentice to Trump after separating himself from the pack in events that included prepping a new class for Bally's Fitness ("Let's Get Physical"), designing an ad for Lamborghini ("There's No 'I' in Team"), and working on a tech expo for Best Buy ("Something Old, Something New").

In the fifth season of *The Apprentice*, there was another parade of eighteen contestants, who in turn had to successfully market Sam's Club ("Summer of Sam's"), create a commercial for Norwegian Cruise Lines ("Cruise Control") and market a new pizza at 7-11 convenience stores ("A Slice of Heaven"). A man from London named Sean Yazbeck was the eventual winner.

Despite a ratings dip in the fifth season, which saw the lowest numbers for a season finale yet at just 11.2 million viewers[3], NBC has nonetheless announced plans for a sixth season of *The Apprentice, slated* to commence in January 2007.

The series' first season has been made available on DVD.

ARRESTED DEVELOPMENT

(FOX) (CANCELED) (30 minutes) (Mondays at 8:00 pm, EST; September 19, 2005-February 10, 2006) Imagine/The Hurwitz Company/20th Century Fox. Created by: Mitchell Hurwitz. Executive Producers: Brian Grazer, Ron Howard, Mitchell Hurwitz, David Nevins. Co-Executive Producers: Richard Day, John Levenstein, Richard Rosentock, Jim Vallely. Produced by: Barbie Adler, John Amodeo, Brad Copeland, Victor Hsu. Camera: Greg Harrington. Film Editors: Stuart Bass, Lee Haxall, Mark Scheib. Music: David Schwartz. Written by: Richard Day Jake Farrow, Michael Hurwitz, Sam Laybourne, Tom Saunders, Robert Weiner. Directed by: John Amodeo, Rebeca Asher, Bob Berlinger, Paul Feig, John Fortenberry, Arlene Sanford, Lev L. Spiro.

CAST
Jason Bateman (Michael Bluth)
Portia de Rossi (Lindsay Bluth)
Will Arnett (George Bluth II/"GOB")
Michael Cera (George Michael Bluth)
Alia Shawkat (May)
Tony Hale (Byron Bluth)
Jeffrey Tambor (George Bluth, Sr.)
Jessica Walter (Lucille Bluth)

The problem with the very funny sitcom *Arrested Development*, canceled after an abbreviated third season of thirteen episodes, is simply that critics always liked it better than average audiences did. It's a smart series, and in a world wherein *King of Queens* remains on the air for nearly a decade, that's not necessarily a good thing.

That *Arrested Development* resolutely remains a highly insular series, one with in-jokes alluding to past events, also makes it difficult for a newbie to embrace it and jump in, even if that's the sincere desire. The best way to enjoy this show is simply to start from the beginning.

Reviewing the third season, *Entertainment Weekly* readily admitted any explanations of *Arrested Development* just wouldn't make sense if you hadn't been following all along. Although this batch "featured some ingenious left-field comic turns, none of them would make even a lick of sense if we detailed them here. Let's just say the climax of "Mr. F"—featuring a mole costume, a jet pack, and four befuddled Japanese businessmen—is reason alone to mourn *Development*'s demise. RIP."[4]

Arrested Development is the woeful tale of Michael Bluth (Jason Bateman), the only sane member of a big, insane family. He's a widower with a young son, George Michael (Michael Cera), but his big problems rest with the remainder of the family. The SEC hauled dad, George Sr. (Jeffrey Tambor), to jail following illegal business dealings. Now Michael's mother (Jessica Walter) is struggling to sustain her rich lifestyle without his income. Michael's brother, nicknamed "GOB," is a failed magician, er, "illusionist." Michael's stuck-up sister Lindsay (Portia de Rossi) is a sucker for all the wrong causes in the world. May (Alia Shawkat) is her daughter, who has a knack for mischief.

The final season of *Arrested Development* involved a story about a summer cabin in Nevada ("The Cabin Show"), and Michael's trip to England ("For British Eyes Only"), where he is called an ugly term by a would-be girlfriend, although it doesn't mean what he thinks it means ("Notapussy"). The final episodes also involve the chance of Michael having a long-lost sister.

There was much speculation in the press about ABC or HBO picking up *Arrested Development* for a fourth season. No such last-minute reprieve came. Although not quite the same, FOX did soon report that MSN had acquired the rights to offer all fifty-three episodes of the half-hour series as downloads.

All three seasons are available on DVD.

THE BACHELOR

(ABC) (RENEWED) (60 minutes) (Mondays at 9:00 pm, EST; January 9, 2006-February 27, 2006) New Entertainment/ Telepictures Productions. Executive Producers: Mike Fleiss, Lisa Levenson. Co-Executive Producer: David Bohnert. Produced by: Russ Breitenbach, Alycia Rossiter. Camera: Zack Kozek, Bruce Ready, Tony Sacco, Matt Sohn. Film Editor: Hilary Scratch. Directed by: Ken Fuchs.

CAST
Chris Harrison (Host)

CONTESTANTS
Travis Lane Stork (The Bachelor), Sarah Stone, Moana Dixon, Allie Garcia-Serra

The implausibly named Travis Stork, a 33-year-old Duke University graduate and doctor at Vanderbilt Medical Center in Nashville, Tennessee, is the bachelor looking for love in this eighth season of ABC's durable reality show franchise. This season, *The Bachelor* lasted for only seven episodes, and was set in a 14th century French Chateau, near Paris.

At the start of *The Bachelor*, hosted by Chris Harrison, five limos pull up to the Chateau and Travis is introduced to a whopping twenty-five women as potential dates. After the first hour episode, he is forced to cut their ranks by half...down to twelve. Keeping true to the format of the series, he asks each of the dozen remaining women to stay by offering them a rose.

Over the next few weeks, there are more eliminations. By week three Travis's two best (doctor) friends show up in France to weed the number down to eight. By Episode Five, just four women remain, and the show then leaves France so that the Bachelor can see each women in their home town in America, their "natural environs."

By Week Seven—the final week—Travis has only two choices remaining. His parents and his sister's family arrive in France at the Chateau to help him choose between the nice gal, Sarah, and the more mysterious Moana.

At the end of the seventh episode, Travis made his choice and presented a 2.2 diamond carat ring to... Sarah.

A ninth season returned to ABC on October 2, 2006, but the series is not yet available on DVD.

BATTLESTAR GALACTICA

(SCI FI Channel) (RENEWED) (60 minutes) (Fridays at 9:00 pm, EST; July 15, 2005–March 10, 2006) R & D TV/USA Cable Entertainment LLC. Based on Battlestar Galactica, created by: Glen Larson. Developed by: Ron Moore. Executive Producers: David Eick, Ronald D. Moore. Co-Executive Producers: Mark Verheiden, Michael Angeli. Produced by: Harvey Frand, David Weddley, Bradley Thompson. Camera: Stephen McNutt. Film Editors: Andy Sekliri, Jacques Gravett. Written by: David Eick, Toni Graphia, Ronald D. Moore, Dawn Prestwich, Carla Robins, Ann Cofell Saunders, Bradley Thomson, Mark Verheiden, David Weddle, Nicole Yorkin. Directed by: Ron Hardy, Allan Kroeker, Sergio Mimica-Gezzan, Michael Nankin, Michael Rymer, Reynaldo Villalobos, Jeff Woolnough, Robert Young.

CAST
Edward James Olmos
   (Commander William Adama)
Mary McDonnell (President Laura Roslin)
Katee Sackhoff (Lt. Kara "Starbuck" Thrace)
Jamie Bamber (Captain Lee "Apollo" Adama)
James Callis (Dr. Gaius Baltar)
Tricia Helfer (Number Six)
Grace Park (Lt. Boomer)
Michael Hogan (Colonel Tigh)
Aaron Douglas (Chief Tyrol)

Although fans of the original Glen Larson 1978–1979 ABC space opera *Battlestar Galactica* continue to term Ronald Moore's low-budget, reimagined series GINO (or "*Galactica* In Name Only") and "*The West Wing* in Space," mainstream critics and a tiny minority of vocal fans have welcomed this reboot with open arms. In 2006, the SCI FI Channel's remake was honored with a Peabody Award as it completed its second season.

On matters of popularity, however, the numbers tell a different story: the original *Battlestar Galactica* drew 65 million viewers to the television for its premiere in September 1978, and remained among the top-twenty-five rated shows for its entire first run. By contrast, the new *Battlestar Galactica* only brings in a little over 2 million fans per episode. Given the splintering of TV with cable stations over the years, that modest number is considered satisfactory; though were *Galactica* to air on the big three networks, it likely would be pulled off the air after a few episodes.

Perhaps defensive over his show's less-than-stellar reception with the established science fiction community, Ronald Moore has compared the original series to popcorn, noting: "We've eaten a lot of popcorn over the years. We're ready for a bigger meal," thus indicating that the new *Battlestar Galactica*, with its increased sex quotient, soap opera plotting and politically relevant stories is somehow more mature than the mythology-based source material. "If you agree with us," sayeth Moore, "then this is the show for you. If not, then thanks for coming, but the popcorn is in a different aisle."[5]

Okay, see you later then…

But seriously, *Battlestar Galactica* concerns a race of human-appearing intelligent machines called Cylons who have launched a catastrophic attack on mankind in a solar system far away. The devastating nuclear attack on the human home planet Caprica has forced the last 50,000 or so humans to flee their home for outer space in a rag-tag fleet of ships. Commander Adama (Edward James Olmos) leads the refugees to the stars in the decommissioned warship, *Galactica*, in hopes of finding a mythical world called "Earth."

Adama's top staff includes two pilots: the rage-filled Kara "Starbuck" Thrace (Katee Sackhoff) and his estranged son, Lee "Apollo" Adama (Jamie Bamber). Commander Adama's first officer is an alcoholic, Colonel

Michael Trucco in "The Farm," an episode of the re-imagined **BATTLESTAR GALACTICA**.

Tigh (Michael Hogan), his science advisor, Baltar (James Callis) is the very man who betrayed the Colonists to the Cylons in the first place, and the President of the Fleet, Laura Roslin (Mary McDonnell) is a woman of faith who is fighting the intergalactic malady known as breast cancer. Meanwhile Chief Tyrol (Aaron Douglas) doesn't know it but he's sleeping with the enemy, a Cylon infiltrator named Boomer (Grace Park).

The second season picks up right where the first season cliffhanger left off. The "sleeper agent" Boomer has attempted to assassinate Commander Adama, who clings to life. Meanwhile, Apollo and President Roslin are locked in the brig for mutiny, and Colonel Tigh has assumed command of the *Galactica*. Starbuck is still trapped back on Cylon-occupied Caprica. The *Galactica* is separated from the rest of the fleet in the premiere, "Scattered," while crewmen are trapped on the planet Kobol, where human life is rumored to have begun in the galaxy.

In follow-up episodes, Tigh imposes martial law ("Fragged"), a Cylon baby is born ("Downloaded"), and Adama's restored command is once more threatened by the arrival of Admiral Caine and the *Battlestar Pegasus* ("Pegasus") in a tale right out of the original series, though then titled "Living Legend." The final two-parter of the season, "Lay Down Your Burdens," covers the Presidential election which finds Roslin fighting Baltar for office. A flashforward at the end of the season sets up for Season Three: humankind, led by the treacherous Baltar, living under Cylon occupation.

The guest stars on the second season of *As the Galactica Turns*—er, *Battlestar Galactica*—include original series star Richard Hatch, who portrays a Nelson Mandela–type rebel leader, Tom Zarek, and Michelle Forbes as Commander Cain. Former *Xena* (1995–2001) star Lucy Lawless joins the cast in a recurring role with the episode "Final Cut" as a journalist named D'Anna Biers. She may also be—*uh oh*—a Cylon agent!

The first half of *Battlestar Galactica's* second season has been released on DVD. Also in 2006: The SCI FI Channel announced it would air a spinoff from the new *Galactica* called *Caprica*. This series will eschew space battles and instead be a dramatic soap opera set fifty years before the events of *Battlestar Galactica*. The focus of the series will be the Adama family, and the "birth" of the malevolent Cylons.

The first half of the second season is available on DVD.

BEAUTY AND THE GEEK

(WB) (RENEWED) (60 minutes) (Thursdays at 9:00 pm, EST; January 12, 2006–March 9, 2006) Fox 21/3 Ball Productions/Katalyst Films. Executive Producers: John Foy, Jason Goldberg, Ashton Kutcher, Todd A. Nelson, J.D. Roth, Nick Santora. Co-Executive Producers: Eli Holzman, Brian Richardson. Produced by: Genevieve Tackenberg. Camera: Mark S. Jacobs. Film Editor: Shawn Chow. Music: Chris Lowe, Neil Tennant. Directed by: Brian Smith.

CAST
Mike Richards (Host)

CONTESTANTS
Joe Block, Cher Tenbush, Tristin Clow, Sarah Coleman, Danielle Gonzalez, Joe Hanson, Josh Herman, Amanda Horan, Jennipher Johnson, Anker Mehta, Tyson Mao, Richard Rubin, Wes Wilson.

That '70s Show star Ashton Kutcher is the mastermind behind this comedy-reality series which lands eight gorgeous women and eight nerdy men together in a Bel Air mansion for a unique competition. The women are "academically impaired" (meaning stupid) but physically remarkable (meaning hot), whereas the males are "socially inept" (meaning goofballs) but brilliant.

Eight teams, each consisting of one beauty and one nerd, compete against each other to win the grand prize of $250,000. But it's not easy, as each of the show's geeky challenges plays directly to the established stereotypes about "beauties" and "geeks." For instance, the women must complete an assignment to assemble a computer, while the guys are left with the unenviable task of redecorating a room.

Another challenge forces the geeks to perform karaoke while the ladies prepare a speech on a political issue they know nothing about. Another episode revolves around a trip to Las Vegas for strip poker; another a trivia contest.

Contestants Josh and Cher won the grand prize.

The series will appear as a midseason replacement on the new CW network for its third season.

Not available on DVD.

THE BERNIE MAC SHOW

(FOX) (CANCELED) (30 minutes) (Fridays at 8:00 pm, EST. September 23, 2006-April 14, 2006) Regency Television/20th Century Fox. Created by: Larry Wilmore. Executive Producers: Peter Aronson, Michael Burkow. Co-Executive Producer: Warren Hutcherson. Produced by: Marc Abrams, Kate Angelo, Bernie Mac, Terri Schaffer. Camera: Victor Nelli Jr., Patricia Lee. Film Editors: Paul Anderson, Micahel Karlich. Music: Stanley A. Smith. Written by: Jerry Collins, Warren Hutcherson, Fred Johnson, Saladin K. Patterson, Terri Schaffer. Directed by: David Grossman, Ken Kwapis, Linda Mendoza, Roger Nygard, Victor Nelli Jr, Keith Truesdell, Millicent Shelton, Ken Whittingham.

CAST
Bernie Mac (Bernie)
Kellita Smith (Wanda)
Camille Winbush (Vanessa)
Jeremy Suarez (Jordan)
Dee Dee Davis (Bryana)

One of TV's sharpest and most delightfully unsentimental sitcoms about parenting, *The Bernie Mac Show* came to an end in the 2005–2006 season. Mac is a towering TV personality and a brilliant comic, and his four-season series never insulted its audience. The jokes were always whip smart, there was no insipid laugh track, and Mac could spin a line to prove absolutely devastating.

The Bernie Mac Show chronicles the only-in-TV-land story of a standup comedian in Los Angeles named—surprise—Bernie. He's happily married to his lovely wife, Wanda (Kellita Smith), who's successful in business. Out of the blue, all this changes. Bernie's sister from the Midwest gets sent to drug rehab and her three children are transferred to Bernie for custody. "Uncle" Bernie becomes a dad to eldest girl, Vanessa (Camille Winbush), Jordan (Jeremy Suarez), and little 9-year-old Bryana (Dee Dee Davis).

Whether he wants to be or not, Mac is now a Daddy times three, and one of the gags of this show has the star addressing the camera directly about his interactions with the children. It's obvious, of course, that he loves them, but he's also immensely irritated by them and surprised by their frequent stupidity.

In the last season of the series, Jordan joins the wrestling team ("Wrestling with a Sticky Situation"), Bernie enters a race for charity ("Marathon Mac"), and Vanessa gets a new car while Jordan visits Comic-Con ("Car Wars"). In a two-part episode, Bernie and wife Wanda decide to get pregnant, but experience issues with infertility ("Exercise in Fertility").

These may sound like fairly typical situation comedy plots (and they certainly are), but Mac is a charismatic star who dominates with tough edges and sharp demeanor.

The first season is available on DVD.

Anthony Anderson guests with Bernie Mac on **THE BERNIE MAC SHOW**.

THE BIGGEST LOSER 2

(NBC) (RENEWED) (60 minutes) (Mondays at 8:00 pm, EST; September 13, 2005–March 15, 2006) NBC Universal. Executive Producers: Al Berman, Dave Broome, John Foy, Todd A. Nelson, J.D. Roth, Ben Silverman. Produced by: Elayne Cilic, Tom Herschko, Fred Pichel, Elizabeth Young. Camera: Bry Thomas Sanders. Music: Mark T. Williams. Written by: Trace Slobotkin.

CAST
Caroline Rhea (Host)
Jillian Michaels (Trainer)
Bob Harper (Trainer)

CONTESTANTS
Andrea, Jeff, Jenn, Kathryn, Matt, Mark, Nick, Pete, Ruben, Ryan, Seth, Shannon, Suzanne, Suzy.

This follow-up to 2004's successful unscripted series, *The Biggest Loser* is actually two shows in one. The first is *The Biggest Loser 2*, and the second is *The Biggest Loser: Special Edition*.

Caroline Rhea is the host as fourteen very overweight and unhealthy contestants arrive at a ranch where they will participate in an effort to lose the most weight, to become, to coin a phrase, the biggest loser.

In *The Biggest Loser* 2, the men and women are separated into two color-coded teams, and each is given a personal trainer. However, encouragement, exercise, and healthy living is only part of the game. The contestants are cruelly tempted by sweets, buffets, and other delicacies. For instance, on one occasion they are told that if they eat high calorie foods, they'll be afforded the opportunity to speak with their families. If it sounds mean-spirited, it is.

Each week, one contestant is eliminated from the competition. When several rounds have gone by, those remaining are no longer working as part of a team, but it's every man (and woman) for him or herself. Among the carrots held out: trips to Vegas and Hollywood-style makeovers. Ultimately, the person who has lost the most weight is the winner of the contest.

The Biggest Loser: Special Edition followed the second edition of the regular series in the Fall of 2005. In this program, one group is pitted against another in direct competition. There was an installment involving military wives duking it out to lose weight, and another series involving engaged couples.

Although the outcome is always good on *The Biggest Loser*—people motivated to exercise, lose weight and eat healthier—one has to wonder at a society that revels in watching overweight people suffer and fight the urge to eat. Still, this second edition garnered huge ratings, drawing 16 million viewers for its finale.

The Biggest Loser is not available on DVD, but a *Biggest Loser* workout is…so jazzercise!

Not available on DVD.

BLUE COLLAR TV

(WB) (CANCELED) (60 minutes) (Wednesdays at 8:00 pm, EST; September 25, 2005-July 26, 2006) Parallel Entertainment/Riverside Productions Inc./Bahr-Small Productions/Warner Bros. TV. Executive Producers: Fax Bahr, Garry Campbell, Jeff Foxworthy, Brian Hartt, Adam Small, J.P. Williams. Co-Executive Producers: Ritch Shydner. Produced by: Emily Cutler, Chris Plourde. Film Editors: Neil Grieve, Michael Tansill, Adam Weiss. Music: Greg O'Connor. Written by: Gary Campbell, Blaine Captach, Emily Cutler, Liz Feldman, Ann Girard, Paul Greenberg, Matthew Harawitz, Laura House, Jason Jordan, Matthew Lawton, Vito Viscom, Hilary Winston. Directed by: Paul Miller.

CAST
Jeff Foxworthy
Larry the Cable Guy
Bill Engvall
Brooke Dillman
Ashley Drane
Ayda Field
Heath Hyche
Peter Oldring
Gary Anthony Williams

This half-hour sketch comedy series about rednecks was inspired by a successful *Blue Collar* tour and then a movie that aired on Comedy Central. The second season aired on WB in 2006, which ran episodes back-to-back on Wednesdays at 8:00 pm (EST) and 8:30 pm.

Each *Blue Collar TV* episode generally followed a unified central theme (like dating, shopping, lying, and birth) and then leapt into a standup routine by series star, Jeff Foxworthy. After that, recurring characters played by the ensemble cast were featured in humorous skits.

Among the routines was a soap opera called *White Trash Days of Our Lives*. Larry the Cable Guy also had his own unique take on national events in "Larry's Rants." Other recurring elements included the redneck "word of the week" and the redneck "yard of the week."

Although the red-state comedy of *Blue Collar TV* was very successful with some audiences, the series did not survive the high-pressure transition from the WB to the more urban CW, and the series was canceled.

You might be a redneck if you find consolation in this fact: *Blue Collar TV: The Complete Second Season* is available on DVD.

Available on DVD.

BOSTON LEGAL

(ABC) (RENEWED) (60 minutes) (Tuesdays at 10:00 pm, EST; September 27, 2005-May 16, 2006) David E. Kelley Productions. Created by: David E. Kelley. Executive Producers: Bill D'Elia, Scott Kaufer, David E. Kelley, Janet Leahy, Jeff Rake. Produced by: Robert Breech, Lawrence Broch, Jane G. Knutsen, Andrew Kreisberg, Phoef Sutton. Camera: James Bagdonas. Film Editors: Michael Hathaway, Philip Carr Neel. Music: Danny Lux. Written by: Corinenne Brinkerhoff, Lawrence Broch, David E. Kelly, Sanford Golden, Andrew Kreisberg, Janet Leahy, Michael Reisz, Jonathan Shapiro, Phoef Sutton. Directed by: Lou Antonio, Adam Arkin, Jeff Bleckner, Jim Badonas, Stephen Cragg, Mel Damski, Bill D'Elia, Mike Listo, Steve Robin, Arlene Sanford, Oz Scott, Jeannot Szwarc, Ron Underwwood, Bob Yannetti.

CAST
James Spader (Alan Shore)
William Shatner (Denny Crane)
Julie Bowen (Denise Bauer)
Mark Valley (Brad Chase)
Rene Auberjonois (Paul Lewiston)
Justin Mentell (Garrett Wells)
Ryan Michelle Bathe (Sara Holt)
Candice Bergen (Shirley Schmidt)

Although critically acclaimed, the first season of David E. Kelley's legal drama, *The Practice* spinoff called *Boston Legal*, didn't have it easy. It was afforded a terrific time slot on Sundays following *Desperate Housewives*, but then saw that berth taken right out from under it by the surprise hit, *Grey's Anatomy*. Although ABC renewed it, a handful of episodes (five to be exact) got left on the shelf.

Still, with a whopping twenty-seven episodes in its arsenal for season two and series star William Shatner awarded an Emmy for Best Supporting Actor, *Boston Legal* got a second chance…and a revamp. David Kelley realized the series functioned better as a comedy than a heavy drama, and made changes accordingly. "As the show evolved this past year, we discovered that the series really wants to be a comedy,"[6] he told Mike Duffy of the *Detroit Free Press*.

Accordingly, regulars Rhona Mitra, Lake Bell, and Monica Potter were let go, to be replaced by the more comedically adroit actress Julie Bowen (late of NBC's *Ed*), who would play a new associate, Denise Bauer. Although this change was promising, ABC still wasn't giving *Boston Legal* a free ride. The network moved the series into the more combative Tuesday night at the 10:00 pm time slot against *Law & Order: Special Victims Unit*, and kept *Grey's Anatomy* in *Legal's* old slot. The plan paid off, however, and *Boston Legal* flourished both creatively and popularity-wise in its second run, a time when it picked up a prestigious Peabody Award.

Boston Legal focuses on the Massachusetts branch of the international law firm Crane, Poole, and Schmidt. Denny Crane (William Shatner) is one of the founding partners and a legendary trial attorney. However, now in his seventies, the conservative Crane is feared to be losing his marbles due the encroachment of Alzheimer's.

A recent addition to the firm is Alan Shore (a character who appeared on the last year of *The Practice*), played by James Spader. Though younger, Shore is as idiosyncratic and individual as his new mentor, Crane, and the two men form a tight friendship. Candice Bergen plays Shirley Schmidt, Crane's ex-wife and a sensible head in the firm…always handling Crane's latest stupid eruption (which in Season Two includes an ill-fated marriage to a character played by Joanna Cassidy). Rene Auberjonois is Paul Lewiston, another sane character who runs the firm, and Mark Valley plays Brad Chase, a sometimes competitor to Shore.

In its second season, *Boston Legal*'s progressive politics came more to the forefront. There was a case taking on American big business, and in particular, credit card companies that charge excessive interest rates in "Legal Deficits." The IRS got sued in "Stick It," and medical privacy was the topic in "Too Much Information."

Characters underwent personal crises as well. Shore underwent a bout of aphasia ("Word Salad Days") and Denny Crane's son, played by Freddie Prinze, Jr. returned to make trouble for his dad. In one instance, Denny went to jail rather than defend an alleged rapist ("Truly, Madly, Deeply") and even shot his client!

Boston Legal's reputation for fine acting and outstanding, humorous scripts brought in an impressive array of guest stars in Season Two, including Betty White, Robert Wagner, and Ed Begley, Jr. Parker Posey played a scheming lawyer, Marlene Stanger, who joined the firm and was known as "The Squid" ("Squid Pro Quo"). Ex-*Boston Public* star Jeri Ryan also turned up as movie star Courtney Rae, who required lawyers after shooting a stalking member of the paparazzi.

Boston Legal was renewed for a third season by ABC, thus ensuring another docket of silly, amusing and ultimately inspiring court room monologues about America today.

Both seasons are now available on DVD.

CHAPPELLE'S SHOW

(Comedy Central) (CANCELED) (30 minutes) (Sundays at 9:00 pm, EST; Wednesdays at 9:00 pm, EST; July 9, 2006-July 25, 2006) Marobru Inc./Pilot Boy Productions. Executive Produced by: Michele Armour, Neal Brennan, Dave Chappelle. Produced by: Tamara Federici, Tsia Moses, Mary Novak, Gina Santonas, Chris Savage. Camera: Dan Shulman. Film Editor: Wyatt Smith. Music: Dead Prez.

CAST
Dave Chappelle
Charlie Murphy (Host)
Donnell Rawlings (Host)

During its first two seasons, the very funny sketch comedy *Chappelle's Show* became one of the most popular series on cable television, earning Dave Chappelle stardom…and a $50 million contract for the production of season three.

But something strange happened. In the spring of 2005, Chappelle quit his own show; at first naming exhaustion as the cause, and later citing racism as a key factor in discontinuing the popular program. All sorts of rumors floated around the industry about Chappelle, and with some suggesting he suffered from mental illness (or maybe drug use). From his sanctuary in Africa, where he had fled, the comic set the record straight about his series, and his feelings that he might never return to it. In particular, he felt he was losing the battle over the creative content of the show to businessmen, and that he was in terrible danger of not shattering racial stereotypes, but actually encouraging them.

Chappelle's relationship with Comedy Central grew more strained in the summer of 2006 when the network aired something they called *Chappelle's Show: The Lost Episodes*, a collection of three half-hour episodes from the aborted third season.

The skits featured in the *Lost Episodes* were assembled without Dave Chappelle's input or approval, and were poorly regarded. In one skit, Chappelle played Democratic politician Howard Dean and repeated his famous campaign-ending "scream." In another skit, entitled "The Fifty-Five Million Dollar Man," he poked fun at his own fame (and the price of it).

The show's "lost" episodes are available on DVD.

CHARMED

(WB) (CANCELED) (60 minutes) (Sundays at 8:00 pm, EST; September 25, 2005-May 21, 2006) Spelling Television. Created by: Constance M. Burge. Executive Producer: Brad Kern. Produced by: Rob Wright. Camera: Jonathan West. Film Editors: Derek Berlatsky, Paul Fontaine, Don Kelly, Stewart Schill, Alan L. Shefland, William Turro. Music: Jake Alston, Jay Gruska, J. Peter Robinson. Written by: Doug E. Jones, Brad Kern, Cameron Litvack, Andy Reaser, Jeannine Renshaw, Liz Sagal. Directed by: LeVar Burton, James L. Conway, Mel Damski, Joel Feigenbaum, Stuart Gillard, Derek Johansen, Jonathan West.

CAST

Holly Marie Combs (Piper Halliwell)
Alyssa Milano (Phoebe Halliwell)
Rose McGowan (Paige Matthews)
Kaley Cuoco (Billie Jenkins)

Many insiders were surprised when the WB renewed the supernatural comedy/drama *Charmed* at the end of its seventh season. The durable series had begun airing in the fall of 1998, but ratings were slowly slipping and the series had weathered massive changes, including the departure of original star, Shannen Doherty. However, there was a last-minute reprieve from the WB and an additional season was commissioned.

By the end of the eighth season in May 2006, the handwriting was *really* on the wall: the Halliwells would cast no further spells after their magical 178th hour-long episode run.

In a sense, *Charmed* remains a genuine under-the-radar phenomenon. Although not generally appreciated by critics, it survived on the air longer than either of its WB supernatural brethren, in particular *Buffy the Vampire Slayer* and *Angel*. Still, in its eighth and final season, the series writers had to work some magic to continue

things after the seventh season wrapup, which had felt particularly final.

Thus the last season of *Charmed* found the Halliwell family (all of them witches living in a lush San Francisco mansion) adjusting to life in a kind of supernatural witness protection program, living "demon free" for the first time ("Still Charmed and Kicking") in years. That accommodation didn't last long, however, and soon the girls—Piper (Holly Marie Combs), Phoebe (Alyssa Milano) and Rose McGowan's Paige were back in the supernatural saddle, even training a new "good" witch, Billie (Kaley Cuoco).

In various eighth season episodes, the Halliwells faced off against a demon who could abduct people and trap them in photographs ("The Lost Picture Show"), a virus that could turn magically inclined people into evil monsters ("Hulkus Pocus"), and even Cupid himself ("Engaged and Confused"). The witches visited the Underworld ("Kill Billie Vol. 2"), fought a demon masquerading as a competitive parent ("Desperate House-witches"), and Paige was engaged to a man named Henry, played by guest star Irvan Sergei.

Finally, on May 21, 2006, the WB (also in its final year) aired the ultimate installment, "Forever Charmed," the series finale which found Piper attempting to turn back time and save her sisters from their untimely demises. This time, things were final. "This was our second chance to end the series properly," said executive producer Brad Kern, who also promised fans "a valentine."[7]

"It's been a hell of a run," Kern added after completing the last episode. "But all good things must come to an end."[8]

No doubt the "power of three" will continue for years to come in reruns and DVD releases, which are now up to the sixth season.

THE CLOSER

(TNT) (RENEWED) (60 minutes) (Mondays at 9:00 pm, EST; June 12, 2006-September 18, 2006) Shepard/Robin Company/Warner Bros. Executive Producer: James Duffy, Michael M. Robin, Greer Shepard. Produced by: Andrew J. Sacks, Gil Carcetti. Camera: Christopher Baffa, Brian J. Reynolds. Film Editors: Butch Wertman. Music: James S. Levine. Written by: Hunt Baldwin, Adam Belanoff, Mike Berchem, James Duff,` John Coveney, Wendy West. Directed by: Arvin Brown, Matt Earl Beesley, Lesli Linka Glatter, Elodie Keene, Gloria Muzio, Michael M. Robin, Rick Wallace.

CAST

Kyra Sedgwick (Deputy Chief Brenda Johnson)
J.K. Simmons (Assistant Police Chief Will Pope)
Corey Reynolds (Sgt. David Gabriel)
Robert Gossett (Captain Taylor)
G.W. Bailey (Detective Provenza)
Tony Denison (Detective Andy Flynn)
Jon Tenney (Detective Fritz Howard)
Michael Paul Chan (Mike Tao)
Raymond Cruz (Detective Julio Sanchez)
Gina Ravera (Detective Irene Daniels)

The number one new cable series of 2005 returned for its second season in 2006. *The Closer* stars sexy Kyra Sedgwick as Deputy Chief Brenda Johnson, a former CIA interrogator from Atlanta, until she moved to the Los Angeles Police Department and joined the Priority Homicide Division there. Although her presence in the division is resented by many of the male officers, Brenda has a reputation to reckon with. Her nickname is "The Closer" because her legendary interrogation skills have a high rate of leading to convictions.

In Los Angeles, Brenda works for an old flame, Assistant Police Chief Pope (J. K. Simmons), but becomes romantically embroiled with Fritz Howard (Jon Ten-

ney), a handsome detective. Other detectives, including Gabriel (Corey Daniels), are not so welcoming, though Brenda quickly proves her usefulness to the department.

In the second season, Brenda and the detectives investigate when a jurist dies unexpectedly during a mobster's trial ("Mom's Duty"). In "Aftertaste," the wife of a chef is murdered, leaving the husband as the prime suspect, though the suspect pool soon widens.

In "Out of Focus" an obnoxious member of the paparazzi is found dead. His quarry was a top Hollywood star, so did the photographer know a secret the celebrity would murder to keep hidden? The death of a porn star is the subject of "Head over Heels" and "Slippin'" involves a gang-related murder of a college student.

Currently, television is overloaded with crime dramas like *The Closer*, but this series' secret weapon is Kyra Sedgwick, who thoroughly relishes what might accurately be called her first star turn. Sedgwick's portrayal of tough-as-nails Brenda Johnson elevates the series above the rest of the crime pack, and it's a unique angle to focus on "the closer" in the interrogation room. Sooner or later, however, crime series are going to run out of viable angles to keep going. But that's a discussion for another day.

The Closer opened its second season with record-breaking numbers, drawing 8.3 million viewers,[9] thus insuring a third season.

If you want to "open" the file on *The Closer,* the first season has been released on DVD.

Available on DVD.

COLD CASE

(CBS) (RENEWED) (60 minutes) (Sundays at 8:00 pm, EST; September 25, 2005-May 25, 2006) Jerry Bruckheimer Television/Warner Bros. Created by: Meredith Stiehlm. Executive Producers: Jerry Bruckheimer, Jonathan Littman. Meredith Stiehlm. Co-Executive Producers: Paris Barclay, Tyler Bensinder, Andre Newman, Sean Whitesell. Produced by: Merri Howard, Veena Cabreros Sud. Camera: Paul Sommers. Film Editor: Roderick Davis. Music: Michael A. Levine. Written by: Tyler Bensinger, Liz W. Garcia, Andrew Newman, Meredith Stiehlm, Veena Cabreros Sud, Craig Turk. Directed by: Paris Barclay, Kevin Bray, Roxann Dawson, Bill Eagles, Tim Hunter, Jessica Landaw, Mark Pellington, Craig Ross Jr., Michael Schultz, Marco Siegal, Alex Zakrewski.

CAST
Kathryn Morris (Lilly Rush)
Danny Pino (Scotty Valens)
John Finn (John Stillman)
Jeremy Ratchford (Nick Vera)
Thom Barry (Will Jeffries)
Tracie Thoms (Kat Miller)

This series, just completing its third season, studies and reopens cases where leads have dried up over the years, or—as the title suggests, in the lingo of law enforcement, "cold cases." *Cold Case* follows a crack team of investigators looking into these old cases, led by beach blond Lilly Rush (Kathryn Morris). Together, the group solves cases in 1929, 1945, 1968, 1988, and 2001 in the third season alone.

A typical episode of *Cold Cases* is "Death Penalty: Final Appeal." Here, the suicide of a corrupt policeman calls into question one of his arrests from a 1994 case. In that instance, an African-American man, Andre Tibbs, was arrested for the vicious murder of Kate Lange, a teenage girl who had just moved into a new house with her dad. Suspiciously, Andre was at the house that day, working for a moving company that employed ex-cons. Now, Tibbs is due to be executed in three days time, and waits on death row. He claims there is exculpatory evidence in the form of a letter he wrote, if only Lilly and her team can find it.

In an unexpected development, Andre dies before being cleared. But afterwards, the team finds the letter and pins the decade-old crime on the real culprit, Andre's boss at the moving company. He had been estranged from his own daughter, Faith, and was a child molester.

This may sound like an interesting tale, but "Death Penalty" bears all the flaws of the current "crime investigation" format; in particular that it features bland central characters in suits and ties mouthing long chunks of exposition and effortlessly solving straw man crimes. Oddly, this particular crime isn't even a cold case, since a person was convicted for the crime. Maybe the story should have been featured on the short-lived *In Justice* instead.

Anyway, the problem with this story, besides the pop tunes incongruously underlining many scenes, is that it's crushingly obvious Andre is innocent all along. All the clues are telegraphed. Andre dies, in fact, only because of a "black hat" character, an evil ADA who knew the letter was evidence but kept it to himself.

And, along the course of the tale, several clues about the killer's closeness to his daughter Faith are dropped, so the surprise is not a surprise at all. Then, adding insult to injury, every last iota of the crime is spelled out during an interrogation sequence in which the suspected killer not only doesn't ask for a lawyer to be present, but conveniently—*and on cue*—reveals to the investigators his true malevolent colors.

If all this isn't crushingly pedantic enough, *Cold Case* then gilds the lily. The episode ends with the appropriately named Lilly putting away the Kate Lange case in the file room. She then sees just ahead the ghost of that young girl, now looking beatific since justice has been served. After a half-smile, the ghost fades away. Sadly, this insipid moment is then coupled with a weepy country song that leads into the closing montage: that of a slow-motion funeral for Andre. Naturally, the ghost of Andre shows up too.

Other episodes in *Cold Case*'s third season involve the death of a dot.commer in 1999 ("Start Up"), the death of an obese freshman in a dorm fire in 2004, and a case from 1988 involving the demise of a teenage boy. "Honor" explores a 1972 case focusing on the shooting of a Vietnam War vet, and "Debut" is about a girl who died at her "coming out" debutante party in 1968.

Not yet available on DVD.

COPS

(FOX) (RENEWED) (30 minutes) (Saturdays 8:00-9:00 pm, EST; October 1, 2005-July 22, 2006) Langley Productions/ Fox. Created by: John Langley. Executive Producer: Malcolm Barbour. Camera: Scott Jason Farr. Film Editors: Wiliam Cole, Michael Glickman, Bryan McKenzie, Frank Sacco.

Whatcha gonna do when they come for you?

In 2006, one of the oldest reality series on TV, *Cops*, continued airing on FOX. In fact, the network broadcast two thirty-minute episodes back-to-back each Saturday night, immediately preceding another law-and-order series, *America's Most Wanted*. Remarkably, *Cops* has been on the air since 1989, and in 2006 was producing its whopping eighteenth season. Another threshold: *Cops* broadcast its 650th episode this year.

As most TV watchers are aware, *Cops* is unscripted, a kind of half-hour "documentary" (replete with shaky-cam) which follows the activities of real police officers on the beat. It's all unfiltered (or at least it looks that way) as cameras capture life and sometimes crimes unfolding before our very eyes. Domestic disturbances, vandalism, theft, prostitution, high-speed chases, physical altercations—these are all the bailiwick of *Cops*.

During this season, the series followed real police officers in Florida's Lee County, Las Vegas, Atlanta, Pittsburgh, and Spokane. Other locales included Palm Beach and Gwinnett County, Georgia.

The series is not currently available on DVD.

CROSSING JORDAN

(NBC) (RENEWED) (60 minutes) (Sundays at 10:00 pm, EST; September 25, 2005-May 7, 2006) Tailwind Productions/NBC Universal. Created by: Tim Kring. Executive Producers: Allan Arkush, Dennis Hammer, Tim Kring. Co-Executive Producers: Kathy McCormick, Emily Whitesell, Linda Gase. Produced by: Melissa Byer, Treena Hancock. Camera: John Aronson. Film Editor: Donn Aron. Music: Lisa Coleman, Wendy Melvoin. Written by: John Cowan, Linda Gase, Rob Fresco, Tim Kring, Kathry McCormick, Robert Rovner, Emily Whitesell. Directed by: Allan Arkush, Ernest Dickerson, Roxanne Dawson, Jonathan Kaplan, Bethany Rooney.

CAST

Jill Hennessy (Dr. Jordan Cavanaugh)
Miguel Ferrer (Dr. Garret Macy)
Jerry O'Connell (Detective Woodrow "Woody" Hoyt)
Kathryn Hahn (Lily Lebowski)
Ravi Kapoor ("Bug")
Steve Valentine (Nigel)

Crossing Jordan is the tale of beautiful Dr. Jordan Cavanaugh (Jill Hennessy), a brilliant medical examiner who utilizes scientific skills and her keen mind to solve crimes. She works in the Medical Examiner's Office under Dr. Macy (Miguel Ferrer) and frequently collaborates with Detective "Woody" Hoyt (Jerry O'Connell). She shares a mutual attraction with the latter. Lily Lebowski (Kathryn Hahn) is the grief counselor on staff, "Bug" (Ravi Kapoor) an entomologist and Nigel (Steve Valentine) another doctor who helps out on baffling cases.

In its fifth season, Jordan went in search of two missing boys during a storm while fighting the flu in "Under the Weather." That's dedication, huh? She also had to deal with a fussy new medical examiner played by Henry Winkler, and then investigate the prison health system in "Judgment Day." Jordan also went after a cop killer in "Man in Blue" and then there was a confessed killer who couldn't remember the crime he committed in "Total Recall." One episode, "Luck Be a Lady" featured a crossover with the popular NBC series *Las Vegas*. The season finale "Don't Leave Me This Way" found Jordan accused of a murder!

At first, it looked like NBC would hold back *Crossing Jordan* as a midseason replacement. Then, however, there was a change of heart at the network and *Crossing Jordan* was slated on the schedule.

Not currently available on DVD.

CSI

(CBS) (RENEWED) (60 minutes) (Thursdays at 9:00 pm, EST; September 22, 2005-May 18, 2006) Alliance Atlantis/ Jerry Bruckheimer Television/CBS. Created by: Anthony E. Zuicker. Executive Producers: Jerry Bruckheimer, Danny Cannon, Cynthia Chvatal, Naren Shankar. Co-Executive Producers: James Hart, Andrew Lipsitz. Produced by: Louis Shaw Milito, Henry Alonso Myers. Camera: Frank Byers, David Stockton. Film Editors: Lou Angelo, Claude Finkel, John Ganem, Alex Mackie. Music: John M. Keane. Written by: Dustin Lee Abraham, Josh Berman, Danny Cannon, Richard Catalini, Sarah Goldfinger, Jacqueline Hoyt, Richard J. Lewis, Carol Mendehlson, Henry Alonso Roberts, Jerry Stahl. Directed by: Danny Cannon, Duane Clark, Jeffrey G. Hunt, Carol Mendelsohn, Naren Shankar, Alec Smight, Bryan Spicer.

CAST

William L. Petersen (Gil Grissom)
Marg Helgenberger (Catherine Willows)
Gary Dourdan (Warrick Brown)
Jorja Fox (Sara Sidel)
George Eads (Nick Stokes)
Eric Szmanda (Greg Sanders)
Paul Guilfoyle (Captain Jim Brass)
Robert David Hall (Dr. Albert Robbins)

The start of a lucrative franchise, with two spinoffs on the air and a third reportedly in the works. *CSI* or *Crime Scene Investigations* is a ratings blockbuster for CBS. It just completed a sixth season and reveals no signs of diminishing in popularity; even if the idea of a forensic investigative team is now thoroughly played out.

Watching the original *CSI*, one understands why the series gained so much popularity in the first place. It's not just because *Everybody Loves Luminol* (my proposed title for the next spinoff, a sitcom variant) but rather because series leads Petersen and Helgenberger have crafted very interesting, colorful characters. One can't say the same of *Cold Case*, for instance.

In this case, Gil Grissom, a fifteen-year veteran of the Los Angeles crime lab, and Catherine Willows, a divorcee (and ex-exotic dancer)-turned-blood-spatter-expert are actually pretty well-rounded. They evidence a sense of humor, have blind spots, and generally seem like authentic human beings. Though it's endlessly fascinating to see crimes solved with forensics, it's always more interesting to know *who's* doing the solving, and how their personalities inform their breakthroughs.

In the 2005–2006 season, the Las Vegas CSI team investigated the death of a movie star discovered in a hotel room ("Room Service"), questioned in "Bite Me" whether a wife had accidentally died from falling down the stairs or if she received a push from her loving husband. A cult committing mass suicide was the subject of "Shooting Stars" and a corpse with excessive body hair was the subject of "Werewolves."

Bodies showed up in chimneys ("Up in Smoke") and in dumpsters ("Dog Eat Dog"), and the victims included a psychic ("Spellbound") and teen rappers ("Poppin' Tags"). One of the most interesting stories was a two-parter called "A Bullet Runs Through it" in which the gang had to figure out which gun had fired the shot that killed a police officer. I hasten to add, there were *hundreds* of bullets at the scene, so this was like identifying a needle in a haystack.

The season closed with a CSI team member shot, in "Way to Go," a cliffhanger that will pick up in season 7. The first six seasons are available on DVD.

CSI: MIAMI

(CBS) (RENEWED) (60 minutes) (Mondays at 10:00 pm, EST; September 19, 2005-May 22, 2006) Alliance/Atlantis/ Jerry Bruckheimer TV/CBS. Created by: Anthony E Zuiker, Ann Donahue, Carol Mendehlson. Executive Producers: Jerry Bruckheimer, Ann Donahue, Stephen Zito, Anthony E. Zuiker. Co-Executive Producer: Elizabeth Devine. Produced by: Don Tardino. Camera: Eagle Egilsson. Film Editors: Edward R. Abroms, Mark C. Baldwin, Joshua Carson, John Refoua. Written by: Elizabeth Devine, Ann Donahue, Marc Dube, Marc Guggenheim, Krystal Houghton, Corey Miller, Sunil Naya, Barry O'Brien, Dean Widenmann. Directed by: Matt Earl Beesley, Norberto Barba, Duane Clark, Ernest Dickerson, Eagle Egilsson, Karen Gaviola, Jonathan Glassner, Sam Hill.

CAST
David Caruso (Horatio Caine)
Emily Procter (Calleigh Duquesne)
Adam Rodriquez (Eric Delko)
Khandi Alexander (Medical Examiner Alexx Woods)
Jonathan Togo (Ryan Wolf)
Eva La Rue (Natalia Boa Vista)

The second product off the *CSI* assembly line is set in Miami and stars former *NYPD Blue* star David Caruso as the head of the Florida crime investigation unit, the dedicated Horatio Caine. A new twist in the format has these forensic detectives occasionally going after a street gang, the Mala Noche. In the show's fourth season, the gang appears in "Silencer," "Rampage," and the season finale, "One of Our Own."

Otherwise, *CSI: Miami* seems to be flying on creative autopilot; just another program about detective forensic work. At least two episodes in this run involved members of the team being accused of crimes they didn't commit, one of the oldest cliches on television. In "Under Suspicion," Horatio is the last person to have been with the victim and looks like a murderer. In "Deviant," Alexx is the one up for murder, this time of a child molester. The season also features another timeworn cliche, the cross-over with another popular show, in this case the baby of the breed: *CSI: NY.*

A pool boy is the victim in "Three Way," a foreign exchange student in "Blood in the Water," and a nail gun is the murder weapon in "Nailed," if any of that sounds like your forensic cup of tea.

The first four seasons are available on DVD.

CSI: NY

(CBS) (RENEWED) (60 minutes) (Wednesdays at 10:00 pm, EST; September 28, 2005-May 17, 2006) Alliance Atlantis Communications/Clayton Entertainment/Jerry Bruckheimer Television. Created by: Anthony E. Zuiker, Ann Donohue, Carol Mendelsohn. Executive Producers: Jerry Bruckheimer, Andrew Lipsitz, Jonathan Littman, Danny Cannon, Co-Executive Producer: Pam Veasey. Produced by: Timothy Leea, Eli Talbert, Vikki Williams. Camera: Chris Manley. Film Editor: Barry Leirer. Music: Bill Brown. Written by: Elizabeth Devine, John Dove, Peter M. Lenkov, Andrew Lipsitz, Eli Talbert. Directed by: David Von Ancken, Rob Bailey, Norberto Barba, Duane Clark, Steven Depaul, Kevin Dowling, Jonathan Glassner, Scott Lautanen, John Peters, James Whitmore.

CAST

Gary Sinise (Det. Mac Taylor)
Melina Kanakaredes (Det. Stella Bonasera)
Carmine Giovinazzo (Det. Danny Messer)
Vanessa Ferlito (Det. Aiden Burn)
Hill Harper (Dr. Sheldon Hawkes)
Eddie Cahill (Det. Don Flack)

In 2005–2006, *CSI: NY* flew high in the ratings, consistently ranking in the top ten series of the week. The second spinoff from the popular *CSI* drama (after *CSI: Miami*), this series adheres to the format and feel of the other programs down to the letter, although with a more New York (meaning, apparently, *sassy*) vibe.

CSI: NY centers around a dedicated team of forensic scientists at the New York Crime Lab. Like their counterparts on the other *CSI* series, these are the kind of precise investigators who obsess on hair fibers, and ought to buy stock in Luminol. Also like the other series, the dialogue is so "tech" heavy that it borders on camp at times.

One primary weakness of the characters: they all boast encyclopedic knowledge of *every* subject under the sun, not just forensics. For instance, in one episode involving a diplomat at the UN, a character recognizes the name of a series of Islands in the Atlantic, and reels off complex data about it, including the fact that the island nation joined the U.N. in 1991. Smart? *Perhaps*. But not very realistic. How many forensic investigators carry around that brand of knowledge?

Gary Sinise headlines the *CSI: NY* cast as Detective Mac Taylor, a workaholic widower who runs the lab and oversees the investigations. Melina Kanakaredes is Stella Bonasera, one of his lovely detectives, and who arrives on each murder scene with a seen-it-all, know-it-all demeanor that is off-putting. Eddie Cahill is a confrontational young detective, another Hollywood version of the pushy "*New Yawkuh*," and Hill Harper is Dr. Sheldon Hawkes, a black man who examines corpses.

The "evidence" in *CSI: NY* is presented sometimes in zooms and closeups of decayed teeth or hair lice, a trademark of *CSI* as well. In its second season, the series' investigators solve the murder of a roller derby girl ("Jamalot"), an exotic dancer ("Trapped"), a fashion model ("Wasted"), an assistant D.A. ("Fare Game"), a limo driver ("All Access"), and confront topical social issues such as polygamy ("Stealing Home").

The "complete" first season is available on DVD.

CURB YOUR ENTHUSIASM

(HBO) (RENEWED) (30 minutes) (Sundays at 10:00 pm, EST; September 25, 2005-December 4, 2005) HBO Films. Created by: Larry David. Executive Producers: Larry David, Jeff Garlin, Gavin Polone, Robert B. Weide. Co-Executive Producer: Sandy Chanley. Producer: Tom Bull. Camera: Bill Sheehy. Film Editors: Grady Cooper, Jon Corn, Steven Rasch. Written and directed by: Larry David.

CAST
Larry David (Himself)
Cheryl Hines (Cheryl David)
Jeff Garlin (Jeff Greene)

Curb Your Enthusiasm is the story of *Seinfeld* co-creator Larry David—a Jewish liberal writer, and his misadventures in Hollywood. As fans of the series are well aware, Larry is always offending *someone*, or *taking* offense at someone…with the result being verbal fireworks of an intense and often hurtful kind. The series is unique among its comedy brethren because there are no scripts as such, only outlines, and dialogue is often improvised. Actor Paul Dooley, who plays David's father-in-law on *Curb Your Enthusiasm*, told me in an interview for *Best in Show: The Films of Christopher Guest and Company* that the script outlines are closely guarded secrets on the set.

"Larry keeps it to himself," Dooley says. "He and the directors and producers look at it between scenes. '*Well, now we have do this,*' and they share it with the cameraman, but they don't give it to the cast because we don't need to know.'"

The HBO comedy's fifth season follows two story arcs. The first story involves misanthrope Larry David's quest to discover if he's actually adopted. He hires a private detective, played by Mekhi Phifer, to learn the answer. The second story involves David's friend, comedian Richard Lewis, and his urgent need of a kidney transplant. Turns out that Larry is a perfect match. Only thing is, Larry doesn't want to donate a kidney and will do anything to avoid it…including hoping against hope that Lewis's cousin, Louis Lewis, will die in a coma so his organs can be harvested.

Both of these stories climax in the final episode of the season, "The End," which sees David meet the folks whom he believes are his biological parents: corn fed, Red-State Christians from the Midwest. Also, the kidney issue is resolved with a journey to the afterlife.

One of the funniest episodes of the fifth season is the seventh installment, entitled "The Seder." This involves Larry inviting Rick Lefkowitz (*The Daily Show's* Rob Corddry), a convicted sex offender, to a religious dinner celebration. The other guests include a raging conservative and a doctor that David suspects is stealing his newspaper each morning. Plenty of shame, mistakes, and disasters ensue before the half-hour ends.

Seinfeld was always famous for generating new catchphrases; Larry David's *Curb Your Enthusiasm* plays with language in a similar and delightful fashion. This year, audiences meet a character, manager Jeff's ex-girlfriend, who has "an unusually large vagina" ("The Ski Lift") and also learn Jeff and Larry's "double transgression" theory of making your wife mad twice, but only paying for it once. Maybe this stuff isn't as memorable as "*master of your domain,*" but it's amusing.

Come the end of Season Five, it appeared that Larry was destined to meet his maker and face judgment in the afterlife for all the people whom he has crossed swords with during five seasons. As David lay in a hospital bed dying, a rabbi asked him if he wanted to make peace.

Then the series cuts to a lengthy montage of David's previous escapades. This sequence boasted a valedictory feeling of "The End," and again one might consider *Seinfeld* and how that series ended: with all the characters going off to the slammer after videotaping a crime but not lifting a finger to stop it.

Here, Larry David questions his faith and heritage, and sees it restored. He dies, and returns to life. He claims to be a changed man…but we see he hasn't changed at all, as audiences learn when he uses a handicapped bathroom.

That's probably a perfect place to call it quits on *Curb Your Enthusiasm*, with the recognition that even a brush with death will not change Larry David's nature. Available on DVD.

CUTS

(UPN)(CANCELED)(30 minutes) (Thursdays at 9:30 pm EST; September 22, 2005–May 11, 2006) Dick Clark Productions/ Penrose Productions/Paramount Television. Created by: Eunetta T. Boone and Bennie R. Richburg Jr. Executive Producers: Eunetta T. Boone, David Janollari, Bernie R. Richburg Jr. Co-Executive Producer: Kenny Smith Jr. Produced by: Jacque Edmonds, Erica Montolfo, John E. Vohler. Film Editor: Mark West. Music: Richard Wolf. Written by: Jessica Goldstein, Erica Montolfo, Bennie R. Richburg Jr., B. Mark Seabrooks, John Wolf. Directed by: Leonard R. Garner Jr., John Tracy, Ken Whittingham.

CAST

Shannon Elizabeth (Tiffany Sherwood)
Marques Houston (Kevin Barnes)
Shondrella Avery (Candy Taylor)
Rashaan Nall (Walt)
Edward Fordham, Jr. (Ace)

This is a workplace and relationship comedy spun off from the UPN series *One on One*. In *Cuts*, a spoiled (but gorgeous rich girl) named Tiffany reluctantly shares ownership in a Baltimore barbershop with urban, hip-hopper Kevin Barnes (Marques Houston). The two don't get along (although they're clearly attracted to one another), and the series focuses on their hijinks, and the hijinks of their staff. Candy (Shondrella Avery) is the shop manicurist and Ace (Edward Fordham, Jr.) and Walt (Rashan Nall) are comedic barbers.

All the typical situation comedy tropes get dragged out for re-use in *Cuts* as Tiffany and Kevin learn to deal with each other's idiosyncracies, old-school *Odd Couple* style. The duo pretends to be married in "Wife Swap," for instance. Other episodes among the twenty-two aired in the sophomore season include "Mack Daddies," in which Tiffany learns her father is dating a younger woman, and "Hair Tease" in which the shop staff endures a sexual harassment sensitivity seminar.

Cuts was not one of the series that survived the UPN/WB merger, and its 2005–2006 season was its last.

No DVD releases have been forthcoming at this point.

THE DAILY SHOW WITH JON STEWART

(Comedy Central) (RENEWED) (30 minutes) (Weeknights at 11:00 pm, EST; January 4, 2006-Continuing) Mad Cow Productions/Comedy Central. Created by: Madeleine Smithberg, Lizz Winstead. Executive Producers: Ben Karlin, Jon Stewart. Co-Executive Producer: Stewart Bailey. Produced by: Colby Hall, Christian Santiago. Camera: Matt Sohn. Film Editors: Mark Paone, David Small. Music: Rob Mould. Written by: Rachel Axler, Chris Regan, Jon Stewart. Directed by: Christian Santiago.

CAST
Jon Stewart (Host)
Samantha Bee (Correspondent)
Rob Corddry (Correspondent)
Ed Helms (Correspondent)
Lewis Black (Commentator)

Another watercooler show. *The Daily Show with Jon Stewart*, currently finishing its eleventh season, is a half-hour satire of national and global news. Host Stewart derides the series as "fake news" since it adopts the anchorman format of most news programs and then presents headlines and more intricate stories in each segment. "It's even better than being informed," is also one of the show's headlines.

But something funny happened to *The Daily Show*. With all critics of the Bush Administration being compared to terrorists, being labeled unpatriotic or accused of cutting-and-running, the only group that could effectively challenge this rhetoric was…the comedians. Jon Stewart took up that mantle and has crafted a series that for many young people gazes at the news more objectively and more honestly than network news programs. Why? Because, part of Stewart's *modus operandi* is to make politicians accountable for their remarks.

When President Bush says "Heck of a job Brownie" after the disastrous FEMA response to Hurricane Katrina, *The Daily Show* rightly points out, it wasn't a heck of a job. When an official contradicts his story or "flip flops," to use the vernacular, *The Daily Show* hauls out archival footage of the same politician saying the exact opposite thing. In one famous segment on the series, Jon Stewart has Bush the candidate of 2000 debate Bush the President of 2005 to reveal how different they are. Importantly, he allows the President to hang himself. There's very little he needs to say.

When the corporate media in this country stopped holding politicians accountable for their words and contradictions, it was only a matter of time before other outlets began to do their work for them. And that's why *The Daily Show* has become such a phenomenon. It is unremittingly funny, of course, but it also reveals the politicians in a more accurate light than fawning coverage on CNN or FOX News.

Also, in the last several years, Jon Stewart has shifted away from interviewing entertainment personalities (though they still appear) to interviewing political figures, pundits, and authors of serious books on policy and history. In 2005 and 2006, Stewart sat next to such luminaries as Senators Barbara Boxer, Russ Feingold, Ted Kennedy, John McCain, Barack Obama, and Chuck Schumer. He had as guests former President Jimmy Carter, former Vice-President Al Gore, General Toni Zinni, former Secretary of State Madeleine Albright, Minority Leader Nancy Pelosi, and former Governor Howard Dean. He welcomed pundits such as Fred Barnes and Bill Kristol, and authors such as Peter Bergen (*The Osama bin Laden I Know*), and more. These interviews did not lob softballs, either.

The Daily Show features several regular news segments, including "Mess-O'Potamia," which looks at the ongoing war in Iraq and "Evolution Schmevlotion," about the American right's war on science. Correspondents on the series include Rob Corddry, who recently gave a geography lesson on the whereabouts of "Macaca" (It's "next to Ya-peepee"), perpetually pissed off Lewis Black, who editorializes in "Back in Black," as well as Ed Helms, Jason Jones, and Samantha Bee. Alumni of *The Daily Show* include Steve Carell (*The Office*) and Stephen Colbert (*The Colbert Report*).

In 2006, *The Daily Show* was so popular that segments were regularly featured on Internet sites *YouTube* and the blog, *Crooks and Liars*. The right wing, including Bill O'Reilly, have now taken to accusing *The Daily Show with Jon Stewart* of turning people off of politics.

On the contrary, *The Daily Show* calls for a more enlightened form of politics; one wherein elected officials are accountable to the governed. Those in power and those who speak for power (like O'Reilly) are obviously feeling the heat from Stewart's popularity.

Although the show is not available in box sets, compilations, including Election 2004 coverage called "Indecision 2004" are available on DVD.

DANCING WITH THE STARS

(ABC) (RENEWED) (60 minutes) (Thursdays at 8:00 pm, EST; Fridays at 8:00 pm, EST; Sundays at 8:00 pm, EST; January 5, 2006-February 26, 2006) BBC Worldwide. Executive Producer: Conrad Green. Co-Executive Producer: Izzie Pick. Produced by: Rob Wade, Matilda Zoltowski. Film Editors: Sean Basaman, David Timone. Musical Supervisor: Harold Wheeler. Directed by: Alex Rudzinski.

CAST
Tom Bergeron (Host)
Samantha Harris (Host)
Len Goodman (Judge)
Carrie Ann Inaba (Judge)
Bruno Tonioli (Judge)

CONTESTANTS
Tia Carrera & Maksim Chmerkovskiy, Giselle Fernandez & Jonathan Roberts, George Hamilton & Edyta Sliwinski, Stacy Keibler & Tony Dovalani, Drew Lachey & Cheryl Burke, Master P & Ashly Del Grosso, Kenny Mayne & Andrea Hale, Tatum O'Neal & Nick Kosovich, Lisa Rinna & Louis van Amstel, Jerry Rice and Anna Trebunskaya.

The series *Dancing with the Stars* is based on the international TV hit *Strictly Come Dancing*, and was the phenomenon of the summer of 2005 both in terms of ratings and popularity with audiences. The TV hoofer blazed back onto the screen for an even more popular and highly seated second season in the winter of 2006. In the process, it stomped all over Olympics coverage, reducing the ratings for that event some 50 percent below 2002 numbers.

Dancing with the Stars (not to be confused with *So You Think You Can Dance* on FOX), is a contest hosted by Tom Bergeron and Samantha Harris, who replaces last year's co-host, Lisa Canning. In the second season, they introduce audiences to ten couples, each one consisting of a celebrity (or, let's face it, a pseudo-celebrity) and an expert dancer. Each week, the couples perform and one couple gets eliminated by a panel of judges.

Yes, it's the tiresome *American Idol* format once more as judges Goodman, Inaba, and Tonioli make their choices and then, on a results show airing the following night, America puts in its votes.

The winners were Drew Lachey and Cheryl Burke. Sixteen hour-long episodes were aired.

Dancing with the Stars returned for a third season on September 12, 2006. The roster of featured celebrities includes conservative commentator Tucker Carlson, talk show host Jerry Springer, and movie stars Vivica A. Fox and Harry Hamlin, among others.

Not available on DVD.

DEADWOOD

(HBO) (CANCELED) (60 minutes) (Sundays at 10:00 pm, EST; June 11, 2006–August 27, 2006) Roscoe Productions/HBO. Created by: David Milch. Executive Producers: David Milch, Greg Fienberg. Produced by: Ed Bianchi, Ted Mann, Elizabeth Sarnoff, Steve Turner. Camera: Joseph E. Gallagher. Film Editor: Stephen Mark. Written by: Ed Bianchi, Gregg Fienberg, David Milch, Steve Shill. Directed by: Daniel Attias, Ed Bianchi, Adam Davidson, Gregg Fienberg, Tim Hunter, Dan Minahan, Mark Tinker.

CAST

Timothy Olyphant (Seth Bullock)
Ian McShane (Albert Swearengen)
Molly Parker (Alma Garret)
Jim Beaver (Ellsworth)
W. Earl Brown (Dan Dority)
Kim Dickens (Joanie)
John Hawkes (Sol Star)
Brad Dourif (Doc Cochrane)
Anna Gunn (Martha Bullock)
Jeffrey Jones (A.W. Merrick)
Paula Malcomson (Trixie)
Leon Rippy (Tom Nuttall)
Robin Weigert (Calamity Jane)
Powers Boothe (Cy Tolliver)
Gerald McRaney (Hearst)

"I will profane your fucking remains," one character threatens in an episode of *Deadwood*'s third season, entitled "Tell Your God to Ready for Blood." That curse is especially colorful, but so is this gritty, densely layered Western. In case you didn't make the connection, *Deadwood* remains the only Western on television, and this program is unlike any other representative of the form; it's not your Daddy's *Bonanza* (1959–1973) or *Gunsmoke* (1955–1975), that's for certain.

Instead, all the characters actually speak as people in that time might have; and accordingly the series boasts a deep literary-sounding bent. The words and sentences spoken by the characters are beautiful—even when the thought behind them is crude, like that example of cussing. *Deadwood* is a gorgeous series from a visual standpoint too, made to look as if it's authentically lit by candlelight (remember, no electricity was available back then). The series enjoys a rich, nearly golden hue in some carefully illuminated scenes, and it's quite striking.

As are the previous seasons, the third season of *Deadwood* is set at an outlaw "camp"—a dusty strip—that's not yet quite a town…called Deadwood. But the camp is growing, and on the verge of holding its first true elections for the offices of mayor and sheriff, respectively. *Deadwood*'s cast is huge, but one protagonist is a fella named Bullock (Timothy Olyphant), who's running for sheriff. Unfortunately, he's stepping into a turf war between a powerful local warlord named Hearst (Gerald McRaney) and the town's vile and violent saloon-keeper, Swearengen (Ian McShane). There are about a million other subplots going on here as well: at the whorehouse, in the local school, and even on those dusty streets, and the one thing *Deadwood* doesn't do is talk down or insult the audience. This is a series that requires viewers to pay close attention.

And that's probably why HBO canceled *Deadwood* at the end of its third season. Although creator David Milch has reported there will be a TV-movie to tie up loose ends, the series as it exists now is finished, which is a sad fact given its distinctive quality; there's no other show that looks or sounds like this on TV.

The first two seasons are available on DVD.

A glowering Sean Bridgers stars in the late, lamented western, **DEADWOOD**.

DESPERATE HOUSEWIVES

(ABC) (RENEWED) (60 minutes) (Sundays at 9:00 pm, EST; September 25, 2005-May 21, 2006) Touchstone Television. Created by: Marc Cherry. Executive Producers: Marc Cherry, Tom Spezialy. Co-Executive Producers: Chris Black, Joel Murphy, John Pardee, George W. Perkins. Produced by: Alexandra Cunningham, Kevin Etten, Charles Skouras. Camera: Walt Fraser, Lowell Peterson. Film Editor: Andrew Doerfer. Music by: Danny Elfman. Written by: Jenna Bans, Chris Black, Marc Cherry, Alan Cross, Alexandra Cunningham, Kevin Etten, Ellie Herman, Josh Senter, Tom Spezialy, Bruce Zimmerman. Directed by: Stephen Cragg, David Grossman, Robert Duncan McNeill, Arlene Sanford, Larry Shaw, Wendy Stanzler, Paul Thomas, Randy Zisk.

CAST

Teri Hatcher (Susan Mayer)
Marcia Cross (Bree Van De Kamp)
Felicity Huffman (Lynette Scavo)
Eva Longoria (Gabrielle Solis)
Brenda Strong (Mary Alice Young)
James Denton (Mike the Plumber)
Nicollette Sheridan (Edie)
Ricardo Antonio Chavira (Carlos Solis)
Alfre Woodard (Betty Applewhite)
Joy Lauren (Danielle Van De Kamp)
Richard Burgi (Karl Mayer)
Doug Savant (Tom Scavo)

If anything, the second season of the smash hit soap opera *Desperate Housewives* makes one realize just how good, how witty, and how sharp the first season really was. In other words, this is a sophomore slump, and *Desperate Housewives* in its followup season feels like a letdown, a disappointment.

Desperate Housewives is set in wealthy American suburbia, on Wisteria Lane. The neighborhood and its denizens are introduced in voiceover by a dead woman,

Mary Alice Young (Brenda Strong), a fun touch. There's hapless divorcee Susan (Teri Hatcher), just finding her way in life, along with her daughter. There's clutched and uptight redheaded Bree (Marcia Cross). Lynette (Felicity Huffman) is a better executive than she is mother to her monstrous boys, and sexy Gabrielle (Eva Longoria) has been engaging in hot sex with the young lawn boy. Edie (Nicollette Sheridan) is the street's slut. Other characters include handsome plumber Mike (James Denton), who is trying to solve a mystery, and Susan's ex-husband, Karl (Richard Burgi).

Desperate Housewives' first season involved a mystery revolving around these characters, in particular the shocking death of Mary Alice, and later the discovery of a crate containing body parts. With these enigmas resolved, *Desperate Housewives* plunged into its second season looking for new territory, a replacement mystery to keep viewers addicted. It found this MacGuffin in a new character played by the talented Alfre Woodard as a new neighbor from Chicago, Betty Applewhite. Suffice it to say that this subplot was not really an adequate replacement for what had come before, and actually bordered on the absurd. Fortunately, it also ended in the two-part season finale, "Remember."

As for the housewives of Wisteria Lane, they seemed to spend less time together in the second season as well, which ruined the fine and delicate balance of the first year. Still, the wives all had their own storylines to deal with. Susan and Mike start out the year together and breakup. Then Susan finds out that her ex, Karl is sleeping with hussy Edie ("You Could Drive a Man Crazy"). Unexpectedly, Karl and Susan rekindle their romance. Meanwhile, the buttoned-down Bree indulges in a romantic relationship with a pharmacist named George and wages a battle with alcoholism. Latin lover Gabrielle sees hubby Carlos incarcerated in prison, has a miscarriage, and then the couple contemplates adopting a baby. Over at the Scavo household, Lynette goes back to work, and her husband (Doug Savant) does too, at her place of employment.

Guest stars in *Desperate Housewives'* second season include Wallace Shawn and Adrian Pasdar, and various episodes bring up lurid details of life in suburbia. A sex tape surfaces in "Color and Light," the town is beset with burglaries in "The Sun Won't Set," and someone tries to blackmail Bree in "One More Kiss." It's all commendably exploitive, yet has lurched towards camp at the expense of believability. Not surprisingly, *Desperate Housewives* was shut out in terms of Emmy Nominations for its second trip around the block.

But that doesn't mean the third season won't see a dramatic resurgence for these resilient, if increasingly desperate, housewives.

Both seasons are available on DVD.

DOG THE BOUNTY HUNTER

(A&E) (RENEWED) (60 minutes) (Tuesdays at 9:00 pm, EST; Wednesdays at 1:00 am, EST; March 21, 2006-August 29, 2006) Hybrid Films/A&E. Executive Producers: Neil A. Cohen, Nancy Dubuc, Daniel Elias, David Houts, Rob Sharenow. Co-Executive Producers: Boris Lee Kurtonog. Produced by: Po Kutchins, Rick Simigielski. Film Editors: Debra Anderson, Sean Basaman, Neil Gegna, Sinead Kinnane, Keith Sicat. Directed by: Andrew Dunn, David Houts.

CAST
Duane "Dog" Chapman
Beth Smith
Leland Chapman
Duane Lee
Tim Chapman

Duane "Dog" Chapman is a real life bounty hunter who works out of Da Kine Bail Bonds in Hawaii. In the series' third season, which mixes adventure with Chapman's unique homelife, the big-haired, inked, musclebound man-in-black chases down fugitives from the law with his "posse."

In this case, that team includes his fiancee Beth, whom the 53-year-old Dog finally married in May of 2006, his two sons, Leland and Duane Lee, and the man he describes as his "blood brother," Tim Chapman.

During this run of *Dog the Bounty Hunter* episodes, Dog goes after some tough cookies. In "California, Here Dog Comes," the season opener, the bounty hunter sets his sights on a crook named Samu, whom he's been hunting for three years. Just seventy-hours remain till his bond comes due, and Dog could end up owing tens of thousands of dollars if the fugitive is not captured.

"In Sickness and in Health," Dog hunts a fugitive while feeling under the weather. In "Vegas or Bust," our favorite bounty hunter is the keynote speaker at a Bail Agents Convention in Las Vegas, but before he can get there, he needs to apprehend two fugitives: a check forger and a cat burglar.

This unscripted series is a peek at a different breed of (mulleted) guy, and his big-haired woman. As such it can be highly amusing. The chases are interesting, made more so by the fact that the series has a moral component to it. For Dog believes in the law—he believes in America—but on occasion he's asked to hunt down folks who've had a tough spell, and the brawny, bronzed bounty hunter is rarely insensitive to that fact, despite the rampant machismo on display. He's a cool customer in his sunglasses and with his tats, but he's also compassionate about what he does in some weird, basic male way.

In August 18, 2006, Dog got in trouble over one of the cases featured on the third season of the series. While tracking the evasive Samu in "California, Here Dog Comes," Dog allegedly mistook a nightclub owner named Lutu for the fugitive, and the police subsequently arrested him. Lutu filed a civil lawsuit in U.S. District Court in San Diego over the incident. "This is reality TV run amok," Jim Hammer, the plaintiff's attorney, said in an interview with *The San Francisco Chronicle*. "There's got to be a bright line between television entertainment on one hand and real police work on the other."[10]

Chapman may have been a bad dog on this occasion, but judging by the success of this A&E series (beginning a fourth season soon), the bounty hunter is still a policeman's best friend.

Season "best of" compilations are available on DVD.

THE DOG WHISPERER

(National Geographic) (RENEWED) (60 minutes)
(Mondays at 9:00 pm, EST; January 6, 2006-August 4, 2006)
MPH Entertainment Productions. Executive Producers: Mark Hufnail, Jim Milio, Melissa Jo Peltier. Produced by: Sheila Emery, Kay Sumner. Camera: David Hesson, David Newman. Film Editors: Mark Baum, Steven Centacchio, Diana Friedberg, Vicki Hammel, Janelle Ashley Nielsen. Music: Anouk Erni. Written by: Jim Milio, Melissa Jo Peltier. Directed by: Mark Cole, Sue Anne Fincke, Jim Milio.

CAST
Cesar Millan (The Dog Whisperer)

A most special and sensitive individual, Cesar Millan understands dogs. He runs a "Dog Psychology Center" and also pursues a unique philosophy about canine behavior that he terms "Power of the Pack." Basically, Cesar believes that dogs are pack animals, and therefore all of their happiness and all of their problems derive from their status as such. When pups are unhappy, it is often because their human owners do not understand their nature and the dynamics of the pack.

In the second season of the immensely popular *Dog Whisperer*, Cesar continues practicing what he preaches by paying house calls on troubled canines. Whether he's reparenting a dictatorial Chihuahua, helping a fearful Mastiff, reigning in an unpredictable German shepherd, or assisting of a compulsive beagle, he brings to bear his philosophy of the power of the pack.

Perhaps it's the end of decadent Western culture when there's a TV series devoted to helping troubled dogs. Or on the other hand, maybe it's good that mankind is learning to tune back into his environment, and the life around him. Discuss amongst yourselves…

The second season of *Dog Whisperer* began in the summer of '06, and by then had grown so popular that it was being lampooned on *South Park*, which featured an animated Cesar Millan re-educating bad boy Eric Cartman with his patented *Dog Whisperer* techniques.

The complete first season has been released on DVD.

ER

(NBC)(RENEWED)(60 minutes)(Thursdays at 10:00 pm, EST; September 22, 2005-May 18, 2006) Constant C. Productions/Amblin Television/Warner Bros. Created by: Michael Chrichton. Executive Producers: Christopher Chulack, Michael Chrichton, Dee Johnson, John Wells. Co-Executive Producers: Jonathan Kaplan, Richard Thorpe, David Zabel. Produced by: Wendy Spence Rosato. Camera: Arthur Albert. Film Editors: Jacque Toberen, Kevin Casey Tim Tommaasino. Music: Martin Davich. Written by: Janine Sherman Barrois, R. Scott Gemmill, Joe Sachs, Virgil Williams. Directed by: Arthur Albert, Christopher Chulack, Stephen Cragg, Lesli Linka Glatter, Laura Innes, Paul McCrane, Richard Thorpe.

CAST

Goran Visnjic (Dr. Luka Kovac)
Mekhi Phifer (Dr. Gregory Pratt)
Linda Cardellini (Samantha Taggart)
Laura Innes (Dr. Kerry Weaver)
Alex Kingston (Dr. Elizabeth Corday)
Ming-Na (Dr. Hen)
Parminder Nagra (Dr. Neela Rasgotra)
Sherry Stringfield (Dr. Susan Lewis)
Maura Tierney (Abby Lockhart)
Shane West (Ray Barnett)
Noah Wyle (Dr. John Carter)

Having been nominated for more than 100 Emmy Awards in its lifetime (and winning over twenty) *ER* blazed across the screen for its twelfth season in 2005–2006, an amazing accomplishment. It's even more remarkable considering that the series has forsaken little of its breakneck pace or open heart. It would be tempting to write a review that reads, "*this show needs new blood…stat!,*" but such a remark would be inaccurate. Although *ER* boasts almost an entirely different cast than the one it premiered with over a decade ago (with the exceptions of Sherry Stringfield and the recurring Noah Wyle), it's arguably as strong a series as it was in the mid-1990s.

ER focuses on a group of attending physicians at a Level One Trauma Center in County General Hospital. The series blends views of their hectic, crazed professional lives with their often-troubled personal lives. In the twelfth-season premiere, Sam's (Linda Cardellini) diabetic little boy, Alex runs away from home and doesn't have his insulin. That's harrowing enough, but perhaps the most poignant episode of the season stars James Woods as Nate Lennox, a professor suffering from a slow-moving, degenerative disease. "Body and Soul" is told via flashback, as Lennox grows progressively worse from one ER visit to the next. Woods' performance is touching and difficult to watch, and was nominated for an Emmy.

Other stories in *ER*'s twelfth season involve a surrogate mother, who refuses to undergo a critical C-section operation ("Nobody's Baby"), a woman who awakens from a coma after half-a-dozen years ("Blame It on the Rain"), and also a story about the prejudice and ignorance that still surround the AIDS epidemic ("I Do").

The first five seasons are available on DVD.

ENTOURAGE

(HBO) (RENEWED) (30 minutes) (Sundays at 9:00 pm, EST; June 11, 2006-August 27, 2006) Leverage Management/ HBO. Created by: Doug Ellin. Executive Producers: Stephen Levinson, Doug Ellin, Mark Wahlberg. Co-Executive Producers: Rob Weiss, Julian Farino, Marc Abrams, Michael Benson. Producers: Brian Burns, Lori Jo Nemhauser, Wayne Carmona. Camera: Steven Fierberg, Dave Perkal. Editors: Jonathan Scott Corn, Gregg Featherman. Writers: Marc Abrams, Michael Benson, Brian Burns, Doug Ellin, Rob Weiss. Directors: Julian Farino, Craig Zisk.

CAST
Kevin Connolly (Eric Murphy)
Adrian Grenier (Vincent Chase)
Kevin Dillon (Johnny "Drama" Chase)
Jerry Ferrara (Turtle)
Debi Mazar (Shauna)
Jeremy Piven (Ari Gold)

The third season of the critically acclaimed HBO half-hour comedy series *Entourage* continues the misadventures of Vincent Chase (Adrian Grenier), a hunky, curly-haired, up-and-coming movie-star in Hollywood, a veritable stranger in a strange land. Vince thrives navigating the Byzantine byways of modern La-La Land by keeping it "real;" maintaining his ties to the old neighborhood in Queens, NY.

Vince's titular "entourage," his colorful group of hangers-on, include Johnny "Drama" Chase (Kevin Dillon), an out-of-work actor and Vince's brother; Turtle (Jerry Ferrara), the designated driver and a budding entrepreneur; and Eric (Kevin Connolly), the savvy business manager and the only one among the group with even a lick of common sense.

Also among those Vince orbits is Ari Gold (Jeremy Piven), his foul-mouthed agent, who plays all the angles and knows the ropes of the industry. This season, Ari is vexed by a dissolute child actor who wants to date his daughter, and his enemies in the industry who don't want him to build a new and powerful agency. Ultimately, Ari gets rid of the little scoundrel by suggesting to director Penny Marshall (playing herself) that the obnoxious child be cast in the upcoming *Encyclopedia Brown* franchise…conveniently shooting in Kazakhstan.

Entourage's third season involves the premiere (and fallout) of Chase's latest blockbuster movie project, James Cameron's *Aquaman.* The season premiere, "Aquamom," escorts Vince and his buddies to the premiere of that megabudget film, and features red carpet cameos by "King of the World" director James Cameron himself , as well as actor James Woods, who plays the fictional movie's villain and who parodies his off-kilter, temperamental persona.

Follow-up episodes also dramatize the storyline involving Chase's superhero debut. For instance, the second segment, "One Day in the Valley," tracks *Aquaman*'s opening weekend, and the industry concern over the box office numbers. Is the movie going to be another *Spider-Man* (which grossed $114 million on its opening weekend) or fall below expectations (which rest at $95 million)? A series of rolling blackouts on the West Coast nearly scuttles *Aquaman* for good.

As Ari confides in Eric, Vince's business manager, one penny under expectations means Chase's movie is a failure…and Vince might as well leave town. One penny over expectations, and Vince is a conquering hero. The same episode offers a well-crafted riff on a trademark rooftop scene from Cameron Crowe's 2000 rock 'n' roll masterpiece, *Almost Famous,* so it's clear that even as the series ages, *Entourage* continues to have fun with the exigencies of modern Hollywood, as well as film history.

Ari (Jeremy Piven) and star Vincent Chase (Adrian Grenier) debate *Aquaman 2* in **ENTOURAGE**.

Other *Entourage* episodes this season, including "Guys and Dolls" and "Crash and Burn," track Vince through his surreal, Alice-in-Wonderland Hollywood existence as he becomes a prisoner of his own success and instantly becomes typecast as Aquaman. Vince wants to play Pablo Escobar in a passion project, a movie called *Medellin* (directed by Paul Haggis, who also cameos in an episode), but instead must report back to Warner Bros. for shooting on *Aquaman 2,* which is to be directed not by James Cameron…but Michael Bay.

The episode "Dominated" follows Vince to a promotional appearance at a theme park…where he's tasked to open the *Aquaman* roller coaster ride, and it's all quite funny. *Entourage* acknowledges and ribs the odd, bipolar nature of Hollywood. It's a land populated with creative artists, storytellers, and actors, yet dominated by cutthroat, imagination-impaired businessmen. No wonder the town seems so schizophrenic. Watching Vince navigate this minefield is amusing, bewildering, and accurate. *Entourage* is not quite a satire because it observes without histrionics the "real" movie industry, but tickles the funny bone anyway and in intelligent fashion.

Among the guest stars this season are Perrey Reeves, who plays Ari's long-suffering wife, and Nora Dunn, as Ari's therapist. Domenick Lombardozzi offers a scene-stealing stint in "Dominated" and "Guys and Dolls" as Vince's old buddy from back home, Dom…a felon who is welcomed back with not-quite-open-arms by the entourage. James Wood and James Cameron play themselves while Mercedes Ruehl plays Vincent's mom in "Aquamom." The late Bruno Kirby shows up in "Guys and Dolls" as the creator of *Shrek* and *Madagascar,* and directors Paul Haggis, Ed Burns, and Penny Marshall play themselves in "Crash and Burn."

Other running plot lines: Turtle attempts to become a player in the business by repping a rapper called Saigon (playing himself); and Johnny convinces Ari to represent him professionally. In the last episode of the season, after Ari botches a deal for Vincent to star in a bio of The Ramones produced by senile Bob Ryan (guest Martin Landau), Chase does the unthinkable. He fires Ari.

Catch up with Vincent Chase on the first two season box sets on DVD.

EVE

(UPN) (CANCELED) (30 minutes) (Thursdays at 9:00 pm, EST; September 22, 2005-May 11, 2006) The Greenblatt/Janollari Studio/Mega Diva Inc./Warner Bros. Created by: Meg De Loatch. Executive Producers: Robert Greenblatt, David Janollari. Co-Executive Producers: Troy Carter, Meg De Loatch, David W. Duclon, Eve. Produced by: Anthony C. Hill. Camera: Gary D. Scott. Film Editor: Jim McQueen. Music: Missy Elliott. Written by: Michael Ajakwe Jr., Trish Baker, Randi Barnes, David Duclon, Anthony C. Hill, Walt Kubiak, Vivien Mejia, Katrina Weaver, David Wyatt. Directed by: Mary Lou Bell, Kim Fields, Leonard R. Garner, Beverly D. Hunter, Reggie Life, Art Manke, Alfonso Robeiro, Eric Dean Seaton.

CAST

Eve (Shelly Williams)
Jason George (J.T.)
Ali Landry (Rita Lefleur)
Natalie Desselle-Reid (Janie)
Brian Hooks (Nick Delaney)
Sean Maguire (Donovan Brink)

Grammy Award-winning MC "Eve" headlines in this star vehicle, a UPN sitcom starring a cast of African-Americans. Or as, the network describes the premise: "Eve stars as a woman whose fashion career is on the move. But her love life is a work in progress."[11]

Confusingly—since the show is titled *Eve*—Eve actually portrays a character named Shelly, the owner of a clothing boutique called Diva Style. Her best friends and confidantes are Rita (Ali Landry), a former model, and Janie (Natalie Desselle-Reid), a married buddy. On the male side of the equation is Donovan (Sean Maguire), who runs a hot Miami club, J.T. (Jason George), a seemingly content bachelor who really loves Shelly, and Nick (Brian Hooks), another friend.

During the course of this last season of the UPN situation comedy, Shelly contends with a double wedding proposal: one from J.T. and another from a guy named Grant. Shelly chooses her bud J.T., who is also accepted to medical school. Meanwhile, in terms of career, Diva Style premieres a new line of clothing at the South Beach fashion show in "Model Behavior," and Shelly finds out that one of her clothing line distributors employs sweatshop employees ("Brit Better Have My Money").

Not currently available on DVD.

EVERWOOD

(WB) (CANCELED) (60 minutes) (Thursdays at 9:00 pm, EST; September 29, 2005–June 5, 2006) Belanti/Liddell Productions/Everwood, Utah/WB. Executive Producers: Greg Berlanti, Mickey Liddell, Rina Mimoun. Co-Executive Producer: Andrew A. Ackerman. Produced by: David Petrarca. Camera: Bruce Douglas Johnson. Film Editor: Kurt Bullinger. Music: Kathleen York. Written by: Anna Fricke, Tom Garrigus, Bryan Holdman, Rina Mimoun, Josh Reims, Nancy Won. Directed by: Tom Amandes, Arvin Brown, Joyce Chopra, Perry Lange, Peter Markle, David Paymer, Joe Pennella, Ellen S. Pressman, Charlie Stratton.

CAST

Treat Williams (Dr. Andrew Brown)
Gregory Smith (Ephram Brown)
Emily Van Camp (Amy Nicole Abbott)
Debra Mooney (Edna Harper)
John Beasley (Irv Harper)
Vivien Cardone (Delia)
Stephanie Niznik (Nina Feeny)
Scott Wolf (Jake)
Tom Amandes (Harold Abbott)

Everwood is a family drama set among the picturesque Rocky Mountains. It focuses on the relationship of Dr. Andrew Brown (Treat Williams), a widower to his two children, Ephram (Gregory Smith) and Delia (Vivien Cardone). They all moved to the small Colorado town of Everwood, leaving behind the hustle and bustle of New York. It was there that Andy set up a free clinic to service the community. Edna (Debra Mooney) is his nurse and receptionist. Also, *Everwood* focuses on the relationship between Ephram and the girl he loves, Amy (Emily Van Camp), as well as the romance of Andy and Nina (Stephanie Niznik).

At the end of the third season, Ephram fled Everwood for Europe after a breakup with Amy. In season four, he returns, and realizes he still harbors feelings for the young woman. While he attempts to repair the relationship, the family drama continues to cover a number of socially relevant issues, often in relation to Andy's role as physician to the community. Viagra comes up as a topic in "Put on a Happy Face," premarital sex is on the radar in "Connect Four" and "Getting to Know You." Breast cancer ("An Ounce of Prevention") and drunk driving ("Across the Line") are also topics in this fourth and last season.

The first season is currently available on DVD.

EXTREME MAKEOVER:
HOME EDITION

(ABC) (RENEWED) (60 minutes) (Sundays at 8:00 pm, EST; August 14, 2005-May 21, 2006) Endemol Entertainment/ Tom Forman Productions/Greengrass Productions/ABC. Executive Producers: Craig Armstrong, Tom Forman. Co-Executive Procuers: Luis Burreto, Denise Cramsey. Produced by: Pete S. Alexander, Alexander Lipson, Courtney MacGregor, Mark Raines, Emily Sinclair, Kathryn Vaughn. Camera: Therese Sherman, Daryl Studebaker. Film Editors: Jackson Anderer, Marc Cahill, Sean Fanton, Michael Yanovich. Directed by: David Dryden, Patrick Higgins.

CAST
Ty Pennington (Host)

DESIGN TEAM
Paul DiMeo, Paige Hemmis, Tracy Hutson, John Littlefield, Tanya McQueen, Michael Moloney, Ed Sanders, Preston Sharp, Eduardo Xol

Good morning! This is the fourth season of the popular hour-long tearjerker in which do-it-yourself remodeler Ty Pennington and his team of contractors, designers, and landscapers descend upon American families in need without their advance knowledge and builds them a brand new luxury home.

Every episode of *Extreme Makeover: Home Edition* requires a fresh supply of Kleenex as audiences are introduced to kind, decent citizens who have faced trauma in their lives, and achieve a sense of happiness and satisfaction from the generous changes Ty brings into their lives.

While families are away on vacation or some other such cover, Ty and his team and accomplish in seven days what most construction companies would takes four months to achieve. Ty himself usually creates something special, something "customized" for the new (or rebuilt) house, just to grant it a personal touch.

In the fourth season, Ty visits "The Nick Family" with *America's Most Wanted* host, Adam Walsh, and it's a family that's suffered through the traumatic experience of having a child abducted. In "The Rodriguez Family," the crew builds a new home for a handicapped Iraq war veteran living in Tennessee. In "The Tom Family," a woman who cares for children with disabilities is built a new and improved home. In El Segundo, Texas Ty inspires another family, this time rebuilding the home of a police officer whose wife suffers from cancer. In "The Goodale Family," an amputee's load is made lighter by the show's involvement.

Is *Extreme Makeover: Home Edition* schmaltzy? Yes, indeed. But it's also sweet and good. There's no reason why a "feel good" show shouldn't succeed on television, and it's wonderful to watch injured and broken people being helped…even if only for a week. Critics may condescend, but *Extreme Makeover* has heart.

One set is available on DVD.

FAMILY GUY

(FOX) (RENEWED) (30 minutes) (Sundays at 9:00 pm, EST; September 11, 2005-May 14, 2006) Film Roman/Fuzzy Door/Hands Down/20th Century Fox. Created by: Seth MacFarlane. Developed by: Seth MacFarlane and David Zuckerman. Executive Producers: Seth MacFarlane, Daniel Palladino, David Zuckerman. Co-Executive Producers: Craig Huffman, Danny Smith. Produced by: Allison Adler, Steve Callaghan. Film Editors: Rick Mackenzie, John Walts. Music: Ron Jones, Walter Murphy. Written by: Kirk Butler, Matt Fleckstein, Mila Henry, Mark Hentemann, Michael Rowe, Alec Sulkin, Danny Smith, Wellesley Wild, John Viener. Directed by: Greg Cotton, Kurt Dumas, Sarah Frost, Seth Kearsley, Chuck Klein, Zac Moncrief.

VOICE CAST

Seth MacFarlane (Peter Griffin/Stewie Griffin/Brian the Dog); Alex Borstein (Lois Griffin); Seth Green (Chris Griffin); Mila Kunis (Meghan Griffin).

Family Guy is the cult series that won't die. It's been resurrected after cancellation twice, following a 100,000-strong viewer petition and then rocketing DVD sales. It's an animated comedy that's often stood in the long shadow of the more critically acclaimed *The Simpsons*, in part because it also airs on FOX, is animated, and features a strange suburban family going through daily life.

Also, in 2006, *South Park* aired a two-part episode mocking *Family Guy*, crafting a joke about the seemingly random writing style that dominates the popular half-hour series. That episode took Cartman into the staff writers' room and revealed an odd secret.

Such criticism aside, it's difficult to argue with success, and one either "gets" and approves of the humor of *Family Guy* or doesn't. Yes, it's a "domestic" comedy about a family living in Quahog, Rhode Island, but the family issues that dominate the series are handled in an interesting fashion. The humor is actually surreal by definition; oftentimes a memory or even a word triggers an ironic or humorous tangent, and the series erupts into a comic ballet of absurdity. More than a simple family sitcom, *Family Guy* serves as a mile-a-minute, meta-deconstruction of pop culture, with family incidents spurring parodies of popular movies and TV programs.

Now, *The Simpsons* is also a self-aware, reflexive TV series that accounts for pop culture, but the balance is quite different. *Family Guy* features a looser structure, one that permits for a delightfully wide spiral outside the bounds of the strict narrative in question, whereas *The Simpsons* remains more formal and, in a sense, more disciplined in terms of plot structure. Perhaps the best way to understand the difference is this: *Family Guy* bases its humor on a viewer's understanding of pop culture allusions that fly fast and thick; whereas *The Simpsons* is more obviously about the family's adventures, and at the same time, comments on things already happening in the culture. *The Simpsons* is thus a more trenchant and relevant satire.

However, that doesn't mean *Family Guy* isn't funny, especially to Generation Xers who speak in the shared lexicon of the TV generation. This series from Seth MacFarlane is almost comedy by word association at times, and the flights of fancy or never less than inventive. Part of the humor is recognition; and part involves how the reference is marshaled in unpredictable ways.

In its fifth season, the series includes allusions to sources as diverse as *Back to the Future* (1985), *Happy Days* (1974–1984), *Quantum Leap* (1989–1993), *Planet of the Apes* (1968), *Poltergeist* (1982), *The Perfect Storm* (2000), and *The A-Team* (1983–1987). And that's just for starters. Guest stars such as Adam West, Alex Trebek, and Carrot Top also contribute to a sense of freewheeling madness.

Family Guy concerns fat patriarch Peter Griffin (Seth MacFarlane) and his antics with wife Lois (Alex Borstein), creepy son, Chris (Seth Green), oddly talkative baby Stewie (Seth MacFarlane), daughter Meghan (Mila Kunis), and the also-talkative Brian the Dog (MacFarlane again).

In the fifth season, Peter forms his own personal TV network in "PTV," gets a vasectomy in "Sibling Rivalry," writes an erotic novel in "Peterotica" and starts his own church devoted to the worship of the *Happy Days* character Fonzie in "The Father, The Son, and The Holy Fonz." "Petergeist" is a parody of—you guessed it—the 1982 horror film *Poltergeist*, and "Perfect Castaway" blends *Castaway* and *The Perfect Storm*, featuring Peter on a deserted island after Hurricane Ru Paul ruins a fishing trip.

First five seasons are currently available on DVD.

FEAR FACTOR

(NBC) (CANCELED) (60 minutes) (Tuesdays at 8:00 pm, EST; December 6, 2005-September 12, 2006) Endemol Entertainment/Evolution Film/Lock and Key Productions/Pulse Creative. Executive Producers: Joe De Mol, Matt Kunitz. Co-Executive Producers: Kathleen French, Douglas Ross. Produced by: Michael S. Glazer, Tom Heschnko, Scott Larsen, Rebecca Shumsky. Camera: Vincent Contarino, Victor Nelli Jr., Matt Sohn, Monty Woodard. Film Editors: Eric Beetner, Michael Berkowitz, Anthony Carbone, Tom McCudden, Jud Pratt, Julius Ramsey. Music: Russ Landau. Directed by: J. Rupert Thompson.

CAST
Joe Rogan (Host)

If your thing is watching people eat roaches, or drink "worm wine" (worms ground up into a slop and imbibed), then this is the TV show for you! *Fear Factor* is the long-lived reality "game" show that mistakes a healthy gag reflex for applause; nausea for entertainment.

Fear Factor's sixth season finds a very sad Joe Rogan still hosting, as weekly contestants run a gauntlet of various stunts and gags. Sometimes the stunts exploit a fear of water, other times a phobia of heights. Eating buffalo testicles? I don't know anyone who truly has a clinically-diagnosed phobia about that, but *bon appetit!*

Fear Factor punched up its formula in this season and sometimes aired 90-minute shows in hopes of spicing up the ratings. There was a "Blind Date" edition of *Fear Factor* in which four men and four women who were strangers paired up to win $50,000. One of their challenges involved entrapment in a tank with cold water… and large crabs.

Then there was "Psycho Fear Factor," a three-part miniseries that found contestants lodged in The Bates Motel, where Hitchcock's classic *Psycho* (1960) was filmed more than forty years ago. The stunts here were all horrific, as one might suspect. There was a blood shower, reminiscent of Janet Leigh's terrifying experience. More genuinely disturbing, however, was a "buried alive" stunt in which contestants were locked in coffins under tons of dirt with worms and rats. Their partners had to dig them out, and then the buried folks had to crawl out of the coffins. Yikes!

"Disaster Fear Factor," a particularly distasteful entry considering Hurricane Katrina, challenged contestants with floods and wind. Oddly, there was also a contest included wherein the players had to eat roaches. Now that's entertainment.

Ratings were low for *Fear Factor* this season and NBC finally canceled the reality show. But if you can't get your fill of the series, don't forget that there's a "Fear Factor" amusement park ride at Universal Studios.

And if you must relive the eating of buffalo testicles or other highwater marks for the tasteful series, the first season has now been released on DVD.

THE 4400

(USA) (RENEWED) (60 minutes) (Sundays at 9:00 pm, EST; June 11, 2006-August 27, 2006) American Zoetrope/Paramount. Created by: Rene Echevarria, Scott Peters. Executive Producers: Rene Echevarria, Scott Peters. Produced by: Kathy Gilroy-Sereda. Camera: Tony Westman. Film Editor: Paul Day. Music: Elliott Lurie. Written by: Ira Steven Behr, Amy Berg, Andrew Colville, Darcy Meyers, Bruce Miller, James Morris, Frederick Rappaport, Craig Sweeny. Directed by: Morgan Beggs, Colin Buckey, Nick Copus, Aaron Lipstadt, Vincient Misiano, Scott Peters.

CAST

Joel Gretsch (Tom Baldwin)
Jacqueline McKenzie (Diana Skouris)
Mahershalalhashbaz Ali (Richard Tyler)
Laura Allen (Lily)
Chad Faust (Kyle Baldwin)
Conchita Campbell (Maia Rutledge)

The 4400 is a fascinating science fiction mystery-drama from Ira Steven Behr, one of the producers of *Star Trek: Deep Space Nine* (1993–1999). When the series began three years ago, it seemed to concern alien abduction. To wit, one day a passing comet alters course and lands in America…and suddenly—*out of a blinding white light*—4,400 UFO abductees reappear on Earth. They have not aged. In fact, they appear unchanged and have amnesia. They have no recollection at all of their experiences "away." However, before long, some of the "returnees" do begin to evidence psychic and unusual powers.

Accordingly, NTAC (The National Threat Assessment Command) investigates the returnees. Two agents spearheading this project are criminal investigator Tom Baldwin (Joel Gretsch) and a medic, Diana Skouris (Jacqueline McKenzie). By the end of the second season of *The 4400*, there's a shocker: the "returnees" weren't abducted by aliens. Instead, they were taken by future humans and then returned to the past for some mysterious purpose.

In the third season, which aired in the summer of 2006, Skouris and Baldwin delve deeper into this mystery. They end up pitted against a faction of the 4,400 called "Nova Group." This cabal is considered a terrorist organization, but the members see themselves in terms of self-defense; preventing the government from any further mischief. On that front, the government had attempted to chemically suppress the abilities of the returnees.

The 4400 is a fascinating and complicated series, exploring a number of terrific genre concepts. For instance, have the 4,400 been sent back to help us, or does their presence destroy one timeline—a beneficial one—in favor of another? *The 4400* returns for a fourth season in the Summer of 2007.

The first two seasons are available on DVD.

GEORGE LOPEZ

(ABC) (RENEWED) (30 minutes) (Wednesdays at 8:00 pm, EST; October 5, 2005-April 12, 2006) Mohawk Productions Inc./Fortis Films. Executive Producers: Sandra Bullock, Robert Borden, Bruce Helford, Deborah Oppenheimer. Co-Executive Producer: Lawrence Broch, Rick Nyholm, Rachel Sweet. Produced by: Brett Baer, David Finkel, Jim Hope, John R. Morey. Camera: Peter Smokler. Film Editor: Pam Marshall. Music: W.G. Snuffy Walden. Written by: Robert Borden, David A. Captan, Kathy Fischer, Valentina Garza, Jim Hope, Paul A. Kaplan, Luisa Leschin, Michael Loftus, George Lopez, Rick Nyholm, Stacey Pulwer, Mark Torgore. Directed by: Sheldon Epps, Katy Garretson, Victor Gonzalez, Bob Koherr, Joe Regalbuto.

CAST

George Lopez (George Lopez)
Constance Marie (Angie Lopez)
Belita Moreno (Benny)
Masiela Lusha (Carmen Lopez)
Luis Armand Garcia (Max Lopez)
Valente Rodriguez (Ernie)
Emiliano Diez (Vic)

George Lopez is a sitcom about an extended Latino family living in Los Angeles. George (George Lopez) is the patriarch of the family, a man contending with his beautiful wife, Angie (Constance Marie), his two children—16-year-old Carmen (Masiela Lusha), and 13-year-old Max (Garcia)—and his troublesome and meddlesome mother, Benny (Belita Moreno). George works in an airplane parts plant with his buddy, Ernie (Valente Rodriguez). Vic (Emiliano Diez) is Angie's dad.

A family sitcom, and one of the few to focus on the Latino community, *George Lopez* is less aggressively stupid than its male-dominated family sitcom brethren on ABC (namely *Rodney* and *According to Jim*). Lopez is himself a more sympathetic figure, and his family seems less cartoonish (and much less smarmy) than that depicted on the aforementioned situation comedies. In fact, there are episodes of this sitcom that are downright involving, once you get into the swing of it. In "The Kidney Stays in the Picture," little Max experiences a health scare, and in the cliffhanger/season finale, everything gets thrown up in the air. George could lose his job when the plant closes and relocates to Mexico, Angie may be carrying another child, and Benny is in trouble with the law...and flees.

George Lopez's fifth sortie premiered in fall of 2005 to the strongest ratings it had seen in three seasons, a huge improvement in the number of viewers. In fact, *George Lopez* regularly bested *That '70s Show* on FOX and *Still Standing* on CBS, making it one of the few older sitcoms to earn high ratings.

The fifth season also saw interesting guest stars tromp through the Lopez household. Los Angeles mayor Antonio Villaraigosa appeared in the same episode with *Dog the Bounty Hunter* star Duane Chapman. Later, *Desperate Housewives*' cast-member Eva Longoria also guest-starred.

The series has been renewed for a sixth season, but the series is not yet available on DVD.

GHOST HUNTERS

(The SCI FI Channel) (RENEWED) (60 minutes) (Thursdays at 10:00 pm, EST; July 27, 2005-May 31, 2006) Pilgrim Films/ The SCI FI Channel. Executive Producers: Craig Piligian, Tom Thayer, Peter Zasky. Produced by: Jay Bluemke. Camera: Brian Hodge, Jonathan Pezza. Film Editor: Craig Ridenour. Directed by: Jay Bluemke, Tom Thayer, Peter Zasky.

CAST
Jason Hawes
Grant Wilson
Brian Harnois
Steve Gonsalves
Brian Bell

The immensely popular paranormal "documentary" *Ghost Hunters* returned to the SCI FI Channel for a triumphant second season, drawing some of the highest ratings yet catalogued for the network. As fans of the series are aware, *Ghost Hunters* follows a chapter of TAPS, an acronym which stands for The Atlantic Paranormal Society. Our heroes are plumbers by day, ghost trackers by night Grant Wilson and Jason Hawes. Brian Harnois is the troubled child of the group, and at one point during the second season even resigns before crawling back for reassignment.

Basically, Brian and Jason (who have been upfitted with a new van and a new HQ for season two), drive across America investigating allegations of ghostly hauntings and specters. The great thing about these guys, and what makes the show so entertaining, is that they treat their night job just like their day job: without histrionics or, really, melodrama. Their tools aren't wrenches, hammers, tubing or the like, but rather advanced tech-head stuff such as night vision lenses, hand-held DV cameras, laptops, EMF scanners (which read electromagnetic

fields), and on and on. They record audio in all their investigations for EVP (Electronic Voice Phenomenon) and also look for temperature variations (because a chill or cold spot is sign of the supernatural, if we're to believe these guys).

During the second season, these intrepid ghost hunters broadened their horizons and visited locales outside the northeast, where TAPS is headquartered. In one episode, they headed to Myrtles Plantation in Louisiana, reputedly one of the most haunted locations on the continent. Another installment took the TAPS team aboard the battleship *U.S.S. North Carolina*, where there had been reports of noises (ghostly rapping). They also visited an insane asylum in New York, and searched the Queen Mary for signs of spiritual interlopers. Usually, in each hour-long show, two investigations would be highlighted.

When and if ghosts are actually uncovered on camera using scientific gizmos, it's highly unlikely it will be on a somewhat cheesy, basic cable reality show, so *Ghost Hunters* has that working against it. But the no-nonsense attitude of the protagonists makes up for a lot of silly stuff. For instance, Jason and Grant are not so self-important that they can't admit when they've found absolutely nothing. Nor do they attempt to tart up their findings when forced to admit the investigation was a wash. One example of this is the segment set at the Willard Library in Indiana. The TAPS squad was searching for a "Gray Lady" apparition that had been reported for at least half a century. After a nighttime exploration of the entire facility, including a chilling walk through the empty book stacks, they found absolutely nothing. The only "manifestation" they find was light shining in through the windows from a nearby highway.

Other episodes give one the "creeps" in a mild way, as Jason and Grant experience strange things. In one episode set in Grafton, Massachusetts, one of the ghost hunters is inexplicably burned on his back. At that insane asylum in New York, a door shuts of its own volition…twice. If you're alone in the house, and at all inclined to take this stuff, goose bumps will result.

Ghost Hunters has been renewed for a third season. The first season is currently available on DVD.

GILMORE GIRLS

(WB) (RENEWED) (60 minutes) (Tuesdays at 8:00 pm, EST; September 13, 2005–May 9, 2006) Dorothy Parker Drank Here Productions/Hofflund/Polone/Warner Bros. Created by: Amy Sherman-Palladino. Executive Producers: Amy Sherman-Palladino, Daniel Palladino, Gavin Polone. Produced by: Sheila R. Lawrence, Geoffrey Hemwall. Camera: Teresa Medina. Film Editor: David L. Bertman. Music: Sam Phillips, Toni Stern. Written by: Keith Eisner, Rebecca Rand Kirshner, Jordan Nardino, Amy Sherman-Palladino, Daniel Palladino, David S. Rosenthal. Directed by: Jamie Babbit, Bob Berlinger, Stephen Clancy, Jackson Douglas, Linda Mendoza, Kenny Ortega, Amy Sherman-Palladino, Daniel Palladino, Ken Whittingham, Michael Zinberg.

CAST
Lauren Graham (Lorelai Gilmore)
Alexis Bledel (Rory Gilmore)
Melissa McCarthy (Sookie)
Yanic Truesdale (Michel)
Scott Patterson (Luke)
Kelly Bishop (Emily Gilmore)
Edward Herrmann (Richard Gilmore)
Matt Czuchry (Logan)
Sean Gunn (Kirk Gleason)

This popular WB family drama, which boasts some of the cleverest dialogue this side of *Buffy the Vampire Slayer* and *Veronica Mars*, finished its sixth season during the 2005–2006 season. It has developed a rabid fan following because of its quirky sense of humor, beloved characters, and fine performances.

Primarily, *Gilmore Girls* tells the story of Lorelai (Lauren Graham) and Rory Gilmore (Alexis Bledel), a mother and daughter in quaint Stars Hollow. They're a close-knit duo, and both neurotic as hell…but they clearly love each other. Rory is now a student at Yale, and Lorelai runs the Dragon Fly Inn with chef and friend Sookie (Melissa McCarthy). Both Gilmore women are involved romantically, Lorelai with Luke (Scott Patterson), and Rory with Logan (Matt Czuchry). Lorelai has also had to reopen ties to her parents (Edward Herrmann; Kelly Bishop) to pay for Rory's college tuition.

The sixth season picks up where the fifth left off. Rory and Lorelai are estranged after Rory pulled an ill-advised prank involving a yacht…and was arrested. Now she's doing community service, has left Yale and is living in her grandparent's guest house. During the course of the season, both women take steps to re-establish their close bond, but it isn't always easy. Sookie tries to help them by asking them to be godmothers of her children ("Always a Godmother, Never A God").

Meanwhile, Lorelai and Luke plan to get married, but their hopes and dreams are put on hiatus when Luke learns of a daughter named April that he never knew about ("The Prodigal Daughter"). Now he feels bad about getting married at this juncture, and at first doesn't even want April to meet Lorelai. Lorelai is patient but soon tires of Luke's delays.

Rory, who turns 21 this season ("Twenty-One is the Loneliest Number") also copes with the fact that after graduation, Logan will likely have to leave the country and return to England.

Gilmore Girls ends its sixth season on another downer note. Tired of waiting for Luke, Lorelai gives her beau an ultimatum about marriage. It doesn't turn out very well for her…

The seventh season is paired with *Veronica Mars* on the new CW network in the fall of 2006.

The first five seasons are available on DVD.

GIRLFRIENDS

(UPN) (RENEWED) (30 minutes) (Mondays at 9:00 pm, EST; September 19, 2005-May 8, 2006) Grammnet Productions/ Happy Camper Productions/Paramount. Executive Producers: Mara Brock Akil, Kelsey Grammer. Co-Executive Producer: Micahel B. Kaplan. Producer: Dan Dugan. Camera: Donald Dugan. Film Editor: Timothy Moser., Travis G. Rendich. Music: Camara Kambon. Written by: Mara Brock Akil, Kenya Barns, Mark Alton Brown, Deela Duke, Tim Edwards, Karin Gist, Martin B. Kaplan, Linda Mendoza, Prentice Penny. Directed by: Salim Akil, Debbie Allen, Mary Lou Belli, Roger Christiansen, Vito J. Giambalvo, Eric Laneuville, Arlene Sanford, Keith Truesdell.

CAST

Tracee Ellis Ross (Joan Clayton)
Golden Brooks (Maya)
Persia White (Lynn Searcy)
Jill Marie Jones (Toni Childs)
Reggie Hayes (William Dent)

This long-lived UPN urban sitcom has often been termed an African-American version of the popular hit, *Sex and the City*. A valid comparison, only *Girlfriends* has now remained on the air longer than the Carrie Bradshaw comedy.

Girlfriends follows a group of friends as they navigate their way through life in L.A. Joan (Tracee Ellis Ross) runs a restaurant called J. Spot and as the sixth season begins, is re-establishing her friendship with William (Reggie Hayes) after an attempt at romance. Maya (Golden Brooks) is a highly successful author now that her book *Oh, Hell Yes!* has been published. Lynn (Persia White) is in a band, and her sexual orientation is a matter of contention. Toni (Jill Marie Jones) is undergoing a relationship breakup and custody battle, but she doesn't easily take to motherhood either.

In the course of the sixth season, all these characters undergo changes and learn life lessons as they grapple with their particular subplots. Toni's problems with motherhood are a focus of "Latching on and Lashing Out." Maya quibbles with her man, Darnell, and attempts to generate greater book sales by creating a seminar based on her *Oh, Hell Yes!* Joan dates three different men, and faces the possibility that J. Spot will close after the restaurant struggles.

Girlfriends was renewed for a seventh season on the new CW, one of the few African-American-centric UPN situation comedies (along with *All of Us*) to make that transition successfully.

Not currently available on DVD.

Left to right, the sexy cast of **GIRLFRIENDS**:
Lynn (Persia White), Maya (Golden Brooks), Joan (Tracee Ellis Ross), Toni (Jill Marie Jones).

GREY'S ANATOMY

(ABC) (RENEWED) (60 minutes) (Sundays at 10:00 pm, EST; September 25, 2006-May 15, 2006) The Mark Gordon Company/Shonda Land/Touchstone Television. Created by: Shonda Rhimes. Executive Producers: Mark Gordon, Betsy Beers, James Parriott, Shonda Rhimes. Co-Executive Producers: Peter Horton, Krista Vernoff, Mark Wilding. Produced by: Tom Corn, Joan Rater, Tony Phelan. Camera: Adam Kane, Tim Suhrstedt. Film Editors: Briana London, Edward Ornela. Music: Danny Lux, Psapp. Written by: Zoanne Clack, Kip Koenig, Stacey McKee, James D. Parriott, Shonda Rhimes, Mimi Schmir, Gabrielle Stanton, Harry Werksmen, Mark Wilding. Directed by: Rob Corn, Alex Davidson, Mike Dinner, Leslie Linka Glatter, Peter Horton, Jeff Melman, Daniel Minahan, David Paymer, Mark Tinker, Jessica Yu.

CAST

Ellen Pompeo (Meredith Grey)
Patrick Dempsey (Dr. Derek Shepherd)
James Pickens, Jr. (Richard Webber)
T.R. Knight (George O'Malley)
Sandra Oh (Christina Yang)
Katherine Heigl (Isobel Stevens)
Chandra Wilson (Miranda Bailey)
Isaiah Washington (Preston Burke)
Justin Chambers (Alex Karev)

Grey's Anatomy tells the tale of Pixie-ish, *Ally McBeal*-type, young Meredith Grey (Ellen Pompeo), a surgical intern at one of the toughest residency programs in the country, in Seattle. She's supervised at the hospital by Dr. Richard Webber (James Pickens, Jr.), an older man experiencing some degradation of his surgical skills, despite his protestations to the contrary. Meredith is also in love with an attractive young surgeon at the hospital, Dr. Derek Shepherd (Patrick Dempsey), whom she calls "Dr. McDreamy" for his good looks and likeable personality. Unfortunately, Derek is married.

Meredith joins a team of surgical interns, including Isobel (Katherine Heigl) and Alex (Justin Chambers), two attractive youngsters who can't keep themselves from feeding "the beast," meaning having sexual intercourse. Christina Yang (Sandra Oh) is also in the program, a hard-pushing Stanford graduate and top student who is sleeping with a renowned heart surgeon, Preston Burke (Isaiah Washington). George O'Malley (T.R. Knight) is a geeky resident who is in love with Meredith, and Kate Walsh plays Dr. Addison Shepherd, Derek's not-estranged-enough-for-Meredith's-taste wife.

Grey's Anatomy is a chronicle of the work and play of these young doctors in training, as they save patients' lives, blow off steam, and fall in and out of love. "I wasn't interested in focusing on the patient's story," creator Shonda Rhimes told *Essence* Magazine. "I was more into the concept of 'This is your first month, day, year on the job, and you have no idea what you're doing. But in this job, when you mess up, someone dies.' That to me seemed interesting, and I wanted to make a show that I would want to see."[12]

Grey's Anatomy is also the latest in a long line of medical series, from *Marcus Welby, MD* (1969–1976) to *ER*. "I'm a medical junkie," Rhimes noted. "I love to watch all those surgeries on the Discovery Channel and TLC. And I thought there was something really sexy about surgery in the sense that they're kind of cowboys. It's the only job where you literally hold a beat of a heart in your hands. On a bad day, you'll kill someone, and on a good day, you save lives."[13]

Oh, who plays intern Yang, sees matters in a less romantic light. "People need to connect desperately after life and death situations. A friend of mine was doing a medical internship and was sleeping on the cot in a side room when two doctors who'd just finished a really intense surgery came in, screwed on the bed right beside her, and left! It's like war. That's the thing that I hope we keep dealing with. These people are at war."[14]

Sadly, the only war *Grey's Anatomy* seems to be fighting is one to remake the modern medical drama into, literally—*Ally McBeal* in scrubs. Many of the episodes are not merely insulting, but actually offensive in terms of the narcissism displayed by the *dramatis personae*.

Take for example the episode entitled "Into You Like a Train," which is literally and metaphorically a train wreck. The episode concerns a catastrophic train crash in Seattle, as all the interns are called back to the hospital during the crisis. Casualties soon arrive, bloodied and in pieces. Two people are actually speared together by a metal pole, and another patient is missing his leg. The surgeons (Meredith and Isobel) chatter behind a curtain during the crisis, complaining that Addison has selected salmon-colored scrubs for this occasion.

Is this really the opportunity for jokes about fashion disasters? People—*human beings*—are dying all around them, and this is what the surgeons are wasting time over?

Even worse, Yang is assigned the task of locating the missing leg. The series uses this quest as an opportunity for humor. She finds the wrong foot, and the male patient is in danger of having two left feet! Then, she tries again, but comes up with a woman's foot (with painted toe nails) rather than a man's! Isn't that just wacky?

Bad jokes are one thing, but the writing makes it absolutely plain where Yang's concerns truly rest. "It's not about the leg. It's not about the guy," she complains, when she can't find the missing limb. By inference, viewers understand exactly what it's about for this doctor-in-

training: *her career.* She's afraid that if she finds the wrong leg, Webber will kick her out of the program. The patient, the well-being of a living man, is not even in her mind.

It's even worse than that: this episode of *Grey's Anatomy* plays the pain of living beings as a source of humor. Not black humor, but gawking, tongue-in-cheek, freak show humor that would indeed, feel right at home on *Ally McBeal*.

The writing, alas is painfully overwrought and therefore dreary. The same episode features a "crisis" for the doctors as they deal with the two patients impaled on the pole. Only one can live, and the doctors must choose. This is all laid out in a beautiful, engaging (and not maudlin or sentimental) dialogue beautifully vetted by Patrick Dempsey and Isaiah Washington. But then, apparently having no faith in the viewer's ability to comprehend the dialogue just seen and heard, the writer (Krista Vernoff) has Meredith go postal. "How do you choose?" She melodramatically demands. "How do you choose who gets to live?" It's stating the obvious, and proof that *Grey's Anatomy* doesn't trust the audience enough to understand the stories without applying a sledgehammer.

The narcissism in *Grey's Anatomy* is truly astonishing at times. In "Yesterday," Burke gives Oh a speech about how he's the greatest doctor in those parts—brilliant and renowned—and that he's chosen to love *her*. Nice, huh? But what's even more disturbing is the manner that the series plays off patients' pain and suffering as a three-ring circus for the doctors to enjoy and crack jokes about. In "Much Too Much," the condition of priapism (long, uncomfortable erections) is mocked. In the aforementioned "Yesterday," a woman who spontaneously orgasms is made the leering butt of jokes by the interns. It would be fine if the series was trying to make a point about the narcissism and emotional retardation of doctors, but it seems to have no such point of view. *Grey's Anatomy* wants the audience to laugh at the unfortunate patients *with* the doctors. Why else the dopey, comedic soundtrack underscoring most scenes?

Grey's Anatomy is a very popular series, but one wholly lacking in subtlety. Both the score and writing telegraph what emotions the audience should be feeling at every moment, and after all the "wild and crazy" moments, virtually each episode has the audacity to feature a likeable character (patient) die, tugging at the heart strings. Here, that equation just doesn't work because it's obvious these self-obsessed interns don't give a rat's ass about the patients they're supposed to help. It's a sad statement about our times that doctors—whom we have cherished as helpful care givers—are now egocentric clowns.

The first season is available on DVD.

HALF & HALF

(UPN) (CANCELED) (30 minutes) (Mondays at 9:30 pm, EST; September 19, 2005–May 15, 2006) CBS Productions. Created by: Jeffrey Klarik. Executive Producers: Yvette Lee Bowser, Jamie Wooten. Produced by: Jan Dyer, Beverly Rose Kubik. Camera: Bryan Hays. Film Editor: Dennis Vejar. Written by: Yvette Lee Bowser, Tamiko K. Brooks, Michaela Feeley, Winifred Hervey, Heather MacGilvray, David L. Moses, Temple Northup, Geoff Tarson, Carla Bank Weddies, Jamie Wooten. Directed by: Ellen Gittelsohn.

CAST

Rachel True (Mona)
Essence Atkins (Dee Dee)
Telma Hopkins (Phyllis)
Valarie Pettiford (Big Dee Dee)
Chico Benymon (Spencer)
Alec Mapa (Adam)

In this situation comedy, two African-American half-sisters who haven't known each other for long end up moving into the same building. Sexy Mona (Rachel True) always lived with her single and working Mom, Phyllis (Telma Hopkins), and is now a self-made woman in her twenties, a record company executive for Delicious Records. Meanwhile, Dee Dee (Essence Atkins) is the daughter of Big Dee (Valarie Pettiford), a white collar woman with acting aspirations. Dee Dee is more indulged and a little less serious than Mona. She's a law school graduate but she doesn't know what she wants to do with her life.

Spencer (Chico Benymon) is Mona's helpful best friend, and Adam (Alec Mapa) the quirky office assistant at Delicious Records in this series that completed its fourth and final season in 2005–2006. The format is as old as *The Odd Couple*, featuring two very different women getting along together, but the series boasts a warm heart.

All the episode titles of *Half & Half* follow the same format. They begin with the words "The Big…" and end with the word "Episode." In "The Big Gen-Why Me? Episode" Dee Dee is cut off by her Dad when she decides she wants to go back to school rather than get a job, a plotline that has repercussions throughout the rest of the season. In "The Big Training Day Episode," she gets a job as a sports agent.

Meanwhile, Mona spends the season trying to get her social life straight. She attends her ten-year reunion in "The Big State of the Reunion Episode," and in the unresolved series finale must choose between two men she cares for: Chase and Lorenzo.

The show didn't survive the morphing process from UPN to CW, and no series box sets have yet been released on DVD.

HELL'S KITCHEN

(FOX) (RENEWED) (60 minutes) (Mondays at 9:00 pm, EST; June 12, 2006-August 14, 2006) Granada Entertainment USA/A Smith & Co. Productions/Upper Ground Enterprises. Executive Producers: Paul Jackson, Arthur Smith, Kent Weed. Co-Executive Producers: Andrew Scheer, Daniel Soiseth. Produced by: Jordan Beck, Peter Tartaglia. Camera: Chip Goebert. Film Editors: Scott Bloom, Jordan Browne, Carol Carimi, Shawn Gutierrez, Andrew P. Jones, Andrienne MacKillop, Marc Markley, Jennifer Read, Hudson Smith, Jason Thompson.

CAST
Chef Gordon Ramsay

CONTESTANTS
Rachel Brown, Virginia Dalbeck, Keith Greene, Sara Horowitz, Maribel Miller, Tom Pauley, Garrett Telle, Heather West.

The second season of *Hell's Kitchen* (known on screen as *Hell's Kitchen 2*) finds Chef Gordon Ramsay shepherding twelve young contestants through a grueling contest to become a top chef. If they can't stand the heat, the acerbic and demanding Ramsay sends them packing.

The twelve contestants in *Hell's Kitchen 2* competed in 2006 to become the "Executive Chef" at Red Rock Casino and Resort and Spa in Las Vegas, as well get a percentage of ownership in that institution. Ramsay tasked them weekly to create a complete dinner service, a complete lunch service (for rowdy tykes), run the kitchen, and finally, run a restaurant. The episodes began with teams—boys against the girls—but by midseason, it was every cook for him or herself. The winner of *Hell's Kitchen 2* was Heather West, a 25-year-old from New York.

"Heather won *Hell's Kitchen* due to her determination. She stuck to what she knew best and she controlled her kitchen from start to finish," Chef Ramsay revealed "Heather clearly has great leadership qualities and this, for a 25-year-old cook, is a phenomenon — this woman is going to be a big success."[15]

Hell's Kitchen 2 came out of nowhere in the summer doldrums of 2006 and cracked the Nielsen's top twenty. FOX rewarded the series with a quick renewal and the promise that *Hell's Kitchen 3* would emerge hot from the production oven in summer 2007.

The series is not available on DVD.

HOPE & FAITH

(ABC) (CANCELED) (30 minutes) (Fridays at 9:00 pm, EST;
September 30, 2005–May 2, 2006) Touchstone Television/
Industry Entertainment/ABC. Executive Producers: Keith Addis,
Guyman Casady, Michael Edelstein, Nastaran Dibai, Jeffery
B. Hodes. Co-Executive Producers: David Babcock, Peter Mur-
rieta, David S. Rosenthal. Produced by: Alysse Bezahler, Jason
Fisher, Tod Himmel. Camera: Dejan Georgevich, Dick Quinlan.
Film Editor: Art Kellner. Music: Alissa Moreno, John Swihart.
Written by: David Babcock, Nastaran Dibai, Mark Driscoll,
Marc Dworkin, Taylor Hamra, Tod Himmel, Jeffrey B. Hodes,
Cristy Stratton. Directed by: Scott Ellis, Gil Junger, Peter Marc
Jacobson, Don Scardino.

CAST
Faith Ford (Hope)
Kelly Ripa (Faith)
Ted McGinley (Charley)
Harve Presnell (Jack)
Macey Cruthird (Hayley)
Megan Fox (Sydney)
Paulie Litt (Justin)

Faith (Kelly Ripa) was once the gorgeous star of *The Sacred and the Sinful*, a popular daytime soap opera. She played "Ashley Storm" until her character's evil twin killed her off…leaving the actress unemployed and desperate. With nowhere to turn, Faith returned home to Ohio to live with her solid, happily married sister, Hope (Faith Ford), Hope's husband, Charley (Ted McGinley) and their three children of various ages (Macey Cruthird, Megan Fox, Paulie Litt). Now, Faith wreaks havoc on the household, but love will get the family through.

That's the premise of Kelly Ripa's sitcom, *Hope & Faith* which lasted for three seasons on ABC, and which was paired with the failed *Hot Properties* on Friday nights in the 2005–2006 season. It's a family sitcom with an *Odd Couple* matchup between sisters, and the valedictory season saw guest stars return such as Robert Wagner and Regis Philbin (Kelly Ripa's co-host on her *other* show).

On the last year of *Hope & Faith*, Faith milks the celebrity associated with her own fake death (an excuse used by Sydney at school over a late assignment) in "Faith Fairfield (1980–2005)," and chips a tooth in "Love and Teeth." Meanwhile, Hope and Charley hope to spice up their love life, and Hope learns to strip in "Charley's Shirt." Hope and Faith's Dad (Robert Wagner) returns to town with their heretofore unknown half-brother in tow in "Blood is Thicker Than Daughter," and Handsome Hal (Regis Philbin) comes back to audition to co-host a local morning show with Faith in "Homeless Hal."

Inoffensive, yet not particularly funny either, *Hope & Faith* remained on the air about as long as it probably could, given its thin and overfamiliar premise, its looka-like lead blondes, and generally uninspired writing. The show's ratings were never terrible, but they were never great.

The series is not available on DVD.

HOUSE

(FOX) (RENEWED) (60 minutes) (Tuesdays at 9:00 pm, EST; September 13, 2005--May 23, 2006) Heel and Toe Films/Bad Hat Harry Productions/NBC Universal. Created by: David Shore. Executive Producers: Paul Attanasio, Katie Jacobs, David Shore, Bryan Singer. Co-Executive Producers: Doris Egan, Russel Friend, Garrett Lerner, David Semel. Produced by: Lawrence Kaplow, Gerrit van der Meer. Camera: Walt Loyd Newton, Roy H. Wagner. Film Editors: Sue Blainey, Marta Envy, Scott Hahn, Deborah Moran, Tatiana Reigel. Music: Massive Attack. Written by: Doris Egan, David Foster, Liz Friedman, Russel Friend, Garrett Lerner, Lawrence Kaplow, David Shore, Matt Witten. Directed by: Jace Alexander, Daniel Attias, Gloria Muzio, Peter O'Fallon, Seran Sarafian, David Semel, Greg Yaitanes.

CAST
Hugh Laurie (Gregory House)
Omar Epps (Dr. Taylor Eric Foreman)
Lisa Edelstein (Dr. Lisa Cuddy)
Robert Sean Leonard (Dr. James Wilson)
Jennifer Morrison (Dr. Allison Cameron)
Jesse Spencer (Dr. Robert Chase)

Let's face it: Dr. Gregory House is not a very likeable guy. That fact breaks one of the oldest rules about TV programing: you can't have an unlikeable coot as your main character! However, House (as portrayed by Hugh Laurie) is undeniably charismatic; even disarming in his single-minded way. He's sharp-witted, brilliant, acerbic and wholly unconventional...which means the character represents a perfect "antidote" for what ails medical series these days. Also, this character clearly has a little age on him, which deepens the character significantly and is a welcome relief from all the gorgeous youngsters who populate *Grey's Anatomy.*

House (the man, not the show) is an untraditional and sometimes unsavory medical genius, but that's okay, because in a sense he's really another detective like Monk, or Columbo. *House* is a medical mystery show, with House routinely ferreting out facts and solutions, so maybe the ancillary rule to not having likeable lead characters would simply state that it doesn't apply to detectives; even medical ones.

Anyway, Dr. House solves his medical mysteries in this series under the watchful and frequently disapproving eye of the hospital administrator, Dr. Lisa Cuddy (Lisa Edelstein). He's assisted in his efforts by consults with oncology specialist Dr. Wilson (Robert Sean Leonard), immunologist Cameron (Jennifer Morrison) and neurologist Foreman (Omar Epps), but getting a consensus out of these guys isn't easy. And besides, House doesn't need one; trial and error is more his modus operandi.

A typical episode of *House* finds a guest character falling ill (usually collapsing) during the "teaser" and then finding his or her way to House. There's general bafflement at first; then usually a dead end or a blind alley. Finally, in the end, House figures out what's really going in with his patients and saves them. In "Acceptance," the second season premiere, he works on a death row inmate who has fallen ill. His condition looks like tuberculosis, but House soon figures out that he may have a tumor that's stimulating his adrenal gland...the very thing responsible for making him an uncontrollably violent man. Not that House cares about that.

Another episode, "Autopsy" involves a young cancer patient who suddenly experiences hallucinations. The doctors fear that these visions may be caused by a hidden tumor near the heart, but the only way to find out for sure is to conduct an autopsy. And that's exactly what House wants to do. On a living patient.

House has treated women with muscle spasms

("Need to Know") and a drug-addicted supermodel in "Skin Deep." Also, in one episode, House is himself badly wounded when he's shot by someone who doesn't find his probing and experimental medical techniques quite so amusing.

House is—quite simply—one of television's gems. Bolstered by Laurie's terrific, unsentimental performance, the series gives TV Land one of its most distinct and memorable new characters for the media Valhalla.

Both seasons are currently available on DVD.

The doctor is in, but he lacks a bedside manner...it's Dr. **HOUSE**, M.D. (Hugh Laurie).

HUFF

(Showtime) (CANCELED) (60 minutes) (Sundays at 10:00 pm, EST; April 2, 2006–June 25, 2006) Bob Lowry TV/Cannon Entertainment/Sony TV. Created by: Bob Lowry. Executive Producers: Cameron Jones, Bob Lowry, Scott Winant. Co-Executive Producer: Thania St. John. Produced by: Byron Bolasco, Jessica Mecklenburg, Nicole Mirante. Camera: Ronn Schmidt. Film Editor: Elba Sanchez-Short. Music: W.G. Snuffy Walden. Written by: Bryan Balasco, Annie Brunnero, Bob Lowry, Jessica Mecklenburg, Nicole Mirante, Mark Richard. Directed by: Sara Pia Anderson, Tricia Block, Steve Gomer, Dan Lerner, Tom Moore, Gloria Muzio, Scott Winant.

CAST

Hank Azaria (Craig "Huff" Huffstodt)
Paget Brewster (Beth)
Oliver Platt (Russell)
Anton Yelchin (Byrd)
Blythe Danner (Izzy)
Andy Comeau (Teddy)
Kimberly Brooks (Paula)
Faith Prince (Kelly Knipper)

This one-hour drama focuses on a psychiatrist named Huff (Hank Azaria). And it's a good thing that Huff can dispense drugs in his capacity as a mental health professional, because with his life…he needs all the help he can get! His wife Beth (Paget Brewster) is caring for her ill mother, Emmy-nominated Swoosie Kurtz, his teenage son Byrd (Anton Yelchin) is a handful, and his mother, Izzy (Emmy winner Blythe Danner) just had sexual intercourse with Huff's best friend, a sleazy attorney named Russell (Emmy nominee Platt). On top of all this, Huff's schizophrenic brother, Teddy (Andy Comeau) is out of the mental institution and has stolen his brother's car.

When the first season of Showtime's *Huff* culminated, Huff's car was gone, and the usually mild-mannered psychiatrist had just decked Russell, knocking him down a long flight of stairs. As the second season picks up, Russell has his neck in a cast, and his friendship with Huff is in mortal jeopardy.

Back on the job, Huff realizes that he isn't paying attention to his clients—a first in his career—because of all of his personal strife. During the season, Huff tries to heal all the holes in his life. Meanwhile, Russell acquires an aggressive new client, a maneater played by guest star Sharon Stone. Before long, she also turns up as one of Huff's clients. As if Russell doesn't have enough problems, he also learns that a former one-night stand is now pregnant with his unborn child. Anjelica Huston also shows up for a four-episode stint as a psychiatrist who lends Huff a shoulder for support.

Raucous and busy, but unappealingly lit, *Huff* is perhaps as much comedy as drama. It has received numerous critical accolades and yet there's an element of it that is overly precious and stagey.

The first season is available on DVD.

INTERVENTION

(A&E) (RENEWED) (60 minutes) (Sundays at 10:00 pm, EST; October 23, 2005-August 27, 2006) GRB Entertainment/A&E. Created by: Sam Mettler. Executive Producers: Gary R. Benz, Michael Branton, Nancy Dubuc. Produced by: Alison Martin, Amy Woods. Camera:.Chris Baron, Jamie Hall, Allison Martino, Amy Woods. Film Editors: Ben Daughtrey, Ryan Morrell, Greg O'Bryant, Mark Town. Music: The Davenports, Craig Marks, Dominic Messenger.

Intervention is a "documentary series" that, as described on it's A&E "about the show" web page, "profiles people who are losing their battle with their addictions, and whose friends and families feel the only remaining option is to hold an intervention." As it goes, this unscripted series gazes at desperate people and the tidal wave of destruction that follows their bad behavior.

The second season of this hour-long program continues to gaze at a person (or sometimes two) per episode, and attempts to convince them to enter rehab or therapy. "John" concerns a 33-year-old crack addict, "Corrine" is about an 18-year-old addicted to heroine and crystal meth (and also a diabetic). And "Kristen" looks at an alcoholic mom, whose behavior could lose her custody of her young daughter.

"Tim" is a fairly typical episode of *Intervention*. The audience is introduced to a workaholic, self-loathing music producer and crack addict named Tim. Tim is a brilliant pianist, but feels bad about himself and has been on an eighteen-month crack binge. His girlfriend Madyson is also his co-worker: a musician hoping to make it big. She sees what the crack is doing to Tim and her career aspirations and hopes to stage an intervention.

Madyson breaks up with Tim. He goes to her house and physically threatens her dad, also destroying a home computer that he claims belongs to him. The cameras follow Tim as he wanders away from Madyson's house, into the woods, into a river, and into a storm drain. There, in the culvert, he lays down in three feet of water and cries helplessly until a producer intervenes (on camera) and tells him to get up or he's going to call the police.

An *intervention* is staged, and at the last minute, Tim's parents decide to join Madyson and her folks. Tim gladly accepts the help offered and goes to rehab to retake control of his life. The intervention takes place in the last ten minutes or so. The rest of the episode features Tim's bad behavior instead (at one point, he flushes his crack down a motel toilet for fear the cops have found him). This focus on the more dramatic bad behavior rather than the actual intervention tells the viewer just about everything needed to know about the series. On one hand, the series stakes claim to the high ground, claiming to be about confronting and helping people in need. In reality, the show panders to the lowest common denominator and wallows in the histrionics of diseases like alcoholism and drug addiction.

Of all the reality shows, *Intervention* remains one of the most suspect in terms how much is staged. The opening card of the episode "Tim" (and other episodes) make it clear: Tim does not know an intervention is coming, that he will be surprised by it. Oh yeah, then why are cameras following him around for days, catching all his bad behavior? What show does he *think* they're shooting, *Bad Boys on Crack*? Something about this series just doesn't quite ring true…or ethical.

Not currently available on DVD.

IT'S ALWAYS SUNNY IN PHILADELPHIA

(FX) (30 minutes) (Thursdays at 10:00 pm, EST; June 29, 2006-August 17, 2006) RCH/3 Art Entertainment. Created by: Rob McElhenney. Executive Producers: Charlie Day, John Fortenberry, Glen Howerton, Rob McElhenney, Michael Rotenberg. Produced by: Tom Lafaro. Camera: Peter Smokler. Film Editors: Robert Bramwell, John Drisko. Music: Ray Espinola Jr. Written by: Charlie Day, Eric Falconer, David Hornsby, Glenn Howerton, Rob McElhenney, Chris Romano. Directed by: Daniel Attias, Rob McElhenney.

CAST
Charlie Day (Charlie)
Kaitlin Olson (Sweet Dee)
Rob McElhenney (Mac)
Glenn Howerton (Dennis)
Danny DeVito (Frank)
Anne Archer (Barbara)

American comedies are in crisis, and merciless series such as *It's Always Sunny in Philadephia* might just be the cure. Once upon, comedians understood that comedy by its very nature must include two elements: brutality and honesty. One quality serves the other, in a sense. And yet, big box office hits like *Wedding Crashers* (2004) or *The 40-Year-Old Virgin* (2005) gained critical acclaim and wide popularity even though they are neither honest nor brutal. Their *dramatis personae* instead succumb to treacly fables about morality, wherein they learn important lessons about themselves, and most importantly—love.

TV sitcoms can be that way too. How many episodes of *King of Queens*, *According to Jim*, *Rodney* or *Still Standing* end with husband and wife happily and blissfully reconciled after the husband's absurd and thoughtless behavior? How many of these "TV wives" actually get up and divorce their sitcom husbands? No, audiences are led to believe the women think that the male antisocial behavior is cute; and that's why the women stay.

All of this is a long-winded way of stating that *It's Always Sunny in Philadelphia*, which completed its second season in the summer of 2006, remembers that comedy should be brutal and honest. Matters such as sexual politics, political correctness and so forth have no place in a narrative that truly wishes to be funny. For instance, in the first season, there was a hysterical episode about abortion in which a slacker got the bright idea of attending a rally to hit on pro-life abortion-clinic protesters. The second year of the series includes the same genuinely mean streak, thank goodness. There's nothing here off-limits, and so TV conventions are shattered and cliches are laid to rest.

It's Always Sunny in Philadelphia is about four slackers, but these aren't TV slackers…these are real slackers. They have bad hair, wear old T-shirts, and probably don't smell too good. Anyway, between Charlie (Charlie Day), Mac (Rob McElhenney), Dennis (Glenn Howerton), and Dennis's sister Dee (Kaitlin Olson), the foursome manages a bar in Philadelphia. This is the "hub" for their bad behavior and in season two, there's plenty to go around. In one episode, Charlie realizes that wheelchairs are magnets for exotic dancers, and so exploits an injury to stay in one. Another episode involves a blasphemous idea: a stain that some in the gang thinks could make them money because it resembles the Virgin Mary. An episode involving a new zoning ordinance that could close down the bar walks a thin line that some viewers might feel is anti-Semitic.

The second season of *It's Always Sunny in Philadelphia* also throws in some new twists. Danny DeVito joins the cast as Dennis and Dee's absent dad, Frank. Anne

Archer also show's up as their Mom, Barbara. These two veterans fit right in, and add even further luster to a show that's willing to break boundaries and be absolutely uncompromising and unsentimental in its humor.

Other episodes in the second season find Charlie in AA ("The Gang Gives Back") and Frank teaching Dee how to box after she is mugged ("Hundred Dollar Baby").

No decision about renewal had yet been reached by FX when this book was written, but it would be a shame to forsake a true television original. When so much comedy on TV looks plastic, manufactured and dishonest, it's a pleasure to watch a series that has its own texture and aura, and dedication to honesty. Even if, on occasion, it threatens to become rampantly offensive.

Not yet available on DVD.

JAKE IN PROGRESS

(ABC) (CANCELED) (30 minutes) (Monday at 9:30 pm, EST; January 9, 2006) Brad Grey Television. Executive Producers: Tim Doyle, Brad Grey, Jeff Richman, Peter Traugtotti, Austin Winsberg. Produced by: Jeffrey Morton, Michael Spiller, John Stamos. Camera: Blake T. Evans. Film Editors: John Axness, Steve Edwards, Wendy Smith. Music: Mark Kilian. Written by: Bob, Kushell, Austin Winsburg. Directed by: Michael Spiller.

CAST
John Stamos (Jake Phillips)
Ian Gomez (Adrian)
Rick Hoffman (Patrick)
Wendie Malick (Naomi)
Margaret Welsh (Caitlin)
Julie Bowen (Brooke)

Jake in Progress is a situation comedy about a sexy New York publicist named, Jake (John Stamos). A good guy, Jake wants to stop screwing around with supermodels and settle down with the "right" woman. Unfortunately, that's easier said than done, and the series is a record of his dating disasters. Adrian (Ian Gomez) is Jake's married friend and confidante; Naomi (Wendie Malick) his helpful boss.

A handful of episodes of *Jake in Progress* aired in the Spring of 2005 and the series was renewed by ABC for the 2005–2006 season. However, upon its return for a sophomore year, *Jake in Progress* was paired in the 9 o'clock hour on Monday evenings with Heather Graham's *Emily's Reasons Why Not*.

That disastrous sitcom only aired once before the axe of cancellation fell, and *Jake in Progress* shared the same fate. The situation comedy only aired once the whole season. It broadcast "The Lying, The Watch, and Jake's Wardrobe" on January 9, 2006 and then was gone forever, though ABC had initially ordered a half-dozen new episodes.

Not currently available on DVD.

JOEY

(NBC) (CANCELED) (30 minutes) (Thursdays at 8:00 pm, EST; Tuesdays at 8:00 pm, EST; September 22, 2005–March 7, 2006) Bright-San Productions/Warner Bros./Silver and Gold Productions. Executive Producers: Kevin S. Bright, Shana Goldberg-Meehan, Scott Silveri. Co-Executive Producers: Sherry Bilson, Dave Finkel, Ellen Plumber. Produced by: Jon Pollack, Todd Stevens. Camera: Nick McLean. Film Editor: Stephen Prime. Written by: Brett Baer, Michael Borkow, Robert Carlock, Dave Finkel, Matt Hubbard, Vanessa McCarthy, John Quintance, Tracy Reilly, Scott Silveri. Directed by: Kevin S. Bright, Sheldon Epps, Gary Halvorson, Ben Weiss.

CAST
Matt Le Blanc (Joey Tribbiani)
Andrea Anders (Alex Garrett)
Paulo Costanzo (Michael Tribbiani)
Jennifer Coolidge (Bobbie Morganstern)
Miguel A Nunez Jr. (Zach)
Drea de Matteo (Gina Tribbiani)

This spinoff from the immensely popular sitcom *Friends* (1995–2004) lasted one-and-a-half seasons, and in the final analysis, that's better than both *AfterM*A*S*H* (1983–1984) and *Gloria* (1982), which followed up hits *M*A*S*H* (1972–1983) and *All in the Family*, respectively). Still, that's not saying much.

After *Friends* completed its run, *Joey,* starring Matt Le Blanc, picked up the adventures of aspiring actor Joey Tribbiani as the not-very-bright thespian moved to Hollywood to pursue his career. On the West Coast, he hung out with his sister Gina (Drea de Matteo), his brilliant nephew Michael (Paulo Costanzo), and romantic interest Alex Garrett (Andrea Anders).

Response to the first season was tepid, and better days were ahead, promised Le Blanc.

"The motto around here is that the new *Joey* is going to be bigger, faster, and funnier, and I'm really excited about the new series." He reported. "You just can't compare the last season of *Friends* with the first season of *Joey*. You have to compare like with like, and so compare the first season of *Friends* with the first season of *Joey*. You then have two shows where the cast and crew gel [sic] and evolve and the show gets better and better."[16]

In the second season, Miguel A. Nunez, Jr. was added to the cast as Zach, and Joey got a plum job on a major movie. Most of the yucks evolved from his antics on the set making the film. Joey dealt with a scene-stealing child in "Joey and the Spanking," tried to do his own stunts in "Joey and the Stuntman" and complained about his likeness on an action figure in "Joey and the Snowball Fight."

Although it was filmed on the same soundstage that had been home to *Friends* for so many years, *Joey* had little of the predecessor's success. It was ousted from its comfortable slot on Thursday night at 8:00 pm (the night that had nurtured *Friends*) and bounced to Tuesday night at 8:00 pm so that newer situation comedies *My Name is Earl* and *The Office* could take over Thursday along with the final season of *Will & Grace*. On Tuesdays, *Joey* received its lowest ratings ever, in competition with juggernaut *American Idol*, and the series was pulled from the NBC schedule midseason, with just fourteen episodes aired during the year.

The complete first season is available on DVD.

THE KING OF QUEENS

(CBS) (RENEWED) (30 minutes) (Mondays at 8:00 pm, EST; September 19, 2005-May 22, 2006) Columbia Tri-Star/Hanley Productions/Sony/CBS. Created by: David Litt and Michael J. Weithorn. Executive Producers: Tom Herz, Kevin James, Tony Sheehan, Michael J. Weithorn. Co-Executive Producers: David Bickel, Chris Downey, Michelle Nader, Rob Schiller, Ilana Wernick. Produced by: Erin Braun, Rock Reuben. Camera: Wayne Kennan. Film Editor: John Dortt. Music: Josh Goldsmith, Cathy Yuspa. Written by: David Bickel, Chris Downey, Owen Ellickson, Amy Gershwin, Michelle Nader, Rock Reuben, Dennis Regan, Michael Weithorn. Directed by: Mark Cendrowski, Henry Chan, Howard Murray, Rob Schiller, Michael Weithorn, Ken Whittingham.

CAST

Kevin James (Doug Heffernan)
Leah Remini (Carrie Heffernen)
Jerry Stiller (Arthur)
Victor Williams (Deacon)
Patton Oswalt (Spence)
Gary Valentine (Danny)

The situation comedy *The King of Queens* aired its eighth season on CBS in the 2005–2006 season. In the same tradition as *According to Jim* and *Rodney*, it's another "men behaving badly" sitcom that glorifies male stupidity and crude behavior. And, you know it's an ego trip because the dumb central figure, no matter how fat or intellectually impaired, is always married to a drop-dead gorgeous woman.

Apparently, stupidity is like Spanish fly in TV Land when it comes to attracting lovely and understanding mates…

The King of Queens tells the tale of Doug (Kevin James), a fat parcel post delivery man who lives in Queens, New York. This blue collar Joe is married to a long-suffering wife, Carrie (Leah Remini), and also lives with her acerbic dad, Arthur (Jerry Stiller). Doug's buds are Deacon (Victor Williams), Spence (Patton Oswalt), and cousin Danny (Gary Valentine).

This season on *The King of Queens*, Doug convinces Carrie to learn pole dancing in "Pole Lox." He tries to convince her they're ready for a family (meaning a baby) in "Fresh Brood," and goes out for an ill-fated guys night out in "Raygin' Bulls." In "Vocal Discord," one of Carrie and Doug's frequent fights end up as fodder for the public, and the duo thinks about marriage counseling.

The first six seasons are available on DVD.

THE L WORD

(Showtime) (RENEWED) (60 minutes) (Sundays at 10:00 pm, EST; January 8, 2006–March 26, 2007) Anonymous Content/Dufferin Gates Productions/Showtime. Created by: Ilene Chaiken. Executive Producers: Ilene Chaiken, Steve Golin, Larry Kennar. Co-Executive Producer: Rose Troche. Produced by: Mark Horowitz, Elizabeth Hunter, Rob Roe, Rose Lam. Camera: Robert Aschmann, Attila Szalay. Film Editors: Jeff Freeman, Luis Lam, Allan Lee, Lisa Robison. Written by: Ilene Chaiken, Elizabeth Ziff. Directed by: Tricia Brock, Billie Eltingham, Bronwen Hughes, Frank Pierson, Angela Robison, Lynn Stopkewich, Rose Troche.

CAST
Mia Kirshner (Jenny)
Jennifer Beals (Bette)
Laurel Holloman (Tina)
Katherine Moennig (Shane)
Erin Daniels (Dana)
Leisha Hailey (Alice)
Pam Grier (Kit)
Karina Lombard (Marina)
Sarah Shahi (Carmen)
Daniela Sea (Moira)

Showtime's *The L Word* is a drama focusing on a group of beautiful lesbian friends living in Los Angeles. This is the series' fourth season on the air, and it's a year of dramatic changes. Bette (Jennifer Beals) and Tina (Laurel Holloman) have been a happy, settled couple for years but during this season, they deal with the issue of parenting their daughter, Angelica. More dramatically, however, Bette loses her job and Tina hides a secret for a time: she's finding herself increasingly attracted to men. This is a taste Tina acquires more fully on a trip away from Bette. Meanwhile, Tina explores Buddhism, a discipline she'll need to keep herself centered during a turbulent year. The shit really hits the fan, however, after Bette learns about Tina's interest in men, and there's an ensuing (and bitter) fight for custody over Angelica.

Elsewhere, Dana (Erin Daniels), the young tennis player grows ill suddenly, goes through treatment, and before the season ends, dies. This news affects all the friends deeply, and is a shocking twist. Meanwhile, Jenny (Kirshner), who hopes to be a writer, ends up as a waitress in the local hangout, The Planet, and Kit (Pam Grier) learns that she's pregnant. Meanwhile, hairdresser Shane (Katherine Moennig) and Carmen, (Sarah Shahi) an emcee, plan to wed.

The first three seasons are available on DVD.

LAGUNA BEACH:
THE REAL ORANGE COUNTY

(MTV) (RENEWED) (60 minutes) (Wednesdays at 10:00 pm, EST; July 25, 2005–November 14, 2005) MTV. Created by: Gary Auerbach. Executive Producers: Gary Auerbach, Tony Di Santo, Liz Gateley, Dave Sirulnick. Produced by: Todd Darling, Morgan J. Freedman, Tina Gazzerro, Jason Sands. Camera: Hisham Abed, Rob Bruce. Film Editor: Jeff Barstch. Music: Jon Ernst, Alissa Moreno. Directed by: George Plamondon, Jason Sands.

CAST
Jessica Smith
Jason Wahler
Alex Murrel
Taylor Cole
Dieter Schmitz
Lauren Conrad
Talan Torriero

In the ignoble tradition of the long-lived *The Real World* is MTV's coming-of-age reality phenom, *Laguna Beach*, an unscripted "drama" that purports to dramatize the real life of affluent Orange County youngsters (unlike that *other* OC show on FOX). This series focuses on a cadre of rich kids with too much time on their hands. They worry about shopping, sex, surfing, shopping, sex, surfing, shopping, sex, surfing…

Most of the *sturm and drang* generated during *Laguna Beach's* popular second season is over bad boy Jason Wahler. He's dating a girl named Jessica, but likely cheating on her with a girl named Alex. Everyone tries to convince Jessica she's going to get hurt, but, well, she's clearly fixated on the guy.

If the drama on *Laguna Beach* feels manufactured, spiced-up, or make-believe, that's just your imagination. According to producer Di Santo in *The New York Times*: "It's as real as any reality show. These are the real kids. The things they're saying are unscripted; it's what goes on in their lives. What we chose to show or not show is where we are editorializing. And just like any reality show, if two kids say they want to go out to dinner and we know that this one restaurant will not allow us to shoot in there then we can't get the scene. So we may ask them… "Would you mind going to this one where they'll let us shoot?" They say yes or may say no. It's obviously their decision."[17] The show's third season, with a mostly new cast of self-obsessed twentysomethings, was slated for fall 2006.

Season One and Season Two are currently available on DVD box sets.

LAS VEGAS

(NBC) (RENEWED) (60 minutes) (Mondays at 9:00 pm; September 19, 2005-May 12, 2006) Dreamworks Television/ Gary Scott Thompson Productions/NBC Universal. Created by: Gary Scott Thompson. Executive Producers: Justin Falvey, Darryl Frank, Scott Steindorff, Gardner Stern, Gary Scott Thompson. Co-Executive Producers: Michael Berns, Matt Pyker, David Solomon. Produced by: Daniel Arkin, Stephen Sasser. Camera: Buzz Feitshans, Bill Roe. Film Editor: Peter Basinski. Music: Mac Davis, Billy Strange. Written by: Tiffany Anderson, Adrienne Carter, Matthew Miller, Kim Newton, Matt Pyka, Vanessa Reisen, Gardner Stern, Gary Scott Thompson. Directed by: Felix Enriquez Alcala, Milan Cheylov, Mel Damski, Steven De Paul, Paul Michael Glaser, Jefery Levy, Tim Matheson, Tawnia McKiernan, Robert Duncan McNeill, Bryan Spicer, David Straiton, Jeff Woolnough, Craig Zisk.

CAST

James Caan (Ed Deline)
Josh Duhamel (Danny McCoy)
Nikki Cox (Mary Connell)
James Lesure (Mike)
Vanessa Marcil (Sam Marquez)
Molly Sims (Delinda Deline)

This popular NBC series set in the gambling capital of the world picks up its third season with some massive changes at the program's central locale, the Montecito Resort Hotel in Las Vegas. To wit, the hotel has a new owner, draconian Monica Mancuso (Lara Flynn Boyle), and she's set a rigid schedule for reopening. Meanwhile, series star Big Ed (James Caan) implores his former staff, including Danny (Josh Duhamel) to return to the new facility, lest the casino be hit by crooks robbing places up and down the strip ("Viva Las Vegas").

A later episode in the season brings a nasty end to Monica. She's blown off the roof of the hotel, and Danny is accused of her murder ("For Sail By Owner"). Other episodes involve all the tricks and conventions of the casino scene, with counterfeit poker chips playing a role in "Fake the Money and Run," and stolen diamonds turning up in "Bait and Switch." The old urban legend about waking up in a hotel room sans kidneys also comes true in "Urban Legends," and Montecito ends up during the season playing host to a dog show ("Whatever Happened to Seymour Magoon?") and a comic book convention ("Moth Woman").

Perhaps the most interesting episode of the season involves Danny's loving gaze back at the hotel during its heyday in the swinging 1960s. "Everything Old is You Again" not only goes back to the Sixties for costumes and hair cuts, but the camera techniques also echo that era in terms of filmmaking.

Las Vegas has been renewed for a fourth season.

The first three seasons are available on DVD.

LAST COMIC STANDING

(NBC) (RENEWED) (60 minutes) (Tuesdays at 9:00 pm; May 30 2006-August 9, 2006) Executive Producer: Barry Katz. Co-Executive Producer: Al Edgington. Produced by: Noel A. Guerra, Phil Silver. Camera: Jorge Alves Jr., Paul Moncrief. Film Editors: James Bedford, Drew Brown, Noel A. Guerra, Joe Mastromonaco, Claire Scanlon. Directed by: Craig Spirko, Tony Sacco.

CAST
Anthony Clark (Host)

CONTESTANTS
Michael Balan, Ty Barnett, Josh Blue, Rebecca Corry, Bill Dwyer, Joel Gay, Gabriel Iglesias, Kristin Key, April Macie, Chris Porter, Roz, Stella Stopler.

After a disastrous third season plagued by allegations of vote-rigging, complaints that the contestants weren't really "unknowns," and a behind-the-scenes feud with host Jay Mohr, *Last Comic Standing* roared back to life in the summer of 2006 with a highly rated fourth season.

Anthony Clark replaces Mohr as the host of the series, a reality series which seeks to find America's next great standup comedian. The opening ninety-minute show introduced America to the next round of aspirants. After the grueling audition process, the final ten comics selected were then forced to cohabitate in the same house together (and later, on the docked Queen Mary for the July 20 episode).

Each week, a comedian would be eliminated, leading up to the announcement of the winner on the finale, August 9. Of the last two contestants, Ty Barnett and Joseph Blue, it was the self-deprecating Blue who emerged triumphant. As booty for his victory, he was awarded a talent contract with NBC and a comedy special on Bravo.

The ratings were such that NBC announced by the end of August 2006 that *Last Comic Standing* would see a fifth season on the network, one to air sometime in the Summer of 2007.

The series is not yet released on DVD.

LAW & ORDER

(NBC) (RENEWED) (60 minutes) (Wednesdays at 10:00 pm, EST; September 21, 2005-May 17, 2006) Wolf Film/NBC Universal. Created by: Dick Wolf. Executive Producers: Walon Green, Peter Jankowski, Matthew Penn, Dick Wofl, Nicholas Wootton. Co-Executive Producers: Arthur Forney, Chris Levinson, Robert Nathan, Luke Reiter, Richard Sweren. Produced by: Peter Giuliano, Gus Makris. Camera: William Klayer. Film Editor: Chris Brookshire. Music: Mike Post. Written by: Wendy Battles, Phillipe Browning, Rick Ed, Carter Harris, Davey Holmes, Chris Levinson, Greg Plageman, David Slack, David Wilcox, Nicholas Wootton. Directed by: Adam Bernstein, Richard Dobbs, Constantine Makris, Matthew Penn, David Platt, Rosemary Rodriguez, Jean de Segonzac, Don Scardino, Rick Wallace.

CAST

Sam Waterston (A.D.A. Jack McCoy)
Annie Parisse (A.D.A. Alexandra Borgia)
Fred Thompson (D.A. Arthur Branch)
Dennis Farina (Detective Joe Fontana)
Jesse L. Martin (Detective Ed Green)
Alana De La Garza (Connie Rubirosa)
S. Epatha Merkerson (Lt. Anita Van Buren)

This is the king of crime investigation shows, the wellspring that just completed its sixteenth season and is still going strong. *Law & Order* begat *Law & Order SVU, Law & Order: Criminal Intent, Law & Order: Trial By Jury* and *Conviction*. It was no doubt the impetus behind such criminal investigation series as *Bones, Cold Case, Criminal Minds, Close to Home*, etc. Since 1990, it has represented the police drama/trial genre with dignity and style.

Why is *Law & Order* so durable? In likelihood, it all goes back to the finely crafted format. The episodes follow the police/prosecutor's office from one end of the crime to the other. Each episode starts with a crime (a murder, often), then the police arrive and begin detective work. Halfway through or so, they have followed their leads and make an arrest. Then the District Attorney's office steps in, and takes that suspect through trial…right up to verdict. It's a tidy package with good closure, but also a concise package. There's never a lull in the pace. Cases may take months in real life, but *Law & Order* accommodates for that fact with a blackout screen featuring information about the trial, etc. (usually accompanied by two thumping musical notes). A trial can go on for fifty days, but as audience members, we see only the most important days.

All kinds of cases come up in *Law & Order*, but the crimes being investigated are often—in the lingo—"ripped from the headlines." That also makes the series quite fascinating; to see dramatic, fictitious cases rendered out of the nightly news.

In the sixteenth season, "Age of Innocence" was one example of this format conceit. In a case reminiscent of Terri Schiavo's drama in Florida (a woman who was taken off her feeding tube over the protest of far-right fringe groups and far-right Congressmen), the story involved a woman named Karen trapped in a vegetative state. The courts had decided it would be most merciful to remove her feeding tube, as per her wishes and the wishes of her husband. Unfortunately, her husband was then killed in a car bomb, and the detectives of *Law & Order*—Green (Jesse L. Martin) and Fontana (Dennis Farina) had to find out who had planted the pipe bomb. It wasn't a clear-cut mystery either. There was Karen's family, who objected to the plan to remove the feeding tube; a publicity hungry reverend who wanted to make a splash in the media by "saving" Karen's life, and a pro-life bomb maker among the subjects. At one point in the episode, *Law & Order* even worked in a reference to the Eric Rudolph case by introducing a domestic terrorist, here called "Mitch Randolph."

The case ended with the arrest of the bomber. In order to lighten his sentence, he gave over evidence and named the Reverend and Karen's brothers as co-conspirators. The Reverend ended up with a hung jury—a mistrial—but "Age of Innocence" just proved how the makers of *Law & Order* had mastered the legal drama to vet stories that relate to real life.

Other stories in the sixteenth season include one about illegal aliens, ("New York Minute"), another about an abduction ("Red Ball"), a crossover with *SVU*, and the resolution of a decade-old murder, "Ghosts." All of the stories were unswervingly compelling. The characters are not so important or individually drawn here as on *Criminal Intent* for instance, but in many ways, *Law & Order* remains the flagship of the franchise.

The first four seasons, as well as the fourteenth, are available on DVD.

LAW & ORDER:
CRIMINAL INTENT

(NBC) (RENEWED) (60 minutes) (Sundays at 9:00 pm, EST; September 25, 2005-May 14, 2006) Wolf Films/NBC Universal. Created by: Dick Wolf. Developed by: Rene Balcer. Executive Producers: Dick Wolf, Rene Balcer. Produced by: John L. Roman. Camera: Jonathan Herron. Film Editor: Micky Blythe, Dorian Harris, Lauren Schaffer. Music: Atli Orvarsson.

CAST
Vincent D'Onofrio (Detective Robert Goren)
Kathryn Erbe (Detective Alexandra Eames)
Chris Noth (Detective Mike Logan)
Annabella Sciorra (Detective Carolyn Barek)
Jamey Sheridan (Captain James Deaken)
Courtney B. Vance (A.D.A. Ron Carver)

In some ways *Criminal Intent* remains the most psychologically fascinating of various and sundry *Law & Order* series rolled off the Dick Wolf assembly line. That's partly because this endeavor, which gazes at the herculean efforts of the Major Case Squad of the New York Police Department, delves deeper into the well of human behavior than the other programs do. *Law & Order* is very good, but what makes a person defy the former and shatter the latter? *Criminal Intent* is unique among its brethren because it often depicts *how* a crime is committed, and makes audiences aware of why it happens. The criminal mind is in play here.

Also, Vincent D'Onofrio's central detective, Goren—in concept an acknowledged updating of the famous Sherlock Holmes persona—remains a fascinating character played with the kind of brooding, method intensity one expects to see in feature films; not necessarily on television. Goren's a great foil for the criminals, a study in intensity…even if his partner Eames (Kathryn Erbe) suffers a little by comparison. In the just completed fifth season, Goren isn't the only one solving crimes, either. Old franchise hand Chris Noth is back as Detective Mike Logan, and he and his partner, Barek (Annabella Sciorra) alternate cases and sometimes team up with Goren and Eames, as in the episode "The Wee Small Hours," a two-parter which saw all four detectives following the trail of a missing girl from the Midwest back to an unusual—and powerful—suspect.

In the fifth season, episodes involved a string of jewelry store robberies by a mother/son crook combo ("Diamond Dogs") and the mob's involvement in the murder of a cop's son, "Unchained." "Act of Contrition" saw Goren and Eames investigate the murder of a nun.

The first three years are available on DVD.

LAW & ORDER: SVU

(NBC) (RENEWED) (60 minutes) (Tuesdays at 10:00 pm, EST; September 20, 2005–May 19, 2006) Wolf Films/NBC Universal. Created by: Dick Wolf. Executive Producers: Neal Baer, Ted Kotcheff, Peter Jankowski, Dick Wolf. Co-Executive Producers: Dawn De Noon, Arthur Forney, Jonathan Greene, Amanda Green, Patrick Harbinson. Produced by: David De Clerque. Camera: Geoffrey Erb. Film Editor: Nancy Forner, Karen Stern, Jim Stewart. Music: Mike Post. Written by: Neal Baer, Dawn De Noon, Jonathan Greene, Amanda Green, Patrick Harbinson, Jose Malina, Robert Nathan, Lisa Marie Peterson. Directed by: Norberto Barba, Matt Earl Beesley, Arthur W. Forney, David Kotchoff, Peter Leto, Constantine Makris, Michelle MacLaren, David Platt, Rick Wallace.

CAST

Chris Meloni (Detective Eliot Stabler)
Mariska Hargitay (Detective Olivia Benson)
Richard Belzer (Detective John Munch)
Dann Florek (Captain Cragen)
Ice T (Detective "Fin" Tutuola)
B.D. Wong (Dr. George Huang)
Diane Neal (A.D.A. Casey Novak)

Second in the *Law & Order* genealogy, this extremely successful edition of the popular Dick Wolf concept gazes at crimes of a sexual nature (rape, pedophilia, etc.) Chris Meloni's Detective Stabler leads the "Special Victims Unit" in New York. He's a family man disgusted by the things he sees on a daily basis and working hard to make the City better. Hargitay plays Olivia Benson, a top detective who survived sexual abuse herself. Baltimore's Detective John Munch (from *Homicide: Life on the Street*) is also an investigator, as is Detective "Fin" Tutuola, played by Ice T.

The cases in the Special Victims Unit often require the detectives to go undercover into dangerous and unpleasant situations. Olivia goes undercover to catch a rapist in the episode "Starved," for instance, and a retired detective infiltrates a therapy group to catch a child molester in "Demons." Sometimes the detectives get out of hand in their work, and Stabler is suspended for his behavior in the episode "Ripped." In one episode, "Strain," Tutuola grapples with the truth that his son is gay when he investigates the death of two meth addicts…who lost their lives to a powerful new strain of AIDS.

In "Raw," the unit traces the death of a schoolboy back to a white supremacy group, while in "Influence," a Tom Cruise–like celebrity inserts him into one of the cases, which concerns a bipolar woman accused of murder, who was taking psychiatric drugs. In "Storm," survivors of Katrina are abducted from New Orleans, and the unit has to find them.

Chris Meloni and Mariska Hargitay were both nominated for Emmy Awards for their performances here, and Hargitay walked away a winner.

The first five seasons are available on DVD.

LESS THAN PERFECT

(ABC) (CANCELED) (30 minutes) (Tuesdays at 9:30 pm, EST; April 18, 2005–June 6, 2006) Touchstone Television/Wass-Stein Productions. Created by: Terri Minsky. Executive Producers: Terri Minski, Nina Wass, Gene Stein, Christine Zander. Co-Executive Producers: Claudia Lenow, Rob Le Zebnick, J.J. Wall. Produced by: Bob Heath, Dionne Kirschner. Camera: Jim Roberson. Film Editor: Skip Collector. Written by: Dan Cohen, Steve Holland, Claudia Lenow, Rob Le Zebnik, Christine Zander. Directed by: Ted Wass.

CAST

Sara Rue (Claude Casey)
Sherri Shepherd (Ramona)
Patrick Warburton (Jeb Denton)
Andy Dick (Owen Kronsky)
Andrea Parker (Lydia Weston)
Will Sasso (Carl Monari)
Zachary Levi (Kipp)

Less than Perfect, a workplace ensemble comedy set in the world of television, comes to a sad end with this abbreviated fourth season. ABC only aired a handful of episodes and then pre-empted the rest for basketball, making it an inauspicious year for a series that, in years passed, had merited decent reviews.

Less than Perfect focuses on Claude (Sara Rue), a young woman who has worked her way up from a temp to a producer at a local station. Unfortunately, as Season Four opens, Claude's boss (Eric Roberts) is gone, replaced by blowhard and idiot Jeb Denton (Patrick Warburton). Worse, he's hired his obnoxious wife, Lydia (Andrea Parker) to be his producer, meaning Claude is out of a job. Fortunately, her co-workers Owen (Andy Dick), Kipp (Zachary Levi) and Carl (Will Sasso) suggest a backup plan and throw her a lifeline: there's a temp position available, putting Claude right back where she began!

Claude needs a job and decides to stay on, but when the difficult Lydia needs her help on a show ("The Devil Wears Burberry"), Claude realizes she can work as Lydia's assistant…assuming there's a pay raise and some ground rules. A desperate Lydia acquiesces. In the final few episodes of *Less than Perfect*, Claude also sleeps with co-worker Carl ("A Crush Grows in Brooklyn").

Not currently available on DVD.

LIVING WITH FRAN

(WB) (CANCELED) (30 minutes) (Fridays at 9:30 pm, EST; September 16, 2005–March 24, 2006) Regency Television. Executive Producers: Fran Drescher, David Garrett, Jamie Kennedy, Bob Myer, Jason Ward. Co-Executive Producers: Tim Kelleher, Frank Lombardi. Produced by: Josh Etting, David Regal. Camera: Julius Metoyer. Film Editor: Michael Karlich. Music: Paul Buckley. Written by: Yoni Berkowits, Josh Etting, Allison M. Gibson, Tim Kelleher, Drew Levin, Frank Lombardi, David Regal, Diane Wilk. Directed by: Mary Lou Belli, Peter Beyt, Lee Shallat-Chemel, Katy Garretson, Barnet Kellman, Bob Koherr, Ken Whittington.

CAST
Fran Drescher (Fran)
Ryan McPartlin (Riley)
Ben Feldman (Josh)
Misti Traya (Allison)

Living with Fran is the record of a nasal-voiced divorcee's second shot at love. Middle-aged Fran (Fran Drescher) falls in love with a twentysomething boy toy named Riley (Ryan McPartlin), despite her deep misgivings about his youth. Simultaneously, Fran's "Boomerang Generation," 21-year-old son Josh (Ben Feldman) returns home to live with her. Fran is also raising her 15-year-old daughter, Allison (Misti Traya), who is on the cusp of becoming sexually active.

In the second season of the WB's *Living with Fran*, a sitcom paired with *Reba* during the 9:00 pm hour on Friday nights, Fran begins taking serious steps to integrate Riley fully into her life. She introduces him to relatives in "Going to the Bar Mitzvah with Fran" and then—finally—to her parents in "The Whole Clan with Fran." However, these advances don't mean things are easy in age mismatched relationship, and age is always an issue. Fran and Riley attend a community class together with difficulty in "Learning with Fran" and on her birthday, Fran is mistaken for Riley's mother in "Dreaming with Fran." In the season (and series) finale, Riley proposes to Fran...

Living with Fran went on a long hiatus in October 2005 because of low ratings, and rumors were that it was canceled. The series ultimately came back to the same time slot in early 2006, but the impending shutdown of the WB and resurrection as CW meant that low-rated programs like this sitcom didn't really stand a chance.

Not currently available on DVD.

LOST

(ABC) (RENEWED) (60 minutes) (Wednesdays at 9:00 pm, EST; September 21, 2005–May 24, 2006) Touchstone Television/ Bad Robot. Created by: J.J. Abrams, Jeffrey Lieber, Damon Lindelof. Executive Producers: J.J. Abrams, Jack Bender, Bryan Burk, Carlton Cuse, Damon Lindelof. Co-Executive Producers: Jeff Pinkner. Produced by: Sarah Caplan, Jean Higgins, Edward Kitsis, Liz Sarnoff. Camera: Michael Bonvillain. Film Editors: Sue Blainey, Sarah Boyd, Mark Goldman, Stephen Semel. Music: Damien Rice. Written by: Carlton Cuse, Leonard Dick, Adam Horowitz, Edward Kitsis, Damon Lindelof, Steven Maeda, Javier Grillo-Marxuach, Elizabeth Sarnoff, Craig Wright. Directed by: Matt Earl Beesley, Jack Bender, Adam Davidson, Paul Edwards, Eric Laneuville, Alan Taylor, Stephen Williams.

CAST

Adewale Akinnuoye-Agbaje (Mr. Eko)
Naveen Andrews (Sayid)
Emilie De Ravin (Claire)
Matthew Fox (Dr. Jack Shephard)
Jorge Garcia (Hugo/Hurley)
Josh Holloway (Sawyer)
Malcolm David Kelley (Walt)
Daniel Dae Kim (Jin)
Yunjin Kim (Sun)
Evangeline Lilly (Kate)
Dominic Monaghan (Charlie)
Terry O'Quinn (John Locke)
Harold Perrineau (Michael Dawson)
Michelle Rodriguez (Ana Lucia)
Cynthia Watros (Libby)

In the first season of the blockbuster *Lost*, Oceanic Flight 815 crashed under odd circumstances en route to Los Angeles, and about fifty people survived the traumatic destruction of the plane.

Among the castaways are Jack (Matthew Fox), a brilliant doctor with a God-complex; Kate (Evangeline Lilly), a sexy ex-con who was in shackles when the plane went down; Sayid (Naveen Andrews), a former Republican Guard for Saddam Hussein in Iraq; a conman named Sawyer (Josh Holloway); Charlie (Dominic Monaghan), a faded rock and roll star from the band Crank Shaft—and a heroin addict; Hurley (Jorge Garcia), a hugely obese man who had once been in a mental institution after winning the lottery; winsome Claire (Emilie de Ravin), a *very* pregnant woman; and a bickering Korean couple, Jin (Daniel Dae Kim) and Sun (Yunjin Kim).

Also on board the flight was an estranged father and son, Mike (Harold Perrineau) and Walt (Malcolm David Kelley)…and Walt seemed to evidence some unusual abilities. One philosophical castaway, John Locke (Terry O'Quinn) spent much of *Lost's* first season unearthing a mystery in the dirt: a locked hatch in the jungle leading down into a subterranean tunnel. That hatch was blown apart at the end of the first season and the other cliffhanger leading viewers into the long summer of '05 involved the abduction of Walt at sea from his makeshift raft by hostile bearded "Others," a mysterious tribe also living on the island.

Recognized by the Emmys as the best drama of the 2004–2005 season, *Lost* fell from grace in 2005–2006. Stated bluntly, the series experienced a sophomore slump, a disease which also afflicted ABC's other 2004–2005 breakout hit, *Desperate Housewives*. Specifically, the writers on *Lost* seemed to be making up the byzantine plots as they were going along, and the series wallowed in time-wasting flashbacks rather than addressing the mysteries inherent in the narrative. For those few who haven't seen the series, essentially *Lost* is the unscripted version of reality series *Survivor*, only vetted as a fictional, scripted tale.

Lost's second season opened with an episode entitled "Man of Science, Man of Faith," in which Jack learned what was underneath that mysterious hatch: an underground facility built in the early 1980s and populated by one man, a deranged fella named Desmond. The second episode, when viewers expected to see more of this plotline, dropped the ball completely, and *Lost* began toying with its audience, apparently stalling for time. This segment was called "Adrift" and it was an hour unrelated to the first episode that climaxed at precisely the same point as the first episode ended, with Jack's recognition of Desmond. What was "Adrift?" about? It was about forty-two minutes of Sawyer and Michael treading water at sea on the remains of their destroyed raft. It was filler; literally and metaphorically adrift, a cheat.

Forecasting the up-and-down nature of *Lost's* sophomore sortie, the next episode "Orientation," was a strong one which introduced a bizarre sociological concept: a computer inside the hatch and a sequence of "numbers." The confused castaways learned that every 108 minutes Desmond had been typing a code into the underground facility's 1980s-style PC. If the castaways didn't continue to type in the sequence—essentially making themselves slaves to the machine—a disaster would allegedly occur; one which could kill all of them and destroy the island.

The bulk of "Orientation" concerned how two very different men interpreted the same information, which is a timely and trenchant notion given the Red State/Blue State divide in the American culture on everything from evolution/intelligent design to Iraq success/quagmire. On *Lost*, Locke takes a "leap of faith" and believes that everything Desmond has said is absolutely true. That the world will come to an end if someone doesn't sit at that keyboard and type in that sequence of numbers every 108 minutes. Jack, on the other hand, rejects fate and destiny and suspects that this is a psychological project, one that

actually charts the endurance/gullibility of a subject.

After this brilliant episode about human nature, *Lost* again retreated with two weeks of stories that focused on flashbacks by supporting characters of events that preceded the airplane crash. In the tedious "…And Found," the crisis of the week is that Sun loses her wedding ring. This is the third time in the second season (after episodes "Adrift," "Everybody Hates Hugo") that the flashbacks add nothing in terms of characterization or momentum. Sun and Jin are fine characters, but audiences had already seen splendid flashbacks in the first season about how they met, how they fell secretly in love, and how working for her cruel father nearly destroyed his soul. This flashback adds nothing to that equation.

In a later week, *Lost* was back in form again with perhaps the best installment of the season, "The Other 48 Days." Except for a few moments at the end of the hour, it featured no regular cast members and instead focused on the survivors from Oceanic Flight 815's tail section (which went down in the surf). The protagonist for the hour was Ana Lucia (Michelle Rodriguez), a tough-as-nails heroine. Other new characters include a therapist named Abby (Cynthia Watros) and a hulky but spiritual black man called "Mr. Eko" (Adewale Akinnuoye-Agbaje).

As the title indicates, "The Other 48 Days" escorted viewers through the survivors' first month-and-a-half on the island, and the events transpiring closely mirrored and connected to what we already know about the other group of survivors. For instance, there's a "mole" in this tail-section group; just as "Ethan" was the mole in Jack's group early on. There's the discovery of another "Dharma" bunker (though it's less elaborate than the one Locke found), and finally there's the explanation of that

At the lip of the mysterious hatch, Locke (Terry O'Quinn, left), Kate (Evangeline Lilly, center) and Jack (Matthew Fox, right) peer deep inside, hoping—like the audience—for answers. From **LOST**.

mysterious radio contact the deceased character Boone had from the cockpit of a second downed plane. Boone raised somebody on the radio and said he was a survivor of Flight 815. The answer was shocking: "We're the survivors of Flight 815." Now we know who spoke those words: Sam Anderson's character, Bernard, the husband of a survivor named Rose.

Naturally, later in the season, Rose and Bernard got a flashback episode too.

It's illuminating to compare *Lost* to a novel since the series is so heavily serialized. In the first few chapters (the first season of the series), one meets all the characters and learn of the tantalizing, fun plot (a plane crash on a deserted island). As we experience these well-forged, dynamically performed dramatis personae, we learn—via flashbacks—of their sordid histories. Again, this mirrors a fine mainstream novel; we expect when reading a really good thriller to learn about character backgrounds…who these men and women are.

Yet then there comes a time in every good novel when the reader sufficiently understands the characters, knows who they are, and what they represent in the larger story. At this point, the novel must turn focus and address the plot. We want to see the characters address their situation directly (stranded on a mysterious island), not learn in detail everything they did before boarding a plane— where they stopped at a bar to have a drink, and so on. In the case of *Lost*, the plot should be: how do these diverse people survive (or not survive) in their new environs? What kind of community do they build? What do they find on the island? Who do they meet: friends or foes?

This is where the second season of *Lost* has ultimately proven disappointing. Up to and including the season finale, the writers still offer flashbacks and background material instead of narrative. In fact, the writers have so forgotten about the central plot and location of *Lost* (a weird island) that none of the characters evidence the slightest bit of worry, concern, or fear about an invisible monster that roams the forests and rattles treetops. It "appeared" last season and has been all but forgotten.

Instead the stalwart islanders routinely and blissfully walk back and forth without protection, without concern. All alone. Even the pregnant women and the one with an infant go back and forth blithely. Remember, they've only been on the island for sixty days, their time. Would there be a perimeter set up? Guards? Would people be scared, refuse to travel alone? Would people at least be talking about that thing they saw? None of that happens on *Lost*.

This flaw is merely one example where *Lost* has severely lost its sense of internal reality. This season we were introduced to the hatch and the labyrinth below, but like so much of this season, that plot ends with a wash. On the season finale, the computer and the complex (along with the countdown ticker) were destroyed, so this season was essentially a dead end. Furthermore, this season spent time (and several episodes) introducing very interesting new characters (the "Tailies"). By the end of the second season, two of the three are dead and buried. Again…what's the point? We're back to the end of the first season; and this season of *Lost* feels like a very long detour down the wrong rabbit hole. In real life, Watros and Rodriguez were dispatched because they both were arrested for drunk driving, but that's beside the point. In the reality of *Lost*, it's a step backwards.

Lost keeps changing its premises on us, sometimes from week to week. Because of that, the writers are blind to what the characters should be experiencing (like, *duh*—fear). Didn't Jack threaten to build an army in one episode (with Ana Lucia?) Did we EVER see any progress made? No, but it made a hell of an episode-ender, didn't it? And what about The Others being able to miraculously swoop in and steal people up out of thin air? (Remember that? On the trek from the other side of the island?) And what about The Others being total savages (barefoot and all)? Is that a third group?

Lost need not answer all of its mysteries, but a mystery is only fun if there is confidence that the writer remembers why you're watching, and furthermore, that he or she is keeping track of all the clues that have been doled out to you. You can't introduce an invisible monster in the first act and then never have the characters react with fear that it is out there. You can't say "we're gonna build an army" and then never do anything in that regard. You can't spend all season pressing a damn button, then just shove a computer out of the way and reveal a hole in the floor that conveniently leads to a failsafe button that saves the day and mitigates the effect of the button. You can't introduce the idea of a teleporting Walt with possible super powers and then send him off on a boat with his dad, presumably never to return.

That's lousy writing. If it were a novel, I'd put it down and start another one. Bottom line: the writers of *Lost* are embarrassed by the fact that their series is "science fiction." If they address monsters on the island and pirate ships, it is definitely so. But…if they continue with quasi-meaningful and "deep" character flashbacks, they can make the claim that this is a serious character "drama." *Lost* needs to get over itself. It's science fiction. If it isn't, there shouldn't have been a tree-rattling invisible monster in the first place…and now it's too late to pretend like it wasn't there…

Both seasons are available on DVD.

MALCOLM IN THE MIDDLE

(FOX) (CANCELED) (30 minutes) (Fridays at 8:30 pm, EST; September 30, 2005-May 14, 2006) Satin City/Regency/20th Century Fox. Created by: Linwood Boomer. Executive Producer: Linwood Boomer. Co-Executive Producer: Alan J. Higgins. Produced by: Dan Hopelman, Jimmy Simons. Camera: Victor Hammer, Levie Isaacks. Film Editors: Alan Baumgarten, Steve Welch. Music: John Flansburgh, John Linnett. Written by: Andy Bobrow, Matthew Carlson, Michael Glouberman, Alan J. Higgins, Davie Ihlenfield, Eric Kaplan, Jay Kogen, Alex Reid, Neil Thompson, Rob Ulin, David Wright. Directed by: Linwood Boomer, Matthew Carlson, Bryan Cranston, Peter Lauer, Christopher Masterson, David D'Ovidio, Alex Welch, Steve Reid.

CAST

Frankie Muniz (Malcolm)
Bryan Cranston (Hal)
Jane Kaczmarek (Lois)
Christopher Kennedy Masterson (Francis)
Justin Berfield (Reese)
Erik Per Sullivan (Dewey)

Malcolm in the Middle was once the toast of the town. It was a highly rated situation comedy that aired on FOX's Saturday night; a perfect complement to the long-running *The Simpsons*. It garnered several Emmy wins and nominations over its seven-year run, and made a star of its lead actor, Frankie Muniz…who moved up to feature films such as *Agent Cody Banks*. Why, at one point, there was even a discussion about a *Malcolm in the Middle* feature film.

Sadly, those plans didn't come to pass as FOX moved their reliable hit about a crazy family to Friday nights after *Bernie Mac*. Audience numbers dropped precipitously (only 3.5 million people watched on a good night). In 2006, FOX moved *Malcolm* back to Sunday nights, but ratings got even worse. The series finale drew 7 million viewers, but even that was considered an anemic finish for the once-mighty *Malcolm in the Middle*.

Malcolm in the Middle is the story of a seemingly deranged lower-class family. Lois (Jane Kaczmarek) is the vindictive, harsh (but loyal) mother of four (now five) wild children. Hal (Bryan Cranston) is her idiot man-child husband. Her children by birth order are: Francis (Christopher Kennedy Masterson), an alcoholic who was sent away to military school and now spends his time at a collection of odd jobs; Reese (Justin Berfield) an idiot and bully; Malcolm (Frankie Muniz), the genius of the family, going through his awkward teen years, and cunning little Dewey (Per Sullivan), a master manipulator with an adorable face. The numbers of the family swelled when a fifth, Jamie was born.

In the final season, as *Malcolm in the Middle* tipped over the 150-episode mark, there were the usual series of disasters for the financially strapped family. Hal lost his family health care coverage for a weekend ("Health Care"), which proved a dangerous mistake. And Lois learned she was the reason Francis started drinking ("A.A."), In the season finale, all roads led to further disaster, except for Malcolm. Brilliant Malcolm was his class valedictorian, graduation speaker, and Harvard-bound. Reese decided—at grandma's (Emmy winner Cloris Leachman) urging—to become a custodian, and Francis finally found a normal job he was happy with. The big shock: Hal and Lois were pregnant. Again!

The first season is available on DVD.

MEDIUM

(NBC) (RENEWED) (60 minutes) (Mondays at 10:00 pm, EST; September 19, 2005-May 22, 2006) Grammnet Productions/Picturemaker Productions/Paramount. Created by: Glenn Gordon Caron. Executive Producers: Glenn Gordon Caron, Rene Echevarria, Kelsey Grammer, Ronald L. Schwary, Steve Sark. Produced by: Larry Teng. Camera: Ken Kelsch. Film Editors: Warren Bowman, John Duffy. Music: Mychael Danna, Jeff Beal. Written by: Glenn Gordon Caron, Moira Kirland Dekker, Robert Doherty, Rene Echevarria, Peter Egan, Melinda Hsu, Diane Adenu-John, Bernadette McNamara, Bruce Miller, Michael Moore, Rob Pearlstein, Craig Sweeny. Directed by: Lewis H. Gould, Arlis Howard, Elodie Keene, Perry Lang, Aaron Lipstadt, Robert Duncan McNeill, Vincient Misiano, David Paymer, Richard Pearce, Steve Robman, Ronald L. Schwary, Helen Shaver, Ed Sherin, Tim Squyres, Peter Werner.

CAST

Patricia Arquette (Allison Dubois)
Miguel Sandoval (D.A. Manuel Devalos)
David Cubitt (Detective Lee Scanlon)
Sofia Vassilieva (Ariel Dubois)
Maria Lark (Bridgette Dubois)
Jake Weber (Joe DuBois)

Glenn Gordon Caron, the talent behind such brilliant TV initiatives as *Moonlighting* and *Now & Again* (1999) brings viewers the second season of *Medium* in the 2005–2006 season. This dramatic series depicts the life and times of Allison Dubois (Patricia Arquette), a happily married woman and mother of three children. What makes Allison unique is that she also happens to be psychic. Sometimes, so much so that it interferes with the rest of her "normal" life. Dubois brings her uncanny powers to bears on criminal cases in Phoenix, Arizona, where she frequently assists the district attorney (Miguel Sandoval) and a hotshot murder detective named Scanlon (David Cubitt), who only slowly comes to recognize the incredible resource at his disposal.

At home, Allison is married to the patient and long-suffering Joe (Jake Weber)—literally an average Joe—who is now quite accustomed to being awakened in the middle of the night by Allison and helping her work through whatever "psychic" crisis is impacting her dreams. Meanwhile, Joe and Allison worry about their daughters, including Ariel (Sofia Vassilieva) and Bridgette (Maria Lark), watching them both closely for the incipient signs of Allison's otherworldly abilities.

The description above probably makes *Medium* sound cheesy and stupid, like *Ghost Whisperer*, but that's wrong. *Medium* is an abundantly clever, amusing and surprising program that deals intelligently with the concept of precognition and other psychic phenomena in a totally grounded, non-melodramatic fashion. Nor is the series draped in New Age spiritual nonsense about "souls" crossing over to Heaven after leaving trite messages like "I Forgive You" or "I Love You" for the grieving living. Even though this series concerns a family, it's much less cloying and maudlin than Hewitt's imitation series.

Medium experienced a fantastic second season, and truly pushed the envelope in terms of its storytelling. "Still Life" is the episode that received the biggest promotional push, and that's because it was shot utilizing 3-D technology. Also, "Still Life" was introduced in the manner of an old *Twilight Zone* (1959–1964) episode with the late Rod Serling doing the honors in black-and-white. Of course, the long-dead writer boasted a computer-generated mouth so he could say precisely what the *Medium* writers desired him to…which made the whole experience kind of cheesy. But the 3-D was great…

Narratively, "Still Life" concerns a mystery leading back to the genetic heritage of a guest character, the son of guest star John Shea. There's a murder "flashback" set in a kitchen in "Still Life." In it, a maid is brutally attacked with a butcher's cleaver. The weapon is hurled across the room right at the screen/camera (in 3-D), and the effect is a humdinger. Then, there's some creepy dream imagery involving a gnarled old tree where sneakers dangle mysteriously from high branches, hanging on by their laces. Beneath the tree trunk, a gory murder with a shovel occurs. Again, the series pulls no punches in depicting it.

"Reckoning," another second season *Medium* episode, involves a hit and run "accident" and the year-long fallout that follows. A 15-year-old girl, Melanie Davenport, is killed while chasing her dog into the street, and the perpetrator, James Massey, keeps it a secret. This secret has driven his wife to commit suicide (because her husband was the driver!) but now her spirit is back from the grave, demanding to be heard. This episode hangs on several twists (particularly in the third act), and a truly appalling (but fascinating) sequence involves James' police interrogation, wherein he ascribes all the blame on his dead wife. In the "scare" category, the segment is very unsettling. There's an eerie moment wherein hit-and-run driver James stands in his kitchen, casually smoking by the oven when a ghostly face materializes behind him in a wisp of his cigarette smoke. The ending was a high note, a narrative twist with a sense of "cosmic justice" evoking DC Comics.

In "Doctor's Orders," Allison battles a recurring nemesis, the psychic projection, apparently, of a deceased and highly malevolent physician. The character (named Dr. Walker) is portrayed with chilling creepiness by Mark Sheppard. This dark spirit goes to susceptible men like doctors and butchers and urges them to kill women, and in "Doctor's Orders," he nearly gets his vicious claws into

Joe and Allison's eldest daughter, Ariel. Masquerading as her new school librarian, the vengeful spirit encourages the 12-year-old to attend a weekend party with a 14-year-old boyfriend named Todd Grimato over the objections of her parents. This strategy nicely sets up Allison, the only threat to the "good" doctor's killing spree, so that she ends up in jail on charges of assault. Of course, it's all a decoy. What he's really up to is far darker than encouraging a tween's bad behavior. He's the merciless Iago in the ear of an unstable butcher at the Sunfair Grocery Market, and the doctor tries to get the poor guy to carve up a shopper in the back room. For Allison to stop the murder, she'll need to get released from prison first…

"Raising Cain" is another exquisite entry in the second season canon. It opens with a grainy film reel meant to represent a 1950s era "educational film." Lensed in black and white, and replete with a booming voiceover from a VOICE OF AUTHORITY, this "Dubois Educational Film" (really one of Allison's prophetic dreams) sets up the dynamic for the remainder of the episode. The film concerns the social dilemma of "the outsider," a trench coat Mafia–type, disenfranchised youth "who may be tempted to act out" at school. The little film goes on to describe this character in the fashion of documentary shorts on personal hygiene, sexually transmitted diseases, and dating in the 1950s. This is a brilliant and original way to introduce the subject matter of the episode, but the best is yet to come.

The subject of "Raising Cain" is a variation on that classic temporal chestnut about Adolf Hitler. Knowing what Hitler would become as an adult, if you could go back in time and shoot the dictator in his crib, would you? Is it right to kill an innocent because he will one day become a monster? Or, can you change that innocent in a different way—a more positive way—by keeping him alive? Here, Allison is drawn into a criminal case in which a very devout suburban mother ends up shooting her 7-year-old son, Tyler, in the head, because she has experienced the same prescient dream Allison has. She believes Tyler will grow up to become a murderous school shooter, and so therefore attempts to murder the "devil's spawn" before that destiny can arrive.

At first, Allison is horrified by the mother's brutal act. And boy is it brutal. Mom wraps the boy's sleeping (sedated) body up in a plastic bag and tosses it on a trash heap next to a discarded toilet bowl. Then she fires a pistol at him and leaves him to die amongst the dirt and garbage. Later, we see the image of the boy breathing inside the plastic bag, and it's disturbing.

Yet, after a time, Allison comes to wonder what the right answer is in this situation. If she fingers the mother as the shooter, the boy (who has miraculously survived the attempt on his life) could grow up and indeed become a killer. If she doesn't, the mother has a second chance, an opportunity to embrace the boy (instead of condemning him as evil), and take him down a path that could culminate with him the valedictorian of his high school class. Allison sees this second possible fate in another black-and-white 1950s style film entitled "The Power of a Positive Influence."

This is a terrific, involving and difficult dilemma for Allison to deal with, and as always, she seeks guidance and advice from her much-put-upon spouse, Joe. One of *Medium*'s perpetual strengths is the manner in which the series depicts the Dubois marital relationship. It's one of occasional exasperation, petty quarreling…and deep, unspoken love and unending trust. Joe—always looking ruffled and half-asleep—may be awakened by his wife at 2:45 in the morning to talk over a riddle like this; but after his initial irritation, he's on board with Allison's mission, and is there when she needs him. As I've written before, so much of this program's best drama occurs in the Dubois bedroom—at odd hours of the night. During that time when husband and wife speak in whispers to each other about hopes and dreams, fears, and uncertainties.

To continue the comparison with the inferior *Ghost Whisperer*, the marriage on *Medium* isn't cheesy and forced. Allison isn't histrionic about her powers (like Love Hewitt's character), but rather more melancholy. On *Medium* it is fun watching Joe's attempts to keep Allison grounded and her chin up. It also helps that these characters are nearing forty. They aren't TV's typical "young" supermodels, and there's something between the lines here…a world-weariness, humanity, and reality that is entirely missing from *Ghost Whisperer*. Life doesn't resemble a movie backlot on *Medium* or some perfect, blissful existence. For instance, when Allison and Joe play with each other, gently prodding and pushing one another with sarcasm, their love borders on irritation. I also like that they share "brewskies" together after a tough day, and the fact that their house looks like one a middle-class family could actually afford. All the character touches and production design elements on *Medium* are just right, and when combined with the sterling, twist-filled plots, this show is just about perfect, or "insanely good" as one critic pointed out.

Or, as Mark Dawidziak wrote, *Medium* is "not epic storytelling on the scale of the dense and ambitious *Lost*. But it is well-written drama, built on character development, intriguing plots and, yes, a timely scare now and then."[18]

The first season is available on DVD.

MIND OF MENCIA

(Comedy Central) (RENEWED) (30 minutes) (Sundays at 10:00 pm, EST; March 23, 2006-August 6, 2006) Comedy Central. Executive Producers: Carlos Mencia, Robert Morton. Co-Executive Producers: Tommy Blacha, Beth Einhorn, Nikki Kessler, Steve Lookner. Produced by: Kelly Hommon. Written by: Chris McGuire, Pamela Ribon, Brian Rubenstein, Ted Sarnowski, Steve Trevino. Directed by: Kelly Hommon.

CAST
Carlos Mencia (Host)

Colorful Latino comedian Carlos Mencia, who once called himself Comedy Central's "resident beaner" returns for a second season of standup comedy and outrageous sketches in the half-hour program *Mind of Mencia*. This razor-sharp joker always shoots from the hip and skewers hypocrisy wherever he finds it. Frequent topics on the series are race, bigotry, and stereotypes.

In the second season of *Mind of Mencia*, the headline star vets parodies such as *Wetback Mountain* (a satire of *Brokeback Mountain*, a film about a love affair between two gay cowboys), *The Serranos* (a Latino version of HBO's gangster drama *The Sopranos*), and "It's Hard Out Here for a Ho," which jokes about the Academy-Award winning song "It's Hard Out Here for a Pimp" from the motion picture *Hustle and Flow*.

Other comic sketches include "Watching Whitey," The "Stereotype Olympics," "Sheik Rapper" (about an Arab hip-hop artist), and "Drive-By Shooting School." Hot social topics include illegal immigration, and Mencia also takes time to satirize the self-important rapper, Kanye West.

Mencia's guests on the second season include Dave Attel, Peter Boyle, skateboarder Tony Hawk, and Cheech Marin.

The first season is on DVD as "uncensored."

MONK

(USA) (RENEWED) (60 minutes) (Fridays at 9:00 pm, EST; July 7, 2006-August 25, 2006) Mandeville Films/Touchstone/NBC Universal/USA Networks. Created by: Andy Breckman. Executive Producers: Andrew Breckman, David Hoberman, Tony Shalhoub, Rob Thompson. Co-Executive Producers: Fern Feild, David M. Stern, Randall Zisk. Produced by: Jane Bartelme, David Breckman, Phillip M. Goldfarb, Anthony Sante Croce. Camera: Nikos Evdemon, Hugo P. Cortina, Anthony R. Palmieri, Jim Westenbrink. Film Editors: Scott Boyd, Ron Rosen, Craig Webster, Richard Wells. Music: Randy Newman. Written by: Jack Bernstein, Andy Breckman, Hy Conrad, Daniel Dratch, Daniel Gaeta, Lee Goldberg, William Rabkin, Tom Scharpling, Blair Singer, Joe Toplyn. Directed by: Andrei Belgrade, David Grossman, Jerry Levine, Chris Long, Stephen Surjik, Randall Zisk.

CAST

Tony Shalhoub (Adrian Monk)
Traylor Howard (Natalie Teeger)
Ted Levine (Captain Stottlemeyer)
Jason Gray-Stanford (Lt. Disher)
Emmy Clarke (Julie Teeger)
Stanley Kamel (Dr. Charles Kroger)

One of the greatest detectives of the modern world (besides Veronica Mars) is no doubt…Adrian Monk (Tony Shalhoub), a delightful and rich character who populates his own USA Network series. Frankly, it is *Monk* that almost single-handedly revived the TV mystery subgenre after the long reign of *Murder She Wrote*.

Mr. Monk is a very unusual cat. He's a brilliant ex-detective on the San Francisco police force, but a personal tragedy destroyed his mind. Literally. Now he's an obsessive-compulsive phobic; afraid of everything that moves (and everything that *doesn't* move). Despite these disorders, Monk retains his canny and unmatched skill in crime solving, a talent that makes him an invaluable (if nonetheless annoying) asset to S.F.P.D. captain Stottlemeyer (Ted Levine). Monk's just a private consultant now, but frequently called in to solve murders.

Monk is aided by Natalie Teeger (Traylor Howard), a new personal assistant who has an 11-year-old daughter, Julie (Emmy Clarke). Finally, Dr. Kroger (Stanley Kamel) is Monk's long-suffering therapist. He's obviously got a lot of work to do.

During its fifth season, which aired in the summer of 2006, *Monk* retained its droll sense of humor and quirky charm. In "Mr. Monk and the Actor," *Monk* finds out that he'll be portrayed in a movie. In "Mr. Monk and the Big Game," he investigates the death of Julie's school basketball coach. In "Mr. Monk Gets a New Shrink," he explores the death of Kroger's housekeeper…if for no other reason than he doesn't want to break in a new therapist. In "Mr. Monk Goes to a Rock Concert," he solves a murder at a rock concert, and in "Mr. Monk and the Class Reunion," Monk goes to his twenty-five-year reunion…and so on.

Monk was slated to return on the *USA Network* for a sixth season starting January 2007.

The first four seasons are available on DVD in yearly box sets.

MONK madness! Captain Stottlemeyer (Ted Levine, left), draws his weapon while OCD detective Monk (Tony Shalhoub) and assistant Natalie (Traylor Howard, right), get ready for an appointment.

NUMB3RS

(CBS) (RENEWED) (60 minutes) (Fridays at 10:00 pm, EST; September 23, 2005-May 19, 2006) Scott Free Productions/ Paramount. Created by: Cheryl Heuton and Nicolas Falacci. Executive Producers: Brooke Kennedy, Barry Schindel, Ridley and Tony Scott. Co-Executive Producers: Cheryl Heuton, Nicolas Falacci, David W. Zucker. Produced by: John Behring. Camera: Matthew Jenson, Film Editor: Robert McFalls. Music: Charlie Clouser. Written by: Sean Crouch, Andrew Dettman, Nicolas Falacci, Ruth Fletcher, J. David Harten, Cheryl Heuton, Robert Port, Ken Sanzel. Directed by: John Berhing, Bill Eagles, Rod Holcomb, Terence O'Hara, Dennis Smith, Jeannot Szwarc, J. Miller Tobin, Andy Wolk, Alex Zakrezewski.

CAST
Rob Morrow (Don Eppes)
David Krumholtz (Charlie Eppes)
Judd Hirsch (Alan Eppes)
Alimi Ballard (David Sinclair)
Sabrina Lloyd (Terry Lake)
Peter MacNicol (Dr. Larry Fleinhardt)

This investigative drama with a twist returned for a triumphant second season on CBS Friday nights in 2005–2006. An unremittingly smart series, *Numb3rs* is the story of no-nonsense F.B.I. special agent Don Eppes (Morrow), who is assigned to particularly troublesome cases in the Los Angeles area.

He's assisted in his crime-solving endeavors by his brilliant mathematician brother, Charlie (David Krumholtz), a teacher and scientist who is able to reduce evidence, data and even personal motivation to mathematical equations and numbers. Even his more wild hypotheses are rendered understandable (and perfectly clear) by the series' sepia-tone dramatizations of their finer points.

Judd Hirsch plays the senior Eppes, eccentric father to the brothers, and Alimi Ballard is Don's dependable

partner at the FBI, Sinclair. The eccentric Dr. Fleinhardt, played by *Ally McBeal*'s Peter MacNicol is also on hand to provide alternate (and sometimes outrageous) theories about crime and criminals.

Numb3rs represents an interesting variation on the *CSI* formula; only here, mathematics, not forensics, represents the hook or gimmick. Therefore, Charlie discusses things such as chaos theory, quantum physics, and nonlinear dynamics. Which makes the exposition heavy (and sometimes repetitive) but the plots intelligent...and there's simply never enough smart television.

In its riveting second season, the team on *Numb3rs* solves crimes involving the murder of a judge's wife ("Judgment Call") a stalker in pursuit of a pop star ("Obsession"), an Enron-type murder investigation ("Calculated Risk"), a terror attack on the subways ("Soft Target), a card-counting scheme ("Double Down"), biological warfare ("The Running Man") and even a school shooting ("Dark Matter").

These plots indeed sound fairly common in this day and age—the era of endless *CSI* and *Law & Order* proliferation—but *Numb3rs* understands the important distinction that although there may be no new original stories under the sun, there are certainly original ways of dramatizing them. With its fresh perspective on crime and engaging cast, *Numb3rs* should rank high on any viewer's must-see list.

The first season is available on DVD.

NANNY 911

(FOX) (RENEWED) (60 minutes) (Mondays at 8:00 pm, EST; September 13, 2005-December 12, 2005) Granada Entertainment. Executive Producers: Paul Jackson, Bruce Toms. Co-Executive Producers: Garry McKean, Michael Shevloff. Produced by: Suzanne Ali, Thomas Loureiro, Paulette Terry, Stacey Travis. Camera: Laurent Basset, Derek Hoffman, Brett P. Jenkins, Paul Mailman, Dave Stewart. Film Editors: Dave Cannon, Andrew P. Jones, Jennifer Read. Music: David Vanacore.

CAST
Lillian Sperling (Nanny Lillian)
Deborah Carroll (Nanny Deb)
Stella Reid (Nanny Stella)
Yvonne Shove (Nanny Yvonne)

The unscripted series *Nanny 911* was deployed by FOX as a pinch-hitter in the 2005–2006 season, airing only sporadically (just four times), and almost always in slots where other shows had failed dramatically and unexpectedly.

Like *Supernanny*, *Nanny 911* concerns out-of-control children, and failed parental efforts to corral them back from the brink of social unacceptability. Lead Nanny Lillian (Lillian Sperling), a grandmotherly-type, reads a case history from desperate parents, and then—like an early *Mission: Impossible* episode—deploys the right nanny for the right job.

In these circumstances, Lillian has one of three British nannies to choose from, Nanny Stella (Stella Reid), Nanny Deb (Deborah Carroll), or Nanny Yvonne (Yvonne Shove). The assigned nanny then goes to the family directly, observes the situation for a time, and subsequently begins to redress the child's behavior. The next important step is getting the parents to behave correctly while disciplining the child. Each Nanny also gives the troubled families rules to follow, such as "work as a team," "don't whine," and "take care of your own space."

In the four hour-long episodes of *Nanny 911* that aired in 2005, the Nannies dealt with an irresponsible dad, a mom who caved too easily to her children, a family of yellers and—as usual—a very disobedient child.

The third season of *Nanny 911* was slated to begin September 8, 2006 at 8:00 pm.

The series is not yet released on DVD.

NCIS

(CBS) (RENEWED) (60 minutes) (Tuesdays at 8:00 pm, EST; September 20, 2005–May 16, 2006) Belisarius Productions/Paramount. Created by: Don Bellisario, Don McGill. Executive Producers: Don Bellisario, Don McGill. Co-Executive Producer: John C. Kelley. Produced by: Frank Cardea, George Schneck. Camera: William Webb. Film Editor: J. Scott Harvey. Music: Matt Hawkings, Maurice Jackson, Neil Martin. Written by: Richard C. Arthur, Don Bellisario, Jack Bernstein, Steven D. Binder, Frank Cardea, Dana Coen, Gil Grant, John C. Kelley, David Noth, George Schneck, Laurence Walsh, Lee David Zlotoff. Directed by: Colin Bucksey, Stephen Cragg, Leslie Libman, Aaron Lipstadt, Terrence O'Harra, Dennis Smith, Thomas J. Wright, William Webb, James Whitmore Jr.

CAST
Mark Harmon (Leroy Jethro Gibbs)
Mike Weatherly (Tony Di Nozzo)
Pauley Perrette (Abby Sciuto)
David McCallum (Dr. "Ducky" Mallard)
Sean Murray (Timothy McGee)
Cote de Pablo (Ziva David)
Lauren Holly (Jenny Shepard)

NCIS stands for Naval Crime Investigation Service, and it's the division in the military that examines and investigates all crimes that have a connection to the Navy or Marine Corps. Created by veteran producer Don Bellisario, *NCIS* stars Mark Harmon as "Jethro" Gibbs, the head of the NCIS and an ex-Marine gunnery sergeant with a nose for solving crimes.

Gibbs' unit includes Di Nozzo (Mike Weatherly), an ex-homicide detective, Dr. "Ducky" Mallard (David McCallum—*The Man from U.N.C.L.E.*, 1964–1968), an arrogant medical examiner, Abby (Pauley Perrette) a forensic scientist, and McGee (Sean Murray) a tech guy and M.I.T. alum. In the third season, the team is joined by an ex-Israeli agent, Ziva (Cote de Pablo) and the team also gets a new boss in Jenny Shepard, new cast member Lauren Holly. Jenny and Gibbs shared a romantic relationship in the past, so this makes some of their interactions…awkward.

At the end of *NCIS's* second season, a terrorist called Ari killed one of the team, Kate—former regular Sasha Alexander. As the third season picks up, an angry and mourning Gibb leads his team in pursuit of the terrorist in "Kill Ari." Otherwise, the season continues to focus on the crime investigations of the Unit. The NCIS attempts to solve the mystery of a soldier buried alive in "Silver War," explain the shooting death of an officer on the highway in "Switch," solve a crime involving the Internet in "Voyeur's Web," and so on.

Members of the NCIS team go undercover to infiltrate a team of assassins in "Under Covers" and Tony is framed for murder at Quantico in "Frame-Up." Another installment focuses on the suicide (or possible murder) of an official in the Pentagon who may have been a spy ("Untouchable"). Finally, the season finale, "Hiatus," sees Gibbs sidelined by an injury acquired in the line of duty while a deadly terrorist plot unfolds.

The first season is available on DVD. The second season is available as of November 14, 2006.

NIP/TUCK

(FX) (RENEWED) (60 minutes) (Tuesdays at 10:00 pm, EST; September 20, 2005-December 20, 2005) Hands Down Entertainment/Shephard/Robins Productions/Warner Bros. Created by: Ryan Murphy. Executive Producers: Ryan Murphy, Michael M. Robin, Greer Shephard. Co-Executive Producer: Lyn Greene, Richard Levine. Producer: Brad Falchuk. Camera: Christopher Baffa. Film Editors: Tim Boettcher, Bryon Smith. Music: James S. Levine. Written by: Hank Chilton, Brad Falchuk, Lyn Greene, Sean Jablonski, Richard Levine, Ryan Murphy, Jennifer Salt. Directed by: Guy Ferland, Elodie Keene, Ryan Murphy, David Nutter, Jeremy Podeswa, Greer Shephard, Greg Yaitanes, Craig Zisk.

CAST

Dylan Walsh (Dr. Sean McNamara)
Julian McMahon (Dr. Christian Troy)
Joely Richardson (Julie McNamara)
John Hensley (Matt McNamara)
Roma Maffia (Liz Cruz)
Kelly Carlson (Kimber)
Bruno Campos (Dr. Quentin Costa)

This self-proclaimed "deeply superficial" series is anything but. *Nip/Tuck* concerns a plastic surgeon's office in Miami, Florida, where family man Dr. McNamara (Dylan Walsh) has an odd-couple professional partnership with arrogant, unethical and promiscuous hot shot Dr. Christian Troy (Julian McMahon). In the third season, these two plastic surgeons become enmeshed in the hunt for a serial slasher called "The Carver."

The Carver subplot (and resolution of that subplot) carried *Nip/Tuck*'s third season to the series' highest ratings ever. The season finale, which revealed the identity of the monstrous attacker, became the highest rated program on cable…ever.

Season Three of *Nip/Tuck* finds Drs. McNamara and Troy welcoming a new partner to their practice, Dr. Quentin Costa (Bruno Campos), while at the same time dealing with a series of bizarre cases. An obese woman must be surgically removed from her sofa, for instance, in "Momma Boone." In "Derek, Alex, and Gary," a frat prank goes horribly wrong and three students are connected in an inconvenient place.

As the episodes continue, an HIV patient needs his face repaired, and a Down syndrome patient also rotates through ("Tommy Bolton"). On the personal front, McNamara briefly considers entering the Witness Protection Program with a gangster's wife and child, and Troy fends off suspicion that he's the Carver at the same time he plans to marry Kimber (Kelly Carlson). The Carver, who boasts an embarrassing biological abnormality, is finally uncovered in the season finale…and it's a shocker.

Nip/Tuck is smart, snarky, over-the-top and thoroughly enjoyable. Unlike many series, it's improved the longer it has remained on the air. Now, it is nothing less than appointment television.

All three seasons are currently available on DVD.

Is one of these characters the Carver? It's the team from **NIP/TUCK**. Left to right, Dr. McNamara (Dylan Walsh), Julie (Joely Richardson, center), and egotistical Dr. Troy (Julian McMahon).

THE O.C.

(FOX) (RENEWED) (60 minutes) (Thursdays at 8:00 pm, EST; September 8, 2005-May 18, 2006) College Hill Pictures/ Wonderland Sound and Vision/Warner Bros. Created by: Josh Schwartz. Executive Producers: Bob De Laurentiis, McG, Josh Schwartz. Co-Executive Producer: Ian Toynton. Produced by: David Karl Calloway, Mike Kelly. Camera: Buzz Feitshans IV. Film Editors: Susan Godfrey, Jeff Granzo. Music: Richard Marvin. Written by: Mark Fish, Leila Gerstein, Mike Kelly, Cory Martin, J.J. Philbin, Stephanie Savage, Josh Schwartz, John Stephens. Directed by: Norman Buckley, Roxanne Dawson, Tate Donovan, Michael Fresco, Michael Lange, Robert Duncan McNeill, Ian Toynton, Tony Wharmby.

CAST
Peter Gallagher (Sandy Cohen)
Benjamin McKenzie (Ryan Atwood)
Kelly Rowan (Kirsten Cohen)
Adam Brody (Seth Cohen)
Mischa Barton (Marissa Cooper)
Tate Donovan (Jimmy Cooper)
Rachel Bilson (Summer)
Chris Carmack (Luke)
Melinda Clarke (Julie Cooper)

Have you ever seen a corpse walking? If you've seen *The O.C.*, you have. This once-hot prime-time soap opera committed a cardinal sin during the third season of the series. The writers killed off a lead character in the season finale, and *The O.C.* simply can't go on very long without her. This is a reference to Mischa Barton's character, Marissa, the romantic lead of the series, who was paired with McKenzie's character, Ryan Atwood. Who knows what delusion writers and producers on this series suffer under, but that on-again/off-again romantic relationship was the galvanizing relationship for fans of *The O.C.* and basically the organizing principle of the soap.

But let's not get ahead of ourselves. *The O.C.*

premiered in 2003. It's the story of a streetwise young man named Ryan who, when thrown out of his home in L.A., has nowhere to go. He ends up in the exclusive community of Newport Beach, and goes to the house of his hotshot lawyer, Sandy Cohen (Gallagher). Sandy takes him in, even though his wife (Rowan) has concerns over the juvenile delinquent. Ryan quickly befriends Sandy's son, Seth (Brody), and the boys have much to teach other: Seth schools Ryan in the rich, elitist world of the O.C., and Ryan can share something of his life experiences with Ryan. But then, Ryan very quickly falls in love with a gorgeous resident of Newport Beach, a neighbor named Marissa (Barton), who's having parental issues to contend with.

That's the premise of the series in a nutshell, and even as other characters come and go, the romantic relationship between an upper class "have" and a street-smart "have not" is the core of this premise. Can a juvie find lasting love with a princess? That's the question everyone wants to answer.

Killing Marissa on *The O.C.* would be like killing Joey on the third season of *Dawson's Creek*; or killing Kate on the third season of *Lost*. It just doesn't make any sense, because killing this character eliminates the most easily identifiable relationship (and motif) on the show. Let's face it: the series is never going to have a happy ending or decent series finale now. Nope, its best hope is to quietly fade away…

Not unexpectedly, the third season of *The O.C.* is a tumultuous one as Marissa, Ryan and Seth all face senior year and a wide open future. They attend orientation at UC at Berkeley in one episode ("The College Try"), experience a contentious senior prom in "The Party Favor," and graduate in the appropriately named "The Graduates."

Then comes the season finale which involves a melee on the road and a fatal car crash. Marissa dies in Ryan's arms.

Once news of the departure leaked, rumors began to fly. Some insisted Mischa Barton had been forced off the series in an attempt to rejuvenate it and make *The O.C.* appointment TV again. Others claimed Barton had left of her own volition to pursue a movie career.

Very quickly, a fan movement "Save Marissa" popped up, dedicated to bringing the character back to life. After all, she could have just been in a coma right? Or it could have been a dream? She could still survive to wake up in Patrick Duffy's shower stall, couldn't she?

Since production on *The O.C.*'s fourth season has already commenced, and Mischa Barton hasn't been involved, that option doesn't seem realistic. But here's a bad omen for fans: FOX's Entertainment President Peter Liguori at least implicitly seems to agree the series' days are numbered without its number-one fan draw. He's cut down the order of episodes to just sixteen.

"I wouldn't read too much into it,"[19] he told the press. *Right*. Okay. But you can read the handwriting on the wall, can't you?

The first three seasons are available on DVD.

THE OFFICE

(NBC) (RENEWED) (30 minutes) (Tuesdays at 9:30 pm; Thursdays at 9:30 pm; September 20, 2005–May 11, 2006) Reveille Productions/Deedle-Dee Productions/NBC Universal. Created by: Ricky Gervais, Stephen Merchant. Executive Producers: Greg Daniels, Ricky Gervais, Howard Klein, Ken Kwapis, Stephen Merchant, Ben Silverman. Produced by: Michael Schur, Teri Weinberg, Kent Zbornak. Camera: Randall Einhorn. Film Editors: Stuart Bass, Dean Holland. Written by: Jennifer Celotta, Lee Eisenberg, Mindy Kaling, Paul Lieberstein, B.J. Novak, Michael Schur, Gene Stupnitsky, Larry Wilmore. Directed by: Greg Daniels, Dennie Gordon, Charles Feig, Ken Kwapis, Charles McDougall, Victor Nelli Jr., Ken Whittingham.

CAST
Steve Carell (Michael Scott)
Rainn Wilson (Dwight Schrute)
John Krasinski (Jim Halpert)
Jenna Fischer (Pam Beesly)
B.J. Novak (Ryan Howard)

The Office is the little sitcom that could. Initially, it had to overcome built-in and elitist criticism that it could never be as good as the BBC original on which it's based. Secondly, it had to establish it's own unique identity while still being funny. It's a delight to report that this remake has more than achieved those goals. It won the Emmy Award for outstanding comedy August 28, 2006 for its just completed second season and the hosannas are well-deserved.

The Office is set at Dunder-Mifflin in Scranton, a paper company office building replete with warehouse. There, boss Michael Scott (Steve Carell) regularly makes a fool of himself, fails to do his job, and tries desperately to be "popular" with his staff. His number one salesman is the annoying, obsequious, and possibly psychotic Dwight Schrute (Rainn Wilson), a self-important nuisance.

Another salesman, Jim (John Krasinski) takes cruel delight in teasing and mocking Dwight, but bears a secret: he's hopelessly in love with the office receptionist, Pam (Jenna Fischer). Unfortunately, Pam's engaged, even though she fully reciprocates his feeling…a fact she can never share with Jim. Finally, Ryan (B.J. Novak) is the attractive office temp, who doesn't quite know what to make of his bizarre co-workers.

In the second season, things begin going badly at the annual Dundie Awards ("The Dundies"), a mock celebration Michael puts together celebrating the office staff. Unfortunately, he also uses the occasion to test his comedic emcee skills, which are an embarrassing failure. Pam gets drunk at the awards, and Michael sets himself up for public ridicule while also handing out humiliating awards (like stinkiest toilet trip).

In "The Fight," an embarrassed Michael challenges Dwight to a midday fight after Dwight injures him in front of the co-workers. The bout ends with Michael threatening to spit into Dwight's mouth. In "Booze Cruise," Jim makes the mistake of confiding in Michael about his romantic feelings for the engaged Pam, an act which will haunt him for the remainder of the season since Michael can't keep a secret to save his life.

In "The Carpet," someone takes a dump on the carpet in Michael's office (and a co-worker thinks it smells like soup). In "Boys and Girls," Michael comes to regret staging a "Boys" seminar opposite a women's seminar on sexual harassment when the warehouse boys threaten to put together a union.

In the season finale, "Casino Night" Michael finds himself in the odd (and rare) position of having two dates for one event: a casino party to raise money for the charity Comic Relief.

"Pretty much anybody who's ever worked can relate to our show,"[20] Rainn Wilson noted about the burgeoning popularity of *The Office* in its second season (which saw the ratings improve markedly). To satisfy this growing audience, *The Office* began an interesting and pioneering effort in the summer of 2006, when most shows are traditionally reruns, or hibernating. To wit, NBC began streaming a series of ten "2 minute" webisodes through its home page at www.nbc.com.

"I don't even know if we had a budget,"[21] executive producer Daniels reported, but the point was that people at home or work could dial up or log on the Net and get a new "chunk" of their favorite show to tide them over till the Fall. Or, contrarily, newbies could sample the product. Either way, it was a win/win situation, and surely a wave of the future.

Fans of Michael's antics could satisfy themselves further with *The Office: The Complete Second Season* on DVD.

Available on DVD.

ONE ON ONE

(UPN) (CANCELED) (30 minutes) (Mondays at 8:00 pm, EST; September 19, 2005-May 15, 2006) The Greenblatt Janollari Studios/Daddy's Girl Productions/Paramount. Executive Producers: Eunetta T. Boone, Dan Cross, Bob Greenblatt. Co-Executive Producer: Arthur Harris. Produced by: Eric Levy, Kenny Smith Jr. Camera: Richard Brown. Film Editing: Edgar Bennett, Bill Lowe, Jim Miley, Mark West. Music: Kurt Farquhar. Written by: Eunetta T. Boone, Michelle Brown, Dave Hoge, Lee House, Eric Lapidus, Eric Lev, Lisa Muse, Chantel Sartor, Devon Shepard. Directed by: Leonard R. Garner, Katy Garretson, Chip Hurd, Art Manke, Alfonso Rubeiro, Maynard Virgil, Ken Whittingham.

CAST

Kyla Pratt (Breanna Barnes)
Robert Ri'chard (Arnaz)
Jonathan Chase (Cash)
Camille Mana (Lisa)
Ray J. (D. Max)
Nicole Paggi (Sarah)
Flex Alexander (Mark "Flex" Washington)

UPN aired the fifth and final season of *One on One* during the span covered in this book. This comedy with a primarily African-American cast follows pretty and sassy young Breanna Barnes (Kyla Pratt) from Baltimore and high school graduation to California and freshman year at college.

Her boyfriend from back east, Arnaz (Robert Ri'chard) follows with her, and their on-again off-again romantic relationship forms the backbone of this series. Flex (Flex Alexander) is Breanna's Dad, who was more prominent in earlier seasons of the series. This year, Breanna's college buddies, Lisa (Camille Mana), D. Max (Ray J.) and Sarah (Nicole Paggi) are all featured.

In the final season of *One on One*, Breanna and Arnaz look for a place to live in the premiere episode, titled "Remix." Arnaz seeks employment but ends up showing off his body in "Money's Tight and So Are My Abs." Later, Arnaz is cast in a movie "Venice Boulevard of Broken Dreams," and Arnaz and Breanna contemplate having sex in "One on One, Oh! Oh!" Sadly for them, they fail a love test ("Espresso Your Love") and eventually end their relationship ("Tijuana Break-up)." The series ends with Arnaz and Breanna both dating others. Brandy guest stars in a few episodes as Arnaz's new girl.

The show did not survive the transition to the CW, and is not currently available on DVD.

ONE TREE HILL

(WB) (RENEWED) (60 minutes) (Tuesdays at 9:00 pm, EST; October 5, 2005-May 3 2006) Tollin/Robbins Productions/ Warner Bros. Created by: Mark Schwahn. Executive Producers: Brian Robbins, Mark Schwahn, Mike Tollin. Produced by: Ryan De Gard, Chad Fiveash. Camera: Bill Dickson. Film Editors: Warren Bowman, Les Butler. Music: Mark Snow. Written by: Terrence Coli, R. Lee Flemming, Mike Herro, Anna Lott, John Norris, Stacy Rukeyser, Mark Schwahn, David Strauss. Directed by: John Mallory Asher, Janice Cooke, Billy Dickson, Kevin Dowling, Stuart Gillard, Marita Grabiak, Paul Johannson, David Paymer, Greg Prange, Bethany Rooney, Thomas J. Wright.

CAST
Chad Michael Murray (Lucas Scott)
James Lafferty (Nathan Scott)
Hilarie Burton (Peyton)
Barry Corbin (Coach Durham)
Paul Johansson (Dan)
Moira Kelly (Karen)
Craig Sheffer (Keith Scott)
Danneel Harris (Rachel)

A cult TV show increasing in popularity, *One Tree Hill* is a soap opera in the vein of FOX's *The O.C.* Like that show, the topic—at least under the surface—is class warfare.

In *One Tree Hill*, a kid from the wrong side of the tracks named Lucas (Chad Michael Murray), living with his single mom, uses his passion and skills on the basketball court to get a berth on the Ravens, the high school team in the small town of Tree Hill, North Carolina. The only problem is that already ensconced on the team is a jock named Nathan (James Lafferty), a rich kid who happens to be Lucas's half-brother. Worse, the two young bucks end up competing over Nathan's girlfriend, the beautiful Peyton (Hilarie Burton).

It's senior year during the recently completed third season of *One Tree Hill* (just like it was senior year on *The O.C.*) and all kinds of changes occur. There's a mayoral election in town, a new girl named Rachel (Danneel Harris), a fiery redhead bent on making mischief, shows up at school, and Peyton's birth mother also puts in appearance. Before the year is over, the Ravens start their season…and begin losing with captain Nathan accusing Lucas of being the team's big deficit. Also, the teenagers must make choices about college (and understand the repercussions of their selection), and figure out who's going to end up with whom. There's even a hostage situation at the high school followed by a death.

All three seasons are available on DVD.

PIMP MY RIDE

(MTV) (RENEWED) (30 minutes) (Thursdays at 10:30 pm, EST; June 13, 2006–August 24, 2006) MTV. Created by: Bruce Beresford-Redman, Rick Hurvitz. Executive Producers: Bruce Beresford-Redman, Rick Hurvitz. Co-Executive Producer: Larry Hochberg. Produced by: Jennifer Colbert, Tess Gamboa, Mark A. Ryan, Ari Shufet. Camera: Scott Sandman. Film Editors: Mike Bary, Stephen Baumhauer, Josh Belson, Brian York. Music: Jeff Cardoni.

CAST
Xzibit (Host)
Mad Mike (Customizer)

Another unlikely reality TV series, but one boasting an established and enthusiastic fan base (consisting of mostly youngsters between ages 12 and 34). In this half-hour series from MTV, rapper and car enthusiast Xzibit hosts, and his customizer "Mad Mike" gives old junkers a new lease on life.

Each episode of *Pimp My Ride* usually begins with Xzibit and his car crew learning of a young person in the California area who desperately needs his or her old car "pimped," meaning customized and improved. Audiences then get background on these rundown wrecks (including all the things wrong them…), and learn the reasons why the people who own them are too strapped to fix 'em themselves.

Then, it's back to the garage (in Season 1 through 4: West Coast Customs; Here, in Season 5: Galpin Auto Sports) for a vehicular extreme makeover; plastic surgery for a car that includes stripping, painting, and the installation of custom "options." These are extras that usually have something in common with the personality or idiosyncrasies of the owner.

MTV has renewed the highly rated *Pimp My Ride* for a sixth season, licensed an international version of the series, and even produced a video game of the concept.

The complete first season is available on DVD.

QUEER EYE FOR THE STRAIGHT GUY

(Bravo) (RENEWED) (60 minutes) (Tuesdays at 10:00 pm, EST; June 6, 2006-September 19, 2006) Scout Productions/ Bravo. Created by: David Collins. Developed by: David Metzler. Executive Producers: David Collins, Michael Williams, David Metzler, Frances Berwick, Amy Introcaso-Davis, Chrstian Barcellos. Co-Executive Producer: Linda Lea. Produced by: Bradley Holmes. Camera: Frankie De Joseph. Film Editors: Mark Augustine, Deborah Barkow, Tom Patterson, Mark Smith. Music: Wildlife. Directed by: Brandon Carter, Stphen Kijack, Max Makowski, Joshua Seftel, Michael Selditch, Becky Smith.

CAST
Ted Allen
Kyan Douglas
Thom Filicia
Carson Kressley
Jai Rodriguez

Bravo's signature series, *Queer Eye for the Straight Guy*, returned for a fourth season in the Summer of 2006. Its mission: to help more clueless straight men act, dress, and just plain live better. Yep, these five gay icons are "building a better straight man" one fella at a time.

Shouldering this impossible mission are the five paragons among men, a group that has become known collectively and far and wide as "The Fab Five." They are: Kyan Douglas, the "grooming guru," an expert in skin care, health and fitness, and hair styling; Thom Filicia, one of America's top 100 designers—"the design doctor"; Jai Rodriguez, the show's so-called "Culture Vulture" who helps re-educate (and coach) straight guys on how to socialize more gracefully; Ted Allen, the food and twin connoisseur and miracle-worker in the kitchen; and last but not least, the amazing Carson Kressley, the fashion "savant," best-selling author and firecracker of a guy.

Queer Eye for the Straight Guy branches out a bit in its fourth season, stretching its restrictive format. To wit, in the first several episodes, the Fab Five trek out to Las Vegas and with the help of real celebrities (including Kathy Griffin, Rita Rudner, and David Brenner), bring their unique brand of fashion and personal first aid to folks in the desert. They help a poker player get his game on, and fashion a wedding makeover for Asher and Tsiliana, a couple that's just eloped.

Later in the season (during Gay Pride Month), the gurus help make-over a gay man...only the second time in the series they've done so.

Later on in the season, the Queer Eye team helps a wounded and burned fireman celebrate his recovery, fashions a second honeymoon for a couple recovering from a recent cancer scare and then—in another twist—takes on the obesity epidemic in America by helping a very fat couple lose weight.

The big news about *Queer Eye* is that in early August, reports surfaced that the series was canceled; that Bravo had not asked the team back for 2007. Reports in the press indicated that the Fab Five had filmed their 100th episode, signed on to new projects, and were done with the series. However, Bravo itself quickly issued a statement to the website TMZ scuttling the rumor: "Bravo's Emmy Award-winning *Queer Eye* has just wrapped its production cycle. These all new episodes of *Queer Eye* premiere every Tuesday at 10:00 pm ET/PT through the fall season. A whole new season is slated for 2007. *Queer Eye* remains the core of our Tuesday night strategy."[22]

Even after years on the air, *Queer Eye for the Straight Guy* retains its droll sense of humor, sense of uplift, and most importantly—its social importance.

The Fab Five join a wedding party in **QUEER EYE FOR THE STRAIGHT GUY**.

REAL TIME WITH BILL MAHER

(HBO) (RENEWED) (60 minutes) (Fridays at 11:00 pm, EST; February 17, 2006-May 12, 2006) Brad Grey Television/ Kid Love Productions/HBO. Executive Producers: Scott Carter, Brad Grey, Marc Gurvitz, Bill Maher. Produced by: Carole Chouinard, Billy Martin. Music by: Chris "Kid" Reid. Written by: Ross Abrash, Scott Carter, David Feldman, Matt Gunn, Rian Jacobsmeyer, Chris Kelly, Bill Maher, Billy Martin, Ned Rice. Directed by: Keith Truesdell.

CAST
Bill Maher (Host)

Guess where the best political commentary on television can be found? It's right here on HBO, on Bill Maher's hour-long no B.S. follow-up to *Politically Incorrect.*

Real Time with Bill Maher also happens to be the funniest show on television. Although Maher's opponents deride him as a liberal (or in Anne Coulter's case, a liberal traitor), he's actually a common-sense guy who is willing to call foul on public officials from both sides of the aisle if they play fast and loose with the facts.

Real Time with Bill Maher just completed its fourth season on the air, and this year Bill hosted such luminaries as Senators Joe Biden, Russ Feingold, and Mel Martinez, former Secretary of State Madeleine Albright, General Wesley Clark, Helen Thomas, Gloria Steinem, Nicholas Kristoff, Ben Affleck, Richard Clarke, Representives Rahm Emanuel and Cynthia Kinney, Lou Dobbs, Gary Hart, and columnist Nicholas Kristof.

He had plenty of political miscues and fodder to discuss too. He had former Rep. McKinney on to explain her tussle with the Capitol Police, and struck comic gold the week Vice President Dick Cheney shot a man in the face while out hunting. Other topics that came up frequently in the fourth season were the proposed sale of many United States ports to an Arab company (a deal which fell through), and the continuing disaster of the Iraq War.

In each episode of *Real Time*, Bill Maher emerges on stage and introduces the show with a long standup act relating to the issues of the week. After that, he convenes a roundtable with three guest commentators, usually representing all sides of the political spectrum. During the roundtable, Maher will often cut to a satellite feed where he interviews authors, anchors, and columnists not in the studio.

The last section of the show may also be the funniest. It's called "New Rules," and here comedian Maher proposes new laws or rules for public officials. These are often in debatable taste and elicit groans from the audience…but that's free speech, baby.

While so much comedy on television is flat out dumb, *Real Time with Bill Maher* shines like a beacon in the night. Maher's humor is based on knowledge of current events, and never fails to pass intellectual muster.

A fifth season began on August 25, 2006.

Although a compilation DVD called *Bill Maher: New Rules* is available on DVD, *Real Time* has not yet been released.

Not available on DVD.

REBA

(WB) (RENEWED) (30 minutes) (Fridays at 9:00 pm, EST; September 16, 2005-May 5, 2006) Acme Production/20th Century Fox. Created by: Allison M. Gibson. Executive Producers: Matt Berry, Don Beck, Michael Hanel, Mindy Schultheis. Co-Executive Producers: Pat Bullard, Pat Carr, Chris Chase, Reba McEntire, Lara Runnels. Produced by: Chris Alberghini, Mike Chessler, Jason Shubb. Camera: Donald A. Morgan. Film Editor: Andy Zall. Music: Tree Adams, Steve Dorff, Christopher A. Lee. Written by: Chris Atwood, Donald Beck, Pat Bullard, Aimee Jones, Clarence Pruitt, Steve Stajich. Directed by: Robbie Countryman, Will Mackenzie, Christopher Rich.

CAST

Reba McEntire (Reba Hart)
Joanna Garcia (Cheyenne Hart)
Scarlett Pomers (Kyra Hart)
Christopher Rich (Brock Hart)
Steve Howey (Van)
Mitch Holleman (Jake Hart)
Melissa Peterman (Barbra Jean)

Country superstar Reba McEntire boasts a charming if low-key screen presence and grace before the camera, and she puts both those qualities to good use in her warm-hearted and soft, though long-lived situation comedy, *Reba*, which completed its fifth season on the WB.

Reba is the Red State tale of a "blended" family living in Texas. After a two-decade marriage to a dentist, Brock (Christopher Rich), Reba Hart is shocked when her husband divorces her for a younger (and dippier) woman, a dental hygienist, Barbra Jean (Melissa Peterman). Meanwhile, Reba has to raise her three children, Cheyenne, Kyra, and young Jake (Mitch Holleman). Worse, Cheyenne (Joanne Garcia) gets pregnant and marries dopey high school football star Van (Steve Howey). Kyra (Scarlett Pomers), meanwhile, pursues a career in music. It sounds farfetched, of course, but this is the stuff of situation comedies.

In the fifth season, Reba throws a party for her real estate clients but the event goes wrong when she mistakes one of Cheyenne's anti-alcohol pills for her vitamin ("Where There's Smoke"). Hilarity ensues. "As Is" finds Reba going into real estate investments with Van...a big mistake. "And God Created Van," sees Cheyenne and Reba meddling in Van's decision not to go to church. The family adopts a dog that survived Katrina in "No Good Deed," and the season's final episode "Reba's Heart," sees the beloved matriarch rushed to the hospital for high blood pressure.

It looked like the fifth season was going to be Reba's final one, especially since the WB was closing down shop, but there was a last minute reprieve and the CW announced that it would produce thirteen additional half-hours of the series, to be used as a midseason replacement in 2007. As it turns out, that decision to save *Reba* was based not on creativity, but business. *The Hollywood Reporter* explained:

"Canceling *Reba,* which was in the middle of a two-year contract between WB and 20th Century Fox TV, would have been costly for the CW, with sources pegging the penalty at about $20 million, including compensating the studio for lost syndication revenue from the sixth-season episodes that would have not been produced."[23]

The first four seasons are available on box set DVDs.

RENO 911

(Comedy Central) (RENEWED) (30 minutes) (Sundays at 10:30 pm, EST; July 9, 2006-August 27, 2006) Jersey Films. Created by: Ben Garant, Kerri Kenney, Thomas Lennon. Executive Producers: Ben Garant, Keri Kenney, Thomas Lennon. Co-Executive Producers: Peter Principato, Paul Young. Produced by: Penny Adams, Steen C. Grossman, Karen Thornton. Camera: Joe Kessler. Film Editors: Jonathan Scott Corn, Christian Hoffman, Jane Wilcox. Music: Stephen Phillips. Written and directed by: Ben Garant, Karri Kenney, Thomas Lennon.

CAST

Ben Garant (Travis)
Kerri Kenney (Wiegel)
Thomas Lennon (Dangle)
Niecy Nash (Williams)
Cedric Yarbrough (Jones)
Carlos Alazraqui (Garcia)
Wendy McLendon-Covey (Johnson)

The fourth season of this semi-improvised spoof of FOX's reality series *Cops* focuses on the further misadventures of the unruly and bizarre police populating the Washoe County Sheriff's Department in Reno, Nevada.

After resolving some cliffhanger business from season three, the fourth season kicks off with brand new comedic adventure with the gang, including the short-shorts-wearing Dangle (Thomas Lennon). In one half-hour episode, Detective Garcia (Carlos Alazraqui) goes undercover to bust undocumented workers.

In another, the officers argue over the ownership of a new jet ski that's been willed to the department. Guest star Carrot Top goes crazy in one episode ("Wiegel is Pregnant"), laying waste to a hotel room like a latter-day Johnny Depp. Another segment involves a crime wave, and the only man who can stop it: guest star Paul Reubens (Pee Wee Herman!) as Citizen Patrolman Rick.

The first three seasons are available on DVD.

RESCUE ME

(FX) (RENEWED) (60 minutes) (Tuesdays at 10:00pm, EST; May 30, 2006-August 29, 2006) Apostle/The Cloudland Company/Dreamworks Television/Sony. Created by: Denis Leary and Peter Tolan. Executive Producer: Jim Serpico. Producers: Tom Sellitti, Kerry Orent. Camera: Tom Houhton. Film Editor: Joel Goodman. Music: The Von Bondies, Coldplay. Technical Advisor: Terry Quinn. Written by: Evan Reilly, Denis Leary, Paul Tolan. Directed by: Jace Alexander, John Fortenberry, Ken Girotti, Peter Tolan.

CAST

Denis Leary (Tommy Gavin)
Michael Lombardi (Mike Silletti)
James McCaffrey (Jimmy)
Jack McGee (Chief Riley)
Steven Pasquale (Sean Garrity)
Andrew Roth (Janet Gavin)
John Scurti (Lt. Shea)
Daniel Sunjata (Franco Rivera)
Callie Thorne (Sheila Keefe)
Dean Winters (Johnny Gavin)
Charles Durning (Mr. Gavin)
Lenny Clarke (Uncle Teddy)
Tatum O'Neal (Maggie Gavin)

"They save us, but who saves them?" asks the tagline for this sizzling dramatic series (and a far cry from *Emergency*) about the lives of New York firemen. Denis Leary stars as Tommy Gavin, a firefighter whose brother died on 9/11 and who, in the third season, is still grieving over the death of his only son by a drunk driver. Janet (Andrew Roth) is Tommy's estranged wife, and as the season picks up, she is only again beginning to communicate with Gavin following the tragedy.

Gavin also has an ex-girlfriend, Sheila (Callie Thorne). Gavin's Uncle Teddy (Lenny Clarke) and sister Maggie (Tatum O'Neal) also occasionally show up.

Dean Winters plays Johnny Gavin, Tommy's brother and NYPD detective.

In addition to his turbulent personal life, *Rescue Me* gazes at life inside the firehouse. Mike Silletti (Michael Lombardi) is the young "rookie" on the job, Franco (Daniel Sunjata), the hot ladies man. Shea (John Scurti) is recently divorced and experiencing financial difficulties. McGee is Chief Riley, an old pro.

In the thirteen episodes of the third season, which aired in the summer of 2006, Tommy continued to mourn over the death of his son. He puts out fires literally, but starts fires in his emotional life, and nowhere is that more obvious than his interactions with ex-wife Janet. In fact, that relationship became the subject of some controversy after an overheated July episode. To wit, Gavin forced himself on Janet; a favor she returned in a later installment. To some, it smacked of exploitation, abuse, and rape.

Star Denis Leary didn't see it that way, as he told *TV Guide*'s Bruce Fretts. "If people were really watching the show, they wouldn't be calling it the 'rape episode.' The kneejerk reaction is 'Oh my God, he raped his wife and he's condoning spousal rape.' I'm sorry, I've got female friends who have been through it and don't think it's an unhealthy situation. And anybody that says different has either not been through it or is just politically correct and should probably be switching the channel."[24]

Talk about fiery, huh?

Denis Leary was nominated for an Emmy Award for his portrayal of Gavin, and the series was renewed in the summer for a fourth season.

The first two seasons of the fireman drama are currently available on DVD.

ROCK STAR:
SUPERNOVA

(CBS) (RENEWED) (60 minutes) (Tuesdays at 9:00 pm EST; July 5, 2006–August 29, 2006) Mark Burnett Productions. Executive Producers: Mark Burnett, David Goffin, Lisa Hennessy, Tommy Lee, David M. Navarro. Produced by: Zach Green, Lee Metzger, Matt Van Wegeer. Camera: Jay Hunter, David Charles Sullivan. Film Editors: A.J. Dickerson, Andrew Frank, Ryan Hermosura, Rich Remis, Hudson Smith. Directed by: Michael Simon.

CAST
Dave Navarro (Host)
Brooke Burke (Host)
Tommy Lee, Jason Newsted, Gilby Clarke
(Supernova)

CONTESTANTS
Dana Andrews, Maghi Asgeirsson, Zayra Alvarez, Jenny Galt, Jill Gioia, Matt Hoffer, Storm Large, Josh Logan, Chris Pierson, Patrice Pike, Ryan Star, Toby Rand, Dilana Robichaux, Phil Ritchie, Lukas Rossi.

This follow-up to last season's *Rock Star: INXS* finds Tommy Lee (late of Motley Crüe), bassist Jason Newsted (once of Metallica), and Guns N'Roses alum Gilby Clarke searching for a talented lead singer to front their new rock band, called Supernova. Dave Navarro and Brooke Burke host this summer series—another knockoff of *American Idol*—which began airing in July of 2006, and at least once cracked the Nielsen top twenty.

Rock Star's premise is this: fifteen contestants hoping to become Supernova's lead singer share a Hollywood Hills home in this series, and then go on stage to perform tunes for the three judges. There's backstage drama in the unscripted moments and on-stage turmoil (and judge putdowns). Songs from The Who, Soft Cell, Hole, The Kinks, Creed, Johnny Cash, Cheap Trick, Nirvana, Steppenwolf, and Coldplay are sung and sometimes mangled by the contestants, and in each round or episode, one singer is eliminated from the competition.

The series is not currently on DVD.

RODNEY

(ABC) (CANCELED) (30 minutes) (Tuesdays at 8:30 pm, EST; October 4, 2005-June 6, 2006) Touchstone Television. Created by: Rick Swartzlander. Executive Producers: David Himelfarb, Ric Swartzlander. Produced by: Jason Fisher, Mark Goss. Camera: Wayne Kennan. Film Editor: David Halfand. Music: Eric Hester. Written by: Phil Baker, Ed Brown, Maisha Clossur, Glen Ellis, Mark Gross, Mike Larsen, Drew Vauper. Directed by: Shelley Jensen, Gil Junger, Sean Mulcahy.

CAST

Rodney Carrington (Rodney Hamilton)
Jennifer Aspen (Trina Hamilton)
Amy Pietz (Charlie)
Nick Searcy (Barry)
Oliver Davis (Jack Hamilton)
Matthew Josten (Bo Hamilton)

Rodney Hamilton (Rodney Carrington) is happily married to a beautiful but long-suffering wife, Trina (Jennifer Aspen) and has two young sons, Jack (Oliver Davis) and Bo (Matthew Josten). But he's unhappy in his profession and quits his job at a fiberglass plant. He commits himself full-time to his dream of becoming a successful standup comedian, even though that commitment means his wife will have to support the family on her own. Fortunately, Rodney also has a dumb male friend, Barry (Nick Searcy) to confide in.

That's the premise of the working-class comedy *Rodney*, a weekly insult to the intelligence that stars standup comic Rodney Carrington. Like *According to Jim*, its mate on ABC's Tuesday night schedule, *Rodney* is a "man behaving badly" series in which a married man does stupid things, is married to an impossibly lovely wife, and yet—because of his bad manners and bad behavior, is depicted as being authentic and true, and not putting on airs. As the series promotional material noted, Rodney evidences "heartland intelligence."

Remind me never to visit the heartland…wherever it is.

Anyway, Rodney Hamilton is a dumb man, and like Jim on *According to Jim*, damn proud of it. The anti-intellectual strain of the series slaps you in the face. However, at least Jim on Belushi's show has a day job. This series is based on the idea of a married father making the irresponsible decision to quit his job to pursue a dream (and based on Rodney's act, success is indeed a long shot). When he isn't making bad choices like that one, he's forgetting Trina's birthday, or taking a bet to walk nude into a big-box store. It's indecent exposure all right…another example, I guess, of "heartland" intelligence.

Episodes of *Rodney*'s second (and mercifully final) season see Rodney trying to make good at church after all his bad behavior ("To Hell and Back"), and talking to one of his boys about sex ("Who's The Man"). In one episode, "Rodney Comes Out," he plays at a gay club.

I didn't realize they had gay people in the heartland…

Not available on DVD.

SCRUBS

(NBC) (RENEWED) (30 minutes) (Tuesdays at 9:00 pm, EST; January 3, 2006–May 16, 2006) Doozer/Touchstone TV/Towers Productions/20th Century Fox. Created by: Bill Lawrence. Executive Producers: Tim Hobert, Bill Lawrence, Tad Quill. Co-Executive Producers: Bill Callahan, Garret Donovan. Produced by: Janae Bakken, Debra Fordham, Liz Newman, Randall Winston. Camera: Andy Rawson. Film Editors: Rick Blue, John Michel. Music: Tim Bright, Chad Fischer, Chris Link. Written by: Janae Bakken, Aseem Batru, Kevin Beigel, Bill Callahan, Debra Fordham, Neil Goldman, Tim Hobert, Bill Lawrence, Ryan Levin, Angela Nissel, Mike Schwartz, Mark Stegemann. Directed by: Rick Blue, Garret Donovan, Rob Greenberg, John Inwood, Chris Koch, Bill Lawrence, Linda Mendoza, Victor Nelli Jr., Michael Spiller, Randall Winston.

CAST
Zach Braff (Dr. John "J.D." Dorian)
Sarah Chalke (Dr. Elliott Reid)
Donald Faison (Chris Turk)
Ken Jenkins (Dr. Bob Kelso)
John McGinley (Dr. Perry Cox)
Judy Reyes (Nurse Carla Espinosa)
Neil Flynn (Janitor)
Robert Maschio (Todd)
Aloma Wright (Nurse Roberts)

Critically acclaimed though perpetually low-rated, the quirky and offbeat medical series *Scrubs* just completed its fifth round on NBC. The story of young interns—now doctors—at Sacred Heart Hospital, *Scrubs* focuses in particular on navel-gazing J.D. Dorian (Zach Braff), who has just become an attending physician dealing with his own interns. This season, he struggles seeing himself through their young eyes ("My Intern's Eyes").

J.D.'s friends and co-workers include Chris Turk (Donald Faison) and beautiful Dr. Elliott Reid (Sarah Chalke), whom he used to live with. Early in the season, J.D. is forced to move in with Turk and Carla (Judy Reyes) for a time, which is a troublesome development because they're hard at work (literally) trying to get pregnant, a goal they achieve.

Meanwhile, obnoxious and arrogant Dr. Cox (John McGinley) is still around, giving J.D. a hard time and refusing to share lunch with him. The "Janitor" (Neil Flynn) is a particularly odd bird, and he gets an episode this year in which he imagines himself the hospital's savior, inventing devices like the flying "hover hoover"—"where suction meets the sky."

In "My Jiggly Ball" J.D. draws the short straw when it comes to introducing cranky Dr. Kelso (Ken Jenkins) at an awards dinner. There, he struggles to figure out something nice to say about the physician, but it isn't easy. Other episodes find J.D. contemplating his thirtieth birthday ("My Day at the Races"), and asking out the lovely Kim out for a date, but with painful results. Stories see the group struggle over a string of organ transplants that go badly wrong due to rabies, and Turk struggling over his new "baby car"...a minivan. Dr. Cox teases him mercilessly about that.

The first four seasons are available on DVD.

7TH HEAVEN

(WB) (RENEWED) (60 minutes) (Mondays at 8:00 pm, EST; September 19, 2005-May 8, 2006) Spelling Television/ Paramount. Created by: Brenda Hampton. Executive Producers: Brenda Hampton, Aaron Spelling, E. Duke Vincent. Co-Executive Producer: Jeff Olsen. Produced by: Jeff Rogers. Camera: Dennis Smith. Film Editor: Michael F. Anderson. Music: Dan Foliart. Written by: Orlando Bishop, Chad Byrnes, Kevin Brownridge, Brenda Hampton, Victoria Huff, Chris Olsen, Paul Perlove, Jeffrey Rodger, Courtney Turk, Kelley Turke. Directed by: Harry Harris, Ron High, Jeol J. Feigenbaum, Michael Preece, Keith Truesdale, Barry Watson.

CAST
Stephen Collins (Reverend Eric Camden)
Catherine Hicks (Annie Camden)
Beverley Mitchell (Lucy Camden)
Mackenzie Rossman (Ruthie Camden)
George Stults (Kevin)
Tyler Hoechlin (Martin)
Nikolas and Lorenzo Brino (Sam and David Camden)

Its tenth season was supposed to be the last for the wholesome Camden family, featured in the family hit *7th Heaven,* "the longest-running family drama in TV history."[25] The wholesome, morally valuable series—a favorite of Christians—has been on the air since 1996 and been the recipient of awards from the Parents Television Council and the Academy of Religious Broadcasters, and apparently some fans' prayers were answered. Now *7th Heaven* will be back on the CW in fall 2006.

In its tenth year, Pastor Eric Camden (Stephen Collins) and his wife, Annie (Catherine Hicks) continued to deal with their veritable brood of seven children. Although series stars Barry Watson and Jessica Biel are long since gone in regular capacities, that still leaves married Lucy (Beverley Mitchell), Simon (David Gallagher), Ruthie (Mackenzie Rossman), and tiny tot twins Sam and David (Nikolas and Lorenzo Brino) to make trouble for the minister and his wife.

As before, the adventures of the family are set in Oak Dale, a southern California burg. Promotional material for the series indicated that this would be the year the series deals with the issue of teen sex and the responsibilities that come with it. That was seen most fully in a plot concerning Ruthie. She's in love with a boy named Martin (Tyler Hoechlin), who fathered a baby with a girl named Sandy (Haylie Duff).

In "Goodbye" and "And Thank You," the two final episodes of the tenth season, the Camdens learned that "three Camden kids" had "stretched the laws of genetics (and believability) by"[26] carrying twins. That would have seemed a perfect end for the series, but now…it's back.

The first two seasons are available on DVD.

THE SHIELD

(FX) (RENEWED) (60 minutes) (Tuesdays at 10:00 pm, EST; January 10, 2006-March 21, 2006) The Barn Productions/Sony Television/20th Century Fox. Created by: Shawn Ryan. Executive Producers: Charles H. Eglee, Scott Rosenbaum, Shawn Ryan, Kurt Sutter. Produced by: Craig Yahata. Camera: Ron Schmidt. Film Editor: Angela M. Catanzaro. Music: Vivian Romero. Written by: Elizabeth Craft, Charles H. Eglee, Sarah Fain, Adam E. Fierro, Ted Griffin, Emily Lewis, Glen Mazzara, Renee Palyo, Scott Rosenbaum, Shawn Ryan, Tony Soltis, Kurt Sutter. Directed by: Phillip Atwell, Michael Chiklis, D.J. Caruso, Guy Ferland, Stephen T. Kay, Gwyneth Payton, Dean White.

CAST

Michael Chiklis (Detective Vic Mackey)
CCH Pounder (Detective Claudette Wyms)
Catherine Dent (Officer "Danny" Sofer)
Walt Goggins (Detective Shane Vendrell)
Michael Jace (Officer Lowe)
Kenneth Johnson ("Lemonhead"/"Lem")
David Rees Snell (Detective Gardocki)
Benito Martinez (David Aceveda)
Jay Karnes ("Dutch")
Cathy Ryan (Corrine Mackey)

The Shield is the ulcer-provoking urban drama centered round "The Barn," an inner-city L.A.P.D. house where a raft of morally ambiguous cops try to maintain law and order. Prime among these cops is the series protagonist, Vic Mackey (Michael Chiklis), the cynical, rough and morally questionable detective… and leader of the Strike Team. Unfortunately for Vic, in the fifth season of the series his previous decisions and choices on the Strike Team are examined closeup by a probing Internal Affairs officer, Kavanaugh (Forest Whitaker) who will stop at nothing to uncover any malfeasance.

After Glenn Close's star turn as Captain Monica Rawling, the new commanding officer of the Barn in season four, Whitaker turns in an outstanding performance as the determined Kavanaugh. In "Enemy of the Good," he reviews the strike team's history. In "Tapo Boca," Vic can read the handwriting on the law and lawyers up. In "Trophy," Kavanaugh puts surveillance on the team in hopes of catching something illicit. Later in the season, fellow detective "Lem" (Kenneth Johnson) is jailed in "Of Mice and Lem," and Vic fears he's going to spill the beans about the Strike Team to cut down his sentence. This leaves Vic with very few options.

Besides the season-long arc about the heat coming down on Vic from Kavanaugh, *The Shield* also involves several crime investigations and arrests. There's a sex traffic ring in "Jail Bait," an illegal prescription drug ring in "Trophy" and other various and sundry bad behavior. Meanwhile, on the character front, Danny reveals she's pregnant. The Barn also has another new captain, Billings, and the department is suffering under the weight of budget cuts.

The first four seasons have been released on DVD.

THE SIMPSONS

(FOX) (RENEWED) (30 minutes) (Sundays at 8:00 pm, EST; September 11, 2005-May 21, 2006) Gracie Films/20th Century Fox. Created by: Matt Groening. Executive Producers: James L. Brooks, Matt Groening, Al Jean, George Meyer. Co-Executive Producers: Kevin Curran, Greg Daniels, Ian Maxtone Graham, Dan Greaney, Brian Kelly Mike Reiss. Produced by: Dan McGrath. Music: Danny Elfman. Film Editors: Don Barrazo, Ric Eisman, Tim Long, Brian K. Roberts. Directed by: David Silverman.

VOICE CAST

Dan Castellaneta (Voices of: Homer Simpson, Krusty the Clown, Willie the Groundskeeper, Grandpa Simpson); Julie Kavner (Voices of Marge Simpson, Patty and Selma Bouvier); Nancy Cartwright (Voices of Bart Simpson, Todd Flanders, Ralph Wiggum, and Nelson); Yeardley Smith (Voice of Lisa Simpson); Hank Azaria (Voice of Apu, Chief Wiggum, Comic Book Guy, Snake); Harry Shearer (Voice of Principal Skinner, Ned Flanders, Montgomery Burns, Waylon Smithers, Reverend Lovejoy, News Anchor Kent Brockman).

The strange yellow animated creations of Matt Groening returned for their seventeenth season in 2005–2006, an act that made *The Simpsons* the longest-running series currently on television. Even though *The Simpsons* and the denizens of Springfield only have four fingers on each hand, what they continue to represent and reflect with flawless humor and insight is America itself, and the American family today.

This season of *The Simpsons* has gone pretty much like the last several, though critics have accused the series of slipping in quality since 2002. You'll find the Tree House of Horror Halloween episode among the catalog, number sixteen in this format, if you can believe it. There's also plenty of examples of Homer's stupidity, such as the episode in which he wants to film a porn movie in the Simpson house and ends up alienating Marge. There's another story wherein little Maggie gets chicken pox, and Homer wants to sell tickets. As usual, bad luck follows the Simpsons no matter what they do, but—as ever—their love for one another allows them to persevere.

Today, there are many animated families on the tube—from *American Dad* to *Family Guy*, but *The Simpsons* remains the gold standard for such efforts. It flawlessly interweaves sociology, pop culture, and politics into its twisted comedic narratives and emerges as a perfect barometer of our times. In fact, it's been such for nearly two decades now, even though the times keep changing. That's no doubt why it continues to win the Emmy Award as Outstanding Animated Series (as it did in 2006), even after more than a dozen years on the air.

Among the celebrities giving voice to characters on *The Simpsons* in the seventeenth season were: Ricky Gervais, William H. Macy, Dennis Rodman, Lily Tomlin, Susan Sarandon, and Michael York. Gervais—creator of *The Office*—also contributed a teleplay.

The first eight seasons are available on DVD.

SIX FEET UNDER

(HBO) (CANCELED) (60 minutes) (Mondays at 9:00 pm, EST; June 6, 2005-August 21, 2005) Greenblatt Janollari Studios/Actual Size Productions/HBO. Created by: Alan Ball. Executive Producers: Alan Ball, Rick Cleveland, Robert Greenblatt, David Janollari, Bruce Eric Kaplan, Alan Poul. Co-Executive Producers: Scott Buck, Jill Soloway. Produced by: Bob De Valle, Lori Jo Nemhauser, Craig Wright. Camera: Jim Denault, Rob Sweeney. Film Editor: Michael Ruscio. Music: Thomas Newman: Written by: Scott Buck, Rick Cleveland, Bruce Eric Kaplan, Nancy Oliver, Alan Poul, Kate Robin, Jill Soloway, Craig Wright. Directed by: Daniel Attias, Alan Ball, Adam Davidson, Rodrigo Garcia, Mary Harron, Don Minahan, Jeremy Podeswa, Alan Poul, Matt Shakmar.

CAST
Peter Krause (Nate Fisher)
Michael C. Hall (David Fisher)
Frances Conroy (Ruth Fisher)
Lauren Ambrose (Claire Fisher)
Rachel Griffiths (Brenda Chenowith)
Freddy Rodriguez (Federico Diaz)
James Cromwell (George Sibley)
Jeremy Sisto (Billy Chenowith)
Matthew St. Patrick (Keith Charles)

One of TV's finest dramas ended just as the 2005–2006 season began in earnest. *Six Feet Under* has garnered a reputation as being one of the most thoughtful and beautifully written series in television history, and the fifth season lives up to it.

The last season is stirring and heart wrenching. There's an unexpected turn in the saga of the Fishers, a Pasadena-based family that runs its own funeral home. And, though it is incredibly sad it's perfectly in keeping with the series' leitmotif that death is ubiquitous. These characters deal with death every day (even though they don't face it), and so the dramatic death of a main character

in this season is appropriate and "true," even if it hurts.

Six Feet Under finds the Fishers in their usual turmoil. Nate (Peter Krause), the eldest brother, marries Brenda (Rachel Griffiths), even though she has experienced a miscarriage. Later in the season, she gets pregnant again and Nate is unhappy about it, especially when he learns that the pregnancy will be high risk; he's not sure he and Brenda can handle a child with serious health problems.

Meanwhile, Nate's younger brother and co-worker, David (Michael C. Hall) and his partner Keith (Mattthew St. Patrick) are desperate to have a baby together. They consider adoption and surrogacy, but are turned down to be adoptive parents over David's former arrest. Later David and Keith become foster parents to two troubled kids, and get more than they bargained for.

On other fronts, Ruth (Frances Conroy), the matriarch of the family is having trouble accepting the increasing dementia of her husband, George (James Cromwell). Sister Claire ends her relationship with the troubled Billy (Jeremy Sisto) and ends up dating a Republican! Finally, funeral home employee Federico (Freddy Rodríguez) is having troubles at home with his wife, Vanessa, who seems to have lost interest in sex. All of this happens as a constant parade of corpses go by in the funeral house, and death is an ever-present force.

Late in the season, *Six Feet Under* takes its final twist when Nate experience a seizure—a hemorrhage in his brain—and dies. The final episodes involve his family facing death so close to home (again) as those who loved him most mourn Nate. In the last episodes, Nate's child by Brenda is born, and David and Keith must decide the future of the funeral home. Also, Federico charts his own path into the future.

All five seasons are available on DVD.

SMALLVILLE

(WB) (RENEWED) (60 minutes) (Thursdays at 8:00 pm, EST; September 29, 2005-May 11, 2006) DC Comics/ Smallville Films/Tollin/Robbins Productions/Warner Bros. Based on characters created by: Jo Shuster, Jerry Siegel. Executive Producers: Greg Beeman, Joe Davola, Miles Millar, Brian Robbins, Michael Tollin. Co-Executive Producers: Steven De Knight, John Litvack. Produced by: Rob Maier, Brian Peterson, Kelly Souders, David Wilson. Camera: Glen Winter. Film Editors: Andi Armaganian, David Ekstrom, Neil Felder, Ron Spang. Music: Mark Snow. Written by: Steven S. De Knight, Holly Harold, Turi Meyer, Brian Peterson, Todd Slavkin, Kelly Souders, Darren Swimmer. Directed by: Greg Beeman, James Marshall, Terrence O'Hara, Whitney Ransick, Rick Rosenthal, Michael Rohl, Paul Shapriro, Jeannot Szwarc, Tom Welling, Glen Winter.

CAST
Tom Welling (Clark Kent)
Kristin Kreuk (Lana Lang)
Michael Rosenbaum (Lex Luthor)
Allison Mack (Chloe)
John Schneider (Jonathan Kent)
Erica Durance (Lois Lane)
Annette O'Toole (Martha Kent)

The series once derided as "Young Superman" and on convention circuits as "Clark's Creek" has long since fully come into its own as a viable and essential part of the long-lived Superman mythos. Although *Smallville* began its run in the autumn of 2001 as a "freak of the week" show about mutants spawned by meteors, the series has long since reversed that tack and focused on telling superb, serialized stories in the tradition of *Buffy the Vampire Slayer* or *Angel*. And that's all to the good.

Smallville tells the story of young Clark Kent (Tom Welling), who arrived in that small town via spaceship in a meteor shower many years earlier. The boy was adopted and raised by farmers Jonathan (John Schneider) and Martha (Annette O'Toole) Kent, who kept his unique, superhuman and extraterrestrial abilities a secret. Now Clark is a young man with powers such as x-ray vision and superstrength; his only weakness is a proximity to the meteor rocks (kryptonite) that accompanied his landing all those years ago.

Now, Clark is in love with Lana Lang (Kristin Kreuk), his next door neighbor for many years. His best friend is reporter Chloe (Allison Mack), and since Season Three he's known another journalist—Lois Lane (Erica Durance). Clark's friend and sometime enemy is Lex Luthor (Michael Rosenbaum), the son of tycoon Lionel Luthor and a young man with an inferiority complex. He's determined to prove himself a superior businessman, politician—you name it—to the patriarch he despises. His climb to power is also catalogued in *Smallville*.

Despite an often plastic, pre-fab look, one that uncomfortably mimics other sci-fi teeny bopper series such as *Roswell* (1998–2001), *Smallville* often works overtime in its efforts to dramatize Clark's powers as a metaphor for puberty, adolescence and growing pains. Young Clark goes weak in the knees when near his love interest Lana, for instance, but it isn't his hormones, it's the proximity of her kryptonite necklace, and so on. This is a rewarding angle of the series and it elevates the material.

The fifth season of *Smallville* has proven the most eventful run of stories yet. In "Arrival" Clark finds his Fortress of Solitude (putting another piece of the Superman puzzle together) while Kryptonian renegades with superpowers threaten Lana. In "Mortal," Clark is stripped of his otherworldly powers. In "Aqua"—a failed pilot for an *Aquaman* series—a particularly good swimmer shows up in town. In "Splinter," Clark is exposed to silver kryptonite and runs afoul of a new, recurring villain, James Marsters' Professor Fine/Brainiac. Another running plot line sees Clark's Dad running for the Senate against Lex Luthor, a contest that turns exceptionally nasty.

After the election, which Jonathan wins, fate takes an ugly turn when Lana is killed in a car crash (where she meets Mischa Barton). Clark refuses to accept reality as it is and uses his powers at the Fortress of Solitude to go back in time. He saves Lana this time, but the universe must be balanced; in payment for her life, Clark's father loses his. The season ended with an involving cliffhanger that found Lex possessed by the spirit of an evil Kryptonian named "Zod" (where have I heard that name before?) and Lana apparently in cahoots with him.

Smallville made the leap to the CW faster than a speeding bullet, and will be paired on Thursday nights with the hit *Supernatural*. *Smallville* had to deal with Super competition too, leading into the sixth season. Summer 2006 saw the release of Bryan Singer's epic *Superman Returns*, another take on the Man of Steel mythos. Ironically, Brandon Routh, the actor who plays Superman in that film, is younger than Tom Welling, who plays a teenage version of the character on TV!

The first five seasons are available on DVD.

THE SOPRANOS

(HBO) (RENEWED) (60 minutes) (Sundays at 9:00 pm, EST; March 12, 2006-June 4, 2006) HBO/Brad Grey Television/Chase films. Created by: David Chase. Executive Producers: David Chase, Brad Grey, Terrence Winter. Co-Executive Producers: Henry J. Bronchtein, Matthew Weiner. Producers: Martin Bruestle, Gianna Smart. Written by: David Chase, Diane Frolov, Andrew Schneider, Matthew Weiner, Terrence Winter. Directed by: Jack Bender, Steve Buscemi, David Leiner, David Nutter, Tim Van Patten, Steve Shill, Alan Taylor.

CAST
James Gandolfini (Tony Soprano)
Edie Falco (Carmela Soprano)
Lorraine Bracco (Dr. Jennifer Melfi)
Michael Imperioli (Christopher Moltisanti)
Dominic Chianese (Junior Soprano)
Tony Sirico (Paulie Walnuts)
Jamie-Lynn Sigler (Meadow Soprano)
Robert Iler (A.J. Soprano)
Joe Gannascoli (Vito Spatafore)

The Soprano family (of North Caldwell, New Jersey) is back (after a long absence) for the first part of the series' sixth season, which aired in the spring of 2006. As just about everyone in the civilized world now knows, *The Sopranos*—one of the finest and most original dramas in the history of the medium—focuses on a Mafioso family, and in particular, capo Tony Soprano (James Gandolfini). This season is actually the last for *The Sopranos*, but the final eight episodes are not slated to air on HBO until 2007. Therefore—technically—the series is "renewed" for the 2006–2007 year even though those last episodes are part of this sixth season. Got that?

Anyway, the last season of *The Sopranos* begins with some interesting twists and developments. Carmela (Edie Falco) and Tony are reconciling, Christopher (Michael Imperioli) is breaking into the movie industry, and gangster Vito Spatafore (Joe Gannascoli) is out of the closet as a gay man. At least until he's "whacked," that is! Early episodes of the season, including "Join the Club," see Tony fighting for his life in a hospital while his family gathers around him. In his head, in dreams, however, he's living a strange alternate and normal life.

Of course, behind-the-scenes on *The Sopranos*, the drama is almost as intense as the Mafia action on-screen. Several *Sopranos* actors allegedly demanded a salary increase (to the tune of $200,000 an episode) for the last slate of eight episodes, and reportedly Gandolfini was a mediator in negotiations. Since the season was already underway, the actors' demands were an offer that the producers could not refuse. Also, the last eight episodes have been delayed from the original air date of January 2007, if one believes the rumors, because star Gandolfini was involved in a scooter accident and required knee surgery! Now, *The Sopranos* won't return until April of 2007!

The first five seasons of this groundbreaking show are available on DVD.

A.J. (Robert Iler, left) gets in trouble with
THE SOPRANOS senior, Tony (James Gandolfini, center) and Carmela (Edie Falco, right).

SOUTH PARK

(Comedy Central) (RENEWED) (30 minutes) (Wednesdays at 10:00 pm, EST; March 22, 2006-May 3, 2006) Comedy Partners. Created by: Trey Parker and Matt Stone. Written and directed by: Trey Parker and Matt Stone.

VOICE CAST

Trey Parker (Stan Marsh, Eric Cartman, Mr. Marsh, Mr. Garrison); Matt Stone (Kyle, Kenny, Butters).

The tenth season of this popular animated sitcom concerning four foul-mouthed children living in a Colorado town offers more profanity-laced observations both about American pop culture (such as the reality series *The Dog Whisperer*) and politics. Inevitably, the latter part of that equation espouses right wing philosophy, hence the descriptor "South Park Republicans."

This season, the fifth-grade boys—Cartman, Kyle, Stan, and Kenny—deal with the strange and unwelcome return of the character Chef, voiced in the past by Isaac Hayes. In this season premiere, "The Return of Chef," Chef comes home from a mysterious "Super Adventure" Club (a metaphor for Scientology) wanting only...to molest children.

This storyline, as debased as it sounds, represents creator Stone and Parker's attempt to give Chef a memorable sendoff after a controversy involving Hayes over their bashing of his religion (Scientology) in a previous episode. Chef dies in this episode (in innumerable, horrible ways), what some viewers may see as petty revenge over Hayes' decision to quit the show. All of Chef's dialogue in "The Return of Chef" is culled from previous episodes (so as not to utilize the services of Hayes), and cut together to be absolutely and utterly profane.

A later episode in *South Park*'s tenth season reflects the James Frey, *A Million Little Pieces* book controversy that was news for about fifteen minutes in 2006. In this story, "A Million Little Fibers," the pot-smoking ("*wanna get high?*") guest character Towelie fictionalizes his autobiography and eventually appears on *The Oprah Winfrey Show*, where she accuses him of being a liar (echoing real life events with the author of the controversial memoir). Towelie's antics, however, are overshadowed by Oprah's private parts, which take on a very vocal life of their own after she has neglected them for years on end.

In another swipe at liberal politicians and actors, a further episode of *South Park*'s tenth season, "Smug Alert," sees a "perfect storm" descending on the town, created by the "smugness" of George Clooney's Academy Award acceptance speech, and that of all the town's self-satisfied hybrid car owners. Then South Park attacks Al Gore in "Manbearpig," equating his belief in global warming ("a theory which is questioned by precisely 0 scientists") with his belief in a mythical beast. Gore is depicted as an attention-starved, petty man in the episode, one with no friends, despite the fact he won the popular vote in 2000).

If this all sounds terribly one-sided, it is. This season is an unpleasant rarity for *South Park*, since in seasons past the cartoon has often proven a bastion of common sense, bashing *both* dominant political parties with equal aplomb. Who can forget, for instance, the brilliant episode from 2004 in which there are two candidates for school mascot, not Kerry and Bush, but Douche Bag and Turd Sandwich? Or the episode last year which had an original and daring (and even-handed) take on the Terri Schiavo tragedy?

However, this season the chemistry changed radically, with the result being attacks leveled only against the left side of the spectrum. This strange partisan focus shift is all the more baffling since in 2005–2006 liberals control not even one branch of the Federal Government, yet are singled out here as being worthy of scorn and derision. Apparently, *South Park* has nothing to say about Pat Robertson, Tom DeLay, Jack Abramoff, Dick Cheney's hunting "accident," or Rick "Man-on-Dog" Santorum. Nope, it's Al Gore, George Clooney, and hybrid owners who are ruining this country.

Despite such persistently one-sided commentary this year, *South Park* did feature a notable two-part episode this season regarding Muslims and the War on Terror. In an episode entitled "Cartoon Wars" that appears to be an attack on FOX's *Family Guy*, the creators of the series make an impassioned and brilliant plea for freedom of speech, even during a time of war. The same episode also

features a very funny action sequence (and play on Hollywood cliches) involving a Big Wheel chase on an interstate highway. In the ultimate irony, Comedy Central censored this episode, refusing to let series' creators broadcast a cartoon image of the Muslim prophet Muhammad. The *South Park* writers responded by having images of Jesus Christ and George W. Bush shit upon.

South Park was nominated for an Emmy Award in 2006 for "Outstanding Animated Program," particularly its ninth season "Trapped in the Closet" episode (the first Scientology-based episode, which involves Tom Cruise locking himself in a boy's closet). The series also nabbed a Peabody Award along with *Battlestar Galactica* and *The Shield*.

As of this writing, the first eight seasons are available on DVD.

Tom Cruise comes out of the closet in an infamous episode of **SOUTH PARK**.

SO YOU THINK YOU CAN DANCE

(FOX) (RENEWED) (60 minutes) (Wednesdays/Thursdays at 8:00 pm, EST; May 25, 2006-August 16, 2006) 19 Entertainment Ltd./Dick Clark Productions. Executive Producers: Simon Fuller, Nigel Lythgoe, Allen Shapiro. Produced by: Nicole Gaha, Simon Lythgoe. Camera: Jack Messitt. Film Editors: Oren Castro, Gus Comgiys, Bill De Ronde, Narumi Inatsuo, Eric B. Shanks. Directed by: Nigel Lythgoe.

CAST
Cat Deeley (Host)
Nigel Lythgoe (Host)

CONTESTANTS
Brian Friedman, Dan Karaty, Mia Michaels, Ron Montez, Mary Murphy, Doriana Sanchez, Shane Sparks

This *American Idol* and *Dancing with the Stars* knockoff from idol producer Simon Fuller returned for a second season in the summer of 2006, and along with *America's Got Talent* cracked the ratings top ten on a regular basis. This happened in part because many programs during the summer are reruns.

The format of *So You Think You Can Dance* is more *déjà vu* than new. There's the audition stage to start things off, and here the series seeks aspiring dancers in New York, Charleston, South Carolina, Chicago, and Las Vegas. Back in Hollywood, the selected contestants are weeded down to twenty, with two eliminations a week until there are just four dancers left strutting.

Finally, the finale presents to America the top dancer. Also like *American Idol*, there's a kindly host on hand (this year Cat Deeley instead of Laura Sanchez), a panel of judges which follows the *de rigueur* rule including the "mean" Simon Cowell knockoff, here played by Nigel Lythgoe. Finally, the contest is stretched to ludicrous and horrific lengths by featuring two episodes per week, a performance night and a results show where viewers learn the results of voting.

This year, 22-year-old Californian Benji Schwimmer won FOX's dancing competition, edging out Donyelle, a teacher, and Travis, a youngster with experience on Broadway. Benji's prize was $100,000.

Not available on DVD.

STACKED

(FOX) (CANCELED) (30 minutes) (Wednesdays at 8:30 pm, EST; November 9, 2005-January 11, 2006) Executive Producers: Steven Levitan, Jeffrey Richman. Produced by: Seth Katz, Dan Signer. Camera: Tony Yarlett. Film Editor: Tim Ryder. Written by: Steven Levitan, Judah Miller, Murray Miller, Cory C. Myler, Heide Perlman, Dan Signer. Directed by: Scott Ellis, Bob Koherr, Steven Levitan.

CAST
Pamela Anderson (Skyler Dayton)
Elon Gold (Gavin P. Miller)
Brian Scolaro (Stuart Miller)
Marissa Jaret Winokur (Katrina)
Christopher Lloyd (Harold March)

After a successful but brief run in the Spring of 2005, FOX renewed *Stacked*, a workplace ensemble comedy, for a second season of thirteen episodes. The sitcom—which gives new meaning to the term "boob tube"—is the heartwarming life story of sexy Skyler Dayton, a former party girl with a bad relationship history who decides suddenly it's time to settle down and grow up.

And, of course, it's a vehicle for buxom star Pamela Anderson.

One day, Dayton (Pamela Anderson) ends up in the family-owned book shop called "Stacked Books" and before long, she's working for smitten owners and brothers Gavin (Elon Gold) and Stuart (Brian Scolaro). Frumpy Katrina (Marissa Jaret Winokur) is the only other employee in the book store, and *Taxi* veteran Christopher Lloyd portrays Harold March, the store's one regular customer.

In various Season Two episodes, wackiness ensues as drooling men fall all over themselves to get a gander at Anderson's prime assets. One story revolves around Skyler's unfortunate propensity to tell all those around her that she "loves" them, and what that term of affection actually means.

The show was canceled by FOX in May of 2006 and is not yet available on DVD.

STARGATE ATLANTIS

(SCI FI Channel) (RENEWED) (60 minutes) (Fridays at 9:00 pm, EST; July 14, 2006-September 22, 2006) Sony Pictures Television. Created by: Brad Wright and Robert C. Cooper. Executive Producers: Brad Wright, Robert C. Cooper. Co-Executive Producer: Carl Binder. Produced by: Martin Wood. Camera: Andreas Poulsson, Brenton Spencer. Film Editor: Eric Hill. Music: Joel Goldsmith. Written by: Carl Binder, Robert C. Cooper, Martin Gero, Joseph Mallozzi, Paul Mullie. Directed by: Robert C. Cooper, Andy Mikita, William Waring, Martin Wood, Paul Ziller.

CAST
Joe Flanigan (Major John Sheppard)
Torri Higginson (Dr Elizabeth Weir)
David Hewlett (Dr. Rodney McKay)
Rachel Luttrell (Teyla)
Paul McGillus (Dr. Beckett)
Jason Momoa (Ronon Dex)

This spinoff of the popular series *Stargate SG-1* commenced its third season in the summer of 2006. The series is set in the distant Pegasus Galaxy, where a military unit from Earth has used a "stargate" to reach it. The team—only in sporadic contact with the mother planet—have found the location of the mythical Atlantis...a highly advanced city built by a race known as "The Ancients."

Unfortunately, the humans, led by Major John Sheppard (Joe Flanigan) have also discovered a new enemy: the evil Wraith!

In the third season of *Stargate Atlantis*, Sheppard goes head-to-head with the monstrous Wraith—who fly "hive" ships—to prevent them from adding to their territory. In "Misbegotten," an experimental technique to turn the Wraith into human beings is also attempted, with unique results.

Otherwise, the series seems to be treading on overly familiar science fiction TV cliches. One episode, "The Real World," finds a character, Dr. Weir (Torri Higginson) being deceived into thinking that her experiences in another galaxy are all delusional and she's really in an insane asylum. This plot has appeared on *Star Trek: Deep Space Nine* and *Buffy the Vampire Slayer* to name just two. Another hoary story ("Common Ground")—a genre concept so old it creaks—finds Sheppard captured by a new enemy and forced to ally himself with a Wraith in order to escape. This idea was once known as *Enemy Mine* (1985); and later, on *Star Trek: The Next Generation* as the third season story "The Enemy."

The first season is available on DVD.

STARGATE SG-1

(SCI FI Channel) (CANCELED) (60 minutes) (Fridays at 8:00 pm, EST; July 14, 2006-September 22, 2006) Sony Television. Based on the feature film: *Stargate*. Developed by: Brad Wright and Jonathan Glassner. Executive Producers: Richard Dean Anderson, Brad Wright. Co-Executive Producer: Damian Kindler. Produced by: Martin Gero. Camera: Peter Woest. Film Editor: Eric Hill. Music: David Arnold. Written by: Damian Kindler, Paul Mullie, Brad Wright. Directed by: Andy Mikita, William Waring.

CAST

Ben Browder (Lt. Colonel Cameron Mitchell)
Amanda Tapping (Major Samantha Carter)
Michael Shanks (Dr. Daniel Jackson)
Beau Bridges (Major General Landry)
Claudia Black (Vala Mal Doran)
Lexa Doig (Dr. Lam)
Christopher Judge (Teal'c)
Bill Dow (Dr. Lee)

Stargate SG-1 began airing its tenth season in the summer of 2006, a remarkable achievement which makes it one of the longest-running dramatic science fiction series in TV history. The program concerns a military unit's journeys through the titular Stargate, which can land the characters on different worlds, where they face alien threats and meet alien allies.

Major changes occurred at the end of the eighth season when series star Richard Dean Anderson left his leading role and was succeeded by former *Farscape* star, Ben Browder, playing Cameron Mitchell. Another *Farscape* star, Claudia Black joined the series in the tenth season as a regular, playing a sexy space pirate named Vala Mal Doran.

The plots during this season involve a new alien enemy called the "The Ori" and their plans to invade the Milky Way galaxy (hence...Earth). The Stargate team, including old friends such as Major Carter (Amanda Tapping) and scientist Dr. Daniel Jackson (Michael Shanks)—who have been with the series since the early days—learns that the only way to combat these villains is with a weapon forged by the historic Merlin. The team believes that the weapon is hidden on one of the worlds they can reach via the stargate but don't know which one. One episode of the tenth season involves the crew searching for the weapon on the planet Atlantis in the Pegasus Galaxy, thus fostering a crossover with the spinoff series, *Stargate Atlantis.*

Stargate SG-1 reached its epic two-hundredth episode in 2006, and the segment (appropriately titled "200") was an homage to science fiction television in general, with funny allusions to *Star Trek* and even *Farscape*. This good-humored episode was welcomed warmly by fans, but very soon bad news soured the achievement. In late August, the SCI FI Channel announced it would cancel the series (in order to give the *Battlestar Galactica* spinoff *Caprica* a spot, according to gossip). This development horrified fans, not to mention series executive producer Wright, who hopes to continue *Stargate SG-1* for an eleventh season on another network or station.

The first nine seasons are available on DVD.

STILL STANDING

(CBS) (CANCELED) (30 minutes) (Wednesdays at 8:00 pm, EST; September 21, 2005–March 8, 2006) Java Boy Productions/Tea Gal Productions/20th Century Fox/CBS. Created by: Diane Burroughs and Joey Gutierrez. Executive Producers: Diane Burroughs and Joey Gutierrez. Co-Executive Producer: Richard Gurman. Produced by: Randy Cordray, Jay Kleckner, Ben Wexler. Camera: Steven V. Silver. Film Editors: Gary Anderson, Joe Bella, Kirk Benson. Music: Holly Knight. Written by: Chris Bishop, Ellen Byron, Cala Filishia, Adam E. Goldberg, Richard Gurman, Jayne Hamil, Cheryl Holiday, Lissa Kapstrom, Terry Mulroy, Ben Wexler, Ed Yeager. Directed by: Mark Cendrowksi, Gerry Cohen, Bob Koherr, Lynn McCracken, Joel Murray, Ken Whittingham

CAST

Mark Addy (Bill Miller)
Jami Gertz (Judy Miller)
Jennifer Irwin (Linda)
Taylor Ball (Brian Miller)
Renee Olstead (Lauren Miller)
Soleil Borda (Tina Miller)
Joel Murray (Danny Fitzsimmons)

Would you believe yet *another* sitcom about an overweight balding, blue-collar guy married to a wife with supermodel looks? Well, if so, then by all means sample *Still Standing* (while you can), a thirty-minute venture that aired its fourth (and last) season in the year 2005–2006.

The central figures of this domestic situation comedy are all part of the Miller family. There's dopey, immature, and overweight dad, Bill (Mark Addy), and lovely, competent, and patient wife, Judy Miller (Jami Gertz)—no, not the *New York Times* reporter. Together, they're raising three kids. There's eldest daughter Lauren (Jennifer Irwin), rapidly becoming a "woman." Brian (Taylor Ball) is just turning 18 and likewise becoming a "man." The youngest of the brood is Tina (Soleil Borda). Danny (Joel Murray) is Bill's quirky friend who drops in a lot.

Every episode of *Still Standing* opens with the word "Still" in its title (as in the case of "Still Irresponsible"). In "Still Aging," Judy fears growing old after an event with her mother. In "Still the Fun One," Judy and Bill compete for the affection of their new friends. In "Still Flunking," Bill tries to help Brian pass his gym class, with predictable hilarity. There's even that worn out old chestnut (going back to the classic comic strip *Blondie*) about inviting the boss over for a dinner that inevitably proves disastrous. Here, that's the appropriately titled episode "Still Bad."

Still Standing no longer stands. CBS finally put us out of their misery.

The series is not yet available on DVD.

SUPERNANNY

(ABC) (RENEWED) (60 minutes) (Mondays at 8:00 pm, EST; September 23, 2005-April 4, 2006) Ricochet Productions/ABC. Executive Producers: Craig Armstrong, Nick Powell. Co-Executive Producers: Carl Buehl, Amanda Murphy, Tony Yates. Produced by: Tracey Finley, Sara Mast. Camera: Jeff Kurr, David Charles Sullivan. Film Editors: Jon Alloway, Parm Arnot, Jeff Bartsch. Music: Christopher Franke.

CAST
Jeff Bartsch (Announcer)
Jo Frost (Supernanny)

This is the second season of the popular unscripted "family" drama in which a stern (but helpful) British stiff-upper-lipped governess named Jo Frost descends upon families in crisis and helps corral wild, uncontrollable children. Frost's parental philosophy is a kind of tough love, meaning that the parents must stick to their guns on disciplining the wayward children and not indulge them or give in to their whining (or frequent tears.) The so-called "Supernanny" was parodied on an episode of Comedy Central's *South Park* in 2006, but that doesn't seem to have stopped Ms. Frost from working her Mary Poppins-style magic on family units in need.

In *Supernanny*'s sophomore run, Ms. Frost comes to the aid of a child who has been kicked out of daycare for bad behavior, heals a family consisting of three kids where the Dad is "traveling" (meaning virtually absent...), rescues a British family wherein a nine-year-old girl dominates her younger sisters with an iron fist, and prevents a gang of children from running rampant in their parents' family restaurant. There's also an episode of *Supernanny* in this run that deals with autism, and how to cope with the disease.

The first season is currently available on DVD.

SURVIVOR

(CBS) (RENEWED) (60 minutes) (Thursdays at 8:00 pm, EST; September 15, 2005-December 11, 2005; February 2, 2006-May 14, 2006) Mark Burnett Productions/CBS. Created by: Charlie Parson (Format); Executive Producers: Mark Burnett, Charlie Parson, Tom Shelly. Co-Executive Producers: Kevin Greene, Doug McCallie. Produced by: Adam Briles, John Kirhoff, Conrad Riggs. Camera: Various. Editors: Various. Music: Russ Landau.

CAST
Jeff Probst (Himself)

2005 CONTESTANTS
Brandon Bellinger, Danni Boatwright, Margaret Bobonich, Brian Corridan, Bobby Jon Drinkard, Cindy Hall, Gary Hobeboom, Rafe Judkins, Stephenie La Grossa, Jym Lynch, Morgan McDevitt, Lydia Morales, Jamie Newton, Amy O'Hara, Judd Sargeant, Brooke Struck, Blake Towsley, Brianna Varela.

2006 CONTESTANTS
Aras Bakauskas, Dan Barry, Austy Carty, Terry Deitz, Danielle Di Lorenzo, Cirie Fields, Misty Giles, Melinda Hyder, Bruce Kanegai, Bobby Mason, Courtney Marit, Ruth-Marie Milliman, Shane Powers, Tina Scheer, Sally Schumann, Nick Stanbury.

Survivor, the granddaddy of reality television programming, returned to CBS prime time for Seasons Eleven and Twelve in the 2005–2006 season. *Survivor* Season Eleven aired in the fall of 2005 and was set in Guatemala.

There, contestants had to survive weather, food shortages, and backstabbing cohorts against the backdrop of the extinct Mayan civilization…an ominous omen.

The twist in this game was that in addition to surviving in an inhospitable location, the challengers—split into two tribes (Yaxha and Nakum) had the "expert" advice of *Survivor* veterans, in this case alumni Bobby Jon and Stephanie of *Survivor: Palau*. After multiple challenges, and the progression down to the final four survivors in the last show, Danni Boatwright, a young woman, was voted as the ultimate "Survivor."

Season Twelve aired in the Spring of 2006. This time, the series was set in Panama, with an opening gambit on "Exile Island." The gimmick for this version of the nature/survival unscripted series was that there would be four teams instead of two: separated by sex and by age. There was Older Men and Younger Men, Older Women and Younger Women. Ultimately, the winner was a man named Aras; the fellow who survived all the immunity challenges, team switches, and council sessions.

A thirteenth edition of *Survivor* is already in the works as of this writing and was the subject of some controversy because for the first time in series history, the survivor contests would be segregated! That's right, they were to be separated by race!

The first ten seasons are available on DVD.

24

(FOX) (RENEWED) (60 minutes) (Mondays at 9:00 pm, EST; January 15, 2006-May 22, 2006) Imagine Television/Real Time Productions/20th Century Fox. Created by: Joel Surnow, Robert Cochrane. Executive Producers: Robert Cochran, Brian Grazer, Ron Howard, Joel Surnow. Camera: Jeff Mygatt. Film Editors: David Latham, Scott Power, David B. Thompson. Music: Sean Callery. Written by: Robert Cochrane, Manny Coto, Duppy Demetrius, David Ehrman, David Fury, Howard Gordon, Evan Katz, Michael Loceff, Michael Michnovetz, Steven Long Mitchell, Sam Montgomery, Nicole Ranadive, Craig Van Sickle, Joel Surnow. Directed by: John Cassar, Tim Iacofano, Dwight Little, Brad Turner.

CAST

Kiefer Sutherland (Jack Bauer)
Carlos Bernard (Tony Almeida)
Kim Raver (Audrey Raines)
Roger Cross (Curtis Manning)
Mary Lynn Rajskub (Chloe O'Brian)
Gregory Itzin (President Charles Logan)
Jean Smart (First Lady Martha Logan)
James Morrison (Bill Buchanan)
Jayne Atkinson (Karen Hayes)

FOX's high-stake tension-game, *24* won the Emmy Award for best dramatic series in 2006 and with good reason. The fifth season was undeniably the series' best… and that's saying something since the series has always been remarkably strong. Yet nearly every installment in the 2006 season was pitch perfect, both suspenseful as a "standalone" and simultaneously valuable in the overall, developing "arc." In some previous seasons, that wasn't always the case.

For instance, recall with dread, if you will, the first-season blind alley wherein Jack Bauer's doomed wife, Terri, suddenly was overcome with temporary amnesia. Or the now legendary moment in the second season when Jack's daughter, Kim, was suddenly accosted by a mountain lion…

On the one hand, such contrivances are certainly true to *24*'s rock-em/sock-em format. This is a show that occurs in "real time," with a genuine ticking clock tensely counting down hours, minutes, and seconds, and accordingly it skillfully updates the old-fashioned movie cliffhanger with the latest technology and twists. It's probably not wrong for the series to occasionally feature over-the-top *Perils of Pauline* moments given its nature as a pressure cooker. Yet, on the other end, narrative dead ends and tricks tend to undercut the believability factor.

But this discussion is pure prologue. Believability is not a problem or stumbling block in the 2006 season, which sees ex-CTU agent Jack Bauer (Kiefer Sutherland)—formerly believed dead—returned to active duty to do battle with three interesting and powerful villains: a Russian terrorist, Vladimir Bierko (played by Julian Sands); his own former mentor at CTU (Counter Terrorist Unit), Christopher Henderson (Peter Weller); and ultimately, the corrupt President of the United States himself, Charles Logan (Gregory Itzin). Worse, Jack must contend with the Department of Homeland Security's hostile takeover of CTU, a bureaucratic snafu that threatens lives.

Given so much action, there simply wasn't much time for ridiculous melodrama or silliness in *24*'s fifth season, and the series opened with a controversial bang by depicting the dramatic and bloody deaths of beloved characters such as Michelle Dessler and President David Palmer (Haysbert).

From there, *24* continued strongly, featuring the death of Jack's other good friend Tony Almeida (Carlos Bernard), as well as that of loveable and obese tech guy,

Christopher Henderson (Peter Weller), Jack Bauer's mentor, is pressed for information
by Bauer (Kiefer Sutherland, back to us) in **24**.

Edgar Stiles. Then to top it off, *24* went out with fire-works. Various late run episodes featured Jack hijacking a plane and a subsequent emergency landing on a Los Angeles highway, a deadly nerve gas attack on CTU, and more.

Then, the two-hour finale was a true humdinger. Pulse-pounding is a better description. The terrorists and the threat of the Centox nerve gas are finally eliminated after a hair-raising siege on a Russian nuclear submarine. But then, Jack must go toe-to-toe with the President of the United States...and all the powers that high office controls. The best part of this confrontation was the sight of Americans of different stripes banding together to stop a President who was out of control and abusing his power. They did so not as partisans, but as patriots.

The characters in the series all worked in the admin-istration of Charles Logan. Audrey (Kim Raver) is the daughter of the Secretary of Defense; Mike Novick is his Chief of Staff; Aaron Pierce, part of the President's secret service detachment; Martha—the President's wife. When they learned what Logan had done, they didn't defend him by outing Jack Bauer as a covert agent (Valerie Plame, anybody?). They didn't remain a loyal to a "man" at the expense of the country. They didn't attempt to protect the Office of the Executive by shredding the Constitution. They knew precisely what their duty was—to bring down a corrupt man—and they did it without regard to *party affiliation*. Why, even the Attorney General had objectiv-ity and obeyed the law. Who could possibly imagine Bush shill Alberto Gonzales taking a position against his lord and master?

With the President in custody, *24* appeared to finally wind down. However, just when the two-hour finale was nearly over, Jack was abducted, whisked overseas on a boat, and tortured there by the Chinese government for acts he committed during the previous season (an under-cover assault on the Chinese Embassy).

Whew! Take a deep breath, and then relive the first four seasons of *24* on DVD.

All four seasons are available on DVD.

THAT '70S SHOW

(FOX) (CANCELED) (30 minutes) (Wednesdays at 8:00 pm, EST; November 2, 2005-May 18, 2006) Casey-Werner-Mandabach/20th Century Fox. Created by: Bonnie Turner, Terry Turner, Mark Brazil. Executive Producers: Mark Brazil, Marcy Carsey, Rob Des Hotel, Jacki Filgo, Caryn Mandabach, Bonnie Turner, Tom Werner. Co-Executive Producers: Joshua Sternin, Linda Welln. Produced by: Steve Joe. Camera: Ronald W. Browne. Film Editors: Mark Karlich. Music by: Chris Bell, Alex Chilton. Written by: Dean Batali, Ken Blankstein, Alan Dybner, Rob Des Hotel, Mark Hudis, Steve Joe, Sarah McLaughlin, Greg Mettler, Bryan Moore, Kristin Newman, Chris Peterson, Greg Schaffer, Dave Schiff, Philip Stark. Directed by: David Trainer.

CAST

Laura Prepon (Donna Pinciotti)
Danny Masterson (Stephen Hyde)
Mila Kunis (Jackie)
Wilmer Valderrama (Fez)
Kurtwood Smith (Red)
Debra Jo Rupp (Kitty)
Don Stark (Bob)

With series star Topher Grace (playing Eric Forman) missing in action to pursue a movie career, and celebrity Ashton Kutcher (playing Kelso) appearing only occasionally, *That '70s Show*'s swan song and eighth season wasn't all that it could have been. At times, it was hard to understand why the series came back at all, since the primary movers and shakers were gone.

Still, *That '70s Show* attempted to make the best of the time it had left chronicling the last days of disco in the year 1979. The series, as before, focuses on a group of young adults and friends, as well as Eric's Mom (Debra Jo Rupp) and Dad (Kurtwood Smith). Their son's absence was explained by saying that Eric had left America for Africa, after basically jilting girlfriend Donna (Laura Prepon). Accordingly, episodes in the eighth season found Donna attempting (and failing) to move on emotionally.

Other story lines during the year involved preparations for Hyde's bachelor party ("You're My Best Friend"), Red and Kitty celebrating their twenty-fifth wedding anniversary ("Misfire"), and Kitty losing her engagement ring ("Keep Yourself Alive"). Donna attempted to arouse Eric long-distance with sexy photographs of herself, a plan that went awry in "Stone Cold Crazy."

Finally, however, an appropriate sense of closure was established in "That '70s Finale," which was set at the Forman's house (destined now to be sold) on New Year's Eve, December 31, 1979, the last night of the disco decade. Topher Grace returned to play Eric one last time and reconcile with Donna, thus ending the series on a happy note. It was a classy ending, and a wise move to end the series as the Seventies gave way to the Eighties (though a sitcom called *That '80s Show* had already been tried and failed).

That '70s Show has always been to the Nineties and 21st Century what *Happy Days* was for the 1970s, an evocation of nostalgia for a time twenty years gone. *That '70s Show* was always a ratings winner and like *Happy Days* a kind of innocent program. It never had the number of spinoffs that *Happy Days* boasted, but it was still a successful initiative and one whose glory days will be missed.

The first five seasons are currently available on DVD.

TWO AND A HALF MEN

(CBS) (RENEWED) (30 minutes) (Mondays at 9:00 pm, EST; September 19, 2005-May 22, 2006) Created by: Lee Aronsohn, Chuck Lorre. Executive Producers: Lee Aronsohn, Mark Burg, Oren Koules, Chuck Lorre, Eric Tannenbaum, Kim Tannenbaum. Co-Executive Producer: Jeff Abugov, Don Foster, Eddie Gorotedtsky. Produced by: Tracey Ormandy. Camera: Tony Askins, Steven Silver. Film Editor: Joe Bella. Music: Lee Aronsohn, Chuck Lorre. Written by: Lee Aronsohn, Susan Beavers, Don Foster, Chuck Lorre. Directed by: Gary Halvorson, Asaad Kelada, Rob Schiller, James Widdoes, Jerry Zaks.

CAST

Charlie Sheen (Charlie Harper)
Jon Cryer (Alan Harper)
Angus T. Jones (Jake Harper)
Marin Hinkle (Judith)
Melanie Lynskey (Rose)
Conchata Ferrell (Berta)
Holland Taylor (Evelyn Harper)

Call me a philistine, but this situation comedy is actually funny. Which comes as a surprise, because as a critic and a viewer, I'm not a big fan of the traditional sitcom format…except on rare occasions. *Two and a Half Men* is one of those rarities.

Just finishing its third season, *Two and a Half Men* has been a rating bonanza for CBS, regularly finishing in the ratings top ten—through the year and even in summer reruns. I guess viewers will find quality, even amongst the dross.

Two and a Half Men is the tale of Charlie Harper (Charlie Sheen), a womanizing bachelor and playboy with a place on the beach in Malibu. His life is turned upside down when his brother Alan (Jon Cryer) and Alan's son Jake (Angus T. Jones) turn up to live with him after Alan's marriage of twelve years to Judith (Marin Hinkle) comes to an end. Now suddenly, Charlie is put in the position of playing "dad" to Jake, and rearranging his whole life to create a viable family unit for the boy.

Making that a more difficult proposition than it need be are those who surround the Harper boys. Evelyn (Holland Taylor) is their mother, a shrew of a woman with a biting wit and a judgmental bent. Berta (Conchata Ferrell) is Charlie's housekeeper and Rose (Melanie Lynskey) is the next-door neighbor, only she's got an interesting backstory. She slept with Charlie once and is now totally fixated on the guy, so has moved next door to him in hopes of getting him back.

Okay, so it doesn't sound like Shakespeare. Or even Norman Lear. Yet something in this show really clicks. Perhaps it's the expertise of the veteran cast, but for a sitcom circa 2006, this series is surprisingly laugh-out-loud funny.

Season Three finds Jake having trouble in school ("Principal Gallagher's Lesbian Lover") and going out on his first date with a girl ("Just Once with Aunt Sophie"). Alan dates a controlling woman who—inch by nefarious inch—asserts her dominance in the house ("Santa's Village of the Damned") and later he and Judith threaten to become an item again ("Carpet Burns and a Bite Mark.") Meanwhile, Charlie dates the usual bevy of good-looking women.

Two and a Half Men moves to Mondays at 8:00 pm in September of 2006, anchoring the new CBS prime-time lineup.

The series is not yet available on DVD.

VERONICA MARS

(UPN) (RENEWED) (60 minutes) (Wednesdays at 9:00 pm, EST; September 8, 2005-May 9, 2006) Silver Pictures Television/Stu Segall Productions/Warner Bros. Created by: Rob Thomas. Executive Producers: Joel Silver, Rob Thomas. Co-Executive Producers: Jennifer Gwartz, Diane Ruggerio, Danielle Stokdyk. Produced by: Howard Grigsby. Camera: Victor Hammer, Joaquin Sedillo. Film Editor: Jim Gross. Music Editor: The Dandy Warhols, Josh Kramon. Written by: Cathy Belben, John Enborn, Phil Klemmer, Dayna North, Diane Ruggiero, Russell Smith, Rob Thomas. Directed by: Sarah Pia Anderson, Guy Norman Bee, Jason Bloom, Kevin Bray, Michael Fields, Steve Gozem, John T. Kretchmer, Nick Marck, Martha Mitchell, Rick Rosenthal, Rob Thomas, Harry Winer.

CAST

Kristen Bell (Veronica Mars)
Percy Daggs III (Wallace Fennel)
Teddy Dunn (Duncan Kane)
Jason Dohring (Logan Echolls)
Francis Capra (Eli Weevil Navarro)
Ryan Hansen (Dick Casablancas)
Kyle Gallner (Beaver Casablancas)
Tessa Thompson (Jackie)
Enrico Colantoni (Keith Mars)

The complete first season DVD box set describes *Veronica Mars* as "a little bit Buffy. A little bit Bogart," and that's a pretty apt description. This series—debatably the best drama currently airing on television—is set in and around Neptune High School on the West Coast. The campus is a playground for the very rich kids of privilege in sunny California. There, cynical (but sweet) teenager Veronica Mars (Kristen Bell) suffers under the weight of her new status as "unpopular" after being ruthlessly dissed and humiliated by the popular kids in school, including her former boyfriend, Duncan Kane (Teddy Dunn).

You see, Duncan's sister and Veronica's former best

friend, Lilly was murdered last year, and Veronica's dad, Keith (Enrico Colantoni)—formerly the sheriff but now a private eye—fingered Duncan's dad, software/tech billionaire Jake Kane as the culprit. Instinctively protecting its own, the town-at-large didn't care for the accusations, and Keith was thrown out of office in a recall election. Veronica was given the option of renouncing her father and his beliefs to stay popular and "cool," or joining him in exile. She chose exile. Her only friend is Wallace (Percy Daggs III), a new transfer student to Neptune High and her sidekick.

Now, Veronica and Keith work together in his detective agency, solving petty, sleazy cases about adultery and the like. But Veronica still wants to know what really happened to Lilly, as the case was never resolved to anyone's satisfaction (despite a convenient arrest of an obvious patsy by the new sheriff). This is doubly important to Veronica because her Mom split town during the hassle with Keith, and somehow, she's also involved. At the same time, Veronica has another mystery to solve. At a party the previous year, she was drugged at a party and woke up to discover she had been raped. The identity of the rapist is unknown to her, and she wants to make him pay. The suspects in the murder and the rape include Duncan, his scoundrel of a best friend, Logan (Jason Dohring), and Weevil (Francis Capra), Veronica's sometimes ally from "the wrong side of the tracks."

Veronica Mars is entrancing, and addictive as hell. Each episode of this hour-long mystery series moves with grace and humor on a carefully layered double track. On one narrative track is the sort of "case of the week," and on the other is the continuing story arc about Lilly and her death. The mix is damn near perfect, and everything is held together by creator Rob Thomas's noir sensibility

She's got her eye on you. Kristen Bell stars as TV's greatest detective in **VERONICA MARS**.

and the performance of Kristen Bell as Veronica.

Veronica Mars is essentially two series in one. In the first instance, it is a colorful, brilliant, (and tech savvy) updating of the *film noir* genre, replete with *femme fatales*, a private dick, labyrinthian mysteries, and other staples of the form. Noticeably, however, the mysteries featured in the series revolve around a central conceit: how 21st-century gadgets impact crime and crime solving. Wireless computers, iPods, blogs, web pages, cell phones, etc., are crucial tools (and crucial clues) in Veronica's universe.

Secondly, the series offers a trenchant comment on class warfare in America. Neptune High is a microcosm for America at large. Wealth and celebrity are worshiped, the middle class is vanishing, and the poor are screwed. In Neptune High, the very rich hold onto the perks and accuse the poor kids of bad behavior when in fact it's the rich kids who are bleeding the school and the community dry. Veronica is a force of justice by mediating and moving freely between the two groups and defending the innocent.

Veronica Mars herself is a classic TV character. She's Nancy Drew with attitude, and—like Sarah Michelle Gellar on the late, lamented *Buffy the Vampire Slayer*—Bell brings an interesting and potent combination of strength and vulnerability to her performances. Both *Buffy the Vampire Slayer* and *Veronica Mars* adopt as series leads a "post-popularity" high school girl. That is, specifically, a girl who has been inside "the in-crowd" yet ultimately rejected that shallow existence, choosing instead a life of individuality and courage.

This choice (and it is a choice, mind you) isn't easy, and both Buffy and Veronica take their lumps at school because they have moved outside the rigid strictures of cliques, the confines of the popular kids, the accepted norms. But what both characters have found in choosing self over group politics and peer pressure is an inner strength, one that can never be found by "joining" others, but only through, ultimately, doing your own thing in your own way. Accordingly, Buffy and Veronica are both strong role models for not just girls, but any high-school-age kids going through the travails of high school.

The second season of *Veronica Mars* expands the world of the series, by introducing a few new characters. Wallace gets a tricky, not-quite trustworthy friend in Jackie (Tessa Thompson), an African-American daughter of privilege and celebrity. Two rich Neptunian brothers, Dick (Ryan Hansen) and Beaver (Kyle Gallner) also step out of the background to emerge as foils and sometimes friends to Veronica. The central mystery in the second year involves the tragic crash of a school bus. Frighteningly, Veronica was destined to be on that bus (and would have been, but for a twist of fate) and so the accident may in fact have been an assassination attempt; revenge, perhaps for her solution of the Lilly Kane murder at the end of the first season.

The second ongoing mystery in the second season of *Veronica Mars* involves Logan Echolls, now Veronica's sometimes boyfriend. He's been accused of the murder of one of Weevil's gang members, but he has no memory of committing the crime. Has he been framed? Or is he hiding something? "The show's ongoing mystery," wrote *Chicago Tribune* critic Maureen Ryan, "about a bus crash that killed several of Mars' classmates, has been expertly handled, and the weekly mysteries are more whip smart than ever."[27]

Attentive viewers can suss out all the clues and find out all the answers now, because the complete second season was released on DVD August 22, 2006.

THE WEST WING

(NBC) (CANCELED) (60 minutes) (Sundays at 8:00 pm, EST; September 25, 2005-May 14, 2006) John Wells Productions/Warner Bros. Created by Aaron Sorkin. Executive Producer: John Wells. Produced by: Michael Hissirch. Camera: Michael Mayers. Film Editor: Caroline Ross. Written by: Eli Attie, Deborah Cahn, Aleg Graves, Peter Noah, Lawrence O'Donnell Jr., Lauren Schmidt, Josh Singer, Bradley Whitford. Directed by: Andrew Bernstein, Lesli Linka Glatter, Alex Graves, Laura Innes, Matia Karell, Mimi Leder, Nelson McCormack, Christopher Misianso, Steve Shill.

CAST

Martin Sheen (President Josiah Bartlet)
Stockard Channing (First Lady Abigail Bartlet)
Allison Janney (C.J. Cregg)
Bradley Whitford (Josh Lyman)
John Spencer (Leo McGarry)
Jimmy Smits (Matt Santos)
Alan Alda (Senator Arnold Vinick)
Mary McCormack (Kate Harper)
Joshua Malina (Will Bailey)
Kristin Chenoweth (Annabeth Schott)
Janel Moloney (Donna Moss)
Richard Schiff (Toby Ziegler)

2005–2006 was the seventh and final season for the Josiah Bartlet Administration, the fictitious Federal government created by Aaron Sorkin on the political drama *The West Wing*, in 1998. Since George W. Bush was elected President of the United States in 2000, critics have complained that the idea of a "liberal" president like Sheen's Bartlet is out of step with the times. Others have suggested the series lost some of its fast-talking, quick-paced luster when Sorkin left the series. *The West Wing* even had its own built-in replacement air in its last season, the female POTUS drama *Commander in Chief*, starring Geena Davis.

Yet despite a conservative executive in the West Wing,

critical gripes, and a contender for the Oval Office, *The West Wing* finished its run in fine, exquisite form, offering one of the series' best group of episodes since the turn of the millennium. The seventh year of *West Wing* sees Bartlet finishing his term in office and watching from the wings as election season kicks into high gear. The contenders are Vice President Matt Santos (Jimmy Smits), a Latino and liberal Democrat, and Senator Arnold Vinick (Alan Alda), a conservative Republican. While Bartlet's office deals with a press leak in "The Ticket," Santos chooses his running mate, and it's a surprise: longtime presidential advisor Leo McGarry (John Spencer).

In *The West Wing's* most talked-about episode of the final year, "The Debate," Forrest Sawyer moderates the presidential debate between Vinick and Santos. Amazingly, this episode was actually taped live, giving the effect of being spontaneous and off-the-cuff, and it gives both Smits and Alda a chance to shine.

The election came and went in "Election Day," a two-part episode that saw progressive Santos narrowly winning the White House (by an Electoral College tally of 272 to 266), but tragedy struck. His vice-presidential candidate, Leo McGarry also died, an event reflecting the death in real life of actor John Spencer, an outstanding character actor who had been with *The West Wing* since the beginning. McGarry's funeral was held in "Transition," while Santos had to deal with a Republican Senate confirming his new choice of Vice President.

The series ended on an emotional high note in "Tomorrow." President Santos took the oath of office, officially ending two terms of peace and prosperity under President Bartlet, who was given one last opportunity to reflect on what these eight years had meant to him.

The first seven seasons are available on DVD.

WHAT I LIKE ABOUT YOU

(WB) (CANCELED) (30 minutes) (Fridays at 8:00 pm, EST; September 16, 2005-March 24, 2006) Tollin/Robbins/Warner Bros. Created by: Will Calhoun, Dan Schneider. Executive Producers: Will Calhoun, Joe Davola, Caryn Lucas, Brian Robbins, Dan Schneider, Michael Tollin. Produced by: Shelley Zimmerman. Camera: Wayne Kennan, Paul Fetzoldt, Tony Yarlett. Film Editor: Ken Tintorri. Music: Scott Clausen, Ramin Sakurai. Written by: Peter Dirksen, Casey Johnson, Caryn Lucas, Jim Reynolds. Directed by: Rebecca Baughman, Dan Cortese, Shelley Jensen, Leslie Small, Steve Zuckerman.

CAST

Amanda Bynes (Holly Tyler)
Jennifer Garth (Valerie "Val" Tyler)
Wesley Jonathan (Gary Thorpe)
Allison Munn (Tina)
Nick Zano (Vince)
Dan Cortese (Vic)

What is this? *What I Like About You*? How about, *Why Don't I Remember You?* Or *Where Did You Come From?*

In the 2005–2006, the WB sitcom *What I Like About You* completed four seasons on the air (and tallied up over eighty half-hour episodes). The series was scandalously low-rated, which begs the question: why did it last so long? But at least that explains why I never heard of it until I began writing this book.

What I Like About You is the story of a teenager named Holly Tyler (Amanda Bynes) who is shuttled off to live with her older sister Val (Jennie Garth) when her dad takes a job in Japan. Together, they share an apartment in New York City and pine away for handsome, strapping men. Because lovely young women are worth nothing if there are no men in their lives…

Val's man is Vic (Dan Cortese), whom she inauspiciously married in Atlantic City during a drunken stupor prior to the fourth season opener. Holly's true love is the soundalike fella, Vince (Nick Zano). Jeez, how do fans keep these guys straight? Oh wait, there aren't any fans.

Anyway, Holly's confessed her feelings to Vince and in response, he tried to flee the state. However, she joined him on his impromptu road trip and the two got together during the fourth-season run. They officially become a couple during this crop of eighteen episodes, had their first fight ("The Re-Do"), and so forth.

Meanwhile, Val and Vic stay married, to Val's chagrin, though she tries dating other men. In one episode, "The Perfect Date," Val goes out with Charlie, played by Jason Priestley. For those who remember the 1990s, Priestley and Garth played romantic partners on *Beverly Hills 90210*…a long time ago. That's this sitcom's idea of frisson, I guess.

Innocuous and vapid, *What I Like About You* aired its tepid series finale in May 2006, with Valerie finally getting her perfect wedding (oh, at last!), and marrying Vic for real this time.

Now, what was I talking about?

This series is not currently released on DVD.

WIFE SWAP

(ABC) (RENEWED) (60 minutes) (Mondays at 8:00 pm, EST; February 20, 2006-March 27, 2006) Executive Producers: Jenny Crowther, Michael Davies, Stephen Lambert. Produced by: Vanessa Frances, Michael Kaufman, Rick Murray. Camera: Matthew Woolf. Film Editor: Paul Frost. Directed by: Philip Lott.

The second season of the unscripted reality series *Wife Swap* went pretty much like the first season did. In each of the eighteen hour-long episodes that comprise the season, a wife from one family swaps with a wife in another family…taking over all the household duties and raising the children (but not swapping sexual partners, in case you wondered).

The gimmick on *Wife Swap* is always the same and apparently never gets old. The producers make the family switch as uncomfortable as humanly possible by forcing the exchange to occur between ethnically, regionally, and religiously diverse "Moms." Yet in the end, there's *Wife Swap*'s eternal appeal to diversity as everybody in each family generally "learns" something important about themselves and others. There's more than one way to skin a cat after all.

In the second season of *Wife Swap*, a Southern Christian Mom and Liberal Hippie Mom switch places. In another episode, it's a Working Mom and Stay-at-Home Mom who turn the tables. Another installment pits a New York Mom against a North Carolina Mom, and so forth. Outdoor Moms versus Computer Geek Moms, career women vs. home schoolers, atheists versus Christians, you name it. Over and over again. *Ad infinitum. Ad nauseam.*

The series is not currently available on DVD.

WILDBOYZ

(MTV2) (RENEWED) (30 minutes) (Fridays at 9:00 pm, EST; January 6, 2006-February 24, 2006) Dickhouse Productions. Executive Producers: Trip Taylor, Jeff Tremaine. Produced by: Greg Wolf, Shanna Zablon. Camera: Dimitry Elyashkevich. Directed by: Jeff Tremaine.

CAST
Steve-O
Chris Pontius

After *Jackass* folded, kamikaze stuntmen-with-high-pain-thresholds Steve-O and Chris Pontius continued in their own spinoff, the globe-trotting series called *Wildboyz*. In the fourth season (which commenced in January of '06), these extreme sportsmen (who boast a penchant for wearing nut huggers) travel the world and meet all kind of animals…only to get badly hurt by them. On one notorious occasion, these two gents (and I use that term loosely) even baited a great white shark.

The eight half-hour episodes in Season Four take the Wild boys to Argentina and Thailand (for crocodile wrestling); to Russia (where they meet up with *Jackass* star Johnny Knoxville for a zero gravity flight) and to California to meet a real wild thing—*Knight Rider* star David Hasselhoff.

The complete first season is available on DVD.

WILL & GRACE

(NBC) (CANCELED) (30 minutes) (Thursdays at 8:30 pm, EST; September 19, 2005-May 18, 2006) KoMut/Three Sisters/ NBC Universal. Created by: David Kohan, Max Mutchnick. Executive Producers: James Burrows, Adam Barr, David Kohan, Max Mutchnick. Co-Executive Producers: Gary Ganetti, Greg Malins. Produced by: Bill Wrubel, Kate Angeli. Camera: Tony Askins. Film Editor: Peter Chakos. Music: Paul Buckley, Jonathan Wolf. Written by: Sally Bradford, Stan Gabiriel, James Hirsch, Gary Janetti, Jon Kinnally, David Kohan, Gail Lerner, Greg Malins, Max Mutchnick, Robia Rushad, James Rhonheimer, Bill Wrubell. Directed by: James Burrows.

CAST

Eric McCormack (Will Truman)
Debra Messing (Grace Allen)
Megan Mullally (Karen Walker)
Sean Hayes (Jack McFarland)

One of television's most beloved and long-lived situation comedies called it quits after eight years on the air in 2006. *Will & Grace*, an unwavering champion of gay rights (*human* rights, really) and just plain decency, made audiences of all stripes laugh and cry for the better part of the decade, and boasted a wonderful (and emotional) sendoff in its last episode, an hour-long finale that found a tender and unexpected new way to comment on the friendship between gay man Will (Eric McCormack) and his friend, Grace (Debra Messing).

The final season of *Will & Grace* opened with another daredevil act, a live performance (actually two: one per coast). In "Alive and Schticking" (with guest star Alec Baldwin), Grace finds herself attracted to a married man. Other episodes from this swan song season include "I Second That Emotion" which sees Grace go on friend Jack's (Sean Hayes) *Jack Talk* show and inadvertently make a remark that some gay men feel is homophobic, a real joke considering her lifestyle.

Other entries find Grace going out on a blind date ("The Old Maid and the Sea"), Grace seeking counsel from Jack about handling her overbearing Mother ("Swish out of Water"), and *Jack Talk* getting a conservative extreme makeover when it comes under corporate ownership.

The tearjerker finale, which features a flashforward (or is it dream sequence?) two decades from now, nicely punctuates the series' leitmotifs. Although some fans complained, the friendship between these dear friends may have ups and downs, but Will and Grace will always love each other. Longevity is part of friendship, even if sometimes people don't talk for a while.

The first five seasons are available on DVD, as is the series finale on a separate disc.

Left to right: Eric McCormack (Will), Debra Messing (Grace), Megan Mullally (Karen), and Sean Hayes (Jack) in a scene from the final season of **WILL & GRACE**.

WITHOUT A TRACE

(CBS) (RENEWED) (60 minutes) (Thursdays at 10:00 pm, EST; September 29, 2005-May 18, 2006) Jerry Bruckheimer Television/Jumbolaya Productions/Warner Bros. Created by: Hank Steinberg. Executive Producers: Jerry Bruckheimer, Jonathan Littman, Jan Nash, Hank Steinberg, Greg Walker. Co-Executive Producers: David Amann, Timothy Busfield, Scott Williams. Produced by: Scott White. Camera: John Aronson. Film Editor: Jane Kase. Music: Peter Manning Robinson. Written by: David Amann, David H. Goodman, David Grae, Diego Gutierrez, Jan Nash, Gwendolyn Parker, Jan Nash, Scott Williams. Directed by: Timothy Busfield, David Grae, Chad Lowe, Paul McCrane, Mathra Mitchell, John F. Showalter, Jeannot Szwarc, Kate Woods.

CAST
Anthony LaPaglia (Jack Malone)
Eric Close (Martin Fitzgerald)
Poppy Montgomery (Samantha Spade)
Marianne Jean-Baptiste (Vivian Johnson)
Enrique Murciano (Danny Taylor)
Roselyn Sanchez (Elena Delgado)

Without a Trace escorts viewers inside the high-pressure offices of the F.B.I. Missing Persons Squad in New York City. There, top detective Jack Malone (Anthony LaPaglia) is single-minded in pursuit of missing persons; sometimes cracking wise and using harsh language in his interrogation of suspects. He's joined by kind-hearted Martin Fitzgerald (Eric Close) and a team of detectives including Samantha Spade (Poppy Montgomery), Vivian (Marianne Jean-Baptiste), Taylor (Enrique Murciano), and Delgado (Roselyn Sanchez).

Each one of these men and women understands that time in critical, and this is a series that often cuts to insert shots of a timeline diagramed out on paper. It has events intersecting the story line, so the detectives

working the case (and the audience too) can understand what the missing subject was doing and where he or she was leading up to the disappearance. *Without a Trace* also provides small legends at the bottom of the screen keeping viewers abreast of how much time has past. They read, for instance "38 hours since disappearance" or "60 hours since disappearance."

In *Without a Trace's* third season, the Missing Person's Squad has searched for missing paramedics ("Blood Out"), teachers ("Rage"), U.S. Marines ("Odds or Evens"), a Dear Abby–type newspaper columnist ("Check Your Head"), and a pregnant woman ("Expectations"), among others. Not all the cases end up happy, and some end with the missing persons found…dead.

One typical episode of the series is "More Than This," the story of a child of privilege named Breck, who after being cut off from his rich father, seeks work in a shelter for battered women called Shield House. Once there, he becomes so enmeshed in the cause, of finally, for once in his life, being a part of something bigger than his selfish needs, that he goes about raising money for the shelter when it is threatened with closing. Then, suddenly, Breck disappears…

Before long, Jack and his team are on the case, learning all about Breck's history (revealed in flashback). His friends and family are interviewed, and then it's time to hit the streets for good old-fashioned police work. The case takes an odd turn when it is learned that Breck was pimping himself out to rich, lonely wives to raise money for the shelter. Still, this isn't the reason Breck disappeared. Finally, the detectives learn that a friend of Breck's, strung out on drugs, was responsible for a car crash that killed him. They later find his buddy in a gulley off a main road.

Without a Trace is undistinguished, but not cringe-worthy, like another Jerry Bruckheimer series, *Cold Case.* The characters are all dull ciphers, reciting rote information so the audience can follow the clues, but there isn't an abundance of mawkish sentimentality, and that's a good thing. The tagline, "when hope is lost, these are the people who find it," suggests melodrama on a grand scale, but thankfully doesn't deliver on anything more than a refreshing, "just the facts ma'am" approach to storytelling.

LaPaglia is an effective lead, and brings gravitas to his role. This is a nice counterbalance to the Fitzgerald character, because Eric Close (*Dark Skies,* 1996–1997, *Now and Again,* 1999) simply exudes sincerity and genuine decency in the role. Some of Malone's and Fitzgerald's other cases in the third season involve locating a missing teenager who was traumatized by 9/11 ("Safe"), and finding a missing prostitute in "From the Ashes."

The first season is available on DVD.

YES, DEAR

(CBS) (CANCELED) (30 minutes) (Wednesdays at 8:30 pm, EST; September 14, 2005-February 15, 2006) Twilight Studios/20th Century Fox/CBS. Created by: Gregory Thomas Garcia, Alan Kirschenbaum. Executive Producers: Gregory Thomas Garcia, Aln Kirschenbaum. Co-Executive Producers: Diane Burroughs. Produced by: Jay Kleckner. Camera: Vincent Contarino, Tony Yarlett. Film Editor: Gary Anderson. Music: Rick Marotta. Written by: Erika Kaestle, Michael A. Marciano, Patrick McCarthy, Gigi McCreary, Bob Smiley, Bob Stevens, Perry Rein, Eric Zicklin. Directed by: Mark Cendrowki, Miguel Higuera, Jay Kleckner, Jeff Meyer, Mike O'Malley, Liza Snyder.

CAST

Anthony Clark (Greg Warner)
Jean Louisa Kelly (Kim Warner)
Liza Snyder (Christine Hughes)
Mike O'Malley (Jim)

This family life situation comedy focuses on the home lives of two couples who live in uncomfortably close proximity. Greg (Anthony Clark) and Kim Warner (Jean Louisa Kelly) are white-collar yuppies and concerned parents conscientiously raising their young son. Kim's sister, Christine Hughes (Liza Snyder) and her husband Jimmy (Mike O'Malley) are blue-collar folks and live in the Warners' guest house. They have very *laissez-faire* ideas about child rearing, which causes tension. In particular, Jimmy likes to give Greg bad, macho advice on the subject.

Yes, Dear concerns the culture clash between the Hughes and the Warners, and it's a fairly weak premise to hang a sitcom on, yet *Yes, Dear* hung on for six seasons doing just that. In its sixth and final season, Kim and Christine both decide they want more children...a decision the husbands aren't terribly pleased with. In another story, Greg also decides to turn the tables and leech off Jimmy for a while, a switcheroo his brother-in-law doesn't care for.

Low ratings doomed any future Warner or Hughes progeny, and CBS canceled *Yes, Dear*.

The series is not currently available on DVD.

SIGNIFICANT TV-MOVIES AND MINI-SERIES

SIGNIFICANT TV–MOVIES AND MINISERIES

The 2005–2006 season brought essentially four kinds of miniseries and television movies to the screen. First, there were several cheesy "natural" disaster films about storms, epidemics, and other examples of Mother Nature's wrath. Oddly, in virtually all cases, it was a woman scientist—either Gina Gershon, Kim Delaney, or Lucy Lawless—who was pitted against these attacks. Chicks and disaster are apparently a winning combination.

Second, the broadcast networks offered unnecessary remakes of movies now considered classics. To wit: NBC offered a redo of the disaster flick *The Poseidon Adventure* while ABC recrafted the epic *The Ten Commandments*.

Thirdly, twin biopics about Pope John Paul II were rushed to the TV screen to capitalize on the world's canonization of the popular pontiff following his death.

Lastly, this was also the year for dueling films about the events of 9/11. Even as Paul Greengrass's *United 93* played in movie theaters, television offered other variations about that doomed plane in *The Flight That Fought Back*, a hokey narrated re-creation from the Discovery Channel, and the genuinely dramatic, fictionalized account, *Flight 93*.

Despite such extreme repetition and duplication, it was the TV films that were *different* that truly stood out this year. Sprawling *Broken Trail* was an AMC Western miniseries starring Robert Duvall that recalled the glory days of *Lonesome Dove*, and HBO's *Elizabeth I* was a ravishing costume drama that took home a raft of Emmy Awards.

AMBULANCE GIRL

(Lifetime) (September 12, 2005) Von Zerneck/Sertner Films. Written by: Alan Hines. Based on the Novel by: Jane Stern. Directed by: Kathy Bates.

CAST
Kathy Bates (Jane Stern)
Robin Thomas (Michael Stern)

This Lifetime original movie focuses on Jane Stern (Kathy Bates), a woman who's been married for thirty years but begins to see her life fall apart. She's wedded to Michael (Robin Thomas), a recovering alcoholic, and they have many arguments…a complication since they work together professionally as food critics. Feeling neurotic, anxious, and panicked, one day Jane finds the strength to change her life. She decides to become a paramedic, an experience that alters the fundamental nature of her life and relationships.

"When I talked about going on emergency calls, people were really fascinated by how I went from being such an absolute basket case emotionally, physically, and every other way to getting the gumption to do this," the real Jane Stern, who wrote the novel the film is based on, told Lifetime about her story. "I figured it would be not only a good tale but that it would give hope to people who never imagined they could do something so frightening."[1]

Ambulance Girl was promoted as part of Lifetimes's "Be Your Own Hero" campaign, designed to encourage self-confidence and self-esteem in women of all ages. Bates, who also directed, summarized the project in this way: "It's really about the recovery of a marriage and about how two people were able to learn to stand apart, but still be able to love each other and find strength together."

She went on to note that "for Jane on a personal level, it's about a woman who was imprisoned by her own fears and phobias yet was able to overcome them so that she could do the things that she'd always wanted to do in life."[2] Available on DVD.

BROKEN TRAIL

(AMC) (June 25-26, 2006) Butchers Run Films/Once Upon a Time Films/Nomadic Pictures/Sony TV. Written by: Alan Geoffrion. Directed by: Walter Hill.

CAST
Robert Duvall (Print Ritter)
Thomas Haden Church (Tom Harte)
Greta Scacchi (Nola Jones)
Scott Cooper (Gilpin)
Gwendoline Yeo (Sun)
Caroline Chan (Mai Ling)

At the turn of the nineteenth century, old Print Ritter (Robert Duvall) and his nephew, Harte (Thomas Haden Church) shepherd 500 horses across the vast expanse of the American West, en route to Wyoming. On the trail, they encounter five Chinese women who have been condemned to a life of prostitution in a small mining town. The women need their help and suddenly, these two cowboys have much more to protect than mere horses—and more at stake—in this four-hour miniseries from AMC.

Walter Hill, the artist behind *The Warriors* (1979) directs this "elegant"[3] and beautiful genre piece that recalls the grand history of TV westerns, like *Lonesome Dove* (1992). Duvall and Church have great chemistry together, and scenery is gorgeous. Nominated for an Emmy, *Broken Trail's* scale "is appropriately vast, and the light where the horizon meets the sky is one of the few soft, glowing things in a harsh world."[4]

CATEGORY 7:
END OF THE WORLD

(CBS) (November 6 and November 13, 2005) Von Zerneck/Sertner Films. Written by: Christian Ford, Roger Soffer. Directed by: Dick Lowry.

CAST
Gina Gershon (Judith Carr)
Shannen Doherty (Faith Clavell)
Cameron Daddo (Ross Duffy)
Robert Wagner (Ryan Carr)
Randy Quaid (Tornado Tommy)
James Brolin (Donny Hall)
Penny Hall (Swoosie Kurtz)
Tom Skerritt (Colonel Davis)
Adam Rodriguez (Ritter)
Nicholas Lea (Monty)
Sebastian Spence (Gavin)
Kenneth Welsh (Horst)

This is the wholly unnecessary follow-up to the 2004 disaster telefilm *Category 6: Day of Destruction*. It's more Hollywood "disaster porn" (made even more distasteful after Katrina) because it asks audiences to simultaneously be frightened of supposedly real terrors (like Mother Nature gone awry, or terrorist attacks) and awed by the special effects grandeur when The Statue of Liberty's arm breaks off its perch, George Washington's face slides off Mount Rushmore in South Dakota, or some other global monument is destroyed.

In *Category 7*, Gina Gershon heads FEMA (heck, Michael Brown could do it) during a crisis. Increasingly savage storms are detected moving towards Washington D.C. She tries in vain to get the government mobilized, but you just *know* those monuments are going to get destroyed no matter what. Fortunately Gina Gershon calls on her old boyfriend…who just happens to be a scientist specializing in dangerous weather patterns.

"It draws us with the premise of destruction writ large and offers a moral so thin that Chicken Little's tale seems downright theological in comparison," wrote *The Charlotte Observer* in relation to this telemovie. "Like those who chose to hunker down rather then flee an onrushing menace, we are left to watch and marvel at something certain to make us feel small and, in the end, foolish."[5] Available on DVD.

COVERT ONE:
THE HADES FACTOR

(CBS) (April 9, 2006 and April 16, 2006) The Sanitsky Company./Ludlum Entertainment. Based on the novel by: Robert Ludlum and Gayle Lynds. Written by: Elwood Reid. Directed by: Mick Jackson.

CAST
Stephen Dorff (Jon Smith)
Mira Sorvino (Rachel Russell)
Blair Underwood (Palmer Addison)
Colm Meaney (Peter Howell)
Anjelica Huston (President)
Jeffrey De Munn (Steven)
Sophia Myles (Sophie Amsden)

A fast-paced hybrid of the spy drama and the disaster film, this two night miniseries is based on the novel by Robert Ludlum and Gayle Lynds. *Covert One: The Hades Factor* involves the sudden and deadly outbreak of an Ebola-type hemorrhagic fever, meaning that human organs liquefy.

After hot zones erupt in Seattle, Washington, D.C., and Afghanistan, former "disease specialist" Jon Smith (Stephen Dorff), who now works for the top secret "Covert One," investigates the spread of the virus that threatens to wipe out much of the population. Mira Sorvino plays a rogue scientist, Rachel Russell, who attempts to get a sample of the disease. However, she has an agenda all her own…can she be trusted?

Before the battle to save the world from an epidemic is won, Smith will also pay a high personal cost in the form of his dead fiancée Sophie (Sophia Myles), whose death may not have been an accident. Meanwhile, a corrupt U.S. President (Anjelica Huston) takes steps to eliminate a bioweapons program called Scimitar that could be the source of the disease.

Available on DVD.

ELIZABETH I

(HBO) (April 24, 2006) HBO Films/Channel 4. Written by: Nigel Williams. Directed by: Tom Hooper.

CAST
Helen Mirren (Queen Elizabeth I)
Jeremy Irons (Robert Dudley, Earl of Leicester)
Hugh Dancy (Robert Devereux, Earl of Essex)
Ian McDiarmid (William Cecil)
Patrick Malahide (Sir Francis Washington)
Toby Jones (Robert Cecil)
Barbara Flynn (Mary, Queen of Scots)

This period piece set in 1579 describes the life and times of a middle-aged, fortysomething Queen Elizabeth I (Mirren), now a good two decades into her reign. Unmarried, but not uninterested in sex, Elizabeth carries on a romantic relationship first with a top advisor, the Earl of Leicester (Jeremy Irons) and then, scandalously, with a much younger man, Robert (Hugh Dancy).

Still, Elizabeth is pressured to marry for political reasons, the end goal always being the birth of an heir that will secure the line of royal succession.

Mirren expressed to HBO her thoughts on the historical figure, Elizabeth: "She was very feminine, very

vulnerable, kind of slightly silly sometimes, but at the same time, incredibly intellectual and very, very emotional. I mean she would fly off the handle very quickly," Mirren noted. "She loved with great passion, great commitment. And she hated with equal passion and commitment. She was an incredibly explosive character. But I never wanted to play this sort of cold, controlling, sort of slightly mean-spirited sort of granite-like character, because she really wasn't like that."[6]

Ravishing in detail and texture, *Elizabeth I* depicts the world around Elizabeth and the tensions pressing down on her from both within and outside her kingdom. The Catholics are openly hostile to the Protestant monarch and the war with Spain rages. Meanwhile, there's a domestic rebellion from Mary, Queen of Scots (Barbara Flynn).

Elizabeth I took home Emmy Awards for Mirren and Irons, and for best miniseries.

Available on DVD.

FATAL CONTACT:
BIRD FLU IN AMERICA

(ABC) (May 9, 2006) Diane Kerew Productions/Sony Television. Written by: Ron McGee. Directed by: Richard Pearce.

CAST
Joely Richardson (Iris Varnack)
Scott Cohen (Governor Newsome)
Justina Machado (Alma)
Ann Cusack (Denise Connelly)
Stacy Keach (HHS Secretary Collin Reed)

A businessman traveling from the Far East to the United States inadvertently brings home the lethal strain of H5N1 or "avian flu" in this made-for-TV movie that ratchets up the fear factor concerning a bird flu epidemic in America and what it would look like.

Our protagonist in the drama is determined scientist Iris Varnack (Joely Richardson), working not for the CDC but for the EIS (Epidemic Intelligence Service). She's joined by Stacy Keach as the Secretary of Health and Human Services and by the Governor of Virginia (Scott Cohen), but will their efforts be too little too late?

Available on DVD.

FLIGHT 93

(A&E) (January 30, 2006) David Gerber Company/20th Century Fox Television. Written by: Nevin Schreiner. Directed by: Peter Markle.

CAST
Jeffrey Nordling (Tom Burnett)
Brennan Elliot (Todd Beamer)
Ty Olson (Mark Bingham)
Colin Glazer (Jeremy Glick)
Kendall Cross (Deena Burnett)

On September 11, 2001, four airliners were hijacked by terrorists; only one missed its target. That was Flight 93, a plane that, according to the official story, was recaptured by brave American passengers just moments prior to its crash in a Pennsylvania field. Had those Americans not succeeded in capturing the cockpit, the plane would have struck the Capitol Building in Washington, D.C.

The Discovery Channel blended reenactments, narration, and photographs to create their own version of the terrifying flight, called *The Flight That Fought Back* (which aired on September 11, 2005), but this is a "movie" version of those events. The initial *Flight 93* broadcast preceded the theatrical release of *United 93* by several months. When it aired on A&E, it drew that channel's largest audience in history, nearly six million viewers.

Flight 93 is absorbing and nerve-wracking, not so much because the filmmakers are particularly skilled—they're not; they're merely workmen—but because all Americans live with the knowledge that it could have been any one of us aboard that plane that day. It's impossible not to put ourselves in the shoes of those doomed citizens, who—sooner than the rest of us—realized a war had begun.

Flight 93 adheres closely to the facts of that day as we understand them, but there are many things about that doomed journey that Americans still don't know. There have been persistent rumors that Flight 93 was shot down by the U.S. Air Force, for instance. Nevertheless, this sincere work will resonate with all Americans.

Nonetheless, *United 93* remains a much better film than this TV effort—better directed and more technically accomplished.

Available on DVD.

HAVE NO FEAR:
THE LIFE OF POPE JOHN PAUL II

(ABC) (December 1, 2005) Five Mile River Films. Written by: Michael Hirst and Judd Parkin. Directed by: Jeff Bleckner.

CAST
Thomas Kretschmann (Pope John Paul II)
Bruno Ganz (Cardinal Wyszynski)
Jasper Harris (Young Wotjyla)
Ignas Survila (Teenage Wotjyla)
Joaquim De Almeida (Romeo)
John Albasiny (Father Dzwisz)

This is one of two TV movies which raced to broadcast in hopes of cashing in on popular audience interest surrounding Pope John Paul II following his death.

This ABC effort (which beat the other film to air by mere days) unfolds in a flashback-style narrative with the Pope recalling the travails of his youth, including the death of his mother and the rise of Nazism.

Variety's Brian Lowry wrote of this effort—filmed on location in Rome and Lithuania—that "there's virtually no character development" and concluded that "the pope himself is rendered somewhat mundane by his utter saintliness, failing to capture the charisma and sparkle that prompted even non-Catholics to respond enthusiastically"[7] to the pontiff.

Catholic Online called *Have No Fear* "a less than fully fleshed-out picture of Pope John Paul. Yet, despite the hurried pace and rough strokes, what emerges from the tableaux is a beautiful mosaic of courage, conviction and compassion."[8]

Available on DVD.

HUMAN TRAFFICKING

(Lifetime) (October 24–25, 2005) Muse Entertainment. Written by: Agatha Dominik and Carol Doyle. Directed by: Christian Duguay.

CAST
Mira Sorvino (Kate Morozov)
Donald Sutherland (Bill Meehan)
Robert Carlyle (Sergei Karpovich)
Laurence Leboeuf (Nadia)
Sarah-Jeanne Labrosse (Annie)

This two-part miniseries (which Lifetime advertised as a "gritty crime drama") looks, feels (and smells) uncomfortably like an overlong pilot for a new crime investigation TV series. *Law and Order: Human Trafficking*, or some such thing.

Human Trafficking concerns Immigration and Customs Enforcement Agent Kate Morozov (Mira Sorvino), a determined rookie who with supreme idealism attempts to bring down the sex trade running rampant in Eastern Europe. In particular, her sights are on human trafficker Karpovich (Robert Carlyle).

The film goes to great length to depict attractive young women (often scantily clad) being abducted all over the world (Ukraine, the Philippines, etc.) and forced into lives of involuntary prostitution. No doubt sex slavery is a troublesome issue in the globe, but this hysterical miniseries plays up the lascivious and sexual angles of the subject while at the same time condemning sexual slavery by noting that women are abducted against their will every day.

In essence, the movie panders to an audience's baser instincts by reveling in the flesh, and then attempts to make the audience feel good about the fact they've been educated about an "important" issue.

Available on DVD.

IN FROM THE NIGHT

(CBS) (April 23, 2006) Hallmark Hall of Fame Productions/ McGee Street Productions. Written by: Susanna Styron, Bridget Terry. Directed by: Peter Levin.

CAST
Marcia Gay Harden (Vicki Miller)
Taylor Handley (Bobby)
Kate Nelligan (Vera)
Regina Taylor (Dr. Gardner)
Thomas Gibson (Aidan)

In this saccharine TV movie from the Hallmark Hall of Fame (its 227th production), Vicki Miller (Marcia Gay Harden) is surprised when her 16-year-old nephew— apparently a runaway—shows up on her doorstep in

ICE (Immigration and Customs Enforcement) Agent Kate Morozov (Mira Sorvino)
is after an international sex slave ring in **HUMAN TRAFFICKING**.

need of room and board. Vicki is emotionally closed off to Bobby (Taylor Handley) at first, in part because she's working on a book with a writing partner she's uncomfortably attracted to, Aidan (Thomas Gibson).

Before long, however, Vicki realizes that Bobby is dealing with a history of abuse, and this revelation leads Vicki to understand some things about her own family history. With a help of a kind therapist, Dr. Gardner (Regina Taylor), the family's secrets are exposed and reckoned with.

"Two people come out of their respective caves in this movie," as director Levin described the treacly movie. "It isn't only Bobby who has a problem—although his is the most obvious. Vicki has cut herself off from her family in order to write. Bobby forces her to deal with her family's ghosts. And Vicki, in turn, helps Bobby out of the cave that he's been locked in because of the damage that's been done to him."[9]

Available on DVD.

A LITTLE THING CALLED MURDER

(Lifetime) (January 23, 2006) Grand Productions/Stonemade Entertainment/20th Century Fox. Based on the novel *Dead End: The Crime Story of the Decade* by Jeanne King. Written by: Teena Booth. Directed by: Richard Benjamin.

CAST

Judy Davis (Sante Kimes)
Jonathan Jackson (Kenny Kimes)
Chelcie Ross (Ken Sr.)
Cynthia Stevenson (Beverly Bates)

Not your average Lifetime fare. At all. This is a lurid but also involving chronicle of a true life American crime spree. Sadistic Sante Kimes (Judy Davis), who may just be evil incarnate, involves her poor son Kenny (Jonathan Jackson) in all manners of violent crimes over his lifetime. She's guilty of enslaving her maids(!), shoplifting, arson, passing bad checks, grand larceny, fraud, and murder to name a few of her trespasses. Star Judy Davis juicily plays the ultraviolent woman while wearing a truly alarming fright wig, and there's a camp touch to the portrayal. However, that seems appropriate given the almost mythic scope of Kimes' assorted crimes.

A Little Thing Called Murder follows Sante from her early days to her time on the lam pursued by the police, to her ultimate incarceration in the twenty-first century, following her trial. In the end, she blames her spree on Kenny, a laughable assertion, since the apple doesn't fall far from the tree.

Not available on DVD.

MRS. HARRIS

(HBO) (August 1, 2006) Killer Films/Number 9 Films. Written and directed by: Phyllis Nagy.

CAST

Annette Bening (Jean Harris)
Ben Kingsley (Herman Tarnower)
Frances Fisher (Marge Jacobson)
Cloris Leachman (Pearl)
Frank Whaley (George Bolen)
Lawrence O'Donnell (Judge Leggett)
Ellen Burstyn (Ex-Lover)

Inspired by the novel *Very Much a Lady* by Shana Alexander, *Mrs. Harris* concerns the 1980 murder of "Scarsdale Diet" doctor, Herman Tarnower (Ben Kingsley) by socialite Jean Harris (Annette Bening).

Mrs. Harris is dominated by a flashback structure, which interweaves scenes of Harris and Tarnower first meeting with preparations for the trial, court testimony, and the like years later. The two lead actors are powerful in their roles, but *Mrs. Harris* ends up an overwrought disaster thanks to neophyte director Nagy's insistence on tarting up the material with inappropriate camera angles and campy touches that undercut the sincerity of the project.

Close-ups often appear distorted, like fish-eye views of the characters; at one point Nagy adopts the old Spike Lee technique of having an actor "glide" through a scene, while others watch. Although powerful in cinema such as *Malcolm X*, the gliding sequence here (involving Kingsley striding through a shower room) merely comes off as funny and inappropriate.

Instead of relying on gimmicks and tricks, Nagy should have relaxed and let her actors tell the story. Indeed, the performances are serious and accomplished, which is quite jarring compared to the hokey, stilted way they're rendered on screen.

Despite such problems, the scene in which Harris drives home in the rain and in a comedy of errors ends up shooting Tarnower remains fascinating and well handled. *Mrs. Harris* was (bafflingly) nominated for several Emmy Awards, so it was a bad year for TV movies; but the year's biggest scandal erupted over the nomination of Ellen Burstyn as best supporting actress for *Mrs. Harris*. She appears in the TV movie for all of fourteen seconds.

Turns out, she was certainly the year's smartest actress.

Available on DVD.

POPE JOHN PAUL II

(CBS) (December 4 and December 7, 2005) Grupa Filmowa Baltimedia/Studio Filmowe Projektor/RAI. Written by: John Kent Harrison, Francesco Contaldo. Directed by: John Kent Harrison.

CAST
Jon Voight (Pope John Paul II)
Cary Elwes (Karol Wojtyla, 18-50 Years of Age)
Christopher Lee (Wyszynski)
Ben Gazzara (Casaroli)

John Paul served as Pope for a quarter-century and died on April 2, 2005. This is the second of the year's dueling Pope productions, a miniseries that spanned two nights on CBS and was ultimately trounced in the ratings by ABC's *Desperate Housewives*. *Pope John Paul II* is also the Pope biopic that received the Vatican's stamp of approval and filmed on location at St. Peter's Square and inside the Sistine Chapel.

The film opens with the assassination attempt on the Pope's life in the early 1980s, and then escorts viewers into a series of flashbacks illuminating the Polish man's life. Cary Elwes plays the future pope in the early days, and Jon Voight takes over once Wojtyla becomes Pontiff. Some of the details include the Nazi invasion of Poland, Wojtyla's passion for performance and—like *Have No Fear*—the death of his mother. This effort is generally considered the better of the two productions, in part because Jon Voight's resemblance to John Paul II is uncanny, and the actor does a remarkable job chronicling the Pope's later life and battle with Parkinson's disease.

Available on DVD.

THE POSEIDON ADVENTURE

(NBC) (November 20, 2005) Silverstar Ltd. Productions/Larry Levinson Productions/Hallmark Entertainment. Written by: Bryce Zabel. Based on the novel by: Paul Gallico. Directed by: Jon Putch.

CAST
Adam Baldwin (Mike Rogo)
Rutger Hauer (Bishop Schmidt)
Steve Guttenberg (Richard Clarke)
Bryan Brown (Jeffrey Eric Anderson)
C. Thomas Howell (Dr. Robert Ballard)
Alexa Hamilton (Rachel)
Peter Weller (Captain Gallico)

This overlong and undersuspenseful remake of the 1972 disaster epic starring Shelley Winters rushed to reach air before Wolfgang Petersen's big budget remake, *Poseidon* (2006) made it into theaters for the summer.

Alas, this version of the ocean-based adventure about a capsized cruise liner has been updated to include silly and "relevant" 21st century touches. Now it's a terrorist cell that detonates bombs on board the Dulcet cruise craft during New Year's Eve which upends the vessel, rather than original's tidal wave.

Our hero is Mike Rogo (Adam Baldwin), now an agent for the Department of Homeland Security, and one of the survivors, played by Bryan Brown, is the producer of a reality show like *Survivor*, which is supposed to be ironic. This "War on Terror"–era redo of the classic story doesn't even really make sense. Why attack the *S.S. Poseidon* in the middle of the Indian Ocean if the idea is to generate "terror" among Americans? There would be nobody nearby in the ocean to see the ship sink!

Almost as ludicrous as this notion (and the bad

digital effects), is the sight of family man Steve Guttenberg making love to a massage therapist as the ship rolls over. I half-expected him to ask her if the Earth moved.

The Richmond Times-Dispatch dubbed the telefilm: "three hours of the dark side of *The Love Boat*."[10]

Now that's scary.

Available on DVD.

STEPHEN KING'S DESPERATION

(ABC) (May 23, 2006) Sennet/Gernstein Entertainment/Touchstone Television. Based on the novel by: Stephen King. Written by: Stephen King. Directed by: Mick Garris.

CAST
Tom Skerritt (Johnny)
Steve Weber (Steve)
Annabeth Gish (Mary Jackson)
Ron Perlman (Sheriff Entragian)
Charles Durning (Tom Billingsley)
Henry Thomas (Peter Jackson)
Matt Frewer (Ralph Carver)
Shane Haboucha (David Carver)
Kelly Overton (Cynthia)
Sylva Kelegian (Ellie Carver)

What would a TV year be without an adaptation of a Stephen King book? In this case, director Mick Garris has found himself a doozy, as *Desperation* is one of the master of horror's finest latter-day literary achievements. The story involves a kind of desert "highway to hell" en route to Nevada. There, evil Sheriff Entragian (Ron Perlman) pulls unwary drivers off the road and hauls them back to the town of Desperation for dark purposes.

Unfortunately, everyone back in town is already dead, thanks to the Sheriff, and so there's precious little help for the captured travelers. Worse, something old,

Pray for Salvation! Rutger Hauer plays a priest trapped on a topsy-turvy cruise liner in NBC's remake of
THE POSEIDON ADVENTURE.

evil, and demonic has been released from the old mine in town; something that takes—and needs—human form to exist.

A diverse group of protagonists, including an ex-alcoholic author (Tom Skerritt), a veterinarian (Charles Durning) and a little boy, David (Shane Haboucha)—who seems to possess paranormal powers and awareness, join forces to stop the ancient evil.

Available on DVD.

THE TEN COMMANDMENTS

(ABC) (April 10-11, 2006) RHI Entertainment. Written by: Ron Hutchinson. Directed by: Robert Dornhelm.

CAST
Dougray Scott (Moses)
Naveen Andrews (Menerith)
Omar Sharif (Jethro)
Linus Roache (Aaron)
Mia Maestro (Zipporah)
Padma Lakshmi (Princess Bithia)
Paul Rhys (Ramses)
Richard O'Brien (Tutor)

This is a redo of the perfectly adequate Cecil B. De Mille 1956 classic. The 2006 version finds *The Heist* star Dougray Scott playing the role Charlton Heston once assayed with so much authority.

The Ten Commandments commences with Moses as a baby...cruising down the Nile and escaping the wrath of a dangerous Pharoah. He's rescued and raised as Egyptian royalty with his half-brother, played by *Lost*'s Naveen Andrews. In his adult years, moping Moses comes to understand his heritage and mission: to free the Israelites from servitude and discrimination. All the curses and

parting of large bodies of water one would expect from the tale are depicted here with special effects that could graciously be called modest.

Available on DVD.

10.5 APOCALYPSE

(NBC) (May 21 and May 23, 2006) Pearl Pictures/Jeff/Branstein Films. Written and directed by: John Lafia.

CAST
Kim Delaney (Dr. Samantha Hill)
Beau Bridges (President Hollister)
Frank Langella (Dr. Hill)
Dean Cain (Brad)
Carlos Bernard (Dr. Garcia)
Melissa Sue Anderson (First Lady Megan Hollister)
David Cubitt (Dr. Fisher)

This two-part disaster movie picks where 2004's *10.5* left off. America is in ruins after a huge-magnitude earthquake, and kindly Commander-in-Chief Hollister (Beau Bridges) learns that the aftershock could cause even more damage.

Fortunately, a lovely female seismologist, Dr. Samantha Hill (Kim Delaney), is hard at work solving the problem. Her scientist father, Dr. Hill (Frank Langella) may hold the key to saving the country...but it won't happen before many landmarks and monuments are wrecked courtesy of computer-generated effects. Dean Cain plays a fireman, *24*'s Carlos Bernard a doctor.

Available on DVD.

THE TRIANGLE

(SCI FI Channel) (December 5-7, 2005) Electric Entertainment/Bad Hat Harry Productions/The SCI FI Channel. Written by: Rockne S. O'Bannon. Directed by: Craig R. Baxley.

CAST

Sam Neill (Eric Benerall)
Eric Stoltz (Howard Thomas)
Bruce Davison (Stan Lathem)
Catherine Bell (Emily Patterson)
Lou Diamond Phillips (Paloma)
Michael Rodgers (Bruce Geller)

In this three-part miniseries, a tycoon (Sam Neill) commissions an expedition to the Bermuda Triangle to explain why so many ships (including some from his own fleet) have gone missing there. The millionaire sends on this quest a psychic (Bruce Davison), a doubting Thomas journalist—literally named Howard Thomas (Eric Stoltz), an engineer (Catherine Bell), and a meteorologist (Michael Rodgers). What this team finds lurking within the Bermuda Triangle is one-part derived from *Solaris* (1971) and one part from Nicolas Roeg's *Don't Look Now* (1973), a blending of visions and nightmares that is terrifying and bends the laws of time and space. *The Chicago Tribune* called the television event "A soggy misfire" and observed that the "stilted pacing…sinks the show."[11]

Available on DVD.

VAMPIRE BATS

(CBS) (October 30th, 2005) Violet Blue Productions/Van Zerneck/Sertner Films/Sony TV. Written and directed by: Eric Boss.

CAST

Lucy Lawless (Dr. Maddy Rierdon)
Dylan Neal (Dan Dryer)
Liam Waite (Warden Jay Schuster)
Brett Butler (Shelly)
Timothy Bottoms (Mayor Hank Poelker)
Tony Plana (Sheriff Herbst)

In this sequel to *Locusts*, which aired in Spring of '05, Dr. Maddy Rierdon (Lucy Lawless), another lovely female scientist, unexpectedly faces nature's wrath again. This time, it happens when a swarm of vampire bats invade a small town in Louisiana and attack the college where she's now a professor.

The computer generated bats are a threat right out of "revenge of nature" horror movies from the 1970s such as *Kingdom of the Spiders* (1977) and *Nightwing* (1979), and Lawless has a cheesy good time battling the flying rodents. Timothy Bottoms is on hand to play the wrong-headed town mayor.

Not available on DVD.

WALKOUT

(HBO) (March 18, 2006) Maya Pictures/Y.O.Y. Productions. Written by: Ernie Contreras, Marcus De Leon, Timothy J. Sexton. Directed by: Edward James Olmos.

CAST
Alexa Vega (Paula Crisostomo)
Yancey Arias (Mr. Crisostomo)
Michael Pena (Sal Castro)
Efren Ramirez (Bobby Verdugo)
Edward James Olmos (Julian Nava)
Bodie Olmos (Esparzo)
Veronica Diaz (Yoh)

This HBO drama remembers a Chicano student walk-out that occurred in East L.A.'s Lincoln High School back in 1968. The impetus for the protest is unfair and discriminatory conditions and practices at the school: punishment for speaking Spanish, for instance, and little or no access to restrooms.

Inspired by her teacher, Mr. Castro (Michael Pena) and over the objections of her concerned father (Yancey Arias), a young honor student, Paula (Alexa Vega) musters the courage and support to march for fair treatment. There's a clash with the L.A.P.D., and the events are remembered and orchestrated in vivid detail by director Edward James Olmos.

"Alexa Vega gives a surprisingly strong performance," noted *Film Threat*. "She has range, and the right ability to perform such a complex character, and she pulls it off. Paired with tight writing, and Olmos' great direction, *Walkout* is a very good look at the power of protest."[12]

Available on DVD.

THE WATER IS WIDE

(CBS) (January 29, 2006) Hallmark Hall of Fame/20th Century Fox. Based on a novel by: Pat Conroy. Written by: Jonathan Estrin. Directed by: John Kent Harrison.

CAST
Jeff Hephner (Pat Conroy)
Alfre Woodard (Mrs. Brown)
Julianne Nicholson (Barbara)
Frank Langella (Dr. Piedmont)
James Murtaugh (Bennington)

Pat Conroy's debut novel (already produced as the 1974 film *Conrack*, starring Jon Voight) is brought to life in this adaptation, a human drama about a young man (the author himself, Conroy, as played by Jeff Hephner) who accepts a job teaching middle-schoolers on a small island off the South Carolina shore in the late 1960s. Most of Conroy's students are African-American, speak their own dialect, and are illiterate in terms of English and American history.

A stranger in a strange land, Conroy proves his skills as a teacher by winning the students over, much to the amazement of school principal Brown (Alfre Woodard), and self-important superintendent Piedmont (Frank Langella).

Stories like *The Water is Wide* are a dime a dozen, from *Blackboard Jungle* (1964) to *Dangerous Minds* (1992), but this Hallmark Hall of Fame version gazes honestly at issues involving bigotry and race. Overall, it's a bit predictable, but its heart is in the right place.

Available on DVD.

THE 58TH ANNUAL EMMY AWARDS

THE 2005–2006 EMMY AWARDS

On Sunday, August 27, 2006, the 58th Annual Emmy Awards were held in Hollywood. Conan O'Brien was the host. Full lists of nominees and winners are presented below.

OUTSTANDING **DRAMATIC SERIES**

The Nominees are:

Grey's Anatomy (ABC)

House (FOX)

The Sopranos (HBO)

24 (FOX)

The West Wing (NBC)

And the Winner is...

24

OUTSTANDING **ACTOR** IN A **DRAMATIC SERIES**

The Nominees are:

Peter Krause, *Six Feet Under* (HBO)

Denis Leary, *Rescue Me* (FX)

Christopher Meloni, *Law & Order: Special Victims Unit* (NBC)

Martin Sheen, *The West Wing* (NBC)

Kiefer Sutherland, *24* (FOX)

And the Winner is...

Kiefer Sutherland, *24* (FOX)

OUTSTANDING **ACTRESS** IN A **DRAMATIC SERIES**

The Nominees are:

Frances Conroy, *Six Feet Under* (HBO)

Geena Davis, *Commander in Chief* (ABC)

Mariska Hargitay, *Law & Order: Special Victims Unit* (CBS)

Allison Janney, *The West Wing* (NBC)

Kyra Sedgwick, *The Closer* (TNT)

And the Winner is...

Mariska Hargitay, *Law & Order: Special Victims Unit* (CBS)

OUTSTANDING **SUPPORTING ACTOR** IN A **DRAMATIC SERIES**

The Nominees are:

Alan Alda, *The West Wing* (NBC)

Michael Imperioli, *The Sopranos* (HBO)

Gregory Itzin, *24* (FOX)

Oliver Platt, *Huff* (Showtime)

William Shatner, *Boston Legal* (ABC)

And the Winner is...

Alan Alda, *The West Wing* (NBC)

OUTSTANDING **SUPPORTING ACTRESS** IN A **DRAMATIC SERIES**

The Nominees are:

Candice Bergen, *Boston Legal* (ABC)

Blythe Danner, *Huff* (Showtime)

Sandra Oh, *Grey's Anatomy* (ABC)

Jean Smart, *24* (FOX)

Chandra Wilson, *Grey's Anatomy* (ABC)

And the Winner is...

Blythe Danner, *Huff* (Showtime)

OUTSTANDING **GUEST ACTOR** IN A **DRAMATIC SERIES**

The Nominees are:

Kyle Chandler, *Grey's Anatomy* (ABC)

Christian Clemenson, *Boston Legal* (ABC)

Henry Ian Cusick, *Lost* (ABC)

Michael J. Fox, *Boston Legal* (ABC)

James Woods, *ER* (NBC)

And the Winner is...

Christian Clemenson, *Boston Legal* (ABC)

OUTSTANDING **GUEST ACTRESS** IN A **DRAMATIC SERIES**

The Nominees are:

Kate Burton, *Grey's Anatomy* (ABC)

Joanna Cassidy, *Six Feet Under* (HBO)

Patricia Clarkson, *Six Feet Under* (HBO)

Swoosie Kurtz, *Huff* (Showtime)

Christina Ricci, *Grey's Anatomy* (ABC)

And the Winner is...

Patricia Clarkson, *Six Feet Under* (HBO)

OUTSTANDING **WRITING** FOR A **DRAMATIC SERIES**

The Nominees are:

The Sopranos: "Members Only" (HBO)

Grey's Anatomy: "It's the End of the World, As You Know It. (Parts 1 & 2)" (ABC)

Grey's Anatomy: "Into You Like a Train" (ABC)

Lost: "The 23rd Psalm" (ABC)

Six Feet Under: "Everyone's Waiting" (HBO)

And the Winner is...

The Sopranos: "Members Only" (HBO)

OUTSTANDING **DIRECTING** FOR A **DRAMATIC SERIES**

The Nominees are:

24: "7:00 am–8:00 am" (FOX)
Big Love: "Pilot" (HBO)
Lost: "Live Together, Die Alone" (ABC)
Six Feet Under: "Everyone's Waiting" (HBO)
The Sopranos: "Members Only" (HBO)
The Sopranos: "Join the Club" (HBO)
The West Wing: "Election Day" (NBC)

And the Winner is...

24: "7:00 am–8:00 am" (FOX)

OUTSTANDING **COMEDY SERIES**

The Nominees are:

Arrested Development (FOX)
Curb Your Enthusiasm (HBO)
The Office (NBC)
Scrubs (NBC)
Two and a Half Men (CBS)

And the Winner is...

The Office (NBC)

OUTSTANDING **ACTOR** IN A **COMEDY SERIES**

The Nominees are:

Steve Carell, *The Office* (NBC)
Larry David, *Curb Your Enthusiasm* (HBO)
Kevin James, *The King of Queens* (CBS)
Tony Shalhoub, *Monk* (USA)
Charlie Sheen, *Two and a Half Men* (CBS)

And the Winner is...

Tony Shalhoub, *Monk* (USA)

OUTSTANDING **ACTRESS** IN A **COMEDY SERIES**

The Nominees are:

Stockard Channing, *Out of Practice* (CBS)
Jane Kaczmarek, *Malcolm in the Middle* (FOX)
Lisa Kudrow, *The Comeback* (HBO)
Julia Louis-Dreyfus, *The New Adventures of Old Christine* (CBS)
Debra Messing, *Will & Grace* (NBC)

And the Winner is...

Julia Louis-Dreyfus, *The New Adventures of Old Christine* (CBS)

OUTSTANDING **SUPPORTING ACTOR** IN A **COMEDY SERIES**

The Nominees are:

Will Arnett, *Arrested Development* (FOX)

Bryan Cranston, *Malcolm in the Middle* (FOX)

Jon Cryer, *Two and a Half Men* (CBS)

Sean Hayes, *Will & Grace* (NBC)

Jeremy Piven, *Entourage* (HBO)

And the Winner is...

Jeremy Piven, *Entourage* (HBO)

OUTSTANDING **SUPPORTING ACTRESS** IN A **COMEDY SERIES**

The Nominees are:

Cheryl Hines, *Curb Your Enthusiasm* (HBO)

Megan Mullally, *Will & Grace* (NBC)

Elizabeth Perkins, *Weeds* (Showtime)

Jaime Pressly, *My Name Is Earl* (NBC)

Alfre Woodard, *Desperate Housewives* (ABC)

And the Winner is...

Megan Mullally, *Will & Grace* (NBC)

OUTSTANDING **GUEST ACTOR** IN A **COMEDY SERIES**

The Nominees are:

Alec Baldwin, *Will & Grace* (NBC)

Leslie Jordan, *Will & Grace* (NBC)

Martin Sheen, *Two and a Half Men* (CBS)

Patrick Stewart, *Extras* (HBO)

Ben Stiller, *Extras* (HBO)

And the Winner is...

Leslie Jordan, *Will & Grace* (NBC)

OUTSTANDING **GUEST ACTRESS** IN A **COMEDY SERIES**

The Nominees are:

Blythe Danner, *Will & Grace* (NBC)

Shirley Knight, *Desperate Housewives* (ABC)

Cloris Leachman, *Malcolm in the Middle* (FOX)

Laurie Metcalf, *Monk* (USA)

Kate Winslet, *Extras* (HBO)

And the Winner is...

Cloris Leachman, *Malcolm in the Middle* (FOX)

OUTSTANDING **WRITING** FOR A **COMEDY SERIES**

The Nominees are:

My Name Is Earl: "Pilot" (NBC)

Arrested Development: "Development Arrested" (FOX)

Entourage: "Exodus" (HBO)

Extras: "Kate Winslet" (HBO)

The Office: "Christmas Party" (NBC)

And the Winner is...

My Name Is Earl: "Pilot" (NBC)

OUTSTANDING **DIRECTION** FOR A **COMEDY SERIES**

The Nominees are:

My Name Is Earl: "Pilot" (NBC)

Curb Your Enthusiasm: "The Christ Nail" (HBO)

Entourage: "Oh Mandy" (HBO)

Entourage: "Sundance Kids" (HBO)

Weeds: "Good S*** Lollipop" (Showtime)

And the Winner is...

My Name Is Earl: "Pilot" (NBC)

OUTSTANDING **REALITY-COMPETITION** PROGRAM

The Nominees are:

The Amazing Race (CBS)

American Idol (FOX)

Dancing with the Stars (ABC)

Project Runway (Bravo)

Survivor (CBS)

And the Winner is...

The Amazing Race (CBS)

OUTSTANDING **REALITY PROGRAM**

The Nominees are:

Antiques Roadshow (PBS)

The Dog Whisperer (National Geographic)

Extreme Makeover: Home Edition (ABC)

Kathy Griffin: My Life on the D-List (Bravo)

Penn & Teller: Bullshit! (Showtime)

And the Winner is...

Extreme Makeover: Home Edition (ABC)

OUTSTANDING **VARIETY, MUSIC,** OR **COMEDY SERIES**

The Nominees are:

The Daily Show with Jon Stewart (Comedy Central)

The Colbert Report (Comedy Central)

Late Night with Conan O'Brien (NBC)

The Late Show with David Letterman (CBS)

Real Time with Bill Maher (HBO)

And the Winner is...

The Daily Show with Jon Stewart
(Comedy Central)

OUTSTANDING **INDIVIDUAL PERFORMANCE** IN A **VARIETY** OR **MUSIC PROGRAM**

The Nominees are:

Stephen Colbert, *The Colbert Report*
(Comedy Central)

Craig Ferguson, *The Late Late Show with Craig Ferguson* (CBS)

David Letterman, *The Late Show with David Letterman* (CBS)

Hugh Jackman, *The 59th Annual Tony Awards* (CBS)

Barry Manilow, *Barry Manilow: Music And Passion* (PBS)

And the Winner is...

Barry Manilow,
Barry Manilow: Music And Passion (PBS)

OUTSTANDING **WRITING** FOR A **VARIETY, MUSIC** OR **COMEDY PROGRAM**

The Nominees are:

The Daily Show with Jon Stewart (Comedy Central)

The Colbert Report (Comedy Central)

Late Night with Conan O'Brien (NBC)

The Late Show with David Letterman (CBS)

Real Time with Bill Maher (HBO)

And the Winner is...

The Daily Show with Jon Stewart
(Comedy Central)

OUTSTANDING **DIRECTING** FOR A **VARIETY, MUSIC,** OR **COMEDY PROGRAM**

The Nominees are:

The 78th Annual Academy Awards (ABC)

American Idol: "Finale" (FOX)

The Colbert Report: "Episode # 110" (Comedy Central

The Daily Show with Jon Stewart: "(Episode 10140)" (Comedy Central)

Saturday Night Live: "Host: Steve Martin" (NBC)

And the Winner is...

The 78th Annual Academy Awards (ABC)

OUTSTANDING **MADE–FOR–TV MOVIE**

The Nominees are:

Flight 93 (A&E)
The Flight That Fought Back (Discovery Channel)
The Girl in the Café (HBO)
Mrs. Harris (HBO)
Yesterday (HBO)

And the Winner is...

The Girl in the Café (HBO)

OUTSTANDING **MINISERIES**

The Nominees are:

Bleak House (PBS)
Elizabeth I (HBO)
Into the West (TNT)
Sleeper Cell (Showtime)

And the Winner is...

Elizabeth I (HBO)

OUTSTANDING: **ACTOR** IN A **MINISERIES** OR **TV–MOVIE**

The Nominees are:

Andre Braugher, *Thief* (FX)
Charles Dance, *Bleak House* (PBS)
Ben Kingsley, *Mrs. Harris* (HBO)
Donald Sutherland, *Human Trafficking* (HBO)
Jon Voight, *Pope John Paul II* (CBS)

And the Winner is...

Andre Braugher, *Thief* (FX)

OUTSTANDING **ACTRESS** IN A **MINISERIES** OR **TV–MOVIE**

The Nominees are:

Gillian Anderson, *Bleak House* (PBS)
Kathy Bates, *Ambulance Girl* (Lifetime)
Annette Bening, *Mrs. Harris* (HBO)
Judy Davis, *A Little Thing Called Murder* (Lifetime)
Helen Mirren, *Elizabeth I* (HBO)

And the Winner is...

Helen Mirren, *Elizabeth I* (HBO)

OUTSTANDING **SUPPORTING ACTOR** IN A **MINISERIES** OR **TV-MOVIE**

The Nominees are:

Robert Carlyle, *Human Trafficking* (HBO)

Clifton Collins Jr., *Thief* (FX)

Hugh Dancy, *Elizabeth I* (HBO)

Jeremy Irons, *Elizabeth I* (HBO)

Denis Lawson, *Bleak House* (PBS)

And the Winner is...

Jeremy Irons, *Elizabeth I* (HBO)

OUTSTANDING **SUPPORTING ACTRESS** IN A **MINISERIES** OR **TV-MOVIE**

The Nominees are:

Ellen Burstyn, *Mrs. Harris* (HBO)

Shirley Jones, *Hidden Places* (Hallmark)

Cloris Leachman, *Mrs. Harris* (HBO)

Kelly Macdonald, *The Girl in the Café* (HBO)

Alfre Woodard, *The Water Is Wide* (CBS)

And the Winner is...

Kelly Macdonald, *The Girl in the Café* (HBO)

ENDNOTES

PART I: NEW TV SERIES

1. *America's Got Talent*, www.nbc.com. http://www.nbc.com/Americas_Got_Talent/show/index.shtml#main

2. Marc Berman, "Martha, Martha," *Mediaweek*, September 12, 2005, 42.

3. "Media Watch—Jury Remains Out on Martha's Return to TV," *PR Week*, September 26, 2005, 12.

4. "Trump to Stewart: Take Responsibility," *Yahoo! TV: News and Gossip*, February 19. http://tvyahoo.com/news/ap/20060219/114041262000p.html

5. Keith Naughton, "You Were Terrible," *MSNBC.Com*, February 21, 2006. http://www.msnbc.msn.com/id/11486686/site/newsweek.from/ET/print1/displaymode/10…

6. Robert Bianco, "*Black. White.* Oh, Whatever," *USA Today*, March 7, 2006. http://www.usatoday.com/life/television/reviews/2006-03-07-black-white_x.htm

7. Sid Smith, "Fox's *Bones* Piles on to the Crowded World of TV Detection." *Chicago Tribune*, September 12, 2005.

8. Ray Richmond, "*Bones,*" *Hollywood Reporter*, September 12, 2005, 13.

9. Adam Buckman, "Mommy Dearest," *The New York Post*. October 3, 2005. http://www.nypost.com/tv/28850.

10. S. T. Karnick, "Red-State TV: Pandering to Good Instincts," *National Review Online*. November 22, 2005. http://article.nationalreview.com/ ?q=ODUyNDkxYjdiMWYyOGNhY2M5YTNlMGJiODdmYzQ0MTY=

11. Steve Rogers, "Close Skillfully Probes Suburbia's Dark Side." *The Boston Globe*. October 4, 2005. http://www.boston.com/ae/tv/articles/10/04/close-skilfully-probes-suburbias-dark-side/

12. L. Martinez, "CBS Keeps *Home* Fires Burning for Fall Season," *Ventura County Star*, November 25, 2005, 5.

13. Stephen Colbert, White House Correspondents' Dinner Speech, *Daily Kos*, April 30, 2006.
http://www.dailykos.com/storyonly/2006/4/30/1441/59811

14. Marie Wilson, "Women in Politics: *Commander in Chief?*" The *Washington Post*. September 22, 2005.
http://usf361.mail.yahoo.com/ym…

15. Nicholas Fonseca, "*Commander in Chief*: Returning to TV, Geena Davis has the Two Tallest Tasks of Any Actor This Fall…," *Entertainment Weekly*, September 9, 2005.

16. Hal Boedecker, "Dick Wolf's Sexy Side," *Orlando Sentinel Blog*, January 25, 2006, 1 of 1. http://blogs.orlandosentinel.com/entertainment_tv_tvblog/2006/01/dick_wolfs_sexy.html

17. Tom Shales, "*Courting Alex*: Without Sparking," *The Washington Post*, January 26, 2006, C01.

18. Marc Peyser, "Snap Judgment: Television," *Newsweek*, September 26, 2005, 64.

19. Gloria Goodale, "*Crumbs*," *Christian Science Monitor*, January 13, 2006, 12.

20. Robert Bianco, "Things Get Nutty on *Crumbs*," *USA Today*, January 12, 2006, 12D.

21. "Instead of a Comedic Feast, We Get *Crumbs*," *New York Daily News*, January 11, 2006, 1 of 1. http"//www.nydailynews.com/entertainment/col-v-pfriendly/story/382171p-324425c.html

22. Bill Frost, "*The World Series of Pop Culture*," *Salt Lake City Weekly*, August 3, 2006.
http://www.slweekly.com/editorial/2006/tube_2006-08-03.cfm

23. Josh Rottenberg, "Lord of the *E-Ring*: Dennis Hopper Has Stuck It to the Man in Films like *Easy Rider* and *Apocalypse Now*, But Now He's Working for the Man in NBC's Pentagon Drama *E-Ring*…," *Entertainment Weekly*, September 23, 2005, 40.

24. Brian Lowry, "*E-Ring*," *Variety*, September 19, 2005, 73.

25. Christopher Lisotta, "Demo Denies a Crop of Debuts." *Television Week*, January 16, 2006, 1A-62.

26. Sarah Hall, "ABC's Reasons for Axing *Emily*" *E! Online*, January 18, 2006.

27. "Jeez, Even Chris O'Donnell's Show Lasted Two Episodes," *Newsweek*, January 30, 2006, 67.

28. Christopher Lisotta, "Despite Failures, Studios Hedge Bets With Stars," *Television Week*, March 27, 2006, 5–41.

29. Dalton Ross, "Ready for His Not-So-Close-Up: On His New HBO Comedy, *Extras*, Ricky Gervais Puts Bit Players in the Spotlight," *Entertainment Weekly*, September 23, 205, 75.

30. David Bianculli, "*Extras* Premiering Sunday on HBO," *New York Daily News*, September 23, 2005.

31. Betsy Streisand, "He-he or Dum-Dum?," *U.S. News & World Report*, January 16, 2006, D-12.

32. "Prinze Jr. Disappointed with Tough Sitcom Schedule," *World Entertainment News Network*, October 5, 2005.

33. Paul Katz, "Freddie's Dread: Is Prinze getting pigeonholed on ABC?" *Entertainment Weekly*, August 12, 2005, 22.

34. "Prinze Jr. Bans Young Fans From Sitcom Set," *World Entertainment News Network*, October 6, 2005.

35. Joel Brown, "*Ghost* Popularity is Just Plain Scary," *Ventura County Star*, November 18, 2005, 7.

36. Josh Wolk, "*Ghost Whisperer*: Debuts September 23 on CBS," *Entertainment Weekly*, September 9, 2005, 104.

37. Tom Jicha, "*Ghost Whisperer* Premiering Friday on CBS," *South Florida Sun-Sentinel*, September 22, 2005.

38. Brian Lowry, "*The Ghost Whisperer*." *Variety*, September 19, 2005, 75.

39. Lynette Rice, "One Down: What Happens When All TV Shows Aren't Created Equal?" *Entertainment Weekly*. October 7, 2005, 8.

40. W.M. Steven Humphrey, "A Taste of Evil," *The Portland Mercury*, August 10-16, 2006, 1 of 1.
http://www.portlandmercury.com/portland/content?oid=48742&category=22118.

41. "The Joy of Hex," *TV Zone Special 65*. Fall 2005, 87.

42. Neil Wilkes, "Confirmed: Supernatural Drama *Hex* Axed," *Digital Spy*. April 26, 2006, 1 of 1.
http://www.digitalspy.co.uk/article/ds32090.html#

43. Barry Garron, "How I Met Your Mother," *Hollywood Reporter*, September 19, 2005, 30.

44. Maria Elenea Fernandez, "It's Mother's Day. Hip Sitcom Thrives," *The Journal Gazette*. December 5, 2005, 3D.

45. "*How to Get The Guy*: Love Coaches Offer Tips," *ABC News*, June 12, 2006.
http://abcnews.go.com/GMA/story?id=2065551&page=1

46. Gael Fashingbauer Cooper and Andy Dehnart, "As *Hell's Kitchen* Heats Up, Ramsay Boils Over. Plus: *How to Get the Guy* Didn't Get the Ratings," *MSNBC.com*.
http://msnbc.msn.com/id/13689220/

47. John Leonard, "Catch My Grift," *New York Magazine*, January 16, 2006. http://www.newyorkmetro.com/nymetro/arts/tv/reviews/15485/index.html/

48. Alessandra Stanley, "Charming, Cunning and Ready for a Con," *The New York Times*. February 17, 2006.
http://www.nytimes.com/2006/02/17/arts/television/17tvwk.html?ex=1156737600&en=2d8bdbad5acccd0e&ei=5070

49. Heather Havrilesky, "The Best and Worst of TV," *Salon.com*, December 27, 2005. http://dir.salon.com/story/ent/iltw/2005/12/27/year_end/index.html?pn=1

50. Debra Watson, "New TV Show Explodes Myths: *In Justice* Dramatizes Reality of United State Criminal Justice System," *World Socialist Web Site*, February 22, 2006, 1 of 1. http://wsws.org/articles/2006/feb2006/inju-f22.shtml

51. Greg Hernandez, "All in the Family: NBC Surrogacy Drama *Inconceivable* and ABC Mid-Season Comedy *Crumbs* Acknowledge That, for Many Gays and Lesbians in 2005, It's All About Families," *The Advocate*, September 27, 2005, 58.

52. "NBC Bumps *Inconceivable*," *UPI Newstrack*, October 4, 2005.

53. Glenn Garvin, "Aliens or Not, ABC Drama Invades the Everglades," *The Miami Herald*. September 19, 2005.

54. J. Max Robins, "Winds of Change," *Broadcasting & Cable*, August 1, 2005, 4.

55. "ABC Pulls Insensitive *Invasion* ads," *UPI NewsTrack*, September 1, 2005.

56. "ABC to Air *Invasion* as Planned," *UPI NewsTrack*, September 9, 2005.

57. Barry Garron, "*Just Legal*," *The Hollywood Reporter*, September 19, 2005.

58. Michael Schneider, "Lehman Turns *Killer*; Cook Rolls Dice," *Daily Variety*, July 11, 2005, 3.

59. Phil Rosenthal, "Popcornish Gore," *Chicago Tribune*, September 19, 2005.

60. Ileane Rudolph, "Matt Dallas: The Star of *Kyle XY* Talks About His New Hit, Nude Scenes, and Kissing Mischa Barton," *TV Guide*. July 24, 2005, 18.

61. "*Love Inc.*," *UPN.com*. http://www.upn.com/shows/love_inc/about.shtml

62. Ed Condran, "Comic Mines Desperate House Husbands' Plight," *New York Daily News*. August 18, 2005. http://www.nydailynews.com/entertainment/v-pfriendly/story/338174-p288775c.html

63. Neil Swidey, "Family !@%$#% Ties." *The Boston Globe*, November 27, 2005, 1 of 7. http://www.boston.com/news/globe/magazine/articles/2005/11/27/family_ties?mode=PF

64. "*Miracle Workers*," *ABC.com* http://abc.go.com/primetime/miracleworkers/about.html

65. Tim Goodman, "No Last Laugh for the WB with *Modern Men*," *The San Francisco Chronicle*. March 17, 2006. http://www.sfgate.com/cgi-bin/article.cgi?f=/c/a/2006/03/17/DDGB2HP3AJ33.DTL

66. Glenn Garvin, "Shows Breaking The Rules (Aren't We Lucky?)," *The Miami Herald*, September 19, 2005.

67. Betsy Voyd, "*The New Adventures of Old Christine*," *Daily Variety*, June 14, 2006, A10.

68. Kate O'Hare, "Evil Takes the Upper Hand on *The Night Stalker*," *Zap2IT.com*, July 15, 2005.

69. John Crook, "TV Diagnosis: Slightly more than *One* Viewer," *The Charlotte Observer*, August 13-19, 2006, 3.

70. "Canadian Version of *The One* on Hold," *The Record.com*, August 16, 2006. http://www.therecord.com/NASApp/cs/ContentServer?pagename=record/Layout/Article_Type1&c=Article&cid=1155678615060&call_pageid=1024322089000&col=1024322319351

71. Andrew Ryan. "*One Ocean View*: Single New Yorkers Hit the Beach in a New Reality Series," *The Globe and Mail*, July 29, 2006. http://www.theglobeandmail.com/servlet/story/LAC.20060729.GT31FEAT/TPStory/Entertainment

72. Amy Amatangelo, "Give us a *Break*—Unbelievable Plot Twists Make for Fun Season Finale of Fox's Thrilling Prison Drama," *Boston Herald*, November 28, 2005.

73. Tom Gliatto, "*Prison Break*," *People Weekly*, September 5, 2005, 41.

74. Gary Levin, "*Psych* sees 6.1M viewers," USA Today, July 12, 2006.

75. Latoya West, "Bravo Introduces Us to the *Real Housewives of Orange County*," *About.com*. http://realitytv.about.com/od/realityshowsintheworks/ss/Housewives_3.htm

76. Steve Rogers, "Bravo's *The Real Housewives of Orange County* to Premiere March 21st," *Reality TV World*, January 6, 2006. http://www.realitytvworld.com/news/bravo-the-real-housewives-of-orange-county-premiere-march-21-3897.php

77. Troy Patterson, "Real Wife: Desperate Housewives, Wife-Swappers and the Women of Bravo," *Slate.com*, March 21, 2006. http://www.slate.com/id/2138401/

78. Nellie Andreeva, "Doelger Builds HBO's *Rome*,'" *The Hollywood Reporter*, July 26, 2004, 3.

79. Hal Boedeker, "HBO's *Rome* the best new drama of the fall," *The Orlando Sentinel*. August 26, 2005.

80. "HBO Previews *Rome* After Show for Scribes," *Multichannel News*, July 4 2005, 6.

81. "At HBO, *Rome* Built in a Day," *Broadcasting & Cable*, September 5, 2005, 26.

82. Alan Pergament, "Showtime Plants *Sleeper Cell* in Battle with HBO," *The Buffalo News*, December 2, 2005, C5.

83. Roger Catlin, "*Sleeper* Will Keep You Wide Awake—FBI Infiltrates Terrorist Cell," *The Hartford Courant*, December 3, 2005, D1.

84. Diane Kristine, "Good Show, Bad News: An Interview with *Sons & Daughters* Creator Fred Goss," *Blogcritics.org*, April 12, 2006, 1 of 1. http://blogcritics.org/archives/2006/04/12/073520.php

85. Maureen Ryan, "Dumb logic rules WB's new *Supernatural*," *Chicago Tribune,* September 12, 2005.

86. Latoya West, "Amy Grant to Grant Wishes on NBC Reality Show *Three Wishes, About.com,* 1 of 1. http://realitytv.about.com/od/realityshowsintheworks/a/ThreeWishes.htm

87. Mark Nollinger, "Amy's Wishing Well: Why *Three Wishes* is Deeply Affecting," *TV Guide*, October 9, 2005, 16.

88. "Cheers and Jeers," *TV Guide*, April 10–16, 2006, 24.

89. Tom Gliatto, "*The War at Home*," *People Weekly*, September 19, 2005, 48.

90. "These Kids Today," *The Advocate*. September 27, 2005, 67.

91. Robert Bianco, "*What About Brian*? Well, Not Much." *USA Today*, April 13, 2006.

PART II: RETURNING TV SERIES

1. "ABC's *Alias* Promises Big Series Finale," *Detroit Free Press*, November 26, 2005, 2A.

2. Lisa de Moraes, "Fox Bows to Golden *Idol*," *The Washington Post*, January 19, 2006, C01.

3. Gary Levin, "*Apprentice* needs work," *USA Today*, June 14, 2006, 4D.

4. Brian Raftery, "*Arrested Development: The Complete Third Season*," *Entertainment Weekly*, August 25, 2006, 1 of 1. http://www.ew.com/ew/article/review/dvd/0,6115,1333738_21_0_,00.html

5. Ronald D. Moore, "Dear Scifi.com and *Battlestar Galactica* Fans," *SciFi.Com.* February 24 2003, 1 of 1. http://www.scifi.com/battlestar/mini/about/intro/

6. Mike Duffy, "*Boston Legal* Gets a Change of Venue to Tuesdays," *Detroit Free Press.* July 28, 2005.

7. Kathie Huddleston, "*Charmed* Is Ready to End," *Sci Fi Wire—The News Service of the Sci Fi Channel*, March 10, 2006, 1 of 1. http://www.scifi.com/scifiwire/print.php?id=34903

8. "*Charmed* a Casualty of WB-UPN Change," *Yahoo TV News & Gossip*, March 3, 2006. http://tv.yahoo.com/news/ap/20060303/114143184000p.html

9. Kimberly Nordyke, "*Closer* Draws Record Crowd as Cable Soars," *The Hollywood Reporter—International Edition*, June 14, 2006, 41–42.

10. Gina Serpe, "Dog the Bounty Hunter Bitten by Lawsuit," *E! Online*, August 18, 2006, 1 of 1. http://www.eonline.com/News/Items/0,1,19800,00.html?fdnews

11. "*Eve*," *UPN.com* http://www.upn.com/shows/eve/

12. Tom Terrell, "Shades of *Grey*: Meet Shonda Rhimes, the Creator and Producer of TV's *Grey's Anatomy*," *Essence*, September 2005, 130–131.

13. Aldore Collier, "Shonda Rhimes: The Force Behind *Grey's Anatomy*," *Ebony,* October 2005, 204-205.

14. Nicholas Fonseca, "Playing Doctors: It's Not Brain Surgery, It's Just the Sexiest Hospital Show Ever. How ABC's Surprise Hit *Grey's Anatomy* Made Doctors Desirable Again," *Entertainment Weekly*, September 23, 2005, 26.

15. Steve Rogers, "Heather West Defeats Virginia Dalbeck to Win Fox's *Hell's Kitchen 2*," *Reality TV World*, August 15, 2006. http://www.realitytvworld.com/news/heather-west-defeats-virginia-dalbeck-win-fox-hell-kitchen-2-4287.php

16. "Give *Joey* Another Chance," *WENN*, August 12, 2005, 1 of 1.

17. Margy Rochlin, "An MTV Coming of Age That Went Far on Charm," *The New York Times*. August 30, 2005, Section 3, 1.

18. Mark Dawidziak, "NBC hopes 3-D Episode Spirits *Medium* to New Heights," *The Plain Dealer*, November 20, 2005, J3.

19. Scott D. Pierce, "Is *O.C.* DOA?," *Deseret Morning News,* August 17, 2006, 1 of 1. http://deseretnews.com/dn/view/0,1249,645193465,00.html

20. Bill Keveney, "*The Office* Reports Strong Future Expansion," *USA Today*, January 25, 2006, 1 of 2. http://www.ustoday.com/life/television/news/20060-01-25-office_x.htm?csp=N009&POE=click-refer

21. James Poniewozik, "Get *The Office* at Your Office," *Time*, June 26, 2007, 1 of 3. http://www.time.com/time/magazine/printout/0,8816.1207792,00.html

22. "*Queer Eye* Not Canceled," *TMZ.com,* August 2, 2006, 1 of 1. http://www.tmz.com/2006/08/02/queer-eye-not-canceled/

23. Nellie Andreeva, "CW Mixes Old, New in Sked; Fox Prepares to Thrill," The *Hollywood Reporter*. May 18, 2006, 1 of 1. http://www.hollywoodreporter.com/thr/article_display.jsp?vnu_content_id=1002538533

24. Bruce Fretts, "Denis Leary's *Rescue* Controversy Heats Up," *TV Guide*, July 24, 2006, 6.

25. Christopher Lisotta, "A Second Coming for *Heaven*," *Television Week.* May 15, 2006, 4.

26. Henry Goldblatt, "News & Notes: Resurrection of the Week," *Entertainment Weekly.* May 26, 2006, Issue 878.

27. Maureen Ryan, "*Mars* as Good as *Buffy* Without All the Demons," *Chicago Tribune.* November 30, 2005, 3.

PART III: SIGNIFICANT TV-MOVIES AND MINISERIES

1. Rhonda Hilario-Caguiat, *"Ambulance Girl," Lifetimetv.com,* August 2006, 1 of 1. http://www.lifetimetv.com/movies/originals/ambulancegirl.html

2. "Kathy Bates Stars in Lifetime Movie, *Ambulance Girl,* a True Story," *Women's Funding Network,* September 1, 2005, 1 of 1. http://www.wfnet.org/news/story.php?story_id=281

3. Gloria Goodale. *"Broken Trail." Christian Science Monitor.* June 23, 2006, 149.

4. "Picks & Pans: *Broken Trail*," *People Weekly*, July 3, 2006, 35.

5. Mark Washburn, *"Category 7: End of the World*, Sunday and November 13 on CBS," *The Charlotte Observer.* November 2, 2005.

6. "Exclusive Interview with Helen Mirren," *HBO Online*, 1 of 1. http://www.hbo.com/films/elizabeth/interviews/

7. Brian Lowry, *"Have No Fear: The Life of John Paul II," Variety.* November 27, 2005, 1 of 1. http://www.variety.com/review/ VE1117928959?categoryid=32&cs=1&s=h&p=0

8. David DiCerto, *"Have No Fear: The Life of John Paul II*, Dec 1, ABC," Catholic Online, November 16, 2005, 1 of 1. http://www.catholic.org/ae/tv/review.php?id=17629

9. "Hallmark Hall of Fame Presents *In From the Night*, Premiering April 23, on CBS," *Hallmark Press Room.* http://pressroom.hallmark.com/hhof_in_from_the_night.html

10. Douglas Durden, "Would You Like Fact or Fiction—Sunday Night Offers Disaster in Both Modes," *The Richmond Times-Dispatch*, November 19, 2005, G21.

11. Maureen Ryan, "Sci-Fi's *Triangle* is a Soggy Misfire," *Chicago Tribune*, December 5, 2005, 7.

12. Felix Vasquez Jr., *"Walkout," Film Threat*, March 30, 2006, 1 of 1. http://www.filmthreat.com/index.php?section=reviews&Id=8875

SELECTED BIBLIOGRAPHY

Armstrong, Jennifer. "Love, Labor, *Lost*: This Season Life Gets Harder for the Castaways with Romantic Triangles, Those Creepy 'Others,' and That Maddening Hatch, But Will Viewers Finally Get Some Answers?" *Entertainment Weekly*. September 9, 2005, 28.

Atkinson, Claire. "Everybody Loves Chris; Media Buyers Pick Their Favorites of the New TV Season, but the Biggest Buzz Doesn't Always Result in the Biggest Share." *Advertising Age*. September 19, 2005, S1.

Boedecker, Hal. "*Commander in Chief*, Premiering Tuesday on ABC." *The Orlando Sentinel*. September 23, 2005.

De Moraes, Lisa. "Recall Election: ABC Yanks Its *Commander in Chief*. *The Washington Post*. May 3, 2006, C01.

Flynn, Gillian. "Skeleton Crew: Fox's Drama's Have Lots of Bodies, But Need More Soul." *Entertainment Weekly*. September 16, 2005, 73.

Guthrie, Marisa. "Martha Stewart's *Apprentice* is a Ratings Letdown." *New York Daily News*, October 4, 2005.

Hussein, Terrina. "*Battlestar Galactica* Returns." *Asia Africa Intelligence Wire*. July 3, 2005.

Kronke, David. "Terrorists Replace Tidal Wave in New *Poseidon Adventure*." *Daily News of Los Angeles*. November 20, 2005, U11.

McDermott, Jim. "Fear and Trembling in Oceania: Pondering ABC's *Lost*." *America*. September 12, 2005, 19.

O'Connor, Brian. "David Boreanaz: TV's most famous (and fit) vampire is back—Only This Time He's Taking a Bite Out of Crime as an FBI Agent in Fox's Hot New Show *Bones*." *Men's Fitness*. September 2005, 98.

O'Hare, Kate. "Lucy Lawless Live from *Battlestar Galactica*." *Zap2It.com*. September 7, 2005.

Pennington, Gail. "Made-for-TV Disaster Isn't a Complete Disaster. (The Special Effects Are Good)." *St. Louis Post-Dispatch*. November 20, 205, F5.

Philpot, Robert. "Ho-hum *Poseidon* Soaked in Silliness." *Fort Worth Star-Telegram*. November 20, 2005, D3.

Ryan, Maureen. "*Boston Legal* Presents Its Case on a New Night." *Chicago Tribune*. August 8, 2005.

Sanders, Dusty. "CBS' Papal Tale Feels Realistic." *Rocky Mountain News*. December 3, 2005, 3D.

"News Briefs: *Head Cases* First Cancellation of Season." *Television Week*. September 26, 2005, 6.

"Hillary 2008 Supporters Cast Vote for Geena Davis in ABC's *Commander in Chief*, Count on Series Paving Way for Hillary's Real-Life Starring Role as President; Group Plans Premiere Day 'Thank You' Rally Outside ABC's Times Square Studios." *The America's Intelligence Wire*. September 23, 2005.

INDEX